Homer Simpson Marches on Washington

Homer Simpson Marches on Washington

Dissent through American Popular Culture

EDITED BY
TIMOTHY M. DALE AND JOSEPH J. FOY

Foreword by Kate Mulgrew

THE UNIVERSITY PRESS OF KENTUCKY

Scholarly publisher for the Commonwealth,
serving Bellarmine University, Berea College, Centre College of Kentucky,
Eastern Kentucky University, The Filson Historical Society, Georgetown College,
Kentucky Historical Society, Kentucky State University, Morehead State
University, Murray State University, Northern Kentucky University, Transylvania
University, University of Kentucky, University of Louisville, and Western
Kentucky University.
All rights reserved.

Editorial and Sales Offices: The University Press of Kentucky
663 South Limestone Street, Lexington, Kentucky 40508-4008
www.kentuckypress.com

14 13 12 11 10   5 4 3 2

Library of Congress Cataloging-in-Publication Data

Homer Simpson marches on Washington : dissent through American popular
culture / edited by Timothy M. Dale and Joseph J. Foy ; foreword by Kate Mulgrew.
    p. cm.
    Includes bibliographical references and index.
    ISBN 978-0-8131-2580-0 (hardcover : alk. paper)
    1. Popular culture—Political aspects—United States. 2. Conformity—United
States. 3. Social change—United States. I. Dale, Tim M. II. Foy, Joseph J.
    E169.12.H663 2010
    306.0973—dc22   2009044736

This book is printed on acid-free recycled paper meeting
the requirements of the American National Standard
for Permanence in Paper for Printed Library Materials.

Manufactured in the United States of America.

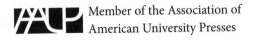 Member of the Association of
American University Presses

CONTENTS

FOREWORD

The Influence of Captain Janeway

Kate Mulgrew

One Thursday afternoon, the phone rang. I picked it up and an unfamiliar voice said, "Captain Janeway, I just wanted to be the first to welcome you aboard. Shooting starts Monday at the crack of dawn. Get some rest. You're going to need it." This voice belonged to the mastermind behind the *Star Trek* franchise, Rick Berman, and though we would occasionally lock horns over the next seven years, it was essentially a love affair. He knew how to work, and so did I. At no point during the entire run of the series did either of us admit defeat. It was a matter of pride, a matter of two type As in silent competition, the confidence of experience pitted against the confidence of conviction. Most important, it was the first time in the history of this multibillion-dollar franchise that a woman had been voted into the captain's seat. Both Paramount and *Star Trek* stood to lose vast sums of money if I failed to attract their most devoted demographic: young men between the ages of eighteen and thirty-five—you know, the guys in charge of the remote control (and the mortgage and the bank account). For the brand-new network labeled UPN, *Star Trek: Voyager* was its flagship show, and I was the first female captain to walk onto the bridge of a starship and issue the signature command, "Engage." I was also the first captain to have more than seven hairdos within a season, a corset sewn into my space suit, and a bra that resembled an alien species. I was puffed and shorn and stuffed and lit and scrutinized by every executive on the lot. I was criticized and cajoled, alternately patronized and petted. It's as if they had all gone out of their way to find this exotic animal who could, in fact, walk and talk and act at the same time, and yet when she appeared on deck, they were stunned to discover that under that feline coat was, God help us, a *feline*. They set about trimming and coaxing and battling this gender problem as only men who stand to lose megabucks do: by straightening my hair, strapping my breasts, raising my heels, and encouraging me to lower my already full and throaty voice. They surrounded me with cohorts of various colors and creeds, but I noted almost immediately that *all* the men were over six feet tall and the two supporting women were small and trim. Then came the real moment of truth. Within six months—hardly enough time to have established that we were lost in an unknown quadrant of space and unlikely to find a gas station anywhere nearby—they sent me a script in which I become stranded on an alien planet for an indeterminate amount of time with my first lieutenant, a strapping, gorgeous Latino named Chakotay. We must do our best to survive, find food, fool around with all things spacelike, befriend a tiny monkey, and, of course, make love. It's a perfect time to make love, one would think: one's ship and its complement of 165 crew are lost in the Delta Quadrant, their organs are being harvested by the Vidians, the Borg queen has threatened to assimilate us all, there is very little food left, and some have already died on shuttlecraft missions. It therefore seems absolutely plausible—if not ideal—that Captain Janeway should lie down on something curiously resembling Astroturf and make mad, passionate love to a Maquis who was her sworn enemy only months before but who now seems to want nothing more than to brush her long and extremely glossy hair and look longingly (read lustfully) into her beautifully lit blue eyes.

Well now, I may have been the first woman starship captain, but I am not the first idiot to have read a script and seen the writing on the wall. So I called a meeting. I asked Rick Berman to gather the key players in his office, and there, on a sunny autumn afternoon, we held our first showdown. I presented my argument quickly and passionately. I said that as a female captain of childbearing age, it was inappropriate to have me cavorting on some planet with my first lieutenant, signifying to the audience that I was not only a negligent and despicable leader but a bimbo to boot. I argued that the male demographic would go elsewhere for their kicks if all we served them was crap, that they were smarter than we were and knew their science fiction, that they loved their captains and understood the nature of epic peril and that this simply would not fly, and that if they persisted in pursuing this absurd line of drama, I would be forced to resist. Some wit mumbled, "Resistance is futile," which was meant to bring down the house but didn't. "Gentlemen," I said, "don't make me plead for what you know is right and correct—give me a chance to lead this crew, to be a captain in my own right, and to inspire the audience to follow me because of my ability to command bravely and authentically, without gender-specific pacifiers or throwbacks. Let's just give it an all-out shot for the rest of the season," I said, "and if, at the end of that time, I have failed to win them over through my merits as a leader, I will agree to revisit this conversation." Rick Berman looked long and hard at me, smiled that slow and naughty smile I would come to love, and held up six fingers. I had six months to prove it. The gauntlet had been tossed.

At first, there was a dip in the ratings. I sensed an underlying tension, but I held my ground and worked hard to endow Janeway with humor and passion and keen intelligence. I studied the Okuda bible, I visited NASA, I read Feynman and Einstein with a view to understanding the scientific mind and its eccentricities. I took the text home every night and battled with the technobabble until I understood and owned it. I developed and nurtured a special friendship with the Doctor, who was a hologram and was the first of his kind to accept and embrace humanity—on my ship and on my watch. I threw myself into the intellectually challenging episodes that confronted issues such as the right to suicide, the loneliness of command and its attendant depression, art versus science, and always, of course, our steadfast devotion to the Prime Directive. I also phasered dozens of aliens, altered course numerous times, lost thousands of light-years, regained them through a vortex, and put my intrepid little starship through more paces than had ever been done before. I did most of my own stunts and stood on my feet for eighteen hours a day, averaging almost eighty-five hours a week, for the entire first season.

Then I received an invitation. First Lady Hillary Clinton inquired as to my interest and availability regarding a speaking engagement at the White House before a group of female scientists being honored for their extraordinary achievements. These women had been culled from research labs, universities, hospitals, classrooms, and space stations. They were the crème de la crème of their species, and Mrs. Clinton thought it would be both fitting and, I think, exciting for them if an actress who played a scientist and a captain on television addressed them from her vantage point of experience. This gave me pause. It would be one thing to address a group of actresses who played scientists on television, but to address the real thing seemed, frankly, suicidal. So of course I accepted. On the plane, I wrote and rewrote my remarks, finally settling on something that I figured was so benign it could neither offend nor impress—the kind of tribute one might find on QVC.

As I approached the podium, I was immediately assaulted by the absurdity of the situation: how could a television actress even begin to impart anything resembling wisdom to these exceptional scientists? So I simply turned to the group and apologized. Whether they thought this was uncharacteristically modest or absolutely appropriate, I'll never know, but as one they burst into applause. This response created an opening for a wonderful dialogue, and I began to talk, directly and honestly, about my experiences as the first female captain of a starship. They listened, rapt, as I went on about my duties, my disciplines, the difficulty of motherhood, exhaustion, the myriad rewards, and the beginning of a profound and enduring respect for science. I spoke of Captain Janeway's ardent love of science and how it endowed her with a courage she might otherwise have lacked. I suggested that science fiction did not run so far afield from what they themselves studied and loved, that science required a leap of the imagination, and that physicists like Einstein and Feynman understood that. I thanked them for their mettle, their fine intelligence, their competitiveness, and their devotion. Then I thanked Mrs. Clinton, who had taken me aside earlier and told me that she and Chelsea were big fans of *Star Trek* and watched *Voyager* religiously. This was enormously satisfying.

Later, mingling with the women scientists, I was surprised and overwhelmed to hear over and over that my performance as a starship captain had been a determining factor in many of their decisions to leave the lab and go into the field. Some spoke of NASA, others of active research, and all of them referred to a "new beginning," the "final frontier," the "joy of pioneering." In that room, on that occasion, there was a very clear sense of a brave new world, and none of these women were talking about microscopes. The talk was of black holes, string theory, life on Mars, space shuttles, and space travel. Some would walk on the moon, and all of them would dream of it.

So, when I'm asked what impact or influence Captain Janeway had on popular culture, I like to revisit that evening in Washington. I see faces, upturned and eager, and I see hope. But most important, I see a new kind of expectation, a very real anticipation of discovering the unknown. That is what this book is about. The authors of these chapters provide insight into the various ways popular culture can change perspectives, influence the way people think, and offer dissenting views of prevailing ideas. If Janeway urged change in the field of science and encouraged even a handful of women to take to the stars, then it seems to me that her influence was considerable. As my father used to say to me, "The sky's the limit, kid." I got to amend that to, "Space is the limit, ladies." And I meant it.

ACKNOWLEDGMENTS

The editors are indebted to the kind support of Anne Dean Watkins and all the good people of the University Press of Kentucky. Your support and guidance on this project are enormously appreciated. We could not ask for a better group of people to work with. We would also like to thank the contributors to and reviewers of this volume for their conscientious efforts and insights.

Joseph J. Foy would like to thank Kristi, Connor, and Dr. Sue and Jim Foy for their unending patience and loving assistance. (Kristi, I promise to let you watch some of your shows now.) Thanks also to Dean A. Kowalski for his help in starting the best research program anyone could ask for; Margaret Hankenson and Dick Flannery for their mentoring and role-modeling; Timothy Dunn, Greg Ahrenhoerster, Phil Zweifel, Chris Roland, Patrick Schmitt, and David Weber for all the pop culture discussions; Bill Schneider for all the anti–pop culture discussions; Scott Silet and the fine staff of the University of Wisconsin–Waukesha library; David Hunt for his comments and insights; Joy Cardin and the good folks of Wisconsin Public Radio for helping to bring academic research to the public conversation in Wisconsin; and Adam Liter for giving me hope that the next generation really does "get it."

Timothy M. Dale would like to thank Amy for putting up with a husband who watches too much TV; his daughter, Ellia, for enjoying football and political talk shows as much as he does; his parents, Carlynn, Mike, Carol, and Doug, for never subscribing to cable television while he was growing up; Ryan for so many years of putting up with his lectures; Fred Dallmayr for countless hours of patient mentoring; his colleagues in the Department of Social Change and Development at the University of Wisconsin–Green Bay for providing a spirited and supportive academic environment in which to teach and research; and anyone who ever fought to have episodes of television shows available for free on the Internet.

This book is dedicated to Connor Joseph Foy and Ellia Danielle Dale. We love you both very much. Don't sit so close to the TV.

INTRODUCTION

Tuning in to Democratic Dissent:
Oppositional Messaging in Popular Culture

Joseph J. Foy

The Simpsons has never shied away from politics. In the seventh episode of its twentieth season, entitled "Mypods and Boomsticks," Bart befriends a young Muslim boy named Bashir whose family has just moved to Springfield from Jordan. Bashir is polite, friendly, and easygoing, but Bart is afraid that his differences will make him a prime target for bullying. Sure enough, when the two run into Dolph, Kearney, and Jimbo, three of Springfield Elementary's notoriously bad eggs, they immediately try to attack Bashir for being Muslim (and for "being the reason [Kearney] can't take toothpaste on an airplane"). The politics of the playground extends to the barflies at Moe's Tavern, as Lenny, Karl, and Moe convince Homer that Bart's new friend is part of a terrorist family looking to destroy America. After seeing Jack Bauer torture a Muslim terror suspect on an episode of *24*, Homer is convinced and lays a trap to try to uncover their plot. Through a series of paranoid misunderstandings, Homer thinks that Bashir's father is going to attempt to blow up the Springfield Mall. He races to the rescue but ends up thwarting a planned demolition of the old mall and destroys a newly constructed bridge to the Duff Brewery in the process.[1]

"Mypods and Boomsticks" was quickly praised by the Council on American-Islamic Relations (CAIR) for its willingness to take on anti-Islamic attitudes and paranoia in the United States and for depicting the respect for difference that is necessary in a multicultural society.[2] The episode will undoubtedly join the ranks of other classic political ones taking on the debates related to homophobia ("Homer's Phobia" and "There's Something about Marrying"), medical marijuana ("Weekend at Burnsies"), gun ownership ("The Cartridge Family"), religion ("Lisa the Skeptic" and "The Monkey

Suit"), animal rights and agricultural production ("Lisa the Vegetarian" and "Apocalypse Cow"), and campaigns and elections ("Sideshow Bob Roberts," "Mr. Spritz Goes to Washington," "Trash of the Titans," "See Homer Run," and "E Pluribus Wiggum"). Even *The Simpsons Movie*, which grossed over $527 million in worldwide box-office receipts, took on controversial issues such as environmental degradation and abuse of power by the U.S. government in the name of security. These are but a few examples of how *The Simpsons* has challenged mainstream cultural and political assumptions, offering a dissenting perspective that seeks to influence the democratic dialogue.

This is perhaps what is most interesting about *The Simpsons*. As a work of popular culture, one might assume that it reflects mainstream attitudes and beliefs so that it will be readily embraced by a wide audience seeking to reaffirm broadly shared and collectively held worldviews. Popular culture is, after all, that which appeals to and is well liked by a mass audience. However, many of the episodes—such as those on homosexuality, animal rights, the war on terror, and religion—actually confront what is culturally accepted and popularly believed in an interesting interplay of popular culture challenging popular convention.

In the 2003 book entitled *Leaving Springfield: The Simpsons and the Possibility of Oppositional Culture*, edited by John Alberti, the theoretical underpinnings of popular culture as a means of fostering social opposition to mainstream views in a manner that is widely accepted and embraced are clearly established.[3] The use of self-critical satire and humorously biting commentary on a range of issues and views has enabled *The Simpsons* to remain popular despite the numerous challenges to dominant views and culture explored by the contributors to *Leaving Springfield*. A theme present throughout the collection is that *The Simpsons* is such a popularly accepted series, despite containing political messages that might threaten to turn some audiences away, because its sociocultural messages of dissent are woven into the fabric of the show in a manner that does not overtly confront popular sensibilities. Instead, the writers and creators of the show internalize the messages of opposition without making their audience feel personally attacked.

Voices of Dissent, Voices of Democracy

The Simpsons is not the only popular culture artifact to take on the role of challenging widely held, commonly shared beliefs and values. Other animated television shows such as *Futurama, Family Guy,* and *South Park* humorously defy sociopolitical norms and conventions, while a dramatic, dark comedy like *Desperate Housewives* attempts to peel back the illusionary veneer in modern America suburbia to offer dissenting perspectives on gender, sexuality, power, and identity. Such perspectives are also reflected on the silver screen. Sean Penn's 2009 Academy Award–winning portrayal of California's first openly gay elected official, Harvey Milk, blends historical footage within a modern take on homophobia and social and political discrimination of the homosexual community.[4] Other movies, such as the 2008 box-office blockbuster *The Dark Knight,* offer a defense of unpopular political tactics used by the Bush administration (wiretapping, extraordinary rendition, and torture) in the name of combating terrorism. Likewise, albums such as Green Day's seventh studio album, *American Idiot,* which reached number one on the American charts and has sold more than 10 million copies in domestic and international markets, openly confront American culture and politics with songs such as "American Idiot," "Holiday," and "Wake Me Up When September Ends." U2's 2009 release, *No Line on the Horizon,* offers tracks that personalize the horrors of war; "White as Snow" comments on the war in Afghanistan from the perspective of a dying soldier, and "Cedars of Lebanon" explores conflict from the perspective of a war correspondent. The aforementioned are just a few examples of how popular culture challenges prevailing political and moral orders. Such expression can be found in a variety of mass media, and whether through television, film, music, or the printed word, these works provide a voice to oppositional views that affect the democratic dialogue.

A liberal society, one that favors progress and individualism, can succeed only to the extent it allows individuals to identify and pursue a variety of goals. This is possible only in a context wherein respect for dissent and difference is maintained. Absent such respect, tyranny will replace pluralism, and individuals will no longer have ways to seek their own personal ends and the collective good through democratic deliberation. Liberal democracy must therefore respect disagreement as much as it pursues consensus. Such tolerance is advanced through the fostering of a culture that not only tolerates dissent but also provides avenues for dissenting views to be freely expressed within mainstream dialogue. When opposition is expressed on a large scale, it is healthy for democracy because it confronts widespread political attitudes and symbols and transforms marginalized views into voices of currency and relevance.

There are likely those who would join the ranks of social commentators and academics Kalle Lasn, Robert Putnam, and Naomi Klein or activist Peter Tatchell in arguing that popular culture and entertainment pacify and insulate the American public from the real obligations and challenges of democratic citizenship.[5] Pop culture, to them, is a commercialized opiate that, in the spirit of Neil Postman, amuses the public to death.[6] However, the purpose of this book is to counter such perspectives and reveal how popular culture can be used to deconstruct or undermine dominant political and social standards. Far from being merely a tool of entertainment or pacification, popular culture is sometimes used by people when they disagree with mainstream attitudes and are looking for a way to express their dissent. In these instances, pop culture becomes a medium for the expression of countervailing ideas in order to advance change and alter the public conversation. When we look at where expressions of dissent are occurring in our society, such as the examples included in this volume, we gain insight into how our society deals with dissenting views, what these views are, and how they are expressed.

Overt Advocacy and Covert Politics in Popular Culture

There are two ways in which popular culture can engage in the expression of social, cultural, and political dissent. The first is through overt messaging in which popular culture is used to advance direct, clear political advocacy. Such messages are openly political without attempting to mask or hide them within a broader entertainment framework. Examples of overt political engagement through popular culture abound. The direct influence of celebrity and popular culture on political discourse is evident in documentary films such as *Darfur Now*, a call to action to end the humanitarian crisis in the Darfur region of Sudan. This documentary prominently features Don Cheadle, who also helped produce the movie, and other celebrity activists, such as George Clooney, who coproduced and narrated another documentary on the crisis, *Sand and Sorrow*. Similarly, Leonardo DiCaprio used his star status to call attention to the ecological crisis resulting from global warming by producing and narrating *The 11th Hour*, which followed on the heels of Al Gore's documentary *An Inconvenient Truth*, exploring similar issues. Likewise, famed director Spike Lee confronts the problems of poverty, racism, poor governmental planning and response, and social perceptions that led to the numerous and widespread problems following

Hurricane Katrina in the HBO documentary *When the Levees Broke: A Requiem in Four Acts,* which features celebrity activists Sean Penn, Kanye West, Harry Belafonte, and Wynton Marsalis alongside public officials and prominent scholars.

In addition to overt political messaging in documentary films, popular corporate brands have begun to promote direct political engagement by marketing products with a clear political message. For example, Product (RED) has created a network of corporate participation involving businesses such as the Gap, Microsoft, Starbucks, and Converse to raise awareness about HIV/AIDS. More important, by tapping into the strategy of a "buycott," which allows consumers to purchase products in a socially conscious fashion to further a particular agenda, (RED) has generated more than $120 million for the Global Fund for HIV/AIDS, which has impacted an estimated 2.5 million lives in Africa.[7]

Political organizations such as MoveOn.org have also embraced the power of popular culture to engage and influence voters by moving away from traditional Beltway political formats of advertising and disseminating information. MoveOn has produced advertisements directed by A-list Hollywood celebrities, comedians, popular music artists, and hip-hop producers. MoveOn has also attempted to work its way into the consciousness of potentially disengaged citizens by placing ads in *Entertainment Weekly, People,* and *Rolling Stone.*[8] Following a similar strategy, Barack Obama famously took out advertising space in the popular video games *Burnout Paradise,* a racing game for X-Box 360 that features an Obama billboard with the Web site voteforchange.com prominently displayed, and *Madden NFL 2009.* He also used both a text-messaging campaign and the social networking sites Facebook and MySpace to reach out to primarily young voters.[9]

It is important to note that the interplay between politics and popular culture has direct social and political effects. A 2008 study released by Christopher A. Cooper and Mandi Bates Bailey found that entertainment news shows have a significant positive effect on civic knowledge among the politically disinterested.[10] Their research is supported by a 2004 Annenberg national election survey that found that voters who watched entertainment news knew more about the policy preferences and positions of presidential candidates than did nonviewers.[11] Likewise, a study by researchers at the Edward R. Murrow College of Communication at Washington State University indicated that the efforts of celebrities such as Beyonce Knowles, Christina Aguilera, and Sean "Diddy" Combs were influential in promot-

The members of U2: Larry Mullen Jr., Adam Clayton, Bono, and the Edge (from left to right). The band is known for its protest anthems, political messages, and a brand of activism that extends beyond the music. (Jerry Ohlinger's Movie Material Store)

ing youth voter turnout, which increased by 12 percent between 2000 and 2008.[12] The researchers concluded that celebrity appeals connect young voters to the political process and help them understand that their actions can make a difference, transforming politics into something that is popular and exciting. Such studies show the important influence of popular culture artifacts, such as Eminem's *Mosh,* a rap song and video to promote youth engagement in the 2004 election, or U2 front-man Bono's numerous calls for public awareness and action on a range of issues, including debt relief for the world's poorest nations, AIDS, and the environment. These overt messages in popular culture are clear and direct and are having an observable impact.

No less important is the second way that popular culture can engage in transforming social and cultural convention, though it is less direct and less obvious. Through the use of covert messaging, which masks political ideas in the guise of entertainment, this strategy engages the political in a far subtler way. Such efforts can introduce oppositional ideas and values without openly or directly confronting audiences, which might cause them to turn away or reject the message outright. These subtle challenges can get individuals to think about their own views, beliefs, values, and priorities. Through covert messaging, we find popular culture attempting to engage the mass public indirectly in social and political discourse.

The influence of popular culture on the politics of mainstream society is well documented. In *Politics and Popular Culture*, John Street describes how popular culture helps organize the values and preferences of society, which also shapes personal and public identities. Street claims that "contemporary politics is itself conducted through the language and the formats of popular culture," and he cites the work of Iain Chambers from a decade earlier when he notes that popular culture offers a "democratic prospect for appropriating and transforming everyday life." Street is careful not to overstate the case. He does not claim that we are forced to imitate the messages or portrayals within popular culture, nor does popular culture serve entirely as a social mirror. Instead, popular culture can be viewed as something woven inextricably into the fabric of democratic society and the lives of its consumers in a manner that allows us to "live through and with it."[13]

Popular culture's ability to challenge social norms and conventions in a manner that covertly influences mainstream perception is evident in portrayals of race. To examine the question "Is America ready for a black president?" National Public Radio ran a segment on *All Things Considered* on January 31, 2008, exploring how Dennis Haysbert's portrayal of President David Palmer in the first through fifth seasons of *24* and Morgan Freeman's role as President Tom Beck in the movie *Deep Impact* may have helped pave the way for acceptance of the notion of an African American president. Neither the television show nor the movie directly advocated that voters change their minds about race, but as Todd Boyd, a critical studies professor at the University of Southern California's School of Cinematic Arts, noted in the segment, such portrayals "may have subconsciously made some things in society seem less troubling."[14] Had the television series *Commander-in-Chief*, starring Geena Davis as America's first female president, been able to resolve some of its time-slot problems and translate its initial number-one rating on Tuesday nights into a regular viewing audience, a similar conversation might have been held about gender.

Like the examples of overt communication, covert political messaging in popular culture is all around us. The focus of this book is on the latter, as the contributing authors show how popular culture works to influence the cultural conversation without directly advocating for change. While some of the chapters show the theoretical connection between popular culture and social opposition, others demonstrate both the affect (the emotional experience invoked by popular culture artifacts to impress a particular perspective on an audience) and the effect (the direct change elicited by popular culture on political beliefs and actions) of dissenting views expressed in popular culture.

Pop Culture and Reactionary Opposition

Many of the chapters in this volume deal with progressive social, cultural, and policy issues rather than reactionary messages within popular culture. That does not mean that reactionary messages do not exist in popular forms of entertainment. One need only turn on the radio to hear conservative voices on entertainment talk shows or turn the dial to country music stations featuring the conservative lyrics of popular artists such as Toby Keith.[15] There are, in fact, numerous examples of popular culture expressing reactionary opposition to prevailing social and political trends.

A common theme in this regard is the expression of dissent against the growth of the state. In *The Power of Myth*, Joseph Campbell points to the character of Darth Vader in the *Star Wars* saga as representing the growth and transformation of the technocratic and overly bureaucratized state. According to Campbell:

> Darth Vader has not developed his own humanity. He's a robot. He's a bureaucrat, living not in terms of himself but in terms of an imposed system. This is the threat to our lives that we all face today. Is the system going to flatten you out and deny you your humanity, or are you going to be able to make use of the system to the attainment of human purposes? How do you relate to the system so that you are not compulsively serving it? It doesn't help to try to change it to accord with your system of thought. The momentum of history behind it is too great for anything really significant to evolve from that kind of action. The thing to do is learn to live in your period of history as a human being. That's something else, and it can be done.[16]

Darth Vader represents a strong conservative fear of the growth of the dehumanized bureaucratic state and the desire to maintain one's individualism and rights in the face of evolving state power.[17] That the rebellion in *Star Wars* seeks to liberate humanity from the all-encompassing, oppressive state reveals a reactionary, conservative message in the film. This message is mimicked in the sci-fi western series *Firefly* and its feature film *Serenity,* as the ruggedly underdeveloped pioneer planets of the outer rim struggle to maintain their identity and freedom from the growing central Alliance.[18]

Also wrapped up in Campbell's assessment of Vader is the assumption that an increasingly technologically driven society would deprive humanity of its true self. The fear of technology as challenging those traditional aspects of humanity has worked its way into numerous artifacts of popular culture. This is most evident in the popularity of the *Terminator* films and the popular Fox spin-off series *The Sarah Connor Chronicles,* which follow humankind's struggle to save itself from the growing threat of machines that will one day wipe out our existence. Likewise, the CBS suspense-thriller *Eleventh Hour* works under the premise that humankind has overcome the forces of nature only to be threatened by the very science and technologies that facilitated civilization's ascension. Such reactionary voices also find their way into less obvious portrayals in film and television. One example is the conclusion of the action film *Rambo: First Blood Part II,* when John J. Rambo (Sylvester Stallone)—himself a symbol for the primal nature of man—opens fire on the computers and equipment in Marshal Murdock's (Charles Napier) command center before threatening to kill the heartless and unfeeling bureaucrat for his lack of concern for the American soldier who sacrificed so much for the state.[19]

A reactionary response to the forces of globalization is also present in many artifacts of contemporary popular culture. The 1990 Academy Award–winning Best Picture *Dances with Wolves* is perhaps the quintessential frontier narrative that highlights the "globalization theme" of an expanding civilization's threat to traditional life and society. We are first introduced to Lieutenant John Dunbar (Kevin Costner) as he fights on the front lines of the American Civil War. After his suicide attempt turns into a heroic ride that captures the attention of his superiors, Dunbar requests a transfer to the western frontier because he would like to see it before it disappears entirely. The story follows his solitary arrival and his communion with the land and its creatures. His animal familiars, Cisco the horse and Two Socks the wolf, represent the natural connection Dunbar has with the frontier, and his slow friendship with the Sioux tribe near the fort represents his immersion in the

John Connor (Christian Bale) from the *Terminator* series symbolizes conservative reaction to the rapid proliferation of technology that has begun to transform society. (MovieGoods)

traditional culture of the American West. But the civilization Dunbar left is close behind him. Soon more soldiers arrive, and they begin to threaten the traditional life of the Sioux. Moreover, the arrival of the soldiers is a harbinger of the expansion of the industrialized East into the western frontier. Eventually civilization will touch all parts of North America; no longer will there be a place to escape its encroachment. *Dances with Wolves* ends with Dunbar and his wife, Stands with a Fist (Mary McDonnell), parting ways with the Sioux tribe, as members of the U.S. Calvary hunt them down. The end of the film gives the impression of a world that is getting smaller, one where the external is always present and with us. This conclusion illustrates the final disappearance of the American frontier, a symbol of the traditional sovereignty and cultural autonomy of an American past that is confronting the omnipresent forces of globalization.[20]

As evidenced in the aforementioned examples, not every form of dissent in popular culture is aimed at progressive social change. Protests from the political Right are usually aimed at reducing the size of government, supporting the values of a traditional moral culture, promoting a certain view of the national American identity, or advancing a realist or isolationist foreign policy. Given these various expressions of reactionary dissent, a reader might wonder why this book does not include an extensive discussion of these voices of protest. There are two primary reasons. First, most of the texts analyzed in this book were produced during the period when conservative politics prevailed in the national political landscape and culture (2000–2006). George W. Bush and a Republican Congress unified government, allowing the pursuit of an aggressive military foreign policy, free-market economics, and a reduction in the size and credibility of the national government (whether through intentional acts of devolution and deregulation or the negligence of executive agencies, as was the case with the response to Hurricane Katrina). A majority of the electorate endorsed or tolerated these policies, and mainstream news reporting rarely questioned or undermined the foreign and domestic policy during this period. Therefore, voices of dissent in popular culture were often aimed at this prevailing conservative politics. If an era of widespread liberal politics were to take over the national political culture in the mass-mediated age, we would expect to see many more popular culture texts reacting to this politics in the form of conservative dissent.

Second, protest and dissent tend to be progressive by their very nature. Progressive politics is about challenging political conventions and conservative ideologies that stand in the way of reform. By definition, *conservative* is that which attempts to preserve what is in place, while *progressive* forces attempt to push society in a direction presumed to be better. Conservatives romanticize the past, while progressives romanticize the future. Dissent aimed at social change, no matter what the era, tends to aim at this future. Dissent does not intend to reinforce the social orders; it intends to change it.

From Culture to the Classroom: The Pedagogy of Oppositional Pop

Just as there are many different ways that popular culture introduces oppositional voices into the social and political mainstream, there are many different approaches to the subject. The contributors to this book are a multidisciplinary team of scholars who bring expertise in the areas of political science and public administration, sociology, criminal justice and law, history, film and media studies, communications, and English. Some of the chapters explain the theoretical ways in which popular culture can be seen as a vehicle for oppositional expression, while others demonstrate the history of the incorporation of popular culture elements into labor and social movements. Some of the chapters explore quantitative data that reveal the direct impact of political representation in popular culture on a viewing audience, while others perform more qualitative case studies of one or two popular culture artifacts. Still others examine some of the covert messages wrapped up in popular culture through a textual analysis of films and television shows. Collectively, the chapters of this book demonstrate the diverse ways pop culture introduces opposition into the social and political mainstream, and they tap into the various themes relevant to an introductory study of the interplay between popular media and politics, identity, culture, and society.

The contributors to this volume join a growing field of scholarly voices and pursuits as academics begin to explore more deeply the interplay between images and messages in popular culture and political and social change. A cursory search through course catalogs and syllabi of colleges and universities across the country reveals a proliferation of courses examining the sociology and politics of popular culture. For example, courses on the Sociology of Popular Culture are being taught at the University of Pennsylvania, the University of Vermont, and Bucknell University; American Popular Culture and Politics: 1940–Present is offered at the University of

Minnesota; and Popular Culture and American Politics is a course at the University of Tennessee–Knoxville. These and a host of other classes being taught on campuses throughout the United States reveal that the cultural interplay between the politics and sociology of popular culture is becoming a serious field of scholarly inquiry. We believe this volume will find a home in those classrooms, and we hope it helps students discover some of those covert messages of social, cultural, and political opposition that are present in contemporary popular media.

The goal of this volume is to explore the dynamics of the expression of dissent and oppositional voices in popular culture and in social and political movements. To accomplish this, the book has been divided into three parts. Part 1 demonstrates how popular culture creates a "public space" wherein democratic debates and dialogue about important issues are waged. Timothy Dale uses social and political theory to explore the notions of a public sphere and demonstrates how popular culture facilitates the democratic discussion of and engagement in ideas of national importance within this public space. Jamie Warner provides a theoretical framework that extends this notion by demonstrating how entertainment news programs such as *The Daily Show with Jon Stewart* introduce oppositional perspectives through comedy and satire to "speak truth to power." Beth Wielde Heidelberg and David Schultz provide a survey of popular political movies to demonstrate how social views of the state and shared societal values and priorities are framed and influenced by the consumption of popular culture. Finally, Paul Cantor examines how popular culture can be viewed in post-9/11 America through a reexamination of the relevant themes and messages in the longest-running science fiction show in television history, *The X-Files.*

Part 2 turns to an examination of how dissent is expressed by means of the social messages conveyed through popular media. Here a variety of views on politics, society, culture, and identity are explored, beginning with a chapter by Sara Jordan and Phillip Gray, who examine oppositional messages against the regulatory state as expressed through the heroic antics of the title character in the series *House.* This is followed by Peter Caster, who uses Spike Lee's film *25th Hour* to explore themes of dissent related to the American prison system and issues of incarceration. Katherine Lehman moves the discussion to an evaluation of identity politics and sociopolitical messaging related to sexual orientation and issues of rights and equality as expressed through the actions of Rosie O'Donnell. Matthew Henry then uses *The Simpsons* as the basis for a discussion about religious debates wrapped up in the larger topic of an American culture war. Finally, Joseph Foy concludes this part with an examination of the environmental messages contained in a genre of film known as "eco-horror" and a textual reading of M. Night Shyamalan's *The Happening* as the basis for exploring American ecological politics and policies.

Part 3 examines how popular culture directly facilitates societal, cultural, and political transformation and change through a look at the dynamics of dissent and social movements. To begin this part, Jeffrey Johnson provides a historical context to the relationship between popular media and political movements by analyzing the use of popular culture by labor organizations and leftist movements at the turn of the twentieth century in America. This historical perspective is extended by Jerry Rodnitzky, who bridges the gap between history and the present through an examination of popular music as a vehicle for protest from Vietnam to the current wars in Iraq and Afghanistan. Next, Tanji Gilliam uses hip-hop as the basis for an inquiry into representation, power, and identity formation within the black community. Isabel Pinedo then examines how popular culture transforms not only the way people understand politics but also how they use popular media to mobilize and express opposition to institutions of power; she does this by looking into the notions of fandom associated with the CBS series *Jericho*. Carl Bergetz explores the transformational effect entertainment media have had on America's mainstream news media. Finally, Diana Relke takes us back to the future with a look into how Gene Roddenberry's *Star Trek* franchise (and *Star Trek: The Next Generation* in particular) influenced perspectives and dialogues on identity, gender, and power in the academy and households across America and around the world.

In the premiere episode of *The Colbert Report,* Stephen Colbert announces that the viewers of his show are "heroes" who know that "something must be done." He then pounds his fist on his C-shaped desk to inform them that they are doing something right now—they "are watching TV."[21] His proclamation might be met with smirks, guffaws, and skepticism, but the authors of the chapters of this book lend credence to this tongue-in-cheek commentary. Although true activism requires mobilized engagement to inspire change, the empowerment of political dissent via mass media and popular culture reflected in these pages provides an argument that true public, democratic action is occurring through popular culture. We merely have to tune in to join the conversation.

Notes

1. "Mypods and Boomsticks," production code KABF20, original airdate November 30, 2008.

2. Bruce Tomaso, "'The Simpsons' Commended for Mocking Islamophobia," *Dallas Morning News,* December 4, 2008, http://religionblog.dallasnews.com/archives/2008/12/ the-simpsons-commended-for-epi.html (accessed February 5, 2009). The original letter from CAIR California to Matt Groening can be found online at http://cair-california.org/ images/stories/thank_you_letter_-_matt_groening.pdf (accessed February 5, 2009).

3. John Alberti, ed., *Leaving Springfield: The Simpsons and the Possibility of Oppositional Culture* (Detroit: Wayne State University Press, 2003).

4. Sean Penn's portrayal of Harvey Milk is a perfect example of the interplay between popular culture as a vehicle for oppositional voices and the challenge it can pose to the social and political mainstream. *Milk,* which was nominated for several awards, drew anti-gay protests from crowds outside the Academy Awards ceremony for its heroic depiction of the homosexual San Francisco supervisor who was assassinated in 1978. Penn criticized the protests in light of California's recent vote to outlaw same-sex marriage. He stated: "For those who saw the signs of hatred as our cars drove in tonight, I think it's a good time for those who voted for the ban against gay marriage to sit and reflect on their great shame and their shame in their grandchildren's eyes if they continue that support. We've got to have equal rights for everyone." David Germain, "'Slumdog' Rules Oscars with 8 Prizes, Best Picture," *Ventura County Star,* February 23, 2009, http://hosted.ap.org/dynamic/stories/O/OSCARS?SITE=CAVEN&SECTION= HOME&TEMPLATE=DEFAULT (accessed February 23, 2009). The interplay between the dominant social and political cultural trends and countervailing views expressed through movies like *Milk* offers further evidence of the democratic role popular culture can have in influencing public discourse.

5. See Kalle Lasn, *Culture Jam: The Uncooling of America*™ (New York: William Morrow, 1999); Naomi Klein, *No Logo* (New York: Picador, 1999); Robert Putnam, *Bowling Alone: The Collapse and Revival of American Community* (New York: Simon and Schuster, 2000).

6. Neil Postman, *Amusing Ourselves to Death: Public Discourse in the Age of Show Business* (New York: Penguin, 1986).

7. News and statistics related to Product (RED) can be found at http://www.joinred. com/Home.aspx (accessed February 6, 2009).

8. Ari Berman, "Populist Politics Meet Popular Culture," *Nation,* August 26, 2004, http://www.thenation.com/doc/20040913/berman (accessed February 6, 2009).

9. Devlin Barrett, "Ads for Obama Campaign: 'It's in the Game,'" MSNBC, October 14, 2008, http://www.msnbc.msn.com/id/27184857/ (accessed February 5, 2009); "Obama Ads Invade Video Games," FOXNews.com, October, 15, 2008, http://www .foxnews.com/story/0,2933,437763,00.html (accessed February 5, 2009); Anne E. Korn-

blut and Ed O'Keefe, "Tale of the Obama Text Message," *WashingtonPost*.com, August 23, 2008, http://voices.washingtonpost.com/44/2008/08/23/tale_of_the_obama_text_message.html (accessed February 5, 2009).

10. Christopher A. Cooper and Mandi Bates Bailey, "Entertainment Media and Political Knowledge: Do Americans Get Any Truth Out of Truthiness?" in *Homer Simpson Goes to Washington: American Politics through Popular Culture,* ed. Joseph J. Foy (Lexington: University Press of Kentucky, 2008), 133–50.

11. Bryan Long, "*Daily Show* Viewers Ace Political Quiz," CNN, September 29, 2004, http://cnn.com/2004/SHOWBIZ/TV/09/28/comedy.politics/ (accessed February 6, 2009).

12. Erica Weintrab Austin, Rebecca Van de Vord, Bruce E. Pinkleton, and Eva Epstein, "Celebrity Endorsements and Their Potential to Motivate Young Voters," *Mass Communication and Society* 11, no. 4 (October 2008): 420–36.

13. John Street, *Politics and Popular Culture* (Philadelphia: Temple University Press, 1997), 6, 4.

14. National Public Radio, "Has Hollywood Helped Pave Way for Obama?" Politics and Society segment, *All Things Considered,* January 31, 2008, http://www.npr.org/templates/story/story.php?storyId=18580711 (accessed February 5, 2009).

15. Although Keith is a registered Democrat, he admits to being "probably the most right [leaning] Democrat in the world." Steve Morse, "He's Not Afraid to Speak Out for His Country," *Boston Globe,* July 23, 2004, http://www.boston.com/news/globe/living/articles/2004/07/23/hes_not_afraid_to_speak_out_for_his_country/ (accessed February 7, 2009).

16. Joseph Campbell, *The Power of Myth* (New York: Anchor, 1991), 144.

17. Sara Jordan and Phillip Gray explore these reactionary themes against the bureaucratic state in their chapter on the television series *House.* Similar themes are evident in Beth Wielde Heidelberg and David Schultz's examination of the portrayals of bureaucratic archetypes in film.

18. In line with more conservative critiques of modern culture and society, *Firefly* and *Serenity,* which tap into the sci-fi western genre pioneered by the original *Star Trek* series (which had the original working title *Wagon Train to the Stars*), exemplify the use of the "frontier narrative." This narrative originally heralded the taming of the savage frontier, as evident in the *Star Trek* series and its spin-offs; it has now begun to critique the expansion of civilization and the threat it poses to traditional cultures and individual identity.

19. At the end of the movie, Rambo is confronted by his mentor and former superior officer, Colonel Samuel Trautman (Richard Crenna), about his hatred toward Murdock and the country he represents. Rambo disabuses Trautman of the notion that he hates his country; in fact, he would die for it. Yet, when asked what he wants, Rambo offers an impassioned plea that embodies the rejection of an unfeeling, dispassionate bureaucratic state: "I want, what they want, and every other guy who came over here and spilled his

guts and gave everything he had, wants! For our country to love us as much as we love it. That's what I want."

20. The Coen brothers' *No Country for Old Men* (2007) also calls on the myth of the Old West and untamed territory. However, rather than being a heroic tale of conquering the frontier, *No Country for Old Men* shows a protagonist, Sheriff Ed Tom Bell (Tommy Lee Jones), struggling against displacement and the oppression of so-called forces of civilization that have no regard for traditional values or the simpler ways of a disappearing past. Interestingly, Ang Lee's *Brokeback Mountain* uses a similar western motif as the setting of the homosexual relationship between Jack Twist (Jake Gyllenhaal) and Ennis Del Mar (Heath Ledger) to demonstrate the oppressive nature of an intolerant society juxtaposed on the liberating backdrop of the frontier. Although Lee's film provides an oppositional perspective on cultural values, given its progressive position on homosexual identity, there is also a conservative call for a simpler time of rugged individualism—a time prior to the dismantling of the personal sphere of private action by the oppressive forces of globalization.

21. *The Colbert Report,* season 1, episode 1, original airdate October 17, 2005.

Part 1

POPULAR CULTURE AS PUBLIC SPACE

1

THE REVOLUTION IS BEING TELEVISED

The Case for Popular Culture as Public Sphere

Timothy M. Dale

The Gil Scott Heron song "The Revolution Will Not Be Televised" begins with the lines "You will not be able to stay home, brother. / You will not be able to plug in, turn on and cop out." As a call to political action, the song takes on the laziness and corporatism of popular culture as inimical to real political change. The song declares a litany of popular culture and media institutions as irrelevant to "the revolution" and suggests that the revolution will require real activism that is impossible within the confines of popular media, music, television, and film. Written before the twenty-four-hour news cycle, the proliferation of cable programming, product placement, and reality television, the lyrics of the Heron song are even more accusing of modern popular culture. Has modern popular culture removed us even further from the possibilities of political activity and prevented us from effecting change in society? With this question, we should consider Heron's warning seriously: if I have "plugged in" and "turned on" my satellite dish, DVD collection, computer, and iPod, have I "copped out"?

The answer depends on how we understand political activity and the public sphere. A traditional understanding of the public sphere is that political discourse is possible only in the realm of traditional political spaces. According to this view, the classic political spaces of picket lines, the halls of government, and conversations at cafés are where the action is. The trappings of popular culture are at best diversions and at worst insidious mechanisms

Norman Lear's *All in the Family*, the highest rated television show of the 1970s, confronted many politically charged issues and frequently encouraged awareness and perspective through its uniquely written characters and comedy style. (Jerry Ohlinger's Movie Material Store)

limiting our creativity and stifling our political imagination. But if political expression can exist in a multiplicity of forms, and exposing injustice and setting discursive agendas are forms of political activity, then perhaps the revolution can be televised after all.

The same year Heron recorded "The Revolution Will Not Be Televised" (1971), millions of American households were tuned in to *All in the Family*, the most popular show on television. The star of the show is Archie Bunker, a working-class (anti)hero who is also an ongoing satire of intolerance. In a notable episode that aired on February 9, 1971, titled "Judging Books by Covers," Archie is convinced that his son-in-law, Michael, has a friend who is gay. Archie bases this assumption on the behavior, appearance, and mannerisms of this friend. It turns out that Michael's friend is not gay, but Archie is even more shocked to learn that his ex–football player drinking buddy is. Situated within sharp, humorous dialogue and well-written characters are serious messages about homophobia, intolerance, and social stigma. Produced years before the gay rights movement became widespread, and at a time when the open discussion of homosexuality was taboo, the episode was clearly intended as a political message by the show's writers. In this case, a popular television show advanced a national dialogue on a controversial issue by exposing the narrowness and inaccuracy of homosexual stereotypes. After the episode aired, people had conversations about this issue in living rooms across the country, and millions were challenged to reconsider their thinking. The episode was remarkable enough that Richard Nixon had a recorded reaction to it in his infamous tapes.[1]

This is one of many examples of *All in the Family* utilizing its popular appeal to encourage a national dialogue about important social issues.[2] Due in part to the controversy the program stirred up, everyone was watching— more than 20 million households tuned in to *All in the Family* each year between 1971 and 1976, making it the number-one-rated show on television. Thus, during this period, the most popular show was also one of the boldest in terms of expressing dissenting views on issues of race, gender, class, and politics. The production of the show was a form of political action, and watching episodes could be politically formative. Can we say, then, that in the case of *All in the Family*, a revolution *was* televised?

The irony of arguing with Heron's premise about the possibility of political activity through popular culture is that "The Revolution Will Not Be Televised" has itself become an artifact of popular culture. Originally recorded as a spoken word poem in 1970, it was rerecorded as a song on an album with musical accompaniment in 1971. The revolution, or at least this one song about it, was also in fact "televised."[3] The song has now become a cultural icon, appearing in the sound tracks to several films, including *The Hurricane* (1999). The song has also been covered by musicians across a range of musical styles, and it is iconically referenced in poetry, song lyrics, news stories, and television shows.[4] Heron's call to action is a political act, and popular culture becomes a mode for communicating, and debating, that call.

An Expanded View of the Public Sphere

Political expression does not always take the form of policy-oriented dialogue, formal political protest, or direct appeals to political representatives. Art and culture are rich with elements that connect individuals with ideas and with communities of meaning. Often created with political intent, these elements can offer alternative avenues for compelling social commentary. Especially for those who express dissent with a message that may not have access at the ballot box, forms of artistic expression can give voice to the otherwise marginalized. Artistic voices do not always exist at the margins, however, and expressions of political dissent become even more salient in the public sphere when they are expressed in modes of popular culture.

This realization is possible, however, only if we conceive broadly of the "public sphere." We engage in political discourse "in public." If political discourse can take many forms, the public sphere can be conceived of as a multiplicity of spaces. Additionally, different messages and forms of communication are intended for and received by different audiences. If we imagine a public sphere in which newspapers, talk radio, and the halls of government account for all public discourse, we will be missing something. When modeled as a concept limited to the place where explicit policy debate and deliberation take place, the public sphere does not necessarily include the forms of political expression and types of political messages that can be found throughout popular culture. If, however, we understand political discourse as that which is expressed in a broader public sphere, including a wide range of ever-expanding modes of discourse, then we can better understand the role of cultural expression as it relates to political institutions and policies.

Such an expanded view of the public sphere is advocated and explored by several contemporary political theorists. They believe that a diversified conception of the public sphere is promising because it includes not only different forms of expression that should be called political but also different groups and messages that may not have widespread access to or acceptance through other means of political communication.[5] Marginalized groups, for example, can create alternative publics to raise issues among themselves and develop their own discursive modes for expressing their perspective. Political dissent expressed among a group of people naturally creates its own public sphere, and the dissent is shaped through participation in the dialogue. Multiple publics then vie for attention, as arguments are made within and among them. The political debates that prevail, and the conclusions that are reached, are the consequence of the interplay among these publics.

Musicians can write political messages into lyrics, for example, that are heard by audiences and spread in digital form. A political message contained therein can have just as much impact as something written on an editorial page, even though it is expressed within this limited "public." For marginalized groups, this method can be especially effective, allowing communities to be created around dissenting ideas and back channels for communication.[6] Additionally, as publics interact, such a message can be spread even further, and if enough people are exposed to the message, we would say that the song has become an artifact of popular culture.

The expanded view of the public sphere also suggests that not every public sphere or collection of political expressions is intended to directly affect decision making. Although we engage in political deliberation about public policy in public, public spheres are also spaces where we form our opinions, and the interactions therein have a significant role in shaping our political identities. That identity, shaped by cultural influences, is the foundation for political activity. Thus, any sharp distinction between "political" public spheres and "cultural" ones misunderstands the nature of political activity and the essential role that identity formation plays in originating political action in the first place. Given the importance of identity for politics, we should consider the political significance of both "strong" and "weak" publics—the former concerned with decision making and the latter with identity formation.[7] As evidenced in the chapters of this book, popular culture is full of politics, and politics is full of popular culture.

Just as the public sphere is not homogeneous, popular culture is heterogeneous as well. As popular culture outlets proliferate, these multiple forms of media circulate a variety of discourses and make them available for analysis.[8] The examples explored in the chapters that follow demonstrate that many political things are happening in popular culture, and they are happening among different audiences, through different messages, and with different political consequences. Thus, even as we refer to "popular culture" as a collection of artifacts and symbols consumed by large portions of the population, they also exist as distinct artifacts of political expression to be analyzed and understood.

Culture, Commercialism, and Co-option

Obviously, not all popular culture contains political content. Much of popular culture is produced to be a diversion, intended as an escape from the matters of everyday life and, more importantly, to sell products for advertisers. Even when there is political content in elements of popular culture, not all of it is effective at bringing about social change, nor does it necessarily challenge prevailing political and moral orders. This is not evidence of the wholesale irrelevance of popular culture for expressions of dissent and political change, however. Dismissing popular culture as irrelevant for understanding the way dissenting views are expressed simply because much of it lacks political content, and because most of it is complicit with established political and economic orders, prevents us from appreciating those instances when popular culture can have a transformative effect on the broader culture and politics.

A visible example of the use of popular culture to promote a political agenda is the work of Bono (U2's front man) to promote awareness of global poverty and other international issues. Bono meets regularly with world leaders, appears at concerts dedicated to international justice issues, and promotes the special products of companies such as American Express, Gap, and Apple, which promise to donate a portion of the proceeds to his favored charities. Are Bono's actions effective political activism? Should it be considered political activism to purchase products or attend concerts?

Such are the questions posed by Naomi Klein and others who challenge the notion that political action can be embodied in consumerism. In her book *No Logo: Taking Aim at the Brand Bullies,* Klein suggests that corporate sponsorship of political activism is merely capitalism finding ways to profit from dissenting political views.[9] Even worse, this co-opting of dissenting views renders them harmless to the prevailing order: people purchase products, feel that they are making a difference, and do nothing else to address social problems. Calling this tendency the "Bono-ization" of political action, Klein argues that "what's been lost . . . is [the] ability to change [global] power structures. There are still the winners and losers, people who are locked in to the power structures and those locked out."[10] This "stadium rock" model of protest is less powerful because everyone affected by it is a spectator rather than a participant.

Klein's argument forces a choice between consumerism and citizenship and claims that the prevalence of marketing in protest movements has allowed the former to take over the latter. But is the dichotomy between citizenship and consumerism accurate? As long as markets have existed, the power of the consumer as a political actor has been utilized to effect political change, though primarily through consumer boycotts. Buying certain products because doing so sends a message, gives money to a cause, and allows us to participate in a particular community of ideas (referred to as "buycotting") is also a political act. Merely because the Gap profits from this exchange does not mean that this form of political action is irrelevant or has been inexorably co-opted by the market. Rather, we could say that the political movement has exploited the market by advancing a particular agenda.

Having a limited view of effective protest activity also neglects the sense in which participation occurs within both weak and strong publics (to use Fraser's terminology described previously). Strong publics, involved in demonstrations and deliberations, require participants rather than spectators. In weak publics, however, everyone is both a participant and a spectator. It is in these publics that one's political identity is formed. This identity has to be formed, and the commitments of the protest movement engendered, before activism within strong publics takes place. Complaining that buying a T-shirt promoting awareness of AIDS or poverty does little to change global power structures seems misplaced.

A person who buys (RED) products at the Gap to fight global AIDS is helping to establish his or her identity as someone who cares about AIDS. This act of purchasing forms an identity and establishes membership in a group. The act of buying the shirt may not do much to combat AIDS—the $25 for a (RED) shirt might be better spent sending a check directly to an AIDS charity—but the ownership and wearing of the shirt is likely to have a greater effect beyond the act of the purchase itself. For example, the person may be more likely to vote for candidates who support African AIDS programs, engage in conversations with friends about global AIDS, and join an activist group as a result of the importance of this issue to his or her political identity. Clearly, the act of buying a shirt is not always simply buying a shirt.

One potential problem with this kind of political protest is the false sense that people are "making a difference" simply by purchasing a product. This is an impossibly difficult standard to uphold, however—that is, in order to be considered worthwhile, political acts must have some measurable effect on the world of political decision making. If the difference I make is merely one of understanding myself and my political commitments with a little more certainty, this too counts as a political act.

Another reason to doubt the political efficacy of popular culture is that certain forms of protest are complicit with the very systems that perpetuate the social problem they are battling (consumerism fighting global poverty, for example). Every protest movement struggles with this dilemma, however: to what extent should it work outside the "system," and to what extent should it use the system to spread its message? Although it is helpful to be reminded that the system itself is flawed, this is not an independent reason to reject the use of consumer culture to spread ideas—even ideas against consumer culture itself. In *No Logo*, Klein describes the use of commercial messages to critique commerce as ironic, but rather than a liability, irony itself can be an instrument for expressing dissent. Dissent needs controversial and engaged activism, as Klein suggests, but it also requires an accessible communication of ideas that reach as many people as possible. The value of the "multiple publics" model is that it does not force us to choose between different forms of political activism as more or less legitimate.

Understanding a model of social change as effective only from the "outside" is limited because it ignores the necessity of cultural transformation in addition to the need to convince decision makers through social pressure. Political expression is about shaping cultural identities and identifying forms of oppression, as well as affecting political decisions.[11] Dissent in popular culture may have a greater effect on the former than the latter, but this is no reason to ignore it as a force of social change. Over the last two decades, for example, the movement for gay rights has been as affected by Ellen DeGeneres, Rosie O'Donnell, and *Dharma and Greg* as it has been by demonstrations or other "engaged" forms of activism, and corporate sponsorship did not diminish these effects.

Exposition, Legitimation, and Agendas

The popular culture artifacts with arguably the greatest potential impact on society are television programs and films. Televisions have become the social and recreational centerpieces of most American homes, and movies are one of the top ways that people seek entertainment outside of television. Because of their widespread consumption, television shows and movies are significant constitutive elements of what we consider popular culture, and because they are viewed by so many, we would expect them to make significant contributions to national dialogues and cultural identities. As such, some of them have been important for communicating dissenting viewpoints to a wider public. (Many of the chapters in this book are dedicated to examining such artifacts.)

In addition to the influence of cultural expressions on the formation of identity, the widely distributed productions of television and film often play an even greater role in shaping the dialogue that occurs in the public sphere (and across public spheres). Regarding political issues, these elements of popular culture can have a threefold effect on how political issues are received and discussed: they can *expose* issues that might otherwise be overlooked, they can *legitimize* issues and viewpoints that might otherwise be considered marginal or inappropriate, and they can *set agendas* for political discussion, forcing issues into a national dialogue that otherwise might not have taken place.

The ability of television and film to reach a wide audience means that the writers, directors, and producers of these media have a powerful tool at their disposal to draw attention to problems or issues that are not yet at the forefront of the national consciousness. These depictions are not always of controversial issues—many shows present what amounts to "public service messages" intended to increase awareness of important topics. The motivation to serve the community led to the widespread use of "very special episodes" by sitcoms in the 1970s, 1980s, and 1990s. In these episodes, a typically comedic show would become serious while the characters dealt with issues such as drunk driving, teen suicide, or drug use.[12] Though usually uncontroversial, except for the advertised "shock value" intended to garner high ratings, these programs demonstrate that popular culture is understood by many as a tool for communicating socially relevant messages.

The power of television and film also makes them useful for communicating more controversial messages that run counter to generally accepted viewpoints or challenge the widely accepted range of appropriate topics for television shows. As discussed in the introduction, *All in the Family* was an early example of dissenting views being expressed on television. Many episodes pushed controversial political and cultural viewpoints to the fore. Homosexuality, racism, and women's liberation were all featured topics in episodes that successfully mixed humor with social commentary aimed at promoting tolerance. The character Mike (whom Archie nonaffectionately referred to as "Meathead") was a frequent mouthpiece for a range of politically charged, dissenting leftist viewpoints, most of which made Archie uncomfortable but all of which were vindicated by the end of the episode. Since *All in the Family,* many other television shows and films have attempted to bring awareness and focus to politically sensitive issues. The film *Crash,* for example, is widely recognized for confronting viewers with insidious racism. *Hotel Rwanda* educated hundreds of thousands of viewers about the horrors of the Rwandan genocide and brought attention to the continuing plight of millions of Africans. With so many people ready

Crash, written and directed by Paul Haggis, portrayed many different attitudes and perspectives on race and racism in the United States and won the Oscar for Best Picture of 2005. (MovieGoods)

to watch television and movies, these are ripe forms of communication for bringing unspoken and marginalized issues to the forefront.

When popular culture artifacts depict a controversial viewpoint, they sometimes legitimize that viewpoint as either worthwhile or accurate. These messages are designed to cause viewers to walk away not only with an awareness of a problem or controversial opinion but also with a changed attitude toward a dissenting view or idea. In these cases, popular culture gives approval to these views or ideas, encouraging viewers to recognize the value of the dissenting political perspective and occasionally bringing these views to national attention through political debate. One of the most famous examples of this was the 1990s sitcom *Murphy Brown,* featuring a sarcastic, hard-hitting news reporter played by Candice Bergen. Although the show frequently referenced political events and issues, at the end of its fourth season it was thrust into the national political spotlight when Murphy (Bergen) gave birth to a child. The day after the episode aired, Vice President Dan Quayle singled out the show as an example of popular culture promoting bad family values by depicting single motherhood as a "lifestyle choice."[13] In response, the following season of *Murphy Brown* began with a series of episodes that took direct aim at the vice president's remarks. The show deliberately featured the struggles and joys of single motherhood, included explicit consideration of the social stigma on single-parent households, and examined a wide range of issues related to the definition of "family values."

When Ellen DeGeneres's character on the show *Ellen* declared that she was a lesbian, she became the first lead character in a popular television show to be openly gay. The "outing" of Ellen created a national stir, with supporters of gay rights defending the show and calling for increased public openness on issues of sexuality, and cultural critics decrying the show for its disrespect for traditional values.[14] Dominating the headlines and gaining big ratings during this period, *Ellen* helped legitimize the "coming out" process and gave many the courage to do the same with family and friends. Since Ellen opened the door to the closet, several prominent figures in popular culture, both fictional and real, have proudly declared their sexuality.

It is important to note, even as we consider dissent in popular culture, that the legitimizing power of popular culture can work both ways. In many cases, it is not dissenting views but prevailing ones that are legitimated through television and film. In the television show *24,* for example, the main character Jack Bauer fights against evil terrorists, allowing him the moral certitude to fight these immoral agents with any means necessary, including the use of torture.[15] The show was so effective at communicating the kind of tactics required when fighting such a war that foreign policy conservatives embraced it as a depiction of the best way to fight the "war on terror." From Rush Limbaugh to the Heritage Foundation, Jack Bauer was glorified as the ultimate hero who legitimized the prevailing arguments in the Bush administration about how to rightly and effectively combat terrorist aggressors.[16] This kind of legitimation can hardly be called dissent, since it authorizes both prevailing and institutionalized views, yet it proves that active legitimation occurs in popular culture from all sides of the political spectrum.[17]

Additionally, it is easy to identify ways that popular culture obscures dissenting voices in favor of a prevailing national culture. This is especially true in times of national crisis, when the value of unity is occasionally pronounced and emphasized through a cooperative cultural defense. After September 11, 2001, for example, much of popular culture united to demonstrate a collective national pride. This unity was embodied in the simulcast of *America: A Tribute to Heroes,* wherein musicians, actors, and other celebrities joined to sing "America the Beautiful" and perform other acts of patriotism for the massive fund-raising effort. This display of a unified cultural voice did not last long, however; as political debate began to occur about the appropriate response to the attack, dissent found its way back into popular culture. For example, ironic humor on late-night talk shows and other comedy programming quickly became popular again. Although popular culture would maintain an enduring reverence for the tragic events of that day, many popular television shows addressed September 11 with humor—*The Daily Show* directing its insulting humor toward the absurdity of the evil perpetrators of the crime, and *South Park* depicting a love affair between Osama bin Laden and a camel.[18]

In addition to bringing visibility to marginalized issues and legitimizing dissenting as well as prevailing views, at its most "political" (in the "strong" sense), popular culture also attempts to set political agendas. When Hollywood produces a film that is politically motivated, it is often with the hope that a national conversation about the film will inspire citizens and lawmakers to instigate political change. The most successful examples of this are popularly distributed documentaries intended both to be entertaining and to effect some kind of social or political change. These include Morgan Spurlock's *Super Size Me* (2004); Al Gore's film about climate change, *An Inconvenient Truth* (2006); and several films made by documentarian Michael Moore.[19] In the case of *Super Size Me*, Spurlock's marathon eating of fast food pressured McDonald's and other fast-food restaurants to add healthier choices to their menus, and several states and cities passed public health laws regarding unhealthy fats and foods that restaurants cannot serve. Gore's *An Inconvenient Truth* also succeeded in advancing the debate about climate change beyond the question of whether global warming is real. Scientists had reached a consensus years before the film, but it took the wide distribution of Gore's cinematic presentation of facts and figures to finally turn the national debate toward solutions.

Popular Dissent in the Public Sphere

When popular films and television shows expose, legitimate, and set agendas for the consideration of dissent, it demonstrates the influence popular culture can have on our political discourse. This discourse is broadened when multiple and diverse political views are communicated through popular forms of culture. Because our public sphere is best viewed as a collection of multiple spheres and forms of expression, we will understand it better when we understand the multiple and dominant sources of information and cultural meaning. Voices of dissent seek listeners, and popular culture is full of voices. We are listening to these voices, and they are affecting us. Sometimes they subtly encourage us to adopt different views,[20] and sometimes we are hit in the face by that with which we disagree vehemently.

Students of politics, social movements, and popular culture are served by analyzing the relationships between marginalized voices and mainstream cultural expressions. An appreciation of the political relevance of popular culture, and a broadened view of the public sphere that includes these cultural expressions, allows new insight into the way our identities, ideas, and politics are shaped by the messages that surround us. Even for political activists and practitioners, an awareness of the productive forces at work in popular culture allows greater understanding of how dissent is expressed, spreads, and draws people toward social movements.

Gil Scott Heron declared that the "revolution will not be televised," but in a world where everything is televised, it is inevitable that the revolution will be as well. These forms of expression deserve analysis because popular culture is full of political voices, many of them dissenting from prevailing views. It benefits us as scholars, students, and participants in this public sphere to understand these messages and their impact on society. We need to recognize that political expression in popular culture can contain a range of productive, counterproductive, and neutral relationships with voices of dissent. Through an understanding of the richness and diversity of popular culture as an important element of the public sphere, we better understand the political significance of popular culture and the multiple modes of expression and artifacts of dissenting voices we find there.

Notes

1. Nixon is recorded as saying, "I don't mind the homosexuality, I understand it. . . . Nevertheless, goddamn, I don't think you glorify it on public television, homosexuality, even more than you glorify whores. We all know we have weaknesses. But, goddamn it, what do you think that does to kids?" See James Warren, "Nixon on Tape Expounds on Welfare and Homosexuality," *Chicago Tribune*, November 7, 1999, http://www.j-bradford-delong.net/Politics/Nixon_on_Tape.html (accessed December 3, 2008).

2. In addition to sex and sexuality, *All in the Family* featured episodes on politics, FBI investigations, racism, rape, crime, gun control, and religion.

3. As of this writing, one of the video versions of the song has been viewed on youtube.com nearly 500,000 times: http://www.youtube.com/watch?v=uTCQSk218bc (accessed December 2, 2008).

4. Among other references, it is the title of Joe Trippi's book about the influence of the Internet on political campaigns (featuring the 2004 Howard Dean presidential campaign), the title of a documentary about a failed coup in Venezuela in 2002, and a frequent "go-to" headline in news stories and scholarly articles on the effects of new media on culture and politics.

5. Many political theorists argue for a more diverse understanding of the public sphere, including those who believe that only a multiplied and varied approach to the "public" allows an understanding of its political significance. See, for example, Nancy Fraser, *Justice Interruptus* (New York: Routledge, 1997); Michael Warner, *Publics and Counterpublics* (New York: Zone Books, 2002); Jodi Dean, "Civil Society: Beyond the Public Sphere," in *Handbook of Critical Theory,* ed. David M. Rasmussen (Cambridge, MA: Blackwell Publishing, 1999), 220–42; Dana Villa, "Postmodernism and the Public Sphere," *American Political Science Review* 86, no. 3 (September 1992): 712–21; and Seyla Benhabib, *Claims of Culture* (Princeton, NJ: Princeton University Press, 2002).

6. Nancy Fraser is well known for theorizing the public sphere in this way, such that "studies of marginal groups as well as unconventional media invite us to adopt Nancy Fraser's assessment of the public sphere as composed of smaller publics, each with particular concerns and channels of communication." Susan Herbst, "Public Expression Outside the Mainstream," *Annals of the American Academy of Political and Social Science* 546 (July 1996): 131.

7. See Nancy Fraser, "Rethinking the Public Sphere," in *The Phantom Public Sphere,* ed. Bruce Robbins (Minneapolis: University of Minnesota Press, 1993), 1–33.

8. See John Fiske, *Media Matters: Everyday Culture and Political Change* (Minneapolis: University of Minnesota Press, 1994).

9. See Naomi Klein, *No Logo: Taking Aim at the Brand Bullies* (Toronto: Knopf Canada, 2000).

10. See Brigid Delaney, "The Bono-ization of Activism," October 12, 2007, http://www.cnn.com/2007/WORLD/europe/10/12/ww.klein/ (accessed December 11, 2008).

11. Trend observes that within the contemporary moral environment, "culture has a dual function. It is both the means by which the oppressed come to know their oppression and the vehicle through which citizens struggle to find methods for change." David Trend, *Cultural Democracy: Politics, Media, New Technology* (Albany: State University of New York Press, 1997), 184.

12. *Diff'rent Strokes* was a notable sitcom featuring many of these special episodes. The most famous starred Nancy Reagan in a "Just Say No" to drugs episode; in another, the young characters had to confront a child molester.

13. Quayle said to the Commonwealth Club of California on May 19, 1992: "It

doesn't help matters when primetime TV has Murphy Brown—a character who supposedly epitomizes today's intelligent, highly paid, professional woman—mocking the importance of fathers, by bearing a child alone, and calling it just another 'lifestyle choice.'" Quoted from an excerpt of the speech at http://www.mfc.org/pfn/95–12/quayle .html (accessed December 6, 2008).

14. Critics succeeded in pressuring ABC to put a parental advisory on the show after Ellen declared that she was gay.

15. For a discussion of *24* as an apologetic for the use of torture in "ticking bomb" cases, see Timothy Dunn, "Torture, Terrorism, and *24*," in *Homer Simpson Goes to Washington: American Politics through Popular Culture*, ed. Joseph J. Foy (Lexington: University Press of Kentucky, 2008), 171–84. Zizek criticizes the show for promoting an "ethics of urgency," thereby legitimizing the unashamed use of unethical techniques justified by states of emergency. See Slavoj Zizek, "Jack Bauer and the Ethics of Urgency," *In These Times*, January 27, 2006, http://www.inthesetimes.com/article/2481/ (accessed December 3, 2008).

16. The show's cocreator Joel Surnow is a Republican, and John McCain (who once made a cameo) and Dick Cheney are fans. This does not mean, however, that the show is completely on the Right. Bauer also dislikes moral absolutes. See James Poniewozik, "The Evolution of Jack Bauer," *Time*, January 14, 2007, http://www.time.com/time/ magazine/article/0,9171,1576853,00.html (accessed December 3, 2008).

17. Another example of this is the film *The Dark Knight* (2008), in which Batman pursues tactics of torture and rendition to save the world from an irrational evil. This depiction of Batman is easily read as "a defense of the (George W. Bush) administration's cursory regard for human rights abroad and civil rights at home, in the cause of reply to attacks from an irrational and inhuman evil." Jonathan Lethem, "The Art of Darkness," *New York Times*, September 20, 2008, http://www.nytimes.com/2008/09/21/opinion/ 21lethem.html?_r=1 (accessed December 10, 2008).

18. See Lynn Spigel, "Entertainment Wars: Television Culture after 9/11," in *Public Culture: Diversity, Democracy, and Community in the United States*, ed. Marguerite S. Shaffer (Philadelphia: University of Pennsylvania Press, 2008).

19. Moore's films are typically motivated by progressive forms of dissent, including corporate responsibility (*Roger and Me* [1989]), gun control (*Bowling for Columbine* [2002]), the war on terrorism (*Fahrenheit 9/11* [2004]), and the health care crisis (*Sicko* [2007]). *Bowling for Columbine*, *Fahrenheit 9/11*, and *Sicko* are three of the four highest grossing documentaries at the box office.

20. A noteworthy example of children's literature that influenced a generation through subtle and not-so-subtle dissent is the writing of Dr. Seuss. See Henry Jenkins, "'No Matter How Small': The Democratic Imagination of Dr. Seuss," in *Hop on Pop: The Politics and Pleasures of Popular Culture*, ed. Henry Jenkins, Tara McPherson, and Jane Shattuc (Durham, NC: Duke University Press, 2002), 187–208.

2

THE DAILY SHOW AND THE POLITICS OF TRUTH

Jamie Warner

"One anchor, five correspondents, zero credibility." So begins the description of *The Daily Show with Jon Stewart* on the Comedy Central Web site. It wraps up as follows: "Don't miss *The Daily Show with Jon Stewart,* a nightly half-hour series unburdened by objectivity, journalistic integrity or even accuracy." In contrast, many media and political heavyweights, such as Ted Koppel, Tim Russert, and Al Gore, argue exactly the opposite: *The Daily Show* is more credible, more objective, more accurate, and more truthful than the politicians it satirizes.

This chapter explores the complicated relationship between truth-telling and the satirical critique of *The Daily Show.* I argue that Jon Stewart embodies a contemporary form of what Michel Foucault calls *parrhesia,* Greek for "truth-telling." This unique form of *parrhesia* could only have emerged in our current political atmosphere: a colonization of the political space by the contemporary spectacle of politics itself, created by campaign consultants, political advertising, and political branding

The Daily Show highlights and satirizes this type of spectacle. This is the "truth" that Stewart and his cast are telling both explicitly and implicitly through parody, epitomizing the show's role as a new type of democratic watchdog. Stewart offers no political alternatives of his own; his contributions are purely diagnostic. He is our guide through the morass of political hype generated by the politicians themselves, calling attention to the spectacle of the permanent campaign by highlighting the artifice of contemporary political discourse. By showcasing this spectacle as artifice and manipula-

Comedy Central's *The Daily Show with Jon Stewart,* the self-proclaimed "most important television show ever," uses comedy and parody to unmask the political spectacle of modern American government and society. (MovieGoods)

tion, Stewart and *The Daily Show* emerge as truth-tellers, despite their protestations to the contrary.

Parrhesia: Telling the Truth

Truth is a complicated concept. From the biblical "The truth will set you free" (John 8:32) to Jack Nicholson's character in *A Few Good Men* shouting "You can't handle the truth," what constitutes the truth, who can give voice to it, and how one can do so have been fraught with layers of often contradictory implications. Even seemingly simple factual truths like "the sky is blue" can become problematic when one examines them more carefully. When dealing with something infinitely more complex—such as politics—what counts as the truth quickly becomes a matter of debate.[1]

Thus, to better understand how a fake news program on Comedy Central can engage in truth-telling, it is first necessary to look more closely at the concept of *parrhesia*, a very specific kind of truth-telling that occurred in ancient Greek and Roman cultures. In the fall of 1983, philosopher Michel Foucault gave six lectures at the University of California–Berkeley in which he discussed the concept of *parrhesia*. He began by briefly examining *parrhesia* as a model of good citizenship in a democracy, then noted the changes in *parrhesia* that can occur in a monarchy and finally the philosophical relationship the *parrhesiastes* must have with himself as a truth-teller, which was Foucault's main concern. In this chapter, however, I am most interested in that which interested Foucault the least: political *parrhesia*, or telling the truth in a democracy.[2]

First, according to Foucault, for truth-telling to be considered *parrhesia*, the telling must be risky and the truth must be a critique of someone more powerful. The risk to the speaker can run the gamut from risking a friendship to risking one's popularity to risking one's life, but there must be some danger present for it to be considered *parrhesia*. Second, the *parrhesiastes* must be frank; it has to be obvious to his audience that what he says is his opinion, and to avoid any confusion, he must use direct, exact, unmistakable language. In the Greek context, Foucault argues, *parrhesia* stands in contrast to mere rhetoric—where the speaker's aim is to convince the audience of his argument regardless of whether he actually believes what he says is true. Finally, the speaker who uses *parrhesia* regards his truth-telling as a duty. He is not telling the truth because he is being forced to do so or because of personal gain. He is free to stay silent, but instead he tells the truth because he believes it is his responsibility and obligation as a person and as a citizen.[3]

Thus, according to Foucault, political *parrhesia* was very important to the Greek conception of democracy. Not only was *parrhesia* a constitutional right of Greek citizens, it exemplified the ethical qualities of a good citizen. A good citizen was considered someone who tells the truth, even if doing so puts his political office, his friendships, his reputation, or even his life in jeopardy.[4]

That's it. Foucault gives no empirical definition of the truth besides the three criteria laid out above. He does not speak to whether the *parrhesiastic* utterances must be empirically verifiable or philosophically universalizable. His only criteria are that the *parrhesiastes* must take a risk by criticizing someone or something more powerful, he must believe what he says and say it plainly, and he must do it for the betterment of his country, not for himself.[5] In the spirit of that definition, I argue that, paradoxically, a fake news show on Comedy Central, *The Daily Show with Jon Stewart,* functions as a contemporary political *parrhesiastes.*[6] To better understand how a fake news program staffed with comedians can fulfill this unlikely role, we must next examine the current political context in the United States, one in which telling the truth has morphed into selling the truth.

The Permanent Campaign: Selling the Truth

When Foucault lectured on *parrhesia,* he talked very specifically about how it worked within the Greek context where it originated. Thus, to examine contemporary versions of political *parrhesia,* we must first look at the contemporary political context.

Political communication has always had a strategic element, but contemporary mass political communication is now saturated with exactly the "rhetoric" against which Foucault defines *parrhesia.* Sidney Blumenthal popularized this move into total strategic rhetoric as the "permanent campaign": image-based, winner-take-all, tactical rhetorical calculations traditionally reserved for political campaigns. These techniques, designed to "sell" a specific politician during the campaign, are now routinely used constantly, even after the politician wins office. And this, according to Blumenthal, "remakes government into an instrument designed to sustain an elected official's popularity."[7] According to this mentality, governing is no longer about legislating and implementing policies helpful to the American people; government is about accruing and keeping power by selling the American people a political product. As George W. Bush said, "See, in my line of work you got to keep repeating things over and over and over again for the truth to sink in, to kind of catapult the propaganda."[8]

It is not controversial to argue that contemporary politics is built on the backs of an army of well-paid, nonelected staff working as general consultants, media consultants, campaign managers, pollsters, public affairs executives, fund-raisers, and the like. In fact, many have become media celebrities in their own right, with recognizable names: Mark Penn, James Carville, Mary Matalin, Dick Morris, Paul Begala, and Karl Rove. Over the past forty years, these political consultants—often with backgrounds in advertising, marketing, public relations, direct mail, and polling—have become integral to the permanent campaign. With the help of their expertise, all communications, all policies, all legislation must be "spun" in a way that highlights the strengths of one politician or political party while, hopefully, drowning out or denigrating one's opponents.

In his book *Words that Work: It's Not What You Say, It's What People Hear,* Republican pollster and strategist Frank Luntz exemplifies the most blatant and overt use of the language of the permanent campaign. (Actually, he thinks we should adopt it not only for governing but also for our lives. In fact, he recommends this book to people who would like to get out of speeding tickets, as does Chris Matthews, discussed later.) The theme of Luntz's book is that all politics is rhetoric: what one says, even what one believes, is not that important. The important thing is what one's audience hears. Thus, one must say things in a very particular (focus group–tested, sound bite–conscious, and overtly manipulated) way to effectively convey one's message. Luntz is probably most famous for his behind-the-scenes work in selling Newt Gingrich's 1994 Contract with America, but he has a long history of manipulating language in the service of the Republican Party. The following is an excerpt from a leaked 2005 memo to Republican congressional spouses entitled "The 21 Political Words and Phrases You Should Never Say Again . . . Plus a Few More":

> Never Say: Inheritance Tax, Estate Tax. Instead Say: Death Tax. While two-thirds of Americans (68 percent) think the "inheritance tax" or the "estate tax" is unfair, fully 78 percent view the "death tax" as unfair. And while a narrow majority would repeal the "inheritance" or "estate tax," an overwhelming majority would repeal the "death tax." If you want to kill it, always refer to it as the "death tax."[9]

Notice that Luntz makes no mention of the fact that this really isn't a "death tax" at all. Ninety-eight percent of Americans will never pay this tax. Only those who own property with a fair market value exceeding $1 million at the time of their death (or the wealthiest 2 percent of all Americans) are affected. Thinking in permanent campaign terms, however, means that the truth of the statement is not as important as the use of a phrase—in this case, "death tax"—that evokes a knee-jerk, negative gut feeling.[10]

The foundational problem with the permanent campaign mentality is that it works against the ideals of democracy, where informed citizens and their representatives debate and compromise to find the best practical solution. Marketing techniques are designed to "win" the consumer-citizen over using emotionally manipulative rhetorical techniques, such as labeling a tax on estates over $1 million a "death tax." The permanent campaign mentality does not encourage compromise, discussion, and working together toward the best solution to a problem: Should we tax property when people die? Why or why not? If not, how will we deal with the shortfall in the treasury? If so, how much tax is appropriate? By manipulating language, the permanent campaign effectively bypasses all these questions. Under these competitive conditions, the dialogue, discussion, and compromise necessary for good governance are actually detrimental, in the sense that they muddy the message the consultants have worked so hard to sell to the public. In fact, the best-case scenario for politicians and their consultants is one in which there is no thinking, no critical examination, and no questioning on the part of the citizen—just a positive emotional reflex. The politician or party has thus become a trusted "brand" that inspires an unreflective loyalty in the mind of the consumer-citizen. Just as the ultimate goal of Geico, Gerber, or Google is for consumers to automatically, consistently, and unthinkingly use their brand, the ultimate goal of the permanent campaign is to create a permanent citizen base that can be counted on to always support the political brand.

In what follows I argue that *The Daily Show* functions as a *parrhesiastes* in our mass media–saturated, consultant-driven political environment, a truth-teller in an environment where no truth goes unspun. Specifically, I argue that Jon Stewart and *The Daily Show* writers and cast meet all three of Foucault's criteria for political *parrhesia*, but in a unique and contemporary way: First, they consistently criticize and ridicule people in positions of power to show how the permanent campaign mentality hurts our democracy. Second, Stewart is frank and tells people what he personally believes to be true (as well as funny). Finally, he does this, in large part, because he feels it is his duty as a citizen and as a human being, thereby functioning as a modern day *parrhesiastes*.

The Daily Show: Parodying the Truth

The Daily Show with Jon Stewart is a popular thirty-minute "newscast" that airs Monday through Thursday at 11:00 P.M. EST on the cable network Comedy Central, with an estimated 1.5 million viewers per night.[11] Although the show has been on the air since 1996, the addition of Jon Stewart as anchor in 1999 resulted in a run of entertainment awards, including ten Emmy Awards.[12] *The Daily Show* has also made journalistic waves, winning two prestigious Peabody Awards for its "Indecision 2000" and "Indecision 2004" election coverage.[13] In addition, Stewart won individual awards from the Television Critics Association for comedy in 2003 and 2005, and in 2004 *The Daily Show* won the Television Critics Award for Outstanding Achievement in News and Information, beating out *60 Minutes* (CBS), *Frontline* (PBS), *Meet the Press* (NBC), and *Nightline* (ABC).[14] *Newsday* even listed Stewart as the most influential media player in the 2004 election, outclassing the likes of Ted Koppel, Sean Hannity, and Tim Russert.[15]

But unlike its competition for these prestigious awards, *The Daily Show* is a funny and often sharply critical satire of a normal news broadcast. It is fake news. It is a parody of cable news, and its host and correspondents are all professional comedians. In fact, in his videotaped acceptance of the 2004 Television Critics Association Award, Stewart recommended that one of the other legitimate nominees—*60 Minutes,* perhaps—should investigate how a *fake* news program won the award for Outstanding Achievement in News and Information.[16] However, it is this odd combination of serious criticism of the politically powerful and news parody designed for laughs that gives *The Daily Show* its unique place as a new type of democratic watchdog. During an interview, Bill Moyers said to Stewart, "I do not know whether you are practicing an old form of parody and satire or a new form of journalism." Stewart responded, "I think, honestly, we're practicing a new form of desperation, where we just are so inundated with mixed messages from the media and from politicians that we're just trying to sort it out for ourselves."[17]

For parody to be effective, one must closely mimic the target, and *The Daily Show* does that. In fact, if you watched *The Daily Show* with the sound muted, you might not realize that it is a fake news program. Jon Stewart sits at an anchor desk, where he reads the news and interviews correspondents and guests. The set is designed in the ubiquitous red, white, and blue, with a map of the world behind him. There is also a video box that appears over Stewart's right shoulder with video clips that complement his commentary. However, turn up the volume, and you would soon be alerted to the fact that this is not an ordinary news program. For example:

> STEWART: When you combine the new mandate that criticizing the commander in chief is off limits in wartime with last year's official disbanding of the Democratic Party, we're left at the all-time low in the good old-fashioned debate category. Now I know you're thinking: But Jon, every time I want to have a calm,

honest discussion about these kinds of issues, I'm shouted down and harassed by the Dixie Chicks and their ilk. Well, tonight it all changes. . . . So first, joining us tonight is George W. Bush, the 43rd president of the United States. . . . Taking the other side, from the year 2000, Texas governor and presidential candidate, George W. Bush.

[Split screen of Governor Bush on the left and President Bush on the right, with a "Bush vs. Bush" logo between them]

STEWART: Mr. President, you won the coin toss. The first question will go to you. Why is the United States of America using its power to change governments in foreign countries?

PRESIDENT BUSH: We must stand up for our security and for the permanent rights and the hopes of mankind.

STEWART: Well, certainly that represents a bold new doctrine in foreign policy, Mr. President. Governor Bush, do you agree with that?

GOVERNOR BUSH: Yeah, I'm not so sure that the role of the United States is to go around the world and say, "This is the way it's gotta be."

STEWART: Well, that's interesting. That's a difference of opinion, and certainly that's what this country is about, differences of opinion. Mr. President, let me just get specific: Why are we in Iraq?

PRESIDENT BUSH: We will be changing the regime of Iraq for the good of the Iraqi people.

STEWART: Governor, then I'd like to hear your response on that.

GOVERNOR BUSH: If we're an arrogant nation, they'll resent us. I think one way for us to end up being viewed as the ugly American is to go around the world saying, "We do it this way, so should you."[18]

This is obviously not your grandmother's newscast.

Risky Business

According to Foucault, in the context of ancient Greece, *parrhesia* entailed a certain amount of risk because the truth being told was a criticism of someone in power. The danger need not rise to the level of risking one's life, although it could if the truth-teller criticized a powerful tyrant. There had to be, however, some risk in the confrontation: to one's friendships, one's reputation, or one's livelihood. Within the contemporary context, *The Daily Show* meets this criterion by consistently criticizing the permanent campaign mentality of those in power, as well as the mainstream media that often unproblematically disseminate their messages. Here, Stewart clearly expresses his opinion of the watchdog role of the media while interviewing "senior media analyst" Stephen Colbert about the coverage of the U.S. invasion of Iraq in March 2003:

> STEWART: What should the media's role be in covering the war?

> COLBERT: Very simply, the media's role should be the accurate and objective description of the hellacious ass-whomping we're handing the Iraqis.

> STEWART: Hellacious ass-whomping? Now to me, that sounds pretty subjective.

> COLBERT: Are you saying it's not an ass-whomping, Jon? I suppose you could call it an "ass-kicking" or an "ass-handing-to." Unless, of course, you love Hitler.

> STEWART [stammering]: I don't love Hitler.

> COLBERT: Spoken like a true Hitler-lover—

> STEWART: I'm perplexed. Is your position that there's no place for negative words or even thoughts in the media?

> COLBERT: Not at all, Jon. Doubts can happen to everyone, including me, but as a responsible journalist, I've taken my doubts, fears, moral compass, conscience, and all-pervading skepticism about

the very nature of this war and simply placed them in this empty Altoids box [produces a box]. That's where they'll stay, safe and sound, until Iraq is liberated.[19]

Although Stewart's main target for criticism is frequently the hapless mainstream media, he also highlights how the Bush administration has become a master of using the media's weaknesses to its advantage to get the administration's version of events to the public. The following example illustrates how *The Daily Show* splices together a sequence of videos to highlight one of the most pervasive tactics of the permanent campaign—the widespread repetition of talking points—and to show how this can be detrimental to democratic conversation. In this excerpt from 2004, Stewart offers an editorial on the origins of what he calls "conventional wisdom":

STEWART: Let's take the example of the addition of John Edwards to the Democratic ticket: I don't know how to feel about that. I don't know what it means. Here's how I will:

[Cut to video clip of CNN reporter, standing in front of the White House]

CNN REPORTER: This is 28 pages from the Republican National Committee. It says, "Who is Edwards?" It starts off by saying "a disingenuous, unaccomplished liberal." We also saw from the Bush-Cheney camp that they had released talking points to their supporters.

STEWART: Talking points: *that's* how we learn things. But how will I absorb a talking point like "Edwards and Kerry are out of the mainstream" unless I get it jackhammered into my skull? That's where television lends a hand [laughter].

[Cut to a series of video clips]

FOX NEWS: He stands way out of the mainstream.

CNN, TERRY HOLT, BUSH CAMPAIGN SPOKESMAN: . . . way out of the mainstream.

CNN, NICOLE DEVENISH, BUSH-CHENEY '04 COMMUNICATIONS
DIRECTOR: . . . that stands so far out of the mainstream.

CNN, LYNN CHENEY: . . . that he is out of the mainstream.

CNN, TERRY HOLT AT DEMOCRATIC NATIONAL CONVENTION: . . . out
of the mainstream.

CNN, FRANK DONATELLI, GOP STRATEGIST: . . . well out of the
mainstream.

STEWART [a glazed expression on his face; laughter]: I'm . . . I'm
getting the feeling . . . I think . . . I *think* they're out of the
mainstream.[20]

The manipulative nature of the Bush administration's rhetoric is also
showcased in the next example, where Stewart is interviewing "senior military analyst" Stephen Colbert in June 2005.[21] This time, Stewart is calling
attention to the rhetoric of two high-ranking administration officials who
seem to be making contradictory points:

STEWART: When the vice president says that the insurgency is in its
last throes and Donald Rumsfeld says that that could mean twelve
years, isn't that contradictory?

COLBERT: Well, Jon, as a member of the cynical, knee-jerk reaction
media, liberal, Ivy League, Taxachusetts elite, I can see how
you would find a discrepancy between the words "last throes"
and "twelve-year insurgency." But your mistake is looking at
what's happening in Iraq on a human scale. The administration
is looking at it from a *geological* perspective. After all, it took a
billion years for the earth to cool.[22]

If we the American people are supposed to choose our leaders based on their
decisions, how can we do so if we don't know the truth? If we would like to
rationally discuss the pros and cons of the Iraq war, how can we talk about it
and judge it accurately if we don't know the truth? Is the insurgency almost
over, or should we prepare ourselves for a much longer, more expensive,

and potentially more violent conflict? Which statement is the sales pitch, and which statement is the truth?

Since Vice President Cheney frequently made the most starkly (and, as we would later learn, wildly) optimistic pronouncements about the Iraq war—pronouncements repeated over and over in the media to attest to the wisdom of invading Iraq—he was the subject of many *Daily Show* segments raising questions about the truth of his statements. The following aired in March 2007, questioning the vice president's continuing "clout":

> STEWART: As it happens, the media is atwitter when it comes to Cheney. . . . Surely, the Libby conviction must have reduced the vice president's clout. His chief of staff was convicted of lying! Is there any other instance involving Cheney that should have had a clout-loosening effect? . . .

> [Cut to a series of video clips of Cheney]

> CHENEY [August 29, 2002]: Simply stated, there is no doubt that Saddam Hussein now has weapons of mass destruction.

> CHENEY [March 16, 2003]: My belief is that we will, in fact, be greeted as liberators.

> CHENEY [May 2, 2005]: I think that they're in the last throes, if you will, of the insurgency.

> STEWART: So I think we're beginning to see the pattern. Cheney causes some high-level embarrassment or makes a completely erroneous statement about American policy. His clout is questioned and yet his clout goes on. All of this does beg the question: *What the fuck?* Why does this man still have any clout? At all? . . . Cheney has been wrong about *everything*: his ideas, his execution. I've been fired from jobs for being *late*. This man is very, very ungood. The only thing I would trust Cheney for advice on is [pause] if I had a dead hooker in my hotel room.[23]

Calling the vice president "ungood" and claiming that he has been wrong about everything is obviously a criticism of the powerful Bush administration and its manipulation of language. How can we talk intelligently about Iraq if the people in power are more interested in selling the policy, in spinning the reasons for the invasion, and in minimizing the difficulty, duration, and expense of the war than in having a serious nationwide discussion about it? If you believe Scott McClelland, White House press secretary from 2003 to 2006, a serious nationwide conversation was not the goal. In his 2008 memoir, he talks candidly about getting caught up in the sales pitch of the permanent campaign:

> When you mount a campaign, you aim at deploying your strongest arguments. It's a bit like the strategy a courtroom lawyer uses. . . . He focuses purely on his most compelling arguments, even if this means presenting a one-sided picture of the case. That's his job. The search for the ultimate truth is in other hands—those of the judge and the jury.
>
> And that is the spirit in which the Bush Administration approached the campaign for war. The goal was to win the debate, to get Congress and the public to support the decision to confront Saddam. In the pursuit of that goal, embracing a high level of candor and honesty about the potential war—its larger objectives, its likely costs, and its possible risks—came distant second.[24]

Since the mainstream media had all but abandoned their watchdog role after 9/11 and in the lead-up to the Iraq war, *The Daily Show* highlighted the weaknesses in the administration's arguments and underscored contradictions between the language used and the actual events on the ground.[25]

You Be Frank and I'll Be Earnest

The second criterion for *parrhesia* is frankness. According to Foucault, the *parrhesiastes* is as direct as possible with his audience and stays away from the artificial nature of rhetoric that would allow him to win an argument that he himself does not believe. In the contemporary political context, where the rhetoric of the permanent campaign is the norm and where almost all information is spun in some way, how can one effectively tell the truth?

This criterion could pose a problem for *The Daily Show's parrhesiastes* status, as its discourse is not necessarily frank or earnest. The show is not a real newscast, and much of the discourse within it is satirical—meaning that the cast members do *not* always say what they really mean. Satire is an indirect, ambivalent, ambiguous mode of communicating meaning, making it problematic for a contemporary *parrhesiastes*. However, this indirectness is actually advantageous in a complicated and artificial rhetorical regime because it can embed "a threatening idea in a non-threatening form" that is unlikely to be taken out of context and respun by those who disagree.[26] In fact, the ambiguity of satire, combined with its often playful yet critical attitude, makes it less likely to be addressed, or even noticed, by those who are the object of the criticism. In addition, the ambiguous, double-layered construction of satire means that it always has the ability to retreat back to the literal, if need be. As Stewart himself remarked: "Here's the way I look at it. President Bush has uranium-tipped bunker busters and I have puns. I think he'll be OK."[27] Instead of overt criticism of powerful people, satirical pieces can circulate as ridiculous suggestions—as jokes—though hopefully, some will know better.[28]

This last point is worth emphasizing. According to George Test, satire requires a public—or a counterpublic, in this instance—that understands the second nonliteral layer of meaning. The double-layered nature of satire asks its audience to be "sophisticated about the context in which the satire transpires, sensitive to the means at work, and sympathetic in sharing the aggression and judgment."[29] This creates what Wayne Booth calls a "tight bond," a knowing wink and a nod between the author and the audience that gets the joke.[30] The top, literal layer of discourse is meant for the ears of those in power, while the underlayer of meaning can be used to question that same power. Thus, when Colbert says that the media are going to put all their doubts and fears about the Iraq war into an empty Altoids box, or when he calls Stewart a member of the "cynical, knee-jerk reaction media, liberal, Ivy League, Taxachusetts elite," the audience knows not to take this literally. Indeed, it is the disjuncture between the literal meaning and the meaning behind it that spurs the audience to laugh. Stewart's discussion with "senior White House correspondent" Dan Bakkedahl in February 2007 further illustrates how this can function:

> STEWART: With more on the White House reaction, we're joined by
>   senior White House correspondent Dan Bakkedahl. Dan, thank
>   you for joining us. Dan, this administration has been very slow
>   to accept the reality of climate change despite the overwhelming
>   evidence.

BAKKEDAHL: No Jon, *because* of the overwhelming evidence [laughter].

STEWART [looking puzzled]: What does that mean?

BAKKEDAHL: Well, we all saw what happened the last time this administration was told that the evidence for something was a "slam dunk," a gathering threat demanding immediate action. Oh, no, no, no [smiling and shaking his head]. We're not falling for that again. No, we go down that road and the next thing you know we're locked in an intractable war against fossil fuels.

STEWART: But aren't we supposed to be cutting back on fossil fuels?

BAKKEDAHL: Oh no. Conserving right now would send the wrong message to the earth, Jon. That just emboldens our planet.

STEWART [still looking confused]: Yes. That would embolden our planet, the source of all that is life-giving.

BAKKEDAHL: You're a cut and walker, you know that, Jon? We've got to show the earth that we mean business: more emissions, more greenhouse gases, more of those plastic six-pack things for dolphin killing. The earth has got to know that we've got the stomach for this fight.

STEWART: So because the war in Iraq hasn't worked out, Bush is not going to heed the global warming study?

BAKKEDAHL: Exactly, Jon. As the president once said, "Fool me once, shame on . . . you? Fool me . . . Fool me twice, uh, can't be fooled again?" I don't know. I'm probably misquoting him, Jon. I'm sure he said it far more eloquently.[31]

Bakkedahl obviously does not mean to be taken literally, but the audience has no trouble understanding the segment's true meaning.

Jon Stewart plays an interesting role in these double-layered skits. To offset his correspondents, who are speaking in a completely exaggerated and satirical manner, Stewart often plays the straight man. Thus, the second way *The Daily Show* demonstrates the frankness of a *parrhesiastes* is for Stewart himself to be unusually direct. This is the role he often plays as interviewer: the voice of common sense in a crazy, artificial world. His October 2, 2007, interview with Chris Matthews, the host of MSNBC's *Hardball* and author of the book *Life's a Campaign,* exemplifies this blunt and open quality, much to the exasperation of Matthews, who laughingly calls this absolutely the worst interview he's ever had:

> STEWART: Now if I read this correctly, and I believe that I read this book [*Life's a Campaign*] correctly, what you are saying is, people can use what politicians do in political campaigns to *help* their lives. . . . This strikes me as fundamentally wrong. It strikes me as a *self-hurt* book, if you will [audience laughter]. Aren't campaigns fundamentally contrivances?

> MATTHEWS: Yeah, campaigns can be, but the way politicians get to the top is the real thing. They know what they're doing. You don't have to believe a word they say, but watch how far they got, how did Clinton get there, how did Hillary get there, how did all these guys get there. Reagan. They have methods to get there and you can learn from those methods.

> STEWART: So you're suggesting—even if no one believes a word you say, you can be successful.

> MATTHEWS: Yes. . . . [Life] *is* a campaign. Everything about getting jobs is about convincing someone to hire you, right? It's about getting promotions; it's about selling products. It's always a campaign. It's a campaign to get the girl of your dreams. It's a campaign to do everything you want to do in life.

> STEWART: But there has to be some core of soul in there. Otherwise—

> MATTHEWS: I'm not denying that [Stewart laughs]. I'm saying that you can learn. You are, you are a hard sell, but let me tell you: Watch the Clintons, watch how successful they are, and watch

what they do. They do listen to people. Hillary Clinton went on a listening tour of upstate New York and won a Senate seat.

STEWART: No, labeling something a "listening tour" doesn't mean you're *listening*. That's what I'm saying. . . . President Bush had a sign that said "Mission Accomplished"; that doesn't make it accomplished . . . [audience laughter]. What campaigns are are photo opportunities that are staged and there's nothing in this book about, uh, be good, be competent—

MATTHEWS: That's called the Bible. It's been written.

STEWART: Oh my God [laughing]. . . . This book has been written too, it's called *The Prince*.[32]

In this example, and unlike many interviews of authors on the perfunctory book promotion circuit, Stewart blatantly disagrees with the political premise behind Matthews's book—that life itself is a permanent campaign. At one point Stewart even remarks that he is not trashing Matthews's book, he is trashing his philosophy of life, which gets a big laugh from the studio audience. Matthews's (also laughingly) incredulous reaction shows that he isn't ready for such a candid discussion.

Another example of Stewart's forthrightness comes from the scandal over the July 2008 *New Yorker* cover in which Barack Obama is portrayed as a Muslim extremist giving a fist bump to his wife, who is dressed as a militant black radical complete with Afro, machine gun, and bandolier. The *New Yorker*'s editor, David Remnick, said that the cover was satire and was intended to target "distortions, misconceptions, and prejudices" about Barack Obama. This was not how either the McCain or the Obama campaign interpreted the cover. Both they and the vast majority of the mainstream media condemned it as stupid, offensive, or worse.[33] Stewart's take was a little different: "Obama's camp initially agreed that the cartoon was 'tasteless and offensive.' [Stewart looks perplexed and shakes his head.] Really? You know what your response should have been? It's very easy. Here, let me put the statement out for you: 'Barack Obama is in no way upset about the cartoon that depicts him as a Muslim extremist, because you know who gets upset about cartoons? *Muslim extremists*. Of which Barack Obama is not.' It's just a fucking *cartoon*."[34] Again, Stewart is very direct, clearly conveying his opinion about the situation and doing so in an unmistakable form.

The Daily Show as Good Citizen

The final criterion Foucault lays out for *parrhesia* is that the truth be told out of a sense of duty, and Jon Stewart clearly feels that it is his duty to point out the artificiality of political spin. Certainly one could argue that *The Daily Show* is simply a vehicle to make money and thus Stewart is being provocative because it is lucrative rather than because he feels obligated to do so. The show's enormous popularity with the coveted eighteen- to thirty-four-year-old demographic is attractive to advertisers and has made *The Daily Show* a very profitable show and Stewart a very wealthy man. However, both the content of Stewart's jokes (like the ones quoted above) and his own words in interviews bespeak an interesting sincerity. For example, Stewart both downplays his importance and demonstrates his motivation in an interview with Bill Moyers: "I think of myself as a comedian who has the pleasure of writing jokes about things that I actually care about. And that's really it. . . . I have great respect for people who are in the front lines and the trenches of trying to enact social change. I am far lazier than that. I am a tiny, neurotic man, standing in the back of the room throwing tomatoes at the chalk board. And that's really it." And Stewart has consistently taken issue with those who accuse *The Daily Show* of fostering cynicism: "People criticize our show for breeding cynicism, but there's nothing at all disingenuous about what we're doing. If anything is cynical, it's suggesting that your policy has never been 'stay the course' when we have thousands of hours of tape showing you using 'stay the course' as a talking point."[35]

Of course, the most blatant example of Stewart's sense of civic responsibility is his now infamous appearance on CNN's *Crossfire* on October 15, 2004. In this instance, Stewart was again astonishingly direct (and, according to *Crossfire* cohost Tucker Carlson, not funny) in his criticism of *Crossfire*: "You're hurting America," Stewart told Carlson and his cohost Paul Begala. "You're doing theater, when you should be doing debate. . . . What you do is not honest. What you do is partisan hackery." Certainly, this appearance can't be explained by a financial motive; being a guest who is so obviously critical of both the show and the hosts is not correlated with increased profits, especially for *Crossfire*, which was canceled several months after that episode. Interestingly, Stewart, a comedian, increased his credibility when he wasn't funny at all. He felt it was his responsibility to be blunt and honest, and he acted on it.[36]

Like the Greeks, American citizens have a constitutional right to free speech. And also like the Greeks, we have embedded in our definition of a good citizen the notion that we need people who will dare to criticize the powerful if they think it is necessary for good government. The Greeks called this type of truth-telling *parrhesia.* Although Foucault confines this concept to the specific Greek context, I believe that we still need those with enough courage to tell the truth. In fact, I would argue that they are especially necessary in a context where practically every political communication is vetted, focus group tested, and compacted into a sound bite before being endlessly repeated.

I have argued that a fake news program on Comedy Central acts as a modern-day *parrhesiastes,* speaking the truth about some very powerful people. Within our current milieu, it seems perfectly logical, as well as a little sad, that someone who is admittedly a "fake" seems more "real" than both the politicians and the media that disseminate their messages. Rather than being discouraged by such a situation, however, I find the very existence of *The Daily Show* a cause for hope. It suggests that no matter what the context, no matter the speed of the technology, the sophistication of the marketing techniques, or the intensity of the spin, someone will step up and have the courage to tell what he sees as the truth.

Notes

1. On whether the sky is actually blue, see http://www.sciencemadesimple.com/ and http://math.ucr.edu/home/baez/physics/General/BlueSky/blue_sky.html.

2. These lectures are compiled in written form from tape recordings in *Fearless Speech* (Los Angeles: Semiotext(e), 2001). It is also important to note that Foucault's discussion of truth and truth-telling in these lectures is very different from his discussion of truth in his earlier work, where truth is inexorably bound up with power and where the criteria we use in a certain time and place to decide whether a statement is true—what Foucault calls "the analytics of truth"—are always coercive. In contrast, in these lectures Foucault talks about the truth from a different perspective. Rather than thinking about how modern institutions such as the prison, the asylum, the hospital, and so on use the "truth" to make us docile and useful subjects, here Foucault looks to the history and evolution of the Greek notion of *parrhesia,* where telling the truth is an ethical decision to criticize someone more powerful, and it is a decision made consciously by the truth-teller, often in the face of great risk.

3. Foucault, *Fearless Speech*, 12.

4. For scholarly work that examines Foucault's concept of *parrhesia*, see Michael Peters, "Truth-telling as an Educational Practice of the Self: Foucault, *Parrhesia*, and the Ethics of Subjectivity," *Oxford Review of Education* 29, no. 2 (2003): 207–23; Nancy Luxon, "Truthfulness, Risk, and Trust in the Late Lectures of Michel Foucault," *Inquiry* 47 (2004): 464–89; Alison Ross, "Why Is 'Speaking the Truth' Fearless? 'Danger' and 'Truth' in Foucault's Discussion of *Parrhesia*," *Parrhesia* 4 (2008): 62–75. For scholarly work that looks specifically at political *parrhesia* outside the Greek context, see David R. Novak, "Engaging *Parrhesia* in a Democracy: Malcolm X as a Truth-teller," *Southern Communication Journal* 71, no. 1 (March 2006): 25–43; Antonia Szabari, "Rabelais *Parrhesiastes*: The Rhetoric of Insult and Rabelais's Cynical Mask," *MLN* 120 Supplement (2006): 84–123; Pam Christie and Ravinder Sidhu, "Governmentality and 'Fearless Speech': Framing the Education of Asylum Seeker and Refugee Children in Australia," *Oxford Review of Education* 32, no. 4 (September 2006): 449–65; Gae Lyn Henderson, "The *Parrhesiastic* Game: Textual Self-Justification in Spiritual Narratives of Early Modern Women," *Rhetoric Society Quarterly* 37 (2007): 423–51.

5. Foucault's definition of truth here is intentionally and, I believe, purposely and provocatively broad. Although he discusses only Greek notions of truth in these lectures, I believe that he intended to start a discussion about the purpose and method of telling the truth in the political arena, rather than ending the discussion with a definitive, narrow, or banal empirical or philosophical definition of truth. Thus, using this definition, one could argue that Rush Limbaugh can be characterized as a *parrhesiastes*. I would not characterize him this way, but the claim could be made—perhaps persuasively. Regardless of the political bent of the claimed *parrhesiastes*, it is incumbent on those making the claim to defend it through argumentation, not simply through appeals to empirical or transcendental truth.

6. Bárcenas and Jordan argue that Foucault's discussion of the Cynics' *parrhesia* is a better description of *The Daily Show* than his earlier discussion of political *parrhesia*. See Alejandro Bárcenas, "Jon the Cynic: Dog Philosophy 101," in *The Daily Show and Philosophy* (Malden, MA: Blackwell, 2007), 93–103; Matt Jordan, "Thinking with Foucault about Truth-telling and *The Daily Show*," *Electronic Journal of Communication* 18, nos. 2–3 (August 2008).

7. Sidney Blumenthal, *The Permanent Campaign* (New York: Simon and Schuster, 1982), 7. For a well-written history of the permanent campaign, see Hugh Heclo, "Campaigning and Governing: A Conspectus," in *The Permanent Campaign and Its Future* (Washington, DC: American Enterprise Institute and Brookings Institution, 2000), 2.

8. Quoted in Dan Froomkin, "The Ostrich Approach," *Washington Post*, May 25, 2005, http://www.washingtonpost.com/wp-dyn/content/blog/2005/05/25/BL2005052501250.html (accessed August 10, 2005).

9. Frank Luntz, *Words that Work: It's Not What You Say, It's What People Hear* (New York: Hyperion, 2007), 282.

10. See Internal Revenue Service, "United States Department of the Treasury Overview of the Estate Tax," http://www.irs.gov/businesses/small/article/0,,id=164871,00.html (accessed August 4, 2008).

11. "Jon Stewart's Nielsen Ratings Down 15 Percent; Colbert's Up 11 Percent," *New York Magazine,* January 9, 2008, http://nymag.com/daily/entertainment/2008/01/stewarts_ratings_down_15_colbe.html (accessed August 4, 2008).

12. A listing of the awards won by *The Daily Show* can be found at http://www.imdb.com/title/tt0115147/awards (accessed August 4, 2008).

13. David Carr, "'60 Minutes II' Wins Peabody Award, Raising Eyebrows," *New York Times,* April 8, 2005, http://www.nytimes.com/2005/04/08/arts/television/08peabody.html (accessed August 4, 2008).

14. Television Critics Association, n.d., http://www.awardsavenue.com/telestreet/critics/ 2004/tvcritics.htm (accessed August 2, 2004).

15. Daniel Bauder, "Stewart Delivers News to Younger Viewers," Associated Press, February 29, 2004, LexisNexis database (accessed October 19, 2005).

16. Howard Kurtz, "No Holds Barred: Alternative News Outlets Smack Down Convention Coverage," *Washington Post,* July 27, 2003, C1.

17. "Jon Stewart," Bill Moyers Journal Archive, July 11, 2003, http://www.pbs.org/moyers/journal/archives/jonstewartnow.html (accessed August 4, 2008).

18. http://www.thedailyshow.com/video/index.jhtml?videoId=117373&title=Bush-V.-Bush (accessed December 1, 2008). All transcriptions of *The Daily Show* videos are my own.

19. Laura Miller, "TV's Boldest New Show," *Salon*.com, April 8, 2003, http://dir.salon.com/story/ent/tv/feature/2003/04/08/stewart/ (accessed August 4, 2008).

20. http://www.thedailyshow.com/video/index.jhtml?videoId=115760&title=talking-points (accessed August 4, 2008).

21. Stephen Colbert wears many hats on the show. He is also senior war correspondent, senior religious correspondent, senior UN analyst, senior White House correspondent, senior psychology correspondent, senior "death" correspondent (for stories that report on the death penalty), and senior child molestation expert (for stories on the Catholic Church). His correspondent persona was so popular that it was spun off into its own show, *The Colbert Report,* in October 2005. For more information, see http://www.comedycentral.com/colbertreport/about.jhtml (accessed August 4, 2008).

22. http://www.thedailyshow.com/video/index.jhtml?videoId=124201&title=semantics&tag=generic_tag_dick_cheney&itemId=104995 (accessed August 4, 2008).

23. http://www.thedailyshow.com/video/index.jhtml?videoId=83639&title=cheneys-clout (accessed August 4, 2008).

24. Scott McClelland, *What Happened? Inside the Bush White House and Washington's Culture of Deception* (New York: Public Affairs, 2008), 132–33.

25. There is an emerging literature that details the media's failure to question the Bush administration's version of both 9/11 and the Iraq war. See, for example, Barbie

Zelizer and Stuart Allen, eds., *Journalism after September 11* (New York: Routledge, 2002); David Dadge, *Casualty of War: The Bush Administration's Assault on the Free Press* (Amherst, NY: Prometheus, 2004); William A. Hatchen, *The Troubles with Journalism: A Critical Look at What's Right and What's Wrong with the Press* (Mahwah, NJ: Lawrence Erlbaum, 2005); Lisa Finnegan, *No Questions Asked: News Coverage Since 9/11* (Westport, CT: Praeger, 2006); Helen Thomas, *Watchdogs of Democracy? The Waning Washington Press Corps and How It Has Failed the Public* (New York: Scribner, 2006); W. Lance Bennett, Regina G. Lawrence, and Steven Livingston, *When the Press Fails: Political Power and the News Media from Iraq to Katrina* (Chicago: University of Chicago Press, 2007).

26. Andrew Boyd, "Truth Is a Virus: Meme Warfare and Billionaires for Bush (or Gore)," http://www.culturejamming101.com/truthisavirus.html (accessed August 4, 2008).

27. Maureen Dowd, "America's Anchors," *Rolling Stone,* October 31, 2006, http://www.rollingstone.com/news/coverstory/jon_stewart_stephen_colbert_americas_anchors/page/3 (accessed August 4, 2008).

28. The classic example and one of the most famous uses of satire is, of course, "A Modest Proposal," and Jonathan Swift is one of the most celebrated satirists in Western literature. See Jonathan Swift, *Gulliver's Travels and Other Writings,* ed. Louis Landa (Boston: Houghton Mifflin, 1960). For discussions of more current satire, see Jamie Warner, "Political Culture Jamming: The Dissident Humor of *The Daily Show with Jon Stewart,*" *Popular Communication* 5, no. 1 (Spring 2007): 17–37; Margaret Farrar and Jamie Warner, "Spectacular Resistance: The Billionaires for Bush and the Art of Political Culture Jamming," *Polity* 40, no. 3 (July 2008): 273–96.

29. George Test, *Satire: Spirit and Art* (Tampa: University of South Florida Press, 1991), 32.

30. Wayne Booth, *A Rhetoric of Irony* (Chicago: University of Chicago Press, 1974), 11.

31. For the full clip, see http://www.thedailyshow.com/video/index.jhtml?videoId=81734&title=hot-topic (accessed August 4, 2008).

32. For the full clip, see http://www.thedailyshow.com/video/index.jhtml?videoId=104548&title=chris-matthews (accessed August 4, 2008).

33. See, for example, http://latimesblogs.latimes.com/washington/2008/07/obama-muslim.html (accessed August 4, 2008).

34. For the full clip, see http://www.thedailyshow.com/video/index.jhtml?videoId=176628&title=obama-cartoon (accessed August 4, 2008).

35. Dowd, "America's Anchors."

36. Lisa de Moraes, "Left Hooks and Right Jabs: Stewart Tangles with Carlson," *Washington Post,* October 16, 2004, http://www.washingtonpost.com/wp-dyn/articles/A37042-2004Oct15.html (accessed August 4, 2008).

3

MR. SMITH GOES TO THE MOVIES

Images of Dissent in American Cinema

Beth Wielde Heidelberg and David Schultz

Terrorists have hijacked a plane. They force everyone to the back, isolating passengers and taking control of the flight. On the ground, government officials are in frenzy, trying to figure out how to resolve the situation. Just when all seems lost, a hero rushes in to save the day. Who is this dashing figure ready at the rescue? The president of the United States. In the post-9/11 world, the terrorist scenario seems all too real, and the president as action hero in Wolfgang Peterson's *Air Force One* shows a new type of dissent—where the government is presented *as we wish it could be* rather than as one we don't trust in reality.

Pop culture expresses potent political messages. Though often dismissed as the fluff of celebrity gossip, crass commercialism, or mass consumption, pop culture images serve as a potentially important source of socialization and knowledge about the political world. It may also be a locus of expressing and channeling dissent.

Individuals are politically socialized and express disagreement about their government in at least three ways. First, they obtain firsthand political knowledge through direct experiences such as voting, attending meetings, or participating in rallies or demonstrations.[1] Second, individual knowledge about politics is second-ordered and mediated by the news establishment, obtained by reading newspapers or watching television news.[2] Finally, political knowledge can be third-ordered, mediated by popular culture venues such as television entertainment shows or movies.[3] Given data suggesting low rates of civic engagement for many activities and significant decreases in public consumption of mainstream news, pop culture's influence on political knowledge is significant.[4] Thus, pop culture's role as a way of expressing dissent and disagreement may be more critical than many think.

There is no question that movies are often political vehicles.[5] Leni Riefenstahl's *Triumph of the Will* is by many accounts one of the most powerful political movies ever made. But many other films also express political messages, dissent, or criticism of authority. *Casablanca*'s Rick and the opposition to the German occupation of France come to mind. But films such as *All the President's Men, Three Days of the Condor,* and even Michael Moore's *Sicko* and *Fahrenheit 9/11* all express critical views of authority and government and serve as potential rallying points for political opposition. Yet even "lighter" fare such as *Dave,* where a look-alike imposter takes over the White House, or *Legally Blonde 2: Red, White, and Blonde,* where vapid Elle Woods exposes corruption and works the political process to get an animal protection bill through Congress, contains critical views of government—the processes and people that encompass the political and public service realms.

Oliver Stone's *W,* a movie about President George W. Bush, was destined to be a political film, especially given its planned October 2008 release, barely a month before the presidential election. Like Stone's earlier films such as *JFK* and *Nixon, W*'s impact on political consciousness might be profound. Evidence exists, for example, that viewers of *JFK* were strongly influenced by Stone's account of the assassination of John F. Kennedy.[6] They might be similarly affected by his depiction of Bush and his presidency. But films do not always have to feature or focus on elected officials or politicians. Critical or negative depictions of government administrators or bureaucrats doing their jobs can also express dissent, legitimize disapproval, or simply socialize citizens.

This chapter examines American movies as a tool of political dissent. It does so by analyzing depictions of public officials in American movies from the 1940s to the present. We first determine the frequency of critical depictions of government and public officials in films; then we examine how movies express dissent, based on discussion of contemporary political events. The data show that movies with government-related subjects are actually more common than thought, and these films often reflect contemporary political themes, issues, and facts. Our conclusion is that movies provide an important third-level source of political criticism and knowledge. We also suggest that this cinematic-based political knowledge has implications for citizens' attitudes about and support for the government.

Pop Culture as Political Expression

Pop culture is ordinarily depicted as politically insignificant. In fact it is often dismissed as fluff, just part of the realm of entertainment. However, at least two arguments can be made as to why pop culture, and especially motion pictures, should be reappraised for its political value.

First, pop culture venues, which include television and movies, are vehicles of political socialization. If political socialization is, as Roberta Siegel defines it, "the learning process by which political norms and behaviors acceptable to an ongoing political system are transmitted from generation to generation," then there are many sources from which individuals acquire this information.[7] These sources include the family, the community, and peers. Direct political engagement, such as participating in campaigns, contacting public officials, or seeking out government services, also serves as a tool for learning about politics. But in addition to this first-level knowledge, individuals acquire knowledge about government and politics through the news media.[8] Traditionally, this has meant gathering information from newspapers and television news—a type of second-order knowledge. Then there is a third-order level of socialization that occurs through pop culture venues such as television and movies.[9] It would be fair to say that depictions of government officials in entertainment venues have a significant impact on how people think of and view these characters. For example, Timothy Lenz demonstrated that crime, the police, and law and order themes change over time, either reflecting the public view or helping to mold it with regard to these issues.[10] Recently, some have contended that there is a "CSI" effect, arguing that these shows influence how jurors think about evidence and trial deliberations.[11] Thus, with so many individuals consuming pop culture, its influence on politics and political knowledge should not be underestimated.

Pop culture as a form of art is potentially political. On one level, pop culture in the United States, especially Hollywood and its films, is often at the center of so-called culture wars.[12] But Walter Benjamin argues that art in the "age of mechanical reproduction" takes on a political dimension.[13] More important, one can draw on Antonio Gramsci's concept of hegemony and argue that pop culture lies at the center of a struggle among contending groups, with movies serving as one setting where the war for the hearts and minds of the public is being fought.[14] Thus, movies such as *Triumph of the Will, Sicko, JFK, An Inconvenient Truth,* and perhaps *W* are part of an ideological battle among various groups to communicate their messages to the public. These messages may be intended to encourage people to take political action or vote in a specific way, or they may simply be efforts to prime an issue or set an agenda.[15]

Overall, if pop culture is in fact a source of political knowledge and socialization for many, and if one views it as part of a hegemonic battle for political influence or dominance, it is also possible to contend that it is a source of expressing dissent. This may be especially true when it comes to films. As Ernest Giglio points out, movies have long been seen as embodying political messages and as being intertwined with images and themes both supportive and critical of the government.[16] Yet studies such as Giglio's have looked mainly at the intersection of movies and politics; they have not examined how often the government and its officials (nonelected) are depicted in film and what types of images are offered. Additionally, these studies generally do not look at films as a source of dissent or as part of the hegemonic battle for political influence. It is to this topic we now turn.

Government as a Theme in Film

An evaluation of research into the depiction of government and public service in film reveals a critical void—specifically, whether there is valid statistical evidence that government-related themes are prevalent in popular culture media. There is no shortage of authors who have examined politics and other aspects of government in popular culture film, but most of them used anecdotal evidence and other nonrandom sampling methods as the basis of evaluation.[17] To determine whether film provides the third-order feature of voicing dissent, it is important to determine how important government in film actually is to popular culture. We used latent content analysis rather than the traditional anecdotal method to develop such evidence.

To determine the popularity of government in film, we derived a data population from the top twenty films from 1945 to 2005 based on gross domestic box-office receipts (with the exception of ten missing data items from 1950 and 1951, where the records indicate only the top ten). First, a data source (boxofficemojo.com) was selected to provide the raw data. Internet databases have been used in peer-reviewed journals in prior studies about film and culture and provide a consistent method of raw data collection.[18] To narrow down the 1,210 films from this raw data, the plot description of each title was investigated and cross-referenced on two film databases (imdbpro.com and allmovie.com). Plot descriptions were checked for specific keywords that indicated governmental themes in the story line. Forty-five percent of the films in the sample were identified as having governmental themes, including foreign and fantasy governments. This was broken down further, as shown in Figure 1, to identify the percentage of films with specifically U.S. government–related themes.

Figure 2 shows the specific breakdown of the most frequently depicted governmental themes in the top twenty films, with political themes accounting for 9 percent. Action-based governmental activity, particularly military and public safety divisions such as police and fire, have been particularly popular at the box office.

Over time, the various sectors of government have been represented at different rates. Figure 3 shows, by decade, the U.S. government sectors being shown most frequently to domestic audiences.

Government as a film theme is clearly commonplace in the ever-changing

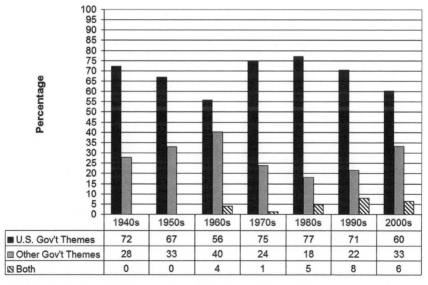

	1940s	1950s	1960s	1970s	1980s	1990s	2000s
■ U.S. Gov't Themes	72	67	56	75	77	71	60
▦ Other Gov't Themes	28	33	40	24	18	22	33
▨ Both	0	0	4	1	5	8	6

Figure 1. U.S. Government versus Other Government Depictions in the Twenty Top-Grossing Domestic Films, 1945–2005.

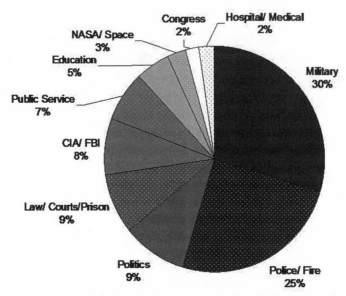

Figure 2. Breakdown of Government-Related Themes in the Twenty Top-Grossing Domestic Films, 1945–2005.

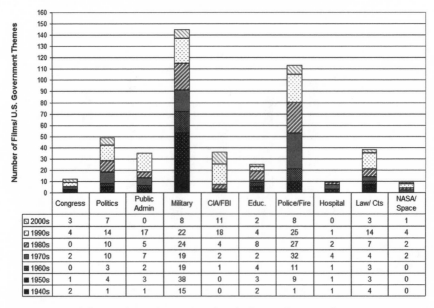

	Congress	Politics	Public Admin	Military	CIA/FBI	Educ.	Police/Fire	Hospital	Law/ Cts	NASA/ Space
⊡ 2000s	3	7	0	8	11	2	8	0	3	1
▢ 1990s	4	14	17	22	18	4	25	1	14	4
▨ 1980s	0	10	5	24	4	8	27	2	7	2
▪ 1970s	2	10	7	19	2	2	32	4	4	2
▪ 1960s	0	3	2	19	1	4	11	1	3	0
▪ 1950s	1	4	3	38	0	3	9	1	3	0
▪ 1940s	2	1	1	15	0	2	1	1	4	0

Figure 3. Breakdown of Government-Related Themes by Decade, 1940s–2000s.

political climate, with almost half of all films in the sample having some sort of governmental theme, and a high percentage of them having U.S. government–specific themes each decade. Measuring the prolific nature of these government-themed films against public sentiment toward government lays the foundation to determine whether film is a tool of dissent or whether it provides a picture of government as we want it to be.

Dissent on Screen

There are at least two ways films can be viewed as tools of dissent. The first simply documents the percentage of films overall with negative depictions of government officials or with specific instances of characters described critically. The second way is to examine film's interrelationship with public opinion about government over time.

To determine whether there is a parallel between public opinion and how film depicts government and the people who operate it, we examined data from the National Election Survey (NES) to see whether depictions tend to increase during times when people's attitudes toward government are favorable. Figure 4 shows the trend in decade averages for NES responses from the 1960s to the 2000s (NES data were not compiled until 1958, so the 1940s and 1950s are not included; for the 2000s, 2004 was the most recent year surveyed). Then it compares those responses to the number of total governmental depictions in film and specific U.S. government depictions. Figure 4 shows that in times of declining government trust (i.e., when more people trust the government only "some of the time" as opposed to "most of the time"), the frequency of government depictions in film actually increases.

In examining the films from 1945 to 2005, individual government officials were initially depicted positively in 27 percent of the films and negatively in 36 percent. By the end of the movie (as a result of character growth or change), positive depictions grew to 64 percent and negative depictions shrank to 23 percent. Neutral depictions dropped from 37 percent to 13 percent.

This survey of films indicates that government-related themes increase as trust levels decline. Conversely, government themes decrease as trust increases. These trends suggest several interesting hypotheses. For one, when faith in government declines, one way to channel criticism toward it is through films. Disapproval of the government can be expressed in cinematic

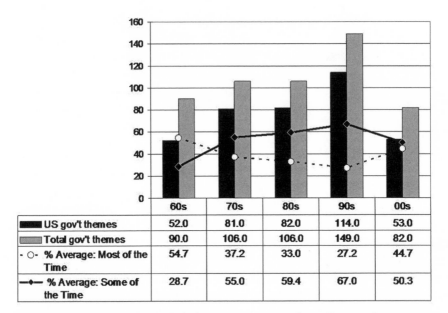

	60s	70s	80s	90s	00s
US gov't themes	52.0	81.0	82.0	114.0	53.0
Total gov't themes	90.0	106.0	106.0	149.0	82.0
- O- % Average: Most of the Time	54.7	37.2	33.0	27.2	44.7
─◆─ % Average: Some of the Time	28.7	55.0	59.4	67.0	50.3

Figure 4. Comparison of National Election Survey Results on Trust in Government and Prevalence of Government-Related Themes in Films, 1960s–2000s.

depictions. Moreover, these depictions can legitimize other forms of dissent or criticism or otherwise validate disagreement in society.

Second, the fact that movies demonstrate mixed negative, positive, and even neutral views of government officials points to their political plasticity. Mixed depictions of government officials show how Gramsci's concept of hegemony is applicable to movies. Contrasting images of government in film speak to an ideological battle for the public's hearts and minds. These mixed images reveal the potential to use films to socialize positive feelings and support for a regime or to provide a basis for legitimizing or channeling dissent and criticism.

Finally, it is important to understand what message audiences are leaving the theater with when they watch these films. For instance, our 2007 study enumerated seven distinct types of depictions of government and the people who operate behind its grand Corinthian columns. Many of these depictions are negative, but some are positive, demonstrating that movies may be one tool to fight our culture wars and express disapproval of the current regime.[19]

Government Depictions

Latent content analysis of government-themed films from 1945 to 2005 reveals six different character types—some positive, some negative, and some neutral.[20] These different images of public officials are important expressions of how films can educate the public about government, with negative character portrayals expressing dissent and disagreement.

Ivan Reitman created the quintessential "Bad Government" depiction in the 1984 film *Ghostbusters* and its 1989 sequel. In the original film, Environmental Protection Agency (EPA) agent Walter Peck oozes with animosity toward the ghost-capturing clan, flexing his governmental muscle whenever he can and managing to both jail the Ghostbusters and shut down their containment system (unwittingly heralding the destruction of New York City by the Stay-Puft Marshmallow Man).

Reitman's films illustrate exactly how the film industry paints a vivid

Ghostbusters, tapping into the zeitgeist of the 1980s, pits its protagonists against both specters and bureaucratic overregulation. (Jerry Ohlinger's Movie Material Store)

portrait of the government worker, the politician, and the governmental process—for better or worse. We viewed the twenty films in our sample to determine whether there are trends in this type of characterization.[21] Six distinctive characteristics emerged from these screenings, and *Ghostbusters'* Walter Peck represents one of the two negative types, the "Monstercrat." *Ghostbusters* shows the Monstercrat as the embodiment of "big government" flexing its proverbial muscle to demonstrate its strength. Sometimes this preening is for self-interest or career advancement, but sometimes it is just out of spite or as a strong-arm tactic to say, "Watch out, we're stronger." But while Monstercrats may use or abuse the power of their office, they stay within the realm of the law, unlike their even less desirable relatives, the "BlackHatocrats."

BlackHatocrats not only use their office for self-interest, monetary gain, career advancement, or self-preservation; they also break the law to achieve their devious goals. In *Enemy of the State* (1998), "regular Joe" Robert Dean (portrayed by Will Smith) gets entangled in a cover-up when the National Security Agency (NSA) tries to hide its involvement in the murder of a congressman who advocates a bill blocking the expansion of law enforcement's surveillance powers (seeing it as encroaching on individual privacy). Dean unwittingly comes into possession of a videotape of the murder, and the NSA uses all its means—legal (observation, pursuit) and illegal (breaking and entering, attempted murder)—to retrieve it. These BlackHatocrats are self-serving and conspiratorial and have little regard for ethics or the public welfare. As long as they achieve their end goal, it doesn't matter what technique is used or who is hurt in the process. This is a typical BlackHatocrat function—to depict government as a system that can get away with murder—but in the film world, the "big, bad government" often gets what it deserves.

In the movies, corrupt governments and public officials often receive their just punishment. And with real-life government scandals and campaign mudslinging, that third-order knowledge may be seen as a relief to some and a fantasy to others, depending on their first- and second-order political opinions. Directors Ivan Reitman (*Ghostbusters*) and Tony Scott (*Enemy of the State*) leave no evil deed unpunished. EPA agent Peck is given a spectacular comeuppance: he is forcefully ejected from the mayor's office, doused by the goo of the melted Stay-Puft Marshmallow Man, and vaporized by the Ghostbusters after a Godzilla-like rampage. The NSA agents are outwitted by Dean, despite their technological resources. They are gunned

Robert Dean (Will Smith) is an "enemy" of the expansion of state power as hypersurveillance encroaches on the privacy and civil liberties of a vast majority of Americans in the 1998 political action thriller *Enemy of the State*. (MovieGoods)

down by a mafioso whom Dean has been working with in a mistaken-identity shoot-out. Those who survive the shoot-out are jailed, and the plot is exposed to the FBI. Such comeuppances usually involve less marshmallow and more jail time, removal from office, or public humiliation. In contrast, one of the reasons *Chinatown*'s end is so unsettling is that the BlackHato-crats do not get reprimanded for their actions—the corruption shown in the film is left unresolved.

The "Obsessocrat" represents a neutral depiction; it is negative in that the character has no discernible life outside of public office, but positive in terms of a strong dedication to public service—to the point where the character rejects self-interest or personal gain. However, this dedication has a downside: an almost robotic, obsessive focus on public service. In *Apollo 13,* flight director Gene Kranz (based on a real person and portrayed by Ed Harris) begins the mission with one focus: to achieve the third manned moon landing. He begins the mission with staunch professionalism; the only indication of an outside life is when he receives a vest sent by his wife—with the mission patch sewn onto it. Even after the spacecraft accident, Kranz is not shown in panic mode; he exhibits only a fierce determination to abort the original mission in favor of a new one—to get the astronauts home safely. He is all business until this new mission is accomplished.

Whereas Kranz personifies the Obsessocrat's determination to accomplish a job, the "Romanticrat" often starts off with this type of fierce government loyalty, but some outside influence—usually a handsome rogue or a stunning ingénue—chips away at that single-minded focus on governmental duty. The Romanticrat is typically a bureaucratic drone who emerges from the constraints of his or her position to become a romantic figure. In *Music Man,* Marian Paroo does just this. The stoic librarian has a rousing musical number locked inside her; all she needs is a smooth-talking "civilian" to release her from her ways. The Romanticrat shows that there is a person behind that government-issued desk.

In *The Wedding Crashers,* the secretary of the interior (depicted by Christopher Walken) is at first excited by the prospect of his daughter marrying a man of wealth and status and the opportunity to merge two powerful families. But when he sees that she loves someone with little power or status, he realizes that love is more important than the merging of two "power families." The Romanticrat, then, puts feelings ahead of duty or power in a way the Monstercrat, the BlackHatocrat, and, to some extent, the Obsessocrat do not.

Yet the Romanticrat faces no physical threat to his or her person or to the overall public safety. The Romanticrat lives in a safe, secure world ruled by love, whereas the life of the "Herocrat" is a dangerous, action-packed thrill ride. The Herocrat puts life and limb on the line to expose the truth, obtain justice, or save others in distress—all out of a sense of duty. In *Air Force One,* the president embodies the Herocrat. When the plane is hijacked by terrorists, staff members choose to stay on board with the targeted president and his Secret Service agents, much to their mortal peril. The president is shown as an action hero, dodging bullets and fistfighting his way out of danger rather than escaping through the hatch designed for his protection.

In Jon Turtletaub's *National Treasure,* Dr. Abigail Chase, the consummate director of the National Archives, reluctantly aids protagonist Ben Gates in uncovering the founding fathers' hidden treasure, risking life, limb, and the Declaration of Independence in the pursuit of truth. In the end, Chase is not only a Herocrat, having been flung out of vans and maneuvering a rotting staircase, but also an "Ethicrat." When they find the treasure, she refuses to take more than a token 1 percent of the reward, despite the government's offer of 10 percent.

Ethicrats are very similar to Herocrats, but rather than becoming involved in life-threatening situations, they use ethics and a general sense of what's right to guide their decisions and serve the greater good. For instance, in *The Day after Tomorrow* (2004), NASA hurricane paleoclimatologist Jack Hall stands up to the stubborn vice president (to warn him about the impending second ice age and to debate the relative importance of economics and ecological responsibility). His refusal to budge from his position despite disagreeing with his superior in the power structure demonstrates that he values ethics over just going along and doing what he is "supposed" to do.

In *Armageddon* (1998), an asteroid is threatening to wipe out Earth, and the only way to save it is to have oil drillers and amateur astronauts dig 800 feet into the asteroid and plant a nuclear bomb to blow it apart. Ethicrat and NASA civilian executive director Dan Truman disregards presidential and military orders to detonate the nuclear bomb prematurely, correctly insisting that his way will work.

Although the NES data indicate a declining trust in government until an upswing in the early 2000s, the depictions of government cover a spectrum of negative (Monstercrat, BlackHatocrat), neutral (Obsessocrat), and positive (Romanticrat, Herocrat, Ethicrat) images. However, there is a strong trend toward positive depictions at the end of films. Positive depictions tend to be strong even in eras when trust in government is low, such as in the 1990s. Figure 5 shows which depictions tend to be dominant at the end of films—that is, the impression left with audiences as they exit the theater. This illustrates that even when trust in government declined in the 1960s, 1970s, and 1990s, government depictions were still strongly positive at the end of films (although in the 1980s, the decline in governmental trust paralleled the Monstercrat and BlackHatocrat depictions). This implies that film, if it is truly a voice of dissent, provides a picture of benign government, where the bad folks get what's coming to them and the good folks prosper.

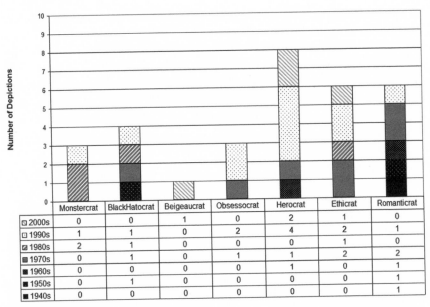

Figure 5. Depictions of Seven Character Types in the Twenty Top-Grossing Domestic Films by Decade, 1940s–2000s.

	Monstercrat	BlackHatocrat	Beigeaucrat	Obsessocrat	Herocrat	Ethicrat	Romanticrat
2000s	0	0	1	0	2	1	0
1990s	1	1	0	2	4	2	1
1980s	2	1	0	0	0	1	0
1970s	0	1	0	1	1	2	2
1960s	0	0	0	0	1	0	1
1950s	0	1	0	0	0	0	1
1940s	0	0	0	0	0	0	1

History and the movie *W* will speak to how the American public ultimately remembers George W. Bush. Cinematic portrayals of government officials offer another way of understanding the relationship between pop culture and politics.

Our examination of the top-grossing American films from 1945 to 2005 demonstrates that the government and its officials are frequent themes. Although this study did not examine American cinema's specific depiction of elected officials, pop culture portrayals of government officials and processes can provide critical insights into politics.

This study reveals an overall mixed—positive, negative, and neutral—depiction of government officials, as well as a number of specific character types that view public officials in various lights. These often ambivalent or perhaps contradictory depictions mean that movies may be a third-order source of knowledge that individuals use to learn about government, standing behind both direct participation and news accounts. But more important, films that offer critical as well as supportive images of the government and its officials demonstrate their Gramscian nature. They are tools of political socialization capable of expressing or channeling dissent or support for a regime. Thus, they serve as one point in the battle for position in culture wars and in political struggles directed at the government.

Notes

1. Roberta Siegel, *Learning about Politics: A Reader in Political Socialization* (New York: Random House, 1970).

2. See Shanto Iyengar and Donald R. Kinder, *News that Matters: Television and American Opinion* (Chicago: University of Chicago Press, 1987); Matthew Mendelsohn, "The Media and Interpersonal Communications: The Priming of Issues, Leaders, and Party Identification," *Journal of Politics* 58, no. 1 (1996): 112–25; M. Margaret Conway et al., "The News Media in Children's Political Socialization," *Public Opinion Quarterly* 45, no. 2 (1981): 164–78.

3. David J. Jackson, *Entertainment and Politics: The Influence of Pop Culture on Young Adult Socialization* (New York: Peter Lang, 2002).

4. See David Schultz, *Lights, Camera, Campaign! Media, Politics, and Political Advertising* (New York: Peter Lang, 2004); Pew Research Center for People and the Press, "Audiences Fragmented and Skeptical: The Tough Job of Communicating with Voters," 2002, http://www.peoplepress.org (accessed October 23, 2008).

5. Ernest Giglio, *Here's Looking at You: Hollywood, Film and Politics* (New York: Peter Lang, 2005).

6. Jim Kelly and Bill Elliott, "Synthetic History and Subjective Reality: The Impact of Oliver Stone's *JFK*," in *It's Show Time! Media, Politics, and Popular Culture*, ed. David Schultz (New York: Peter Lang, 2000), 171–96.

7. Siegel, *Learning about Politics*, 1.

8. Conway, "News Media in Children's Political Socialization."

9. Jackson, *Entertainment and Politics*.

10. Timothy O. Lenz, *Changing Images of Law in Film and Television Crime Stories* (New York: Peter Lang, 2003).

11. CNN, "Toobin: *CSI* Makes Jurors More Demanding: Is Popular Show Guilty of Influencing U.S. Courtrooms?" May 6, 2005, http://www.cnn.com/2005/LAW/05/05/otsc.toobin/ (accessed October 10, 2008).

12. See Giglio, *Here's Looking at You*; Lenz, *Changing Images of Law*.

13. Walter Benjamin, "The Work of Art in the Age of Mechanical Reproduction," in *Illuminations*, ed. Hannah Arendt (New York: Schocken Books, 1978), 211–44.

14. Antonio Gramsci, *Selections from the Prison Notebooks* (New York: International Publishers, 1971), 234–36.

15. Iyengar and Kinder, *News that Matters*.

16. Giglio, *Here's Looking at You.*

17. See ibid.; Michael Rogin, *Ronald Reagan, the Movie and Other Episodes in Political Demonology* (Berkeley: University of California Press, 1987).

18. See, for example, Deborah P. Valentine and Miriam Freeman, "Film Portrayals of Social Workers Doing Child Welfare Work," *Child and Adolescent Social Work Journal* 19, no. 6 (2002): 455–71; B. McCullick, D. Belcher, B. Hardin, and M. Hardin, "Butches, Bullies, and Buffoons: Images of Physical Education Teachers in the Movies," *Sport, Education, and Society* 8, no. 1 (2003): 3–16.

19. Beth Wielde and David Schultz, "Wonks and Warriors: Depictions of Government Professionals in Popular Film," *Public Voices* 9, no. 2 (2007): 61–82.

20. Ibid. Over the course of the study, the term "Beigeauocrat" was merged with "Obsessocrat" because the two character types share the same key characteristics.

21. Ibid.

4

THE TRUTH IS STILL OUT THERE

The X-Files and 9/11

Paul A. Cantor

> What does this science fiction have to do with anything?
> —Special Agent Kallenbrunner, "The Truth," *The X-Files*

From the beginning it was very difficult to separate the significance of the events of 9/11 from the significance of the media representation of them. The impact of what happened that day was bound up with the fact that it largely took place on live television, with the whole world watching. The terrorists who planned the attack no doubt were counting on media coverage to magnify its impact and thus to achieve their sinister purposes. With the media rushing to cover such a shocking event, their commentary quickly turned into meta-commentary, as they began to discuss not just the event itself but also how they were covering it. Within days, if not hours, of the event, media commentators began speculating about how 9/11 would affect American popular culture. At times, the talking heads on television seemed concerned as much about the cultural impact of 9/11 as about its political, economic, and military implications.

Under the stress of a profoundly traumatic event, the media experts were understandably tempted to make apocalyptic pronouncements. Soon a consensus seemed to emerge: *after 9/11, American popular culture would never be the same again.*[1] Cynicism about America was out; patriotism would return to movies and television. The mood of the moment was crystallized in a *Time* magazine article by Roger Rosenblatt with the title "The Age of

Irony Comes to an End" (September 16, 2001). In words that resonated throughout the mediasphere, Rosenblatt powerfully argued that "one good thing could come from this horror"—Americans would wake up from three decades of insisting that "nothing was to be believed in or taken seriously." In opposition to a postmodernist attitude that "nothing was real," the events of 9/11 would serve as a reality check for Americans: "The planes that plowed into the World Trade Center and the Pentagon were real. The flames, smoke, sirens—real." From this perception, Rosenblatt went on to predict a return to patriotism: "The greatness of the country: real."[2] Rosenblatt's eloquent rhetoric struck a responsive chord in America, especially among those who had long felt that movies and television were letting down their country, failing to offer images embodying its traditional values and instead debunking its icons of national greatness. The heroic responses to the 9/11 crisis by firefighters, police, military personnel, and ordinary citizens were genuinely inspirational and, many commentators argued, would serve as new and invigorating models for American popular culture. Many predicted that the traditional all-American hero would soon be returning to movie and television screens.[3]

The events of 9/11 certainly had an immediate impact on television. In the first few days following, broadcasting schedules had to be hastily reshuffled. For example, the Fox Network canceled a showing of the movie *Independence Day* advertised for September 15. The movie's trademark shot of the White House exploding was exactly what Americans did not want to see so soon after witnessing all-too-similar disasters in the real world.[4] Late-night talk-show hosts such as David Letterman and Jay Leno were open about their reluctance to go ahead with their normal comedy routines at a time when the nation was more inclined to grieve than to laugh.[5] To focus on a trivial reflection of a very serious situation: the wacky family sitcom *Malcolm in the Middle* had to retool itself. Since its beginning the show had featured a subplot involving the oldest son in the family (Francis) being exiled to a military academy. The show mercilessly satirized this institution as fascist, with the particularly repellent Commandant Edwin Spangler as a grotesque caricature of an authoritarian personality. When the sitcom began its third season on November 11, 2001, it took only a week for the show to find a way for Francis to flee the military school and head up to Alaska to work at a resort. I may have been the only person to make anything of this development at the time—the country had more important things on its mind—and I have never seen any explanation from the producers of the series. Yet I cannot help thinking that Commandant Spangler was a casualty of 9/11. In its own small way, *Malcolm in the Middle* confirmed what commentators like Rosenblatt had argued. After 9/11, one of the most cynical shows on television now drew the line at making fun of the military in any form.

A more significant and complex case study of the impact of 9/11 on American popular culture is provided by the Fox Network's flagship series, *The X-Files*. In its eight-season run leading up to the fall of 2001, *The X-Files* exemplified what media critics had in mind when they complained about a negative attitude toward government in American popular culture. One of the mottoes of the show was "Trust No One," and that meant especially trust no one in government. The show featured two FBI agents, Fox Mulder and Dana Scully, who were presented as heroic, but only because of their independence from the government, their constant willingness to disobey the orders of their superiors and go it alone in their pursuit of truth and justice. Over the years, *The X-Files* portrayed the FBI and other government agencies such as FEMA as alternately incompetent or sinister. In the seemingly contradictory terms of the show, government agencies were either incapable of handling the simplest problems or involved in complex conspiracies and cover-ups. In the central plot arc of the series, the FBI and other government agencies were shown to be manipulated by a shadowy syndicate masterminding a projected alien takeover of the planet, which involved, among other nefarious schemes, the federal government spying and experimenting on American citizens against their will and without their knowledge. *The X-Files* raised doubts about the conduct of the U.S. government throughout the cold war, often presenting its actions as morally equivalent to those of its evil enemies. In a number of episodes, the show took a cynical attitude toward the first Gulf War, even going so far as to suggest that Saddam Hussein was a puppet of the United States—indeed, its creation.

Thus, if any show was going to run into problems with a changed American public in the wake of 9/11, it was going to be *The X-Files,* and Fox chose to delay the beginning of its ninth season by several weeks. In the event, its ratings plummeted in the 2001–2002 season, with the show averaging 8.5 million viewers, down from 13.2 million the previous season and from a peak average of 18.3 million in 1996.[6] By January 2002, the creator-producer of *The X-Files,* Chris Carter, could see the handwriting on the wall and made the decision to pull the plug on the series. When its last episode aired in May 2002, many commentators chose to view *The X-Files* as another

In uncanny ways, *The X-Files* anticipated the events of 9/11 and their troubling aftermath. In the series finale "The Truth," Fox Mulder (David Duchovny) is represented by Walter Skinner (Mitch Pileggi) in a closed military tribunal completely controlled by the state and Mulder's enemies. (MovieGoods)

casualty of 9/11. In a thoughtful—and appreciative—article on the show, Andrew Stuttaford argued that 9/11 had relegated *The X-Files* to the dustbin of history: "the *X-Files* is a product of a time that has passed. It is a relic of the Clinton years as dated as a dot-com share certificate, a stained blue dress or Kato Kaelin's reminiscences." Echoing Rosenblatt and other media pundits, Stuttaford accused the series of not taking life seriously, pointing to its "cynicism, irony, and a notable sense of detachment." "This is a show where, for all the drama, no one seems genuinely involved—even with each other. . . . This is Po-Mo Sci-Fi. . . . It is *Seinfeld* with flying saucers, another show, ultimately, about nothing. Nothing serious, anyway." Invoking 9/11 as having transformed the world, Stuttaford dismissed the series as having become irrelevant in the twenty-first century: "The *X-Files* was a show for self-indulgent, more complacent times, an entertainment for *before*."[7]

Sorting out causality in the realm of culture is notoriously difficult, and an argument like Stuttaford's risks falling into the fallacy of *post hoc, ergo propter hoc.* Merely because the popularity of *The X-Files* began to decline after 9/11 does not prove that a change in the American public's attitude toward government was responsible for the show's demise. To his credit, Stuttaford admits that other factors may well have been at work. Nine seasons is a long time for any television series to survive. *The X-Files* is, in fact, the longest running science fiction show in TV history (by comparison, the original *Star Trek* lasted only three seasons). Well before 9/11, media critics began wondering whether 2001–2002 would—and should—be the last for *The X-Files*.[8] Many argued that the show had suffered a significant decline in quality ever since its fifth season, or at least since its seventh. For a show that often depended on the shock value of its episodes, *The X-Files* was running out of novel plot twists. Moreover, casting problems threatened to doom the show once its stars, David Duchovny and Gillian Anderson, began to lose interest in continuing in their roles. Duchovny's absence from all but the final episode of the ninth season was probably enough by itself to sink the series. The attempt in the eighth season to introduce two new FBI agents to pick up the slack from Mulder and Scully never really caught on with *X-Files* fans. In short, the show had probably run its course by the 2001–2002 season, and attempts to attribute its demise to a post-9/11 change in mood in the American public probably overemphasize the importance of cultural factors.

More to the point, if Stuttaford's thesis were correct, *The X-Files* should have long since slipped off the pop culture map. Instead, a significant segment of the public continues to be very interested in the show. *The X-Files* has been highly successful in syndication and is still rebroadcast regularly on such channels as SciFi. DVDs of the show have also sold very well in various packaged and repackaged forms. Despite Stuttaford's confident prediction, *The X-Files* has not gone the way of Kato Kaelin, ending up as a mere footnote in pop culture history. On the contrary, *The X-Files* has emerged as a permanent feature of the American pop culture landscape. New television shows and movies continue to draw on its legacy and refer to it in implicit and explicit ways.[9] One might even argue that, far from being made outdated by 9/11, *The X-Files* actually pioneered a model of what post-9/11 popular culture would be like. Some critics were saying this even in the immediate aftermath of 9/11. An October 23, 2001, *New York Times* article on how horror movies might have to change after 9/11 quotes Robert J. Thompson, a professor of media and popular culture at Syracuse University: "The horror movie is going to move away from the age of Godzilla, which personi-

fied this enormous threat of atomic power to destroy things. . . . Instead, it's
going to be much more on the 'X-Files' model, where the villain is elusive
and perhaps conspiratorial."[10]

Perhaps *The X-Files* did not generally receive the credit it deserved for
modeling the post-9/11 world because media pundits did not want to face
up to a disturbing truth—the show had actually predicted a new age of
international terrorism with uncanny accuracy. *The X-Files* was one of the
darkest and most unnerving shows in the history of television, especially
in the way it dwelled on the nightmare aspects of globalization. Its horror
stories often focused on how the increasing dissolution of national borders
was unleashing new and terrifying forces in the contemporary world, forces
that threatened to undermine and destroy the American way of life. *X-Files*
plots often dealt with the migrant as monster and the monster as migrant. In
episode after episode, various forms of alien creatures, whether extraterrestrial or not, penetrated U.S. borders and had to be hunted down by Mulder
and Scully. The show rested on the premise that in the age of globalization,
the nature of the threat to the United States had undergone a fundamental
transformation. Gone were the cold war days when America had faced a
single, clear-cut enemy in the form of the communist bloc and the central
fear was nuclear annihilation. *The X-Files* accurately reflected the fact that
by the 1990s, the enemies of the United States were no longer coming neatly
packaged in the form of hostile nation-states like the Soviet Union.

Again and again *The X-Files* suggested that in a globalized world, threats
would take more shadowy, diffuse, and mysterious forms, difficult to pin
down and hence difficult to deal with. Many episodes centered on the threat
of terrorism, both international and domestic, and the line between the two
was sometimes difficult to draw. *The X-Files* was especially interested in
bioterrorism, and several episodes portrayed the threat of plague and other
forms of disease being spread around the globe by sinister but unidentifi-
able forces. As I summed up the basic situation in *The X-Files* in a book
published in September 2001:

> *The X-Files* portrays a kind of free-floating geopolitical anxiety that
> follows upon the collapse of the clear-cut ideological divisions of
> the Cold War. . . . [It] presents a post–Cold War world that, far from
> being polarized in terms of nation-states anymore, is interconnected
> in all sorts of clandestine and sinister ways that cut across national
> borders. . . . The central image of threat during the Cold War was a

nuclear explosion—destruction that starts at a clear central point and spreads outward. The central image of threat in *The X-Files* is infection—a plague that may begin at any point on the globe and spread to any other—thanks to international air travel and all the other globalizing forces at work today.[11]

Does this sound like a television show that is irrelevant in the post-9/11 world?

In fact, when the events of 9/11 were quickly followed by the anthrax scare, and scenes of personnel in hazmat suits decontaminating whole buildings suddenly filled the airwaves, the real world seemed to have been plunged into an *X-Files* episode. I remember thinking at the time not how outdated the series was but how prophetic it had turned out to be. Life seemed to be imitating art in the form of *The X-Files*. But the most prophetic moment the show produced came not in the series itself but in its spin-off *The Lone Gunmen*. The eponymous heroes of this series were three paranoid conspiracy theorists who ran a tabloid that sought to expose various forms of government cover-ups and evil deeds. Introduced in the first season of *The X-Files* as aides to Mulder in his FBI investigations, the characters were treated semicomically and became very popular with fans of the show. Eventually the *X-Files* team decided to give the Lone Gunmen their own series, produced by the same people who had made the parent show successful (Chris Carter, Frank Spotnitz, John Shiban, and Vince Gilligan).

The new series debuted on March 4, 2001, with a pilot episode punningly entitled "Pilot" because it deals with piloting an airplane. Incredible as it sounds, the episode portrays an attempt to pilot a commercial airliner into the World Trade Center in order to create an international incident. Of course, the episode does not get all the details right—it involves a Boeing 727 rather than a 757 or 767, and the fictional flight is heading for Boston's Logan Airport, not departing from it. Still, the resemblance of the fictional story to the actual events of 9/11 was chilling for anyone who, like me, remembered the *Lone Gunmen* episode on that fateful day in September. It seems to me very odd to claim that 9/11 demonstrated the irrelevance of *The X-Files* to the twenty-first century when the creators of the show had anticipated the details of the disaster better than anyone else in the twentieth century, including U.S. intelligence agencies.

To be sure, in the TV episode, the plane headed for the World Trade Center is being piloted not by Islamic terrorists but by remote control, and at the last moment the Lone Gunmen succeed in freeing the regular pilots to fly the 727 on their own. The plane merely grazes one of the Twin Towers, and disaster is averted. As for the explanation of the "terrorism," true to the conspiratorial worldview of *The X-Files,* in the *Lone Gunmen* episode the plot has actually been hatched by a faction within the U.S. government. As the father of one of the Lone Gunmen explains it: "The Cold War's over, John, but with no clear enemy to stockpile against, the arms market's flat. But bring down a fully loaded 727 into the middle of New York City and you'll find a dozen tin-pot dictators all over the world just clamoring to take responsibility and begging to be smart-bombed."[12] In their commentary in *The Lone Gunmen* DVD set, the producers of the show all talk about how difficult it was for them just to view the episode after 9/11. Frank Spotnitz says: "I actually couldn't bring myself to even look at the episode again until I sat down to prepare for this interview today." They regret having presented a plot so close to 9/11 as planned by the U.S. government itself. Commenting on the episode's explanation of the plot, one of the producers says: "The irony is there are people out there who believe this to be true"—referring to all the conspiracy theories about the 9/11 attacks having been executed by the U.S. government, not by Islamic terrorists.

The deeper irony is that the existence of this *Lone Gunmen* episode has itself fueled conspiracy theories about 9/11. Refusing to accept the idea that the anticipation of 9/11 in this television show could have been a mere coincidence, conspiracy theorists have offered the episode as proof that some people in the United States must have known about the World Trade Center plot ahead of time.[13] Some theorists have seized on the fact that, like *The X-Files, The Lone Gunmen* was broadcast on the Fox Network, which is owned by the wealthy and powerful media mogul Rupert Murdoch. These conspiracy theorists insist that Murdoch must have been actively involved in producing this episode, perhaps trying to warn the public about what turned out to be the 9/11 terrorist attacks, perhaps trying to create disinformation about them in advance. There could be no better example of art and life blurring together than the way in which the pilot episode of *The Lone Gunmen* has become woven into conspiracy theories about 9/11. In this case, television has become part of the reality it is supposed to be merely representing.

But if we are to believe the *Lone Gunmen* producers—and I think that we should—they were as shocked as anybody by what happened on 9/11. In the DVD commentary, Spotnitz says of the morning of 9/11: "My first thought was the *Lone Gunmen*. . . . 'I hope this has nothing to do with what we did on television six months ago. . . . I hope we weren't somehow guilty of inspiring this.'" Given the amount of time required to prepare for the 9/11 attacks, Spotnitz and his colleagues were safe in assuming that they were innocent of having contributed in any way to what happened. Nevertheless, they were troubled by their strange "prediction" of the World Trade Center disaster. A number of government authorities, in defense of their failure to anticipate 9/11 and their lack of any contingency plans for dealing with this kind of attack, have said that such a terrorist act was unimaginable. And yet in working on the *Lone Gunmen* pilot, the *X-Files* team in fact imagined it.[14] As Spotnitz says about his own assumptions at the time: "If we thought about something like this happening, then the government certainly has thought about something like this happening. When it actually happened in real life, six months after this was broadcast, I just was shocked that there was nothing in place . . . to prevent something like this from happening." Unfortunately, the events of 9/11 confirmed not only *The X-Files'* vision of the rise of global terrorism but also its vision of the U.S. government's inability to deal with this development. The kind of bureaucratic infighting and snafus *The X-Files* frequently portrayed in the FBI and other government agencies turned out to be all too real. As subsequent investigations revealed, various government agencies had reason to believe that a terrorist attack was imminent in September 2001, but their failure to share their information and other errors prevented them from doing anything to forestall the disaster.

Perhaps, then, those who chose to dismiss *The X-Files* in the wake of 9/11 were shooting the messenger. Far from being wrong about the world we now live in, *The X-Files* had portrayed it all too accurately. Disturbed by what they saw in that mirror, critics decided to blame the representation for what it revealed about the underlying reality it was representing. As the series approached its final episode, many commentators seized the opportunity to proclaim its irrelevance in the post-9/11 era, but they never bothered to analyze the episode itself.[15] They thereby missed a chance to see whether *The X-Files* might have anything important to say about the post-9/11 world.

I myself found that watching "The Truth" air on May 19, 2002, I was so caught up in the excitement of seeing the last-ever episode of *The X-Files* that I was unable to view it critically. Seeing it again on DVD now, I would have to say that "The Truth" is not an example of *The X-Files* at its dramatic and intellectual best. Chris Carter and his crew were trying to accomplish too many things at once in this episode, and as drama it suffers from being overburdened with retrospective exposition, nostalgia, and the sheer emotional weight of being the last show. Oddly enough, in light of the criticism of the show at the time, the strongest aspect of the final episode is its contemporary relevance. Unwilling to go down without a fight, Carter came out swinging in "The Truth." At a time when movies and television were heeding the media pundits and trying to avoid any content that might be considered antigovernment, the final episode of *The X-Files* remained true to its motto of "Trust No One." "The Truth" has turned out to be almost as prophetic as the "Pilot" episode of *The Lone Gunmen*. Just as the Bush administration's war on terror was ramping up, *The X-Files* chose to deliver a timely warning against its tendency to disregard civil liberties and to deprive people of their fundamental legal rights.

In "The Truth," Mulder breaks into a secret government facility and is put on trial for supposedly killing a soldier in the attempt. The episode is largely devoted to showing how brutally Mulder is treated in detention and how unjustly he is treated during the trial. Early in the episode, he is kept incommunicado in a military prison and is shown wearing the orange outfit that had already become familiar to the American public in images coming out of the U.S. government's detention facility for terrorist suspects in Guantanamo Bay. The parallels with the situation in Guantanamo were obvious at the time and have become only stronger as more information has emerged about how the government has treated its prisoners at the Cuban base. Mulder is being held in secret, with no access to legal counsel and no way to communicate with his friends and allies. In the opening sequence, he is brainwashed by vicious military guards, who, in Orwellian fashion, keep asking him: "What are you thinking?"[16] He is deprived of sleep, beaten, and tormented in an effort to break his spirit and get him to confess his guilt. At a time when most Americans were not inclined to think too closely about what their government was doing in Guantanamo, *The X-Files* was confronting them with images of what can happen when there is no public scrutiny of the treatment of prisoners.

Mulder's friends at the FBI, including Scully and Assistant Director Walter Skinner, finally find out that he is, in Skinner's words, "being held .. . indefinitely" and are able to come to his aid. But they seem virtually helpless in the face of a coalition between the military and the FBI to ensure that Mulder is convicted. FBI Deputy Director Alvin Kersh has always had it in for Mulder, and if that were not enough, he is told by General Mark

Suveg that he will have to preside over Mulder's trial. Suveg makes Kersh's task clear: "I want a verdict—a guilty verdict." Then, in typical *X-Files* fashion, he ominously adds, "There are forces inside the government now that a man would be foolish to disobey." This seems to be Carter's comment on a political turn for the worse in post-9/11 America.

As for Mulder's trial, it is a classic case of a kangaroo court. In the director's commentary on the episode in the DVD set, Kim Manners says that Carter's model for the trial was the Australian movie *Breaker Morant,* a powerful story of military subordinates taking the fall for the misdeeds of their imperialist superiors. In "The Truth," every aspect of the trial is stacked against Mulder. Skinner tries hard to defend him, but any appeal he makes to traditional legal safeguards is rejected by the court. Finally in exasperation, he says to Kersh, "This isn't a secret tribunal; as you so kindly informed me, it's a court of law." But Kersh immediately counters that it is "a military court of law," and it turns out to be a secret tribunal of the worst kind. No written record is being kept at all of the proceedings. The government is never able to produce the body of the soldier Mulder is charged with killing (which would in fact be impossible, since Mulder's "victim" is one of the show's invincible "supersoldiers" and hence cannot be killed). Even when Scully comes up with incontrovertible forensic evidence that the corpse the government claims is Mulder's "victim" is a fake, Kersh refuses to accept her expert testimony. He finally delivers the court's verdict: "Acting fairly and impartially, this panel finds the defendant guilty." But fairness and impartiality are exactly what the episode shows are absent when the government is able to try people in secret, outside the normal justice system.

Condemned to death by lethal injection, Mulder is rescued by his FBI allies (in one of several unprepared for plot developments in the episode, Kersh inexplicably comes to Mulder's aid and helps in his escape). Instead of fleeing to safety through Canada, Mulder heads with Scully to one of the series' favorite locations—the deserts of New Mexico (site of the infamous 1947 UFO incident at Roswell and hence where the story begins for *The X-Files*). Here the episode's plot gets murky, especially for anyone unfamiliar with *X-Files* mythology. In a remote desert cave, Mulder finds none other than the chief villain of the series, the sinister Cigarette Smoking Man. We had every reason to believe that he had been killed off in an earlier episode, but somehow he survived and somehow he has made it to this mountain retreat, where he is cared for by an old Indian woman.

None of this action is well explained, and at this point the plot appears to be driven by considerations not of narrative logic but of thematic symbolism. The most striking fact about the scene is that the hitherto urbane Cigarette Smoking Man, at home in the corridors of power in Washington, D.C., has retreated to a mountain cave. In President Bush's October 7, 2001, address on the first U.S. military operations in Afghanistan, he famously said: "Initially the terrorists may burrow deeper into caves and other entrenched hiding places."[17] Because of its initial implausibility, I offer this interpretation with some hesitation, but in the cave scenes of "The Truth," the Cigarette Smoking Man appears in some weird way to be standing in for Osama bin Laden.[18] He has traded in his standard-issue government bureaucrat's business suit and adopted the pose of an Indian shaman. He is referred to as a "wise man" and looks the part of some Eastern sage with his newly flowing long hair. At the climax of the episode, two military helicopters blast him into flaming oblivion by firing missiles into his retreat. Exactly this kind of scene was very much on the American public's mind at the time this episode aired. The U.S. government was promising to deliver a similar blow to bin Laden in his mountain hideaway in Afghanistan.

I am not sure exactly what point *The X-Files* was trying to make by linking the Cigarette Smoking Man with Osama bin Laden, but a connection that seems logically weak is extremely strong visually in the episode (and television is a visual medium). Just look at the cave scenes with the sound turned off and ask yourself whether what you are seeing was more appropriate to Afghanistan than to New Mexico at the time the show was broadcast. The best I can do to articulate the connection is this: American Indians, especially the long-vanished Anasazi peoples referred to in this episode, always figured prominently in *X-Files* mythology. The show criticized what it regarded as a contemporary American empire by linking it with the conquest and extermination of Indian tribes in the creation of the American nation-state. If "The Truth" was pairing Afghanistan with New Mexico, the suggestion was that the United States was doing to a Third World people in Asia in 2002 what it had done to Indians in America throughout the nineteenth century—namely, using its technological superiority to wipe them out.

As for the destruction of the Cigarette Smoking Man, it seems to be an illustration of the principle of blowback, which was on many people's minds in connection with 9/11. The United States had originally armed and trained the mujahideen in Afghanistan; terrorists were now using those weapons and skills against the United States. Similarly, throughout *The X-Files*, the

Cigarette Smoking Man had participated in one government operation after another directed against indigenous peoples around the world, operations that sometimes bordered on genocide. In the final episode, the government weapons he helped unleash against the world come back to destroy him with a kind of rough justice.

As so often happens in *The X-Files,* opposites come to be equated. Governments turn out to be the mirror images of the evil opponents they rail against; sometimes governments generate the very enemies they fight. In "The Truth," the Cigarette Smoking Man has retreated to his cave because unusual mineral deposits in the area will protect him against the aliens and the government's supersoldiers. He explains to Mulder: "Indian wise men realized this over 2,000 years ago. They hid here and watched their own culture die. The original shadow government." These words take us back to the beginning of the episode, when Skinner explains that the secret facility Mulder broke into, the Mount Weather Complex, is "where they say our so-called shadow government is installed." Two shadow governments—the episode is bookended by images of leaders hiding out in mountain caves, protecting themselves while appearing to be indifferent to the fate of their own people. Ever willing to play two sides against each other, the amphibious Cigarette Smoking Man moves between these two worlds, the government at the center of power and the remote Indian tribes on the periphery. In response to 9/11, there was much speculation about where American leaders would go to keep safe during a national emergency. *The X-Files* could not resist calling our attention to the irony of the fact that our nation's leaders might be hiding in mountain caves even as they were directing air strikes against terrorist leaders hiding in mountain caves in Afghanistan.

The finale of *The X-Files* is characteristic of the series as a whole in the way it blurs the line between the persecutor and the persecuted, showing that the victim is the mirror image of his killer. The protean Cigarette Smoking Man, who had already played many contradictory roles in the series, represents at once both the government and the forces it wants to suppress. In seeking to annihilate him, the government is trying to eliminate the destructive forces it originally set loose itself. In a world of terrorist blowback, the cave scenes of "The Truth" makes a kind of rough sense. After all, in bombing Afghanistan, the United States was trying to wipe out terrorist forces it had originally armed and trained back in the 1980s in an effort to push the Soviet Union out of the country.

If we had any lingering doubts about the contemporary relevance of the final episode of *The X-Files* when it first aired, they have been dispelled by the evidence of a deleted scene in the DVD version. We now know that "The Truth" was originally intended to conclude with a scene of President Bush in the White House overlooking the Washington Monument (with a remarkable look-alike cast in the role of the president). Handed a note that evidently tells him that Mulder has escaped, Bush says, "What do you want me to do? I was told this was being handled. The truth is out there now." The camera then pans to the other figure in the room, and it turns out to be one of the members of Mulder's kangaroo court. Indeed, he is the most sinister of the judges, the one identified by the psychic Gibson Praise as an alien and the clandestine orchestrator of Mulder's railroading in court (in the quaint terminology of *The X-Files*, he is known as the Toothpick Man). It is this dark figure who was originally going to conclude the episode and hence *The X-Files* as a whole with these ominous words, which refer to two of the show's mottoes: "The truth has always been out there, Mr. President. The people just don't want to believe."

Even by the normally harsh standards of *The X-Files*, this scene is extraordinarily cynical about the U.S. government. It is the only time in the long history of the series that a U.S. president is shown actively engaged at the heart of the great conspiracy the program purported to chronicle. With the words "What do you want me to do?" the Bush figure suggests that the president is merely the puppet of shadowy forces of which the American public is willfully ignorant. One of the commentators on the deleted scene says, "I'm so happy we cut this scene," and perhaps this decision is evidence that even *The X-Files* felt a need to exercise some self-restraint in the wake of 9/11. Yet further comments on deleting the scene suggest that the real reason for doing so was aesthetic, not political—they wanted to end the episode and the series with the highly emotional exchange between Mulder and Scully that actually brought the original broadcast to a close. But for whatever reason it was deleted, the mere existence of the Bush scene gives some insight into the political attitudes of *The X-Files* and emphasizes how much it was engaged with the realities of the post-9/11 world. Precisely when media pundits were calling for movies and television to get on board with the program and become cheerleaders for Team America, *The X-Files* had the courage to remain true to its long-term mission of providing a voice of dissent in popular culture.

In sum, even though the plot and the symbolism of the final episode of *The X-Files* are often murky and perhaps inconsistent, it is still clear that the series was engaging with some of the fundamental issues that had been raised by 9/11 and its aftermath. The attitude the show took toward those issues may not have pleased media pundits at the time, and they had every right to criticize the show's position, but it was unfair to say that *The X-Files* had simply been made irrelevant by 9/11. In some ways, we can now say that it had become more relevant than ever. Up to and including "The Truth," the show continued to have something to say about global terrorism and the U.S. government's efforts to combat it. The course the war on terror has taken since *The X-Files* went off the air has unfortunately confirmed what the series was trying to say about the danger to civil liberties posed by government policies, as well as about the government's ineffectiveness at eradicating terrorism at its roots. In particular, in its portrait of a globalizing world, the show cautioned that the nation-state is no longer the appropriate unit of analysis in geopolitical conflict. Some would argue that one of the basic errors in the U.S. government's post-9/11 antiterrorist policy has been to look for nation-states to punish, while ignoring ways in which the threats against America have been fundamentally altered, thereby requiring new modes of response that take into account the amorphous and global nature of the new forces arrayed against the United States.

As for the prediction of a total transformation of American popular culture after 9/11, very little of what the pundits prophesied in the fall of 2001 has come to pass.[19] As we have seen, in the immediate weeks and months after 9/11, there were many signs of movie and television producers altering their plans in an effort to avoid upsetting and displeasing a traumatized American public. But as for the long-term effects of 9/11 and its aftermath, one could argue that movies and television are more cynical than ever about government. The landscape of popular culture is constantly changing. As I am writing this chapter in the summer of 2008, the biggest blockbuster of the season is the new Batman movie *The Dark Knight*, a film that in its scenes of urban destruction on a mass scale clearly evokes 9/11. Insofar as it is an allegory of a post-9/11 world, it suggests that the good guys have become virtually indistinguishable from the bad guys. Batman must operate outside the law and resort to the tactics of the villains in Gotham City in order to combat them successfully. In particular, the Caped Crusader must rely on morally and legally dubious practices, such as kidnapping foreign citizens on foreign soil and eavesdropping on a massive scale on the citizens of Gotham City in the name of protecting them. The Joker is a chilling portrait of a terrorist—a man who is not interested in money or any of the other usual goals of criminals but is destructive because "some people just want to watch the world burn." The Joker is actually shown triumphing in the film, because he manages to turn the most upright man in Gotham City, District Attorney Harvey Dent, into Two-Face, a crazed vigilante who seeks vengeance at any price. After Dent dies, the only way justice can prevail in the world of the film is for the authorities to cover up his crimes to preserve the myth of him as a decent and just civic official. _The Dark Knight_ may end up endorsing the need to violate civil liberties in order to combat terrorism, but its portrait of government officials comes very close to what _The X-Files_ tried to show.[20]

Two other popular superhero movies from the summer of 2008—_Iron Man_ and _The Incredible Hulk_—portray the federal government in general and the military-industrial complex in particular in a sinister light. In both cases, the government literally produces monsters and unleashes them to wreak havoc on its own cities on a scale that dwarfs the devastation of 9/11. _Iron Man_ explicitly connects the operations of the U.S. military-industrial complex with terrorist threats coming out of Afghanistan from a group called Ten Rings. Both movies provide powerful metaphors of geopolitical blowback. One review of another blockbuster hit from the summer of 2008, _Indiana Jones and the Kingdom of the Skull_, begins: "Steven Spielberg's fourth Indiana Jones adventure is the best very special episode of _The X-Files_ ever!"[21] (Notice how _The X-Files_ continues to be a reference point with regard to popular culture.) It is not just that Spielberg's movie heavily borrows its plot elements from _The X-Files_, with references to the 1947 Roswell incident, alien autopsies, and extraterrestrial forces colonizing the earth in earlier periods of history. The film is cinematically nostalgic, with a loving re-creation of the 1950s as it was visualized in film, including a teenage hangout perfect in all the details. It takes us back to the "simpler" days of the cold war and even features that most 1950s of movie treats—a nuclear explosion. But the film does not take a 1950s attitude toward the 1950s. The main villains are from the Soviet Union, but it portrays its FBI agents as their moral equivalents; just as in _The X-Files_, the McCarthyism of the FBI is presented as the mirror image of the Stalinism of the KGB.[22]

To turn briefly to television, the popular Fox series _24_ is frequently offered as the alternative to _The X-Files_ and an example of a patriotic response to 9/11.[23] The show celebrates the actions of a government Counter Terrorist Unit and makes a hero out of Jack Bauer for risking everything, including his own family, to foil terrorist plots against America. But in fact, *24* is much closer to *The X-Files* than it may at first appear. Bauer is actually much like Mulder and Scully—he succeeds not because of but in spite of the government agencies he works for and with. And *24* goes just as far as *The X-Files* ever did in showing how bureaucratic incompetence and infighting hamstring the government's efforts to deal with terrorism. Hence Bauer is, if possible, even more insubordinate than Mulder and Scully and even more of a lone wolf and a loose cannon. As for the show's portrait of the federal government, it offered a very attractive model of a president in the figure of David Palmer, but let us not forget that it went on to show Palmer assassinated on the orders of his successor, Charles Logan. In Logan, *24* created perhaps the most loathsome portrait of a U.S. president ever offered in popular culture—a figure who is obviously meant to conjure up memories of Richard Nixon but who, in the end, makes "Tricky Dick" look like Mr. Nice Guy by comparison. Logan turned out to be literally a traitor to the United States, colluding with the Russians and countenancing a terrorist strike against American citizens in a conspiracy that would have shocked even Fox Mulder. Looking carefully at *24,* one would conclude that the spirit of *The X-Files* is very much alive in American popular culture in the post-9/11 era.[24]

At a party celebrating the conclusion of the broadcast run of *The X-Files,* Sandy Grushaw paid tribute to its creator: "Chris Carter didn't just create a show for our time, but for all time."[25] A Fox executive is not exactly the most objective judge of one of his own network's series, and Grushaw's evocation of Ben Jonson's famous encomium to Shakespeare may be a trifle over the top. As with all cultural products, only time will tell how enduring the achievements of *The X-Files* will turn out to be in the history of television. But I think that it is already safe to say that the rumors of its death in 2002 were exaggerated. The continuing relevance of *The X-Files* is a tribute to the vitality of popular culture and its ability to perform a gadfly role in American society. The pilot episode of *The Lone Gunmen* is a powerful reminder that popular culture may sometimes glimpse truths about our world that have eluded those in power who are supposed to be on the lookout for just such truths. The critics of *The X-Files* in 2001–2002 may have mistaken political dissent for cynicism about politics. In political terms, popular culture is at its best when it provides not a chorus unanimously singing the praises of America and its values but lone voices raising the kinds of question that must be asked if democracy is to continue to function.

Notes

1. For example, NBC Entertainment president Jeff Zucker was quoted in "The Robins Report" in *TV Guide*: "This is a watershed moment, where everything in popular culture changes" (October 13, 2001, 37).

2. I quote the article from http://time.com/time/printout/0,8816,175112,00.html (accessed July 13, 2008).

3. See, for example, Suzanne Fields, "A Reformed Hollywood? More Wholesome Entertainment Poised to Sell," *Washington Times,* October 1, 2001, A21.

4. For a detailed article on how one show, *The Agency,* struggled to adapt to the post-9/11 environment, including script and cast changes, see Stephen Battaglio, "Tactical Maneuvers," *TV Guide,* December 15, 2001, 43–44, 60–61. For attempts by the Bush administration to influence Hollywood productions after 9/11, see Dana Calvo and Rachel Abramowitz, "Hollywood May Enlist in Unconventional Warfare," *Los Angeles Times,* November 10, 2001, A6, which discusses a meeting between Bush's senior adviser Karl Rove and high-level Hollywood executives such as Sandy Grushaw of Fox and Sherry Lansing of Paramount.

5. For the way TV comedians reacted to 9/11, see Matt Roush, "Reality Check," *TV Guide,* October 20, 2001, 28–32. The article quotes late-night host Conan O'Brien as saying: "I have no idea how we're going to get back to doing this [comedy] again. I make a living acting like an ass, generally. No one's looking to me to put this in perspective" (29). At the time, only Jon Stewart of Comedy Central's *The Daily Show* seemed willing to challenge the "end of irony" thesis: "Maybe we should wait to make pronouncements about what will happen to us culturally until the fire is completely put out. Why did irony have to die? Why couldn't puns have died? Or would that have been too devastating to Mr. Al Yankovic?" (30). Just a month later, in its November 20, 2001, issue, *TV Guide* was already reporting a return to normalcy among TV comedians in Mark Laswell's "Laughing Matters." The article ends with a heavy dose of irony about the end of irony: "*Vanity Fair* editor Graydon Carter, whom many blame for starting the epidemic of eulogies for contemporary humor, has since issued a deft retraction in the *Washington Post.* 'Only a fool would declare the end of irony. I said it was the end of the age of ironing,' Carter said, adding a new wrinkle to the debate" (28).

6. Allan Johnson, "Secret Agents Won't Reveal All in the Finale of *The X-Files,*" *Chicago Tribune,* May 19, 2002, Arts & Entertainment (section 7), 5.

7. Andrew Stuttaford, "The Ex-Files: Mulder and Scully's Exit," National Review Online, May 17, 2002, http:www.nationalreview.com/stuttaford/stuttaford051702.asp (accessed January 6, 2006). Among media pundits taking this line on the demise of *The X-Files* at the time (indeed, on the very same day), I notice in my files an authority I generally find unimpeachable: "Paul A. Cantor, a University of Virginia English professor, said that the end of the series reflects a change in the mood of the country, which has

less cynicism about the government after Sept. 11 than it did during the drama's heyday." Greg Braxton, "Closing the Files," *St. Petersburg Times,* May 17, 2002, F30.

8. As early as February 12, 2000, Matt Roush was writing in *TV Guide* of *The X-Files:* "an exhaustion factor has set in among fans" (20). In his predictions in the September 9, 2000, issue of *TV Guide* for the start of the eighth season of *The X-Files,* he wrote, "this seems like an excellent opportunity for Carter to find a way for Duchovny and Anderson to bow out gracefully" (8). Responding to Carter's decision to end the series, Roush wrote in the February 9, 2002, *TV Guide:* "Nothing on TV lasts forever, not even a landmark like Fox's marvelously inventive *The X-Files.* . . . Yes, I will miss the show when it signs off in May after nine seasons, a wise but overdue decision. The sorry fact is that I've been missing the series—at least as it was in its prime—for some time. The decline dates back to the fatal decision last season to continue without Duchovny's full-time services . . . , a move that coincided with the unsatisfying announcement of Scully's miracle pregnancy: two 'jump the shark' moments for the price of one" (10). On Duchovny's absence causing the show's decline, see also Johnson, "Secret Agents," 5.

9. In the fall of 2005, for example, no fewer than six shows debuted that were clearly derived from *The X-Files* in one way or another: *Bones, Supernatural, The Night Stalker, Invasion, Threshold,* and *Surface.* I discuss these shows in relation to *The X-Files* in my essay "Un-American Gothic: The Fear of Globalization in Popular Culture," in *The Impact of Globalization on the United States,* vol. 1, *Culture and Society,* ed. Michelle Bertho (Westport, CT: Praeger, 2008), 109–27.

10. Rick Lyman, "Horrors! Time for an Attack of the Metaphors? From Bug Movies to Bioterrorism," *New York Times,* October 23, 2001, E3.

11. Paul A. Cantor, *Gilligan Unbound: Pop Culture in the Age of Globalization* (Lanham, MD: Rowman and Littlefield, 2001), 184–85. This book contains a long analysis of the show in the chapter "Mainstreaming Paranoia: *The X-Files* and the Delegitimation of the Nation-State" (111–98). The scholarly literature on *The X-Files* has become quite extensive. I particularly recommend two collections of essays on the show: David Lavery, Angela Hague, and Marla Cartwright, eds., *"Deny All Knowledge": Reading the X-Files* (Syracuse, NY: Syracuse University Press, 1996), and Dean A. Kowalski, ed., *The Philosophy of* The X-Files (Lexington: University Press of Kentucky, 2007). Of the many valuable essays on the show, see in particular Michael Valdez Moses, "Kingdom of Darkness: Autonomy and Conspiracy in *The X-Files* and *Millennium,*" in *The Philosophy of TV Noir,* ed. Steven M. Sanders and Aeon J. Skoble (Lexington: University Press of Kentucky, 2008), 203–27.

12. I transcribed all quotations from "Pilot" from the 20th Century Fox DVD set *The Lone Gunmen: The Complete Series* (2004). The quotations from the producers are from either their commentary on the pilot episode or the retrospective feature "The Making of *The Lone Gunmen.*"

13. By their nature, these conspiracy theories are of dubious provenance and questionable in terms of both authority and motive—and they are mostly to be found on the

Internet. I shudder to dignify them by citation, especially since some of them involve anti-Semitic claims. Nevertheless, in the interests of scholarship, and because some of them offer excerpts from the relevant moments in the *Lone Gunmen* pilot, I cite three of the sources I consulted: http://www.cloakanddagger.de/media/LONE%20GUNMEN/ Killtowns.htm, http://www.thetruthseeker.co.uk/print.asp?ID=1130, and http://www .davidcogswell.com/Media Roulette/Lone Gunmen.html (all accessed July 13, 2008). If one is interested in the subject, all one need do is Google "Lone Gunmen and 9/11."

14. The pilot was not the only episode of *The Lone Gunmen* that conjured up images that came to be associated with 9/11. "Tango de los Pistoleros" contains this remarkable line about a Department of Defense composite material that confers invisibility: "Saddam Hussein could build a Cessna out of this stuff and fly it right into the White House." The imaginations of *The Lone Gunmen* staff were evidently in high gear in 2001 and attuned to the zeitgeist.

15. See, for example, Jesse Walker, "X-Files, R.I.P.," Reason Online, May 20, 2002, http://www.reason. com/news/printer/32603.html (accessed May 29, 2008).

16. I transcribed all quotations from "The Truth" from the 20th Century Fox DVD set *The X-Files: The Complete Ninth Season* (2004). The quotations from the producers are from their commentary on this episode or from the documentary "The Making of The Truth."

17. George W. Bush, "Address on Initial Operations in Afghanistan," http://www .americanrhetoric.com/ speeches/gwbush911initialafghanistanops.htm (accessed July 21, 2008).

18. I owe this insight to Michael Valdez Moses, who has often guided me through the mysteries of *The X-Files*.

19. One of the post-9/11 predictions that turned out to be way off the mark was the widespread opinion that the attacks spelled the doom of reality shows on TV—the subject of two editions of the "Robins Report" in *TV Guide* (October 13 and 20, 2001). One "senior network executive" was quoted as saying of reality television: "My gut tells me it's over. After what's happened here, the audience is going to want uplifting programming—not endless faux reality, where people succeed by screaming and double-crossing." Tom Wolzien, a senior media analyst at the investment-research firm Sanford C. Bernstein & Co., made this comment: "Millions of Americans watched thousands of people die in ghastly terrorist attacks in their own backyard. After this kind of unprecedented horror, you have to wonder if anybody will want these reality shows the networks have bet so much on." USA Network president Doug Herzog joined the chorus: "We know we've entered a whole new terrain. . . . You have to ask if the values people want to see now are represented in a lot of these reality programs. Do we still want to see people stabbing each other in the back to win a million dollars?" (The three preceding quotations are from "Robins Report," *TV Guide,* October 13, 2001, 37–38.) Polls at the time seemed to confirm these predictions. J. Max Robins reported that a poll taken by Initiative Media "found that since September 11, 57 percent of those surveyed say their taste for

these types of [reality] shows has diminished." ABC Entertainment cochairman Lloyd Braun went on to say: "The pettiness and interpersonal dynamics of people are one of the really interesting parts of these shows. But you have to wonder, after September 11, whether people will look at that now and say, 'Please, we don't care.'" (The two preceding quotations are from "Robins Report," *TV Guide*, October 20, 2001, 57–58). All these reports of the death of reality programming on TV proved to be premature; in fact, the genre is now flourishing more than ever. With the benefit of several years' hindsight, it is easy for us today to laugh at the confidence with which these experts made their predictions about the demise of reality TV, but I can understand why they made them at the time. Still, the way all these commentators woefully misread the future of reality TV is good evidence for the wisdom of Jon Stewart's caution at the time not to rush to judgment and, literally and figuratively, to wait for the dust to settle before making apocalyptic pronouncements about the course of pop culture.

20. Debate over the relevance of *The Dark Knight* to U.S. foreign policy quickly came to focus on the issue of whether the film's Batman is a portrait of George Bush and, if so, whether it is a favorable or unfavorable portrait. See, for example, Andrew Klavan, "What Bush and Batman Have in Common," *Wall Street Journal*, July 25, 2008, A15. In Chris Nashawaty, "Knight Fever," *Entertainment Weekly*, August 1, 2008, the director of *The Dark Knight*, Christopher Nolan, quotes Michael Caine, the actor who plays Batman's butler, making what I regard as the single most intelligent comment on the film: "Superman is the way America sees itself, but Batman is the way the world sees America" (24).

21. Steve Warren, "Indiana Jones and the Kingdom of the Crystal Skull," *The Hook*, July 10, 2008, 60.

22. In reviewing the movie blockbusters of the summer of 2008, I cannot, alas, include *The X-Files: I Want to Believe*. In fact, the movie did more poorly than expected at the box office, perhaps effectively ending the franchise. The disappointing showing of the film might be taken as strong evidence for the claim that *The X-Files* has become irrelevant in the post-9/11 world. But in fact, the situation is more complicated than it at first appears. Having themselves bought into the "*X-Files* and 9/11" thesis, the producers went out of their way to avoid any possible element of government conspiracy in the new film and dropped most of the trademark themes of the TV series. The advance publicity for the film stressed the absence of antigovernment sentiment in it. For example, Frank Spotnitz assured the potential audience, "I don't think you're going to worry about the government in this one," in a prerelease interview (Whitney Pastorek, "The Truth Is in Here," *Entertainment Weekly*, August 1, 2008, 36). It is ironic that, even as the real summer blockbusters were presenting the U.S. government in an extremely negative light, *The X-Files* deliberately blunted its political edge and may have thereby destroyed its chances for success. There were other reasons for the film's poor showing at the box office. It had the misfortune of opening one week after the new Batman film *The Dark Knight*, which emerged as one of the greatest box-office successes of all time

and no doubt drained some of the potential audience for a new *X-Files* film. Moreover, *I Want to Believe* is a deeply dark, unnerving, and depressing film, with almost none of the humor or light touches that brought comic relief to many of the TV episodes. With very few of the characters remaining alive from the series, the film offered little to die-hard fans other than the chance to see Mulder and Scully reunited and a glimpse of Skinner coming to the rescue. *I Want to Believe* may have been an excellent movie—a very serious reflection on profound issues of religion and science—but it was not a good *X-Files* movie. Therefore, it would be unfair to judge the relevance of the original TV series to our world on the basis of how this theatrical film performed at the box office. For a review of *I Want to Believe* that makes a strong case for the quality of the movie and its intellectual depth, see Michael Valdez Moses, "Modern Day Frankensteins: The Return of Mulder and Scully," Reason Online, August 11, 2008, http://www.reason.com/news/show/128028.html (accessed September 29, 2008).

23. For an analysis of *24* in relation to 9/11, see Ina Rae Hark, "'Today Is the Longest Day of My Life': *24* as Mirror Narrative of 9/11," in *Film and Television after 9/11*, ed. Wheeler Winston Dixon (Carbondale: Southern Illinois University Press, 2004), 121–41.

24. As I am annotating this chapter in the fall of 2008, the most ballyhooed new show on television at the moment is Fox's *Fringe*, created by J. J. Abrams, the man who brought *Lost* to the screen. With its female FBI agent paired with a maverick scientist investigating bizarre phenomena somehow linked to government cover-ups and a mysterious multinational corporation, the show is such an obvious rip-off of *The X-Files* that the production team has been on the defensive in interviews. One of the writers, Roberto Orci, admitted, "*The X-Files* was an inspiration" (*TV Guide*, July 14, 2008, 33–34), and Abrams tried to differentiate his show from *The X-Files* is this rather lame fashion: "But I do think that a government agent investigating weird stuff is kind of where the similarities end" (*TV Guide*, September 8, 2008, 42). See also James Hibberd's *The Live Feed* for July 14, 2008, where the *Fringe* producers protest a bit too much that they did not copy *The X-Files* (http:www.thrfreed.com/2008/07/fringe-x-files.html [accessed September 17, 2008]).

25. This quotation is from *The X-Files* DVD documentary "The Making of The Truth."

Part 2

POPULAR CULTURE AND OPPOSITIONAL NARRATIVES

5

UNPACKING THE *HOUSE*

Images of Heroism against the Regulatory State

Sara R. Jordan and Phillip W. Gray

Gregory House, M.D., is not the type of doctor most people would want to meet. He is rude, condescending, and curmudgeonly—not the type of man anyone would want for a colleague, either. His general view of humanity is straightforward—"everyone lies"—and his favorite term for others is "moron." Yet this unattractive central character of the popular television show *House, M.D.* attracts millions of viewers. Whether viewers tune in to *House* weekly, record it via DVR, or purchase the series on DVD, the show appears to have a dedicated viewer population.[1] In this chapter we attempt to ascertain what accounts for the series' dedicated viewership.

Communications and media researchers advance a number of hypotheses on the psychological appeal of television dramas. Here we advance another, based on the political-psychological effects of this particular drama and its genre. Without delving into an empirical assessment of its appeal, which is beyond the scope of this chapter, we argue that the appeal of *House* originates from a desire for professionals to escape the confines of the regulatory state. What millions of health care professionals and representatives of various other professions cannot do, House does. The attitude that so many people hide behind their e-mail and professional personae is the public image he cultivates. *House* has intuitive psychological appeal to an audience whose psyches are entangled in red tape. We do not argue that the creators of the character designed House as a purposeful emblem of rebellion against the regulatory state—the character's exoteric appeal is his unique antisocial genius charm. We argue that the esoteric

Dr. Gregory House (Hugh Laurie) personifies one man's struggle against the over-regulated state and professionalized health care system. (Jerry Ohlinger's Movie Material Store)

meaning of the series is an insider's rebellion against modern regulation and professionalism.

Diagnosing Viewer Motivation

If House (Hugh Laurie) is an abrasive character whose professional and private personae are emblems of a purposeful violation of law and convention, what draws viewers to the screen episode after episode? Communications scholars such as Graber and McQuail suggest that viewers have multiple motivations for their choice of television programs.[2] Based on a survey of the relevant research, Dhavan Shah provides the following summary: "Many theorists suggest a four-part typology of media use and gratifications: an information function, a personal identity function, an integration and social interaction function, and an entertainment and diversion function." Shah further develops these categories, describing the use of television media "to achieve social empathy and a sense of belonging, find a basis for conversation and social interaction, carry out social roles, or connect with family, friends and society."[3] Although the literature on viewer motivation and gratification is too rich to delve into here, the hypothesis we espouse to explain the *House* phenomenon is that viewers get a sense of rebellious catharsis in the behavior of the main character. That is, viewers tune in to displace their own dissatisfaction with their regulated professional or personal lives onto the screen and the character House.

In this chapter we describe the contours of catharsis gained through *House* viewership. By *catharsis*, we mean a psychological release from pain or frustration. The origin of the pain and frustration that viewers feel is multifaceted, but we hypothesize that it is rooted in frustration with their totally administered existence. The totally administered existence is the modal condition of modern humankind; subsumed by the blob of the extensive household administration that is a social policy–focused state, men and women know little of the comparative freedom of a polis or a Roman republic.[4] The normative claims for or against the administered state are largely left to the side here, but the basal assumption is that the psychological effects of the totally administered existence posited by Arendt, Hummel, Marcuse, Oakeshott, Strauss, and others are nominally true. Although the argument in this chapter is descriptive, we hope that this empirical claim might be substantiated by further research.

A Rebel without a Heart

The story line of the archetypal medical drama is the compassionate caregiver working in the cold, cruel "system." Shows such as *ER*, *M*A*S*H*, and *Grey's Anatomy* replicate variations on this archetype, to clear viewer applause. The story line of *House, M.D.* is a contradiction—an unalloyed uncompassionate character, surrounded by emblems of compassion, works purposefully against the standard. As suggested above, the character is contrarian to the point of rebelliousness. Yet the question arises: can such a character represent conscientious dissent? Importantly, can this representation have cathartic effects for those who cannot do so? There are various facets of the character that make House unique. He is part *übermensch*, part Oakeshottian "responsible man," part Rousseauian "noble savage," and part reincarnation of La Mettrie, the cynical French physician-philosopher. While House acts out with Nietzschean disregard for the sensibilities of those around him, his intention is not a "transvaluation of values."[5] Although he has a Zarathustrian influence on those around him, he himself is not interested in disciples. His obsessive drive to solve puzzles derives from his well-developed notion of truth as an outside, objective force. For House, the right answer is always out there, even if it is not known or, further, *cannot be known*. What cannot be known is often the result of intentional obfuscation—"everyone lies" because they cannot accept this difficult obligation to the truth. As the converse to those around him, House's pride centers on his recognition of this responsibility.

In his sense of responsibility to the truth, House resembles Oakeshott's "responsible man."[6] Rather than expecting others to take on these burdens, as "mass man" does, House accepts the responsibility that comes with acknowledging the obligatory nature of the "right answer." House embodies this sense of responsibility in himself, while holding a contempt of mass man similar to Ortega y Gasset.[7] When presenting a radical and usually dangerous method of treatment for a patient, House offers the option without diplomacy, without lies: "Either we do this, or she dies." The scorn heaped on the mass man is not reserved for the layperson; it extends to colleagues as well. Anyone who tries to hide from the brutal nature of this truth gains House's disdain as a coward and will be circumvented.

In his isolation from others and his intuitive drive for truth, House shares similarities with Rousseau's "noble savage."[8] In rejecting the social order's norms and institutions, without desiring to overturn them to further his own will-to-power, House liberates himself from false constraints and hypocrisies of administered society. Like La Mettrie, he reserves for physicians the privilege of diagnosing social order and disorder. Only physicians, he says, echoing the philosophe Frenchman, can know human nature well enough to diagnose individuals and societies.

And, echoing each of the philosophers whose personae and theories he embodies, House's expertise is not limited to the realm of medicine. Throughout the series, we see indications that he is skilled in sundry other fields, including statistics, music appreciation and performance, analytic philosophy, history, comparative anthropology and cultures, languages, and (before his thigh infarction) various sports.[9] One result of this breadth of knowledge is House's willingness to address, and usually offend, the philosophical, religious, legal, and moral proclivities of those around him. More to the point, House is comfortable not only ignoring the administered state but also launching a cogent attack at its foundations. Putting to the side his manipulative use of conventions and norms when trying to get what he wants, House expresses his disgust at the administered state through direct or oblique attacks, euphemism, and irreverence.

Few, if any, individuals completely conform to expectations. Nonconformity seems to be a basic human trait shared by all. What differentiates the nonconformist from the dissenter is the degree to which one rejects norms and one's motivation for doing so. For the purposes of this chapter, *nonconformity* means loosely applied contrarianism or rejection of norms as part of an adolescent growing process. Nonconformity, *pace* theorists of the household as political space, is a household matter. Dissent is public; it is meant to be political and representative of the agonistic nature of politics, whereas nonconformity is less than this.

Dissent, as theorists of politics recognize, comes in various forms. As a modal form of political expression, dissent is, as Camus describes it, "the affirmation of a borderline beyond which one cannot go"; it is a "movement of rebellion . . . founded simultaneously on the categorical rejection of an intrusion that is considered intolerable and on the confused conviction of an absolute right which, in the rebel's mind, is more precisely the impression that he 'has the right to . . .'. Rebellion cannot exist without the feeling that, somewhere and somehow, one is right."[10] In more Foucauldian terms, rebellion is a reassertion of confidence and camaraderie with the criminal, a rejection of the "invincibility of power."[11] As such, dissent need not be an ideologically motivated form of expression, though an ideology can be its frontispiece. Dissent is an individual's conscientious move against expectations and against the direction in which she or he is pushed. Dissent is going against the tide under one's own sails, guided by one's own interpretation that the present or prevailing tide flows in an unfortunate direction that one cannot follow.

Based on this definition of dissent, how does the character House dissent? What distinguishes House's form of dissent is its anti-ideological nature. House is not an altruist pursuing a "public interest" or a common good. Indeed, House seems to be dissenting against the expectations of a physician as a professional whose purpose is to protect a modal public interest in "health" (however defined). His rebellion is against the belief that following the rules and conforming to expectations are somehow protective of life as such and a life well lived. Like the tragic heroes of so many novels now eclipsed by the plastic characters of reality television, House's dominant desire is truth—specifically, to determine the answer to puzzles of human nature, medical or otherwise. His dissent is against the unreal nature of existence according to expectations. As a result, he disregards or belittles any obstacles that come between him and his answers. One episode that embodies this dissenting attitude well is "Half-Wit" (season 3, episode 15), starring Dave Matthews. In this episode, House swims against the tide to recommend that a musical savant undergo radical surgery to remove half his brain in order to recoup the basic minimal functions necessary to live independently. Contrary to the expectation that special gifts trump ordinary abilities, and contrary to the expectation that disabled individuals' guardians are always their best advocates (an issue that appears in a number of episodes), House recommends the ordinary life of buttoning one's shirt independently over the exceptional life lived only with constant management. The esoteric theme of the episode seems to be that a life of ordinary independence is what is actually extraordinary.

Obstacles to the ordinary and extraordinary, whether ordinary misery, ordinary independence, or extraordinary medical treatments, crop up regularly in the drama. These obstacles often include people, but looking beyond the characters as such, those that represent obstacles are embodiments of rules and norms. One character that exemplifies this is Lisa Cuddy (Lisa Edelstein), the endocrinologist turned dean of medicine that House seeks to circumvent or subvert regularly. In House's quest for truth, all that matter are solving the puzzle and determining the right answer, whether in compliance or not with rules, laws, expectations, or norms. In that quest, a regulation-implementing boss is certainly an obstacle. For instance, in the episodes "Euphoria" parts one and two, House makes multiple appeals to Cuddy to contravene a quarantine and instructions for handling an unknown agent imposed by the Centers for Disease Control. In this episode and others, what thwarts House's quest for truth is the firm hand of regulation.

Against the Administered Life

To paraphrase the arguments of Arendt and, later, Pitkin, the contemporary state is the totally administered blob. A morass of administrative offices supervising the conduct of household tasks, the state is less a sovereign creature and more a social, regulatory creature. By *social*, we mean an amorphous, all-encompassing entity that describes the location for the lives of human beings whose right to self-determination has been stripped by the steady accumulation of mass culture, mass politics, and the mass man's power (also noted, in different language, by Oakeshott). Living in the mire of the social, contemporary man is trapped in a gilded cage—secure in his sustenance, but insecure in his being.

The life of the professional in present-day America is the life of the socialized human. Reflecting on the arguments posited by Caiden in "What Really Is Public Maladministration?" we can recognize this existence for its pathology.[12] Overly specialized, highly routinized, dependent on the direction of others, and stripped of the autonomy of free, rational choices, the bureaucratized person is an automaton, a cog in a machine. And at last count, the number of cogs was in the millions. Further, particularly through the mechanisms of "contracting out" or the formation of "public-private partnerships," the number of bureaucratized people has expanded greatly. As noted in a study from 2006, the total number of employees in the federal bureaucracy alone (including employees in the military, postal service, contractors, and others) stood at 14.6 million.[13]

For each man and woman working in or for public bureaucracies, there are untold numbers of regulations applicable to them, and they are creating even more regulations to control others. Apropos of the present context, the medical profession is the most heavily regulated. According to the U.S. Bureau of Labor Statistics, there were nearly 6.9 million health care practitioners and technicians employed in the United States in 2007, and another 3.6 million people employed in health care support occupations.[14] Given that this accounts for approximately 3.5 percent of the total American population, the sheer size of the medical-industrial complex is clear. Compound this by the number of individuals employed in the Department of Health and Human Services and the number of regulations pertinent (at the federal level alone) to medical care, devices, technology, and pharmaceuticals, and the magnitude of the totally administered existence becomes abundantly and frighteningly clear. There is, it seems, no escape from the attack of the blob.

As described in the introduction to this chapter, our primary hypothesis is that House's performances act as a catharsis for all professionals who feel suffocated by the administered life and its regulated structures, constraining any creativity they may wish to impart to their day-to-day activities. Although we do not systematically prove the decidedly empirical claim that all professions are heavily regulated, most readers would vigorously nod in the affirmative if asked whether their profession is heavily regulated.

By contemptuously ignoring the hierarchies, the norms, and the mundane obligations cum bureaucratic procedures that inhibit him, House acts as an inspiration to the misanthropic desires inculcated in overly regulated professionals. *House* serves as a therapeutic release by giving professionals in all fields the vicarious experience of revolt against procedural systems that appear insurmountable.

By combining the traits of independence, genius, and sarcasm, House provides a psychological release for viewers. The audience gains this release from two themes in the program. The first theme is the personality of the character himself. Locked in the position of the administered mass man, viewers can vicariously experience the emancipation of the autonomous, flippant genius. Few people will ever have the intelligence, learning, or audacity to act remotely similar to House, as they are habituated and trained to behave in ways more conducive to the administered state. But in the character of House, the audience can briefly experience the liberation not dissimilar to the freedom Camus describes in his absurdist existentialism. The second theme is the success of the character. The catharsis experienced by the audience derives not only from House's personality but also from his victories against the crushing bureaucracy he loathes. It is in his accomplishments—forcing the representatives of his profession's regulatory norms to acknowledge not only his autonomy but also the validity and accuracy of his methods—that the audience gains vindication.

It is against this startling backdrop that the medical drama comes into focus. As suggested by Burke so many years ago, we marvel at the sublime magnificence of difficulty. In a stroke of both terror and reverence, we perceive the voice of the dissenting medical professional as representing the possibility of sublime salvation from our own eventual consumption, or the pathway out of the gut of the Leviathan.

How Far Dissent?

House's rebellion against regulatory norms is best compared to his main antagonist in the third season: Detective Michael Tritter (David Morse). After House humiliates the detective in a clinic examination room, Tritter dedicates himself to investigating House. In the process, he catches House driving a motorcycle without a license, carrying a large amount of painkillers (having forged a prescription for Vicodin using his friend Wilson's pad), and taking a bottle of OxyContin prescribed to a dead man. Although Tritter collects a damning amount of evidence, and House's antisocial behavior aggravates the case against him, House avoids a trial in the end. In large measure, House evades indictment through the assistance, or at least the complacency, of his colleagues. The character Wilson (Robert Sean Leonard), who epitomizes the altruistic drive of the professional, regularly defends and lies for House, up to the point of nearly losing his medical practice. Indeed, House's salvation comes through the regulatory minded Cuddy, who commits perjury to protect her egomaniacal genius doctor. House's dissent pushes his colleagues to rebel in his defense, but his solitary and miserable example prevents them from internalizing his form of resistance.

Throughout the story arc, House shows little or no remorse for what he has done and is in fact self-righteous in the declaration of his innocence. His staff, colleagues, and boss all tell him that he needs help with his Vicodin addiction, yet they spend most of their time attempting to hide from the police House's unethical (and potentially illegal) actions, ranging from omitting information when being questioned by Tritter to committing perjury in court. For House, the arrest and potential indictment are unjust, in that he has done nothing wrong (he needs the exceptional amount of Vicodin he takes for pain), and he sees the entire investigation as merely the result of a "bully" being angry with him. The transvaluation that House inspires is notable in this story arc—while he wants to focus on his medical puzzles, the other main characters spend their time (for the most part) rationalizing and lying about House's drug abuse. When Wilson, facing economic and professional ruin as a result of writing prescriptions for House, works with Tritter to get a better deal from the district attorney, House, Cuddy, and especially Dr. Cameron (Jennifer Morrison), one of House's medical fellows, accuse Wilson of being a traitor and self-interested. In other words, House's utter contempt for regulation, law, and friendship makes his abuse of all of them acceptable, but as soon as Wilson attempts to help himself, he becomes the unethical one—a transvaluation of marked proportions. But Tritter's persecution of House presents a conundrum: how far can dissent be pressed in the administered state?

Tritter and House share various characteristics. Both are antisocial; neither man seems to have much of a life outside of his profession. Both have addictions: House to Vicodin, Tritter (if House's diagnosis is correct) to cigarettes. Both believe that "everybody lies" and are unwaveringly dedicated to finding the truth. But there is one major difference between them: while House ignores and rebels against the regulatory norms of his field, Tritter does not. By remaining within the confines of the regulatory state, abiding by the legal and procedural rules of police work, the detective cannot catch his quarry. House shows himself to be the more dedicated and superior professional, and perhaps the more responsible individual, because he will stop at nothing to find his answers. But this comparison also shows the danger of this type of dissent: If House can blithely ignore the rules, why not Tritter? If the truth is truly what matters, should we not cheer on Tritter as well?

House is a misanthropic hero for the conformist professionals who seek release from the administered life. Through his genius, his self-made autonomy, and his sarcasm, House provides a cathartic release for all those trapped in the regulated life of mass man. Viewers flock to this program to find the type of liberation that can only be imagined but not performed. But by placing the administered state in question, *House, M.D.* may provide opportunities to rehabituate audiences away from the presumption of the normalcy of current regulatory norms.

Notes

1. Statistics on *House, M.D.* viewership are available at http://tvbythenumbers .com/2007/11/18/house-ratings-2007–2008/1816(accessed December 6, 2008) and http://www.nielsenmedia.com/nc/portal/site/Public/menuitem.55dc65b 4a7d5adff3f65936147a062a0/?vgnextoid=c663c5e568522110VgnVCM 100000ac0a260aRCRD (accessed December 6, 2008).

2. Doris A. Graber, *Mass Media and American Politics,* 3rd ed. (Washington, DC: Congressional Quarterly Press, 1993); Denis McQuail, *Mass Communication Theory: An Introduction* (London: Sage, 1987).

3. Dhavan V. Shah, "Civic Engagement, Interpersonal Trust, and Television Use: An Individual-Level Assessment of Social Capital," *Political Psychology* 19, no. 3 (1998): 475.

4. Hannah Arendt, *The Human Condition* (Chicago: University of Chicago Press, 1958).

5. Friedrich Nietzsche, *Beyond Good and Evil,* trans. Walter Kaufmann (New York: Random House, 1989).

6. Michael Oakeshott, *Morality and Politics in Modern Europe: The Harvard Lecturers,* ed. Shirley Robin Letwin (New Haven, CT: Yale University Press, 1993).

7. José Ortega y Gasset, *The Revolt of the Masses,* trans. Anonymous (New York: W. W. Norton, 1932).

8. Jean-Jacques Rousseau, *A Discourse on Inequality* (London: Penguin Books, 1984).

9. Certainly, the creators of *House, M.D.* have purposely given him this polymath nature to parallel another literary figure: Sherlock Holmes. Doyle's creation was not only a brilliant detective but also knowledgeable in chemistry, music, and certain forms of literature, as well as a skilled pugilist. Where House and Holmes appear to differ is in terms of ignorance: Holmes was so strongly focused on criminological pursuits that he was unaware of some basic facts (including that the earth revolved around the sun instead of vice versa). Thus far, House has not shown any such lacunae in his knowledge.

10. Albert Camus, *The Myth of Sisyphus and Other Essays,* trans. Justin O'Brien (New York: Vintage Books, 1991), 12.

11. Michel Foucault, *Discipline and Punish: The Birth of the Prison,* trans. Alan Sheridan (New York: Vintage Books, 1995), 63.

12. Gerald Caiden, "What Really Is Public Maladministration?" *Pubic Administration Review* 51 (1991): 486–93.

13. Christopher Lee, "Big Government Gets Bigger: Study Counts More Employees, Cites Increase in Contractors," *Washington Post,* October 6, 2006, A21.

14. Bureau of Labor Statistics, "Occupational Employment and Wages News Release," May 9, 2008, http://www.bls.gov/news.release/ocwage.htm (accessed November 25, 2008).

6

"I LEARNED PRISON IS A BAD PLACE TO BE"

25th Hour and Reimagining Incarceration

Peter Caster

Midway through Spike Lee's *25th Hour* (2002), the story of a man's final day before beginning a lengthy prison sentence for drug trafficking, main character Monty Brogan (Edward Norton) offers an extended monologue to a bathroom mirror. It is a profanity-laced litany of abuse heaped on every racial, ethnic, and identity group in New York before Brogan concludes that his real anger is directed at himself: "You had it all and you threw it away." The film tracks the dialogue with extradiagetic images of the "Bensonhurst Italians," "Korean grocers," and "uptown brothers" Brogan derides. One line in the rant directed at African Americans—"Slavery ended 137 years ago. Move the fuck on!"—echoes Norton's role as a white supremacist in Tony Kaye's *American History X* (1998), where he asks rhetorically, "Slavery ended like a hundred and thirty years ago, how long does it take to get your act together?" In that film, Norton's character makes an effort at atonement the day after being released from prison for a racially motivated murder. Thus the two films bookend an imagined prison sentence, and *25th Hour* responds to Norton's previous film in particular and to prison films in general by staging a complex representation of criminality nuanced in terms of race and history.

As sociologist Sean O'Sullivan recognizes, *American History X* itself seems to respond to an earlier prison film—*The Shawshank Redemption* (1994), an escapist male melodrama by Frank Darabont. The 1998 film's

Departing from the often sensationalized Hollywood portrayals of life in prison, Spike Lee's *25th Hour* provides a realistic perspective on the complexities of crime and punishment in the United States. (MovieGoods)

"gritty realism" and cinema verité contrast with its predecessor so much that it "could be seen as a mirror image of, or an answer-film to," the prior work. O'Sullivan suggests that the "contrasts between the two are so striking that it is almost as if the makers of *American History X* had set out to make a film that was not *The Shawshank Redemption*."[1] The consistently dark and occasionally documentary style of *American History X* certainly differs from the soft-focus sentimentalism of *The Shawshank Redemption*, but both describe prison as a violent setting of sexual predation, vicious inmates, and cruel corrections officers, a hellish place that paradoxically proves transformative, man-making, and redemptive for the charismatic central characters. Such prison films can be seen to endorse the very system of punishment they seem to critique. Many representations of incarceration—both fiction and nonfiction—rely on lurid portrayals in which crime and punishment are divorced from historical specificity and dynamic relationships of personal agency and cultural circumstances. Lee's film offers a more complex understanding of the causes and effects of incarceration. As this chapter demonstrates, the massive expansion of the criminal justice system in the past three decades has been accompanied by an increased public fascination with actual and imagined prisons. Lee's film departs from more common sensationalist portrayals, focusing instead on equating imprisonment with personal, social, and historical loss. Most important, the film depicts crime, punishment, and race with a historical specificity to counter broadly held but inaccurate assumptions of criminality, wherein criminals are usually black and uniformly guilty of violent offenses, deserving the harsh incarceration that will somehow redeem them.

Prisons Actual and Imagined

Law-and-order–themed films and television programs textured as realistic regularly portray criminals who murder or rob innocents before being apprehended and sent to prison, but more detailed and accurate portrayals of crime and punishment are vital at a time in U.S. history when an unprecedented number of persons live behind bars, many sentenced for nonviolent offenses. The social institution of incarceration creates one the most marginalized groups in the United States, as prisoners are nearly invisible and voiceless in the public sphere. Although prisons and jails hold 2.3 million people at an annual cost to taxpayers of more than $60 billion, and nearly one-third of black men will be incarcerated during their lives, broad critiques of this criminal justice system and its racial inequities rarely get public attention.[2] After all, prisons are largely concealed from public sight by both design and economic necessity. Given that property values in urban areas with the densest crime preclude the construction of large, unprofitable structures there, prisons are relegated to distant rural areas. In addition to the 2.3 million people in correctional facilities, almost 5 million are involved in another phase of the criminal justice system, whether parole, probation, or alternative sentencing.

The numbers have not always been so high; the incarcerated population doubled in the 1980s and again in the 1990s, largely due to extended sentences, increased criminalization of drug-related offenses, decreased alternative sentencing, and trends in population demographics, such as a slight increase in the total number of young men—those most likely to commit crimes. Furthermore, the prison population has expanded even as violent and property crime rates have decreased, and to suggest that the former caused the latter underreads the complexity of the interlocking local, state, and federal criminal justice systems, as well as historical trends, racial inequities, and economic factors.

Although more than 1 percent of the U.S. adult population is in prison or jail, the 99 percent who are not have scarce access to that environment, and that lack of access likely contributes to the popular fascination with seeing inside. Serial television drama and would-be blockbusters do not lend themselves to complexity, substituting sensationalism for ambiguity and sophistication. Certainly prisons have long provided a dramatic setting, and such stories punctuate film history: *I Am a Fugitive from a Chain Gang* (1932), *The Birdman of Alcatraz* (1962), *Cool Hand Luke* (1967), and *Escape from Alcatraz* (1979). An innocent man unjustly imprisoned thematically links many of these films and makes for compelling narrative.[3] Since the fourfold increase in the incarcerated population began, we have seen an increasing number of these stories in films such as *The Shawshank Redemption, Murder in the First* (1995), *American History X, The Hurricane* (1999), and *The Green Mile* (1999). However, the ideological pressure to reinforce the legitimacy of the criminal justice system to appeal to the broadest audience mandates that in many of these stories, prison provides a place of redemption as well as punishment. Television programming plays a role as well, and ABC's 2006 *In Justice* followed Fox's phenomenally successful 2005 series *Prison Break*, both of which featured story lines based on innocent characters escaping from prison through appeal or breakout, continuing a common trend in prison films going back to Hollywood's golden age.

These fictional accounts are accompanied by documentaries from which audiences might expect greater truth value. The rising population of California's prisons serves as the focus of Ted Koppel's Discovery Channel prison documentary *Breaking Point* (2007), where he interviews some of the 173,000 inmates at California State Prison Solano. However, in pursuit of niche market shares, documentaries take their cues from fictional programming, even as prisons become a setting for dramatic situations or generic conventions. Koppel's slice-of-life video journalism joins the cable network's other shows, including *Dinosaurs: Return to Life? Future Weapons,* and *Animal Face-off: Hippo vs. Bull Shark*. Along with its regular expositions of bizarre foods and exotic destinations, the Travel Channel features *Mysterious Journeys,* one episode of which is "Prison of Horrors—Eastern State Penitentiary," which balances the history of the 1829 prison built on Benjamin Rush's eighteenth-century model with contemporary lore of its reported haunting by ghosts. MSNBC features *Lockup,* which shares its name with a Sylvester Stallone innocent-man-in-prison film from 1989, while the National Geographic Channel has *Prison Nation* and Tru TV (with its tagline "Not reality. Actuality") brings audiences *Inside American Jail.*

Prison dramas, documentary or otherwise, saturate the media landscape and become naturalized, concurrent with the expansion of actual incarceration. They become one more place to tell familiar stories. According to the Internet Movie Database, as of the end of 2008, the keyword *prison* resulted in a list of more than 1,500 films. Prison narratives have become a ubiquitous part of the national culture, and for a nation that defines itself by freedom, the loss of liberty is the dark side of the American dream.

Evoking Loss

For Monty Brogan, the main character of *25th Hour,* the dream has become a nightmare. Heroin sales funded his Horatio Alger rise from working-class youth to moderately wealthy businessman; arrested, convicted, and sentenced, he heads for prison in twenty-four hours. Over the course of the day, he bids good-bye to his father, the boyhood friends from whom he has grown distant, the girlfriend he suspects of turning him in to the police, and his Ukrainian mobster connections. He also comes to terms with his past regret—not guilt for selling drugs, but the greed that kept him in the game long enough to get caught—and his fear of the future—prison rape and a life without point or promise. Lee's direction in this, his fifteenth feature, stays very close to its source, the debut novel and screenplay of David Benioff. The novel's extended character study translates well in Benioff and Lee's adaptation, although more of the drama surrounds Monty, and plot proves to be less important than the ensemble performance of complex characters and the richness of the New York setting (familiar in Lee's oeuvre). Aside from a few expressionist flourishes that are among Lee's directorial trademarks, the film adheres to conventions of realism, its story visually evoking the traumatic absence of the World Trade Center, a visual metonymy for Monty's lost future and a direct testament to the film's immediate realness, its historical present, and thus an indirect testament to its truth value.

The two central questions of the film's plot—did the girlfriend sell him out? (no) and will Monty go to prison? (yes)—provide the stage for the film's three-act structure, each of which culminates in increasingly intense conflict. From morning through evening, a series of separate interactions introduce the characters and demonstrate their relationships with Monty. The first act concludes with the central character's extended monologue mentioned earlier. That scene is signature Lee, closely resembling a similar sequence in *Do the Right Thing* (1989), as most reviewers recognized; even Benioff admits that the film may have served as unconscious inspiration.[4] That night, Monty meets his girlfriend Naturelle (Rosario Dawson) and childhood friends Jacob (Philip Seymour Hoffman) and Frank (Barry Pepper), first at a bar and then at a dance club, where they are joined by Jacob's student Mary (Anna Paquin). The group rapidly devolves into pairs and intense, ultimately divisive conversations, especially as Monty discovers that not Naturelle but his partner Kostya (Tony Siragusa) betrayed him. The short final act sees Monty, Jacob, and Frank walking to a park in the early morning, a return to the riverside setting of the film's opening. There, Monty goads Frank into brutally beating him, hoping that disfiguring his boyish good looks will help him escape rape in the first few weeks of life in prison. In the dénouement, Monty's father (Brian Cox) drives him to Otisville Correctional Facility in upstate New York. A five-minute voice-over by Cox narrates an oversaturated montage of what would happen if Monty jumped bail and escaped west to make a new life. One *New York Times* film reviewer called this conclusion as "bittersweet and sincere an evocation of the American dream as I have seen on film."[5]

Loss permeates the film—from the title credit montage, a tableau of light and dark at Ground Zero, to the final dream of a life that will never happen—with Monty's imminent prison term the *causa causans* for all. The adaptation faces a challenge the source text does not, in that the novel's narration rather than staged dialogue can tell readers that the main character is headed for a seven-year term in Otisville, whereas the film seeks to reveal that visually.[6] A daybreak scene opens with a long view of the East River, and the crane shot descends as a distant figure walks to the foreground to meet Monty seated on a bench overlooking the water. The shot emphasizes the perspective of the railing receding in the distance, and when the camera cuts to the next shot from the opposite side of the railing, its vertical slats stay between the camera and Monty, situating him literally behind bars. He refuses to sell drugs to the slovenly and strung-out Simon in a scene with two key matches later—one narrative and one visual. Nearly an hour later in the film, in a flashback to Monty and Naturelle's first meeting, Simon appears briefly in the background as a well-dressed businessman buying drugs from Monty, the implication being that Simon has fallen far in the intervening months. In that scene too, shot in a playground, Monty is situated behind the bars of the fence railing. And at the end of the film, after beating Monty, Frank takes Monty's place sitting on the same bench, presumably to think about his past and his future, to account for the choices he has made.

On-screen it is Norton's film—he appears in the poster and in most scenes, and he starred in *Red Dragon* (2002) in part to develop the capital to help fund Lee's direction. The most charged scenes focus on his character's forthcoming prison sentence, with all the other characters bleakly anticipating his future. His father suggests contacting an old-timer who did time two decades ago, tells his son to "keep your head down," and blames himself for accepting Monty's money. In a dialogue in Frank's condo overlooking the concrete scar of Ground Zero, Frank and Jacob share their sense of what will happen to Monty even as they elliptically discuss the larger social tragedy below them. In a tightly blocked scene consisting largely of a five-minute single shot, the distance between the actors makes the most of the wide aspect ratio; their differences are also marked by the pensive Jacob's gaze out past his prominent mirrored image, contrasted with Frank's turn away from the reflection. Frank's blunt assessment of Monty's future—"He's going to hell for seven years, what are we gonna do, wish him luck?"—leads to his description of Monty's choices: commit suicide, run, or do the time. In any case, he is gone forever, whether dead, vanished, or a fundamentally different man.

Not only the felon, his father, and his friends but also the police themselves anticipate that hellish future in prison. In a flashback to Monty's arrest, a Drug Enforcement Administration (DEA) agent played by Michael Genet, a regular in law-and-order television programming, proposes that Monty can expect to be regularly gang-raped "by a bunch of guys calling you Shirley." Monty shares that expectation, as he tells Frank at the nightclub, though without the braggadocio he displays in the interrogation scene. That conversation between the men, like the earlier exchange between Frank and Jacob, takes place in front of glass overlooking the background below, and again the dialogue focuses on Monty's incarceration, which he relates in racial and gendered terms of power: "Up there, I'm a skinny white boy with no friends." In grim and highly specific detail, he describes his first night: an overcrowded prison, the complicity of the corrections officers, being overpowered by 200 inmates, his teeth knocked out, being repeatedly raped, initiated into seven years of more of the same. As the dialogue plays out, the framing grows tighter and tighter in the film convention of a slow forward track amplifying emotional intensity, and the prison horrors of deprivation, isolation, and regimentation are subsumed under the sign of male rape.

Crime, Punishment, and Racial Difference

That dark sexual fantasy is rooted not only in repeated depictions in films raising the ante on realism and graphic personal trauma—prison films such as *American Me* (1992), *The Shawshank Redemption,* and *American History X*—but also in growing public awareness of the actual practice and an ambivalent response. Numerous studies conducted in the past ten years have generated conflicting results, largely due to the large and difficult-to-access incarcerated population, the differences between prison and jail, male prisoners' reticence to reliably relate incidents, and the overdetermined power dynamics of the criminal justice system, making problematic distinctions between coercion and choice in the homosocial environment of threatened and actual violence, extortion, and a black-market economy. According to a 2006 Associated Press article, a "bitterly disputed, government-sponsored study has concluded that rape and sexual assault behind bars may be rampant in movies and books but are rare in real life."[7] A survey of county jails the next year by the U.S. Department of Justice placed the rate of sexual assault at less than 3 percent for male inmates, whereas other analyses indicate frequencies ten times that rate.[8] John Edgar Wideman describes the tension between imagination and actuality, pointing out that the good-evil symbolism of prisons and their same-sex organizations set the stage for them to operate with racially charged sexual violence: "Men must go to other men for sex, and given this necessity, prisons reify behind their locked doors the unspoken drama of homo-erotic interpenetration and exchange—the white fantasy of assault by the black males and assaulting black males. In the collective imaginary, prisons become a site of conflicted sado-masochistic desire."[9] In *25th Hour,* the "skinny white boy" recognizes that racism can reverse its trajectory within prison walls, where disproportionate rates of incarceration turn minorities into majorities and "the man" into a threatened boy.

That power reversal is one of several in the film involving racial difference and criminality. Lee is well known as one of the first directors working outside the blaxploitation genre to showcase largely African American casts, but *25th Hour* is his first effort to feature primarily white actors. It is also a departure from his tradition of working with familiar talent; none of the cast appeared in Lee's earlier work—a first for his fictional features. Also, Lee and his longtime casting partner Aisha Coley switch the pervasive racial binary of white cops–black criminals by making all the film's offenders white and the prominent drug enforcement agents African American. Drug dealer Monty, partner Kostya, addict Simon, head mobster Uncle Nikolai, and all his henchmen are (in the simplest terms) white, while the two DEA agents with speaking roles are black. That seemingly simple switch counters more than thirty years of racial expectation in history and imagination. That is, as early as 1969, American Correctional Association (ACA) sociologists demonstrated that white expectations of black crime created demands for expanding law enforcement, even when white ignorance and fear rather than statistical actuality shaped those concerns, and more recent articles reproduce those findings.[10] As Carole Stabile concludes in *White Victims, Black Villains,* "By the waning years of the century, U.S. society has created a narrative of fear and denial that had entirely transformed the political challenges that the Civil Rights Movement had presented into a saga about African Americans' inherent criminality."[11] For the film, Lee consciously reverses the racial expectation not only for criminals but also for law enforcement; in Benioff's novel, "There were four men, all white. . . . They showed Monty their badges, DEA."[12] The importance of such a gesture is underscored in other recent law-and-order adaptations. For instance, John Carpenter's *Assault on Precinct 13* (1976) features a black police officer and his white prisoner, but the 2005 remake switches to a white officer and a black prisoner, perhaps a capitulation to popular expectation. Lee resists the conventional racing of criminality that has in part contributed to the vast overrepresentation of black men in prison through practices such as racial profiling.

We have, then, a number of misconceptions and related ambivalences regarding crime and punishment on which *25th Hour* places pressure. First, long-standing racism creates self-fulfilling expectations of black men as criminals requiring punishment, but the film portrays white crime. Second, long prison sentences generally presume violent crime, but Monty's drug trafficking, though affiliated with the violence of the Ukrainian mob, involves none of the murder, rape, or robbery so prevalent in films. Third, the presumption of criminals' inherent moral evil makes their brutal sexual assault part of the "just deserts" model of incarceration prevalent since the 1970s, wherein prisoners get what they deserve.[13] However, Monty hardly seems deserving of the seven years of beating and sexual assault that friends, criminals, police, and the felon himself anticipate, and how such punishment functions as any sort of rehabilitation escapes reason. His expectation to be released as "a 38-year-old punked-out ex-con with government-issue dentures" presents a throwback to what Michel Foucault describes as *old regime* punishment, the pre-Enlightenment approach of bodily torture that gave way to mental discipline in the nineteenth century.[14] The lack of violence in the crime and Norton's charismatic performance imply that the tacit torture violates the Eighth Amendment regarding cruel and unusual punishment and the accompanying Enlightenment principles of justice and self-ownership. And although the anticipation of such misery may function as a deterrent, it in no way resembles the intention to rehabilitate that led the American Prison Association to change its name to the American *Correctional* Association in 1955. The film's narrative voice, its commitment to representing a criminal as guilty but not meriting the "just deserts" for which he is headed, speaks against the widespread silent assent to the massive expansion of imprisonment, especially for nonviolent offenses, and the accompanying dangers of overcrowded incarceration.

Lee's *25th Hour* carefully marks the specific legal history contributing to the extended criminalization of drug crimes, expanded prison terms, and jurisprudential dynamics of sentencing. During police interrogation, Monty proposes that as a first-time offender he might earn a light sentence, but Agent Flood (played by *Law and Order* and *The Wire* actor Isaiah Whitlock Jr.) corrects him. As part of an extended exposition, Flood offers to "educate" Monty and, by extension, the audience regarding the differences between A-1 and A-2 felonies: "You don't read the papers much, do you, smart guy? In New York, we've got a wonderful thing called the Rockefeller laws. . . . Fifteen years to life minimum, first offense. Now with that much spread in the sentencing guidelines, the judges take their cues from the prosecutors—who take their cue from the DEA." This dialogue occurs only in Lee's film, not in the novel. Lee incorporates the history of the actual laws implemented by Governor Nelson Rockefeller in the early 1970s that expanded the criminalization of drug offenses, switched from treatment to incarceration for users, and instituted draconian minimum sentences (though slightly short of Rockefeller's intent to impose life sentences on first offenders for marijuana possession). These New York laws expanded nationally after Rockefeller became vice president under President Gerald Ford. It is that expansion of criminalization and the harsh sentences for drug crimes, not an increase in violent or property crimes, that led the incarcerated population described in 1977 by the ACA executive director as a "crisis" to more than quadruple in the decades since.[15] These mandatory minimums worsened with the Anti-Drug Acts of the 1980s, designed to punish users and dealers of crack cocaine, which was widely (and inaccurately) believed to be used primarily by African Americans.

Lee's explicit implication of legal history in the arrest of a white drug dealer by black police officers reverses the all too prevalent racist expectations of criminality. Still, Lee—as well as Benioff's script and Norton's performance—shies away from overtly politicizing the events depicted, and the director's sometimes criticized bombast remains tightly constrained, offering an evenhanded but nevertheless dramatic appraisal that refuses to either glamorize crime in the fashion of *Scarface* (1983) and *American Gangster* (2007) or depict sentenced criminals in redemptive suffering, as in *The Shawshank Redemption* and *American History X*. Historically, crime films demarcate clearly between bad guys and good guys, and films with villains as protagonists tend to portray them as unabashedly, charismatically bad, at once fulfilling the audience's dark fantasies and meeting the cultural need to see the social order maintained in their final punishment. It is not only *25th Hour* that attempts to sort more carefully the racial, ethical, and moral nuances of drug crime. In the early 1970s the ACA pointed to a history of racism as a cause of the overrepresentation of black men in prison. Since the early 1990s the ACA and, to an extent, the American Bar Association have protested racial bias in sentencing, argued to reduce existing mandatory minimums, and proposed alternative sentencing.[16] To a degree, *25th Hour* joins in their dissent by, in its simplest reading, suggesting that white men distribute and consume drugs, taking drugs is bad, selling them is worse, criminals are people who made poor decisions and had worse luck in negative situations, and prison is terrible.

Though thinly marketed and failing to make back its budget in its domestic theatrical run, Lee's film remains a compelling narrative, visual, and cultural achievement, an entry in the genre of the humanist male melodrama. It helped the director become more of an inside man in Hollywood, and it allowed Benioff to join the ranks of celebrity. More pertinent to this collection, the film resists easy answers to commonly held assumptions of crime and punishment too prevalent in popular news and fiction. As head mobster Uncle Nikolai relates to Monty—and he should know, as he has served three sentences—"I learned prison is a bad place to be." U.S. audiences already believe that, but the film invites us to ask, does it need to be as bad a place as it currently is? Popular imagination supposes that (generally black) prisoners are invariably guilty of violent crimes, and prisons are intended to deter crime, separate criminals from the rest of society, punish them, and rehabilitate them to allow their return. Fictional representations often stage the contradiction of innocent protagonists imprisoned for violent crimes but nevertheless experiencing the transformative benefits of incarceration.

In contrast, *25th Hour* offers multiple but invariably bleak expectations of incarceration, descriptions of drug crimes and enforcement based on actual legal history, and an unwillingness to capitulate to simple determinations of race, criminality, and innocence. Academics have lamented the power of film and television to shape popular perception, but movies present the opportunity not only for deflection, distraction, and hegemony but also for dissent.[17] Critics as seemingly disparate as 1998 ACA president Reginald A. Wilkinson and scholar, activist, and former prisoner Angela Davis have disparaged the "misrepresentations" of "grossly sensationalized" fictional prison dramas.[18] For a national audience confronting TV and films saturated with images of incarceration that reproduce existing expectations of race, crime, and punishment, *25th Hour* proposes an alternative discourse and an opportunity to think critically about one of the most important civil rights problems of our time.

Notes

I am grateful to Kathryn McGrath, a former student whose insightful paper on *25th Hour* proved useful in developing this chapter.

1. Sean O'Sullivan, "Representations of Prison in Nineties Hollywood Cinema: From *Con Air* to *The Shawshank Redemption*," *Howard Journal of Criminal Justice* 40, no. 4 (2001): 327. Though both *The Shawshank Redemption* and *American History X* initially did poorly at the box office—the former failed to recoup its marketing costs, and the latter did not even cover its production—they have garnered significant attention since their theatrical releases. They earned a total of eight Academy Award nominations, saw extensive cable network circulation, and received tremendous popular recognition. As of the end of 2008, on the Internet Movie Database's ranking of films by user votes, *American History X* was number 40 (between *Vertigo* [1956] and *American Beauty* [1999]), and *The Shawshank Redemption* was number 1. The latter was the American Film Institute's 72nd best film in its 2007 ranking.

2. The racial disparities in expanded incarceration were the subject of recent national discussion when Barack Obama included sentencing statistics in his primary campaign speeches in 2007. In addition, a widely reported February 2008 report from

the Pew Center relied on U.S. Department of Justice figures to demonstrate that more than 1 percent of the adult population was behind bars. George Will immediately criticized Obama and the Pew report, citing instead the analysis of the conservative think tank the Manhattan Institute in his column "More Prisoners, Less Crime," *Washington Post*, June 22, 2008.

3. As the vast majority of the prison population is male and the overriding concerns of *25th Hour* (both book and film) involve men, this chapter focuses exclusively on masculinity and incarceration.

4. All references to the film are from the DVD *25th Hour* (40 Acres & a Mule/ Touchstone/Buena Vista, 2002); references to the novel are from David Benioff, *25th Hour* (2000; reprint, New York: Plume, 2002). Roger Ebert, among others, pointed out the scene's resemblance to *Do the Right Thing* in his review of *25th Hour* in the *Chicago Sun-Times,* January 10, 2003. In an interview with *Cineaste,* Benioff acknowledges that the earlier film may have shaped the scene in his novel, which he removed from the screenplay; Lee reintroduced it. Paula J. Massood, "Doyle's Law: An Interview with David Benioff," *Cineaste* (Summer 2003): 9.

5. A. O. Scott, "Confronting the Past before Going to Prison," *New York Times,* December 19, 2002.

6. The showing-versus-telling binary is a familiar one in adaptation studies, as Seymour Chatman makes clear in "What Novels Can Do that Films Can't (and Vice Versa)," *Critical Inquiry* 7 (1980–1981). Hutcheon and Leitch have each debunked the presumption that novels tell and films show; see Linda Hutcheon, *A Theory of Adaptation* (New York: Routledge, 2006), and Thomas Leitch, *Film Adaptation and Its Discontents: From Gone with the Wind to The Passion of the Christ* (Baltimore: Johns Hopkins University Press, 2007). The East River scene of *25th Hour*—book and film—embodies some of the variations of exposition in revealing Monty's impending prison sentence.

7. Kim Curtis, "A Disputed Study Claims Rape Is Rare in Prison," *USA Today,* January 17, 2006.

8. Allen J. Beck and Paige M. Harrison, *Sexual Victimization in Local Jails Reported by Inmates, 2007* (Washington, DC: U.S. Department of Justice, 2008); William F. Pinar, *The Gender of Racial Politics and Violence in America: Lynching, Prison Rape, and the Crisis of Masculinity* (New York: Peter Lang, 2001); Donald F. Sabo, Terry A. Kupers, and Willie London, eds., *Prison Masculinities* (Philadelphia: Temple University Press, 2001); Michael Scarce, *Male on Male Rape: The Hidden Toll of Stigma and Shame* (Cambridge, MA: Perseus, 1997); Sandesh Sivakumaran, "Male/Male Rape and the 'Taint' of Homosexuality," *Human Rights Quarterly* 27, no. 4 (November 2005).

9. John Edgar Wideman, "The American Dilemma Revisited: Psychoanalysis, Social Policy, and the Socio-Cultural Meaning of Race," *Black Renaissance/Renaissance Noire* 8, no. 1 (2003): 41.

10. Joseph M. Dell'Olio, "The Public, Crime, and Corrections—Acceptance or Rejection," *Proceedings of the Ninety-ninth Annual Congress of Correction of the Ameri-*

can Correctional Association, 1969 (Washington, DC, 1969); Franklin D. Gilliam Jr., Nicholas A. Valentino, and Matthew N. Beckmann, "Where You Live and What You Watch: The Impact of Racial Proximity and Local Television News on Attitudes about Race and Crime," *Political Research Quarterly* 55, no. 4 (December 2002).

11. Carol Stabile, *White Victims, Black Villains: Gender, Race, and Crime News in U.S. Culture* (New York: Routledge, 2006), 173. Racist expectations of criminality have been documented extensively in criminal justice studies. See Mary Bosworth and Jean Flavin, eds., *Race, Gender, and Punishment: From Colonialism to the War on Terror* (New Brunswick, NJ: Rutgers University Press, 2007); Peter Caster, *Prisons, Race, and Masculinity in Twentieth-Century U.S. Literature and Film* (Columbus: Ohio State University Press, 2008); Dana E. Mastro and Amanda L. Robinson, "Cops and Crooks: Images of Minorities on Primetime Television," *Journal of Criminal Justice* 28, no. 5 (September–October 2000); Julian V. Roberts and Loretta J. Stalans, "Crime, Criminal Justice, and Public Opinion," in *The Handbook of Crime and Punishment,* ed. Michael Tonry (New York: Oxford University Press, 1998).

12. Benioff, *25th Hour,* 41.

13. John M. Sloop, *The Cultural Prison: Discourse, Prisoners, and Punishment* (Tuscaloosa: Alabama University Press, 1996), 63, 91.

14. Michel Foucault, *Discipline and Punish: The Birth of the Prison,* trans. Alan Sheridan (New York: Vintage, 1979).

15. Anthony Travisono, "Prison Crisis—Over 280,000 Men and Women in Our Nation's Prisons," *American Journal of Correction* (May–June 1977).

16. See Caster, *Prisons, Race, and Masculinity,* 108–12, 197–200.

17. Henry A. Giroux has made something of a cottage industry of publishing works about the relationships of social justice, pedagogy, and popular culture, but he never seems to like the films he critiques, and he treats dissent less as encoded within popular films than as embodied in his critical response to them. See Giroux, *America on the Edge: Henry Giroux on Politics, Culture, and Education* (New York: Palgrave Macmillan, 2006), *Breaking into the Movies: Film and the Culture of Politics* (Malden, MA: Blackwell, 2002), and *Disturbing Pleasures: Learning Popular Culture* (New York: Routledge, 1994).

18. Reginald A. Wilkinson, "Best Practices: Tools for Correctional Excellence," in American Correctional Association, *The State of Corrections: Proceedings of the American Correctional Association Annual Conferences, 1998* (Upper Marlboro, MD, 1998), 85; Angela Davis, "A World unto Itself: Multiple Invisibilities of Imprisonment," in *Behind the Razorwire: Portrait of a Contemporary American Prison System,* ed. Michael Jacobson-Hardy (New York: New York University Press, 1999), x.

7

Riveted to Rosie

O'Donnell's Queer Politics and Controversial Antics on ABC's *The View*

Katherine Lehman

Rosie O'Donnell made a splash at Sundance in 2006 as the star of the documentary *All Aboard! Rosie's Family Cruise.* The film features the versatile comedian in a range of roles—from campy stage performer to gracious host to nurturer of her own brood—aboard the inaugural voyage of R Family Vacations, the gay-friendly travel company O'Donnell co-owns with spouse Kelli Carpenter. The same-sex couples captured by the camera seemed more comfortable cuddling babies and swapping wedding vows than sparking political upheaval. O'Donnell, too, chose her battles carefully, speaking about adoption by same-sex couples to a supportive crowd in Key West but refusing to engage fierce anti-gay protesters who greeted the cruise ship when it docked in the Bahamas. O'Donnell feared that confronting the protesters would only lead to negative publicity. "I thought I'd get in a fight with someone," she explained on camera. "If I saw them being rude to a passenger, I would have gone ballistic, and that's all they want, is a little news clip."[1]

With the release of *All Aboard,* the comedian who had risen to prominence while masking her sexual preference was more visible than ever as an openly gay, recently married mother of four representing gay people as parents and consumers. *All Aboard* reached a wide audience through its HBO distribution and film festival screenings, and it attracted the attention of famed telejournalist Barbara Walters. Walters was reportedly so moved by an early screening of the documentary that she approached O'Donnell about joining her as cohost of the ABC daytime panel show *The View.* "There was the warm, thoughtful, intelligent, charming, funny Rosie I've always known," Walters told *Newsweek* in September 2006. "There were discussions with the ABC brass in which we talked about the new Rosie—not the woman who might have been aggressive or belligerent, but the woman I had seen that night. There were some concerns over which Rosie we were getting."[2]

During the six-year run of *The Rosie O'Donnell Show* and through her work with children's charities, O'Donnell had cultivated an accessible, family-friendly image. However, O'Donnell's career took an abrupt turn in 2002 when she publicly announced her sexual orientation, disappeared from daytime TV, and embraced what some saw as an aggressive political agenda. Was the "new Rosie" the affable host who had warmed housewives' hearts, starred as the best friend in romantic comedies, and been dubbed the "Queen of Nice" by *Newsweek* in the mid-1990s? Or was she the acerbic activist who had lopped off her hair and castigated the president for forbidding gay marriage?[3]

Though Walters may have hoped for the former, the news media knew better and braced for a firestorm. Indeed, O'Donnell's eight months on *The View* were marked by conflict and controversy as she battled conservative cohosts, baited powerful celebrities, and espoused a left-wing political agenda rarely voiced on network television. Much of the media coverage and Rosie's own memoir centered on the dramatic moments, such as her duel with Donald Trump and war of words with cohost Elisabeth Hasselbeck; less attention has been paid to the subtle ways she foregrounded gay and lesbian families on a mainstream talk show.

This chapter simultaneously examines O'Donnell's public role as lesbian parent and political pundit. I argue that her brief reign on *The View* directly engaged cultural understandings of gay and lesbian families and challenged expectations of how gay celebrities should behave in the mainstream media. While O'Donnell's status as a middle-aged mother of four made her accessible to a key viewer demographic, her unapologetic advocacy for the normalcy of gay and lesbian families amplified the threat she posed to conservative interests. The network capitalized on the controversy O'Donnell created, welcoming the ratings boost but fearing the backlash her antics might cause. O'Donnell's experience not only provides a fascinating case study of a contemporary lesbian celebrity but also illuminates the political possibilities and limitations posed by the feminized space of the daytime talk and variety show format typified by *The View*. Furthermore, the *View* debacle demonstrates the increasing power of online media to amplify and interpret television: O'Donnell addressed viewers directly from her blog

Rosie.com, and her *View* appearances still provoke debates on streaming video sites such as YouTube.

The Fight for Family Recognition

Long before her return to daytime television, O'Donnell had framed her struggle for family recognition as a political issue. Over the course of *The Rosie O'Donnell Show* (1996–2002), O'Donnell joked about her crush on Tom Cruise and mentioned her friendships with famous lesbians, but she rarely talked publicly about her romantic and family life. That silence ended in early 2002 when she announced her sexual orientation in an off-stage comedy routine and discussed her partner's pregnancy in interviews. O'Donnell ended her show two months later.[4]

Her decision to come out, she claimed, was prompted by Florida's restrictive adoption laws. When O'Donnell and partner Kelli Carpenter were barred from adopting a three-year-old Florida girl they had fostered for nearly two years, O'Donnell became an advocate for same-sex couples denied the opportunity to adopt. As she told Larry King, "When the state of Florida said to me, 'You are unworthy because you're gay,' I said it is time for me to stand up and say this law is wrong." For the next few years, O'Donnell absented herself from daily television to tend to the challenge of raising multiple children. After adopting son Parker on her own, she and Carpenter adopted two more children, Blake and Chelsea. In late 2002 Carpenter gave birth to Vivienne.[5]

In February 2004 O'Donnell and Carpenter were among the first same-sex couples to legally wed in San Francisco. Again, O'Donnell combined her personal life with politics, using the occasion to criticize President George Bush's recent call for a constitutional amendment to ban gay marriage. "I think the actions of the president are, in my opinion, the most vile and hateful words ever spoken by a sitting president," O'Donnell told ABC's *Good Morning America.*[6]

O'Donnell's return to daytime television came on the heels of a heated debate over same-sex marriage. In the 2004 election alone, thirteen states adopted amendments defining marriage as the sole prerogative of one man and one woman; nine of those amendments restricted other rights available to same-sex partners.[7] (As of November 2008, all but six U.S. states had laws or amendments restricting marriage to heterosexual couples.[8]) Bush's reelection, paired with the passage of state laws banning gay marriage and voters' stated concerns about "moral issues," strengthened perceptions that same-sex marriage played a pivotal role in the election.[9]

In opposing same-sex marriage, groups such as Focus on the Family and Concerned Women for America emphasized the relationship between marriage and parenting, framing gay marriage as a "looming threat that endangers children and society." Opponents claimed that same-sex parents deprived their children of opposite-sex role models, accusing lesbians in particular of undermining the importance of fatherhood. Some opponents characterized gay parenthood as inherently abusive because it exposed children to societal discrimination and ridicule and gave them misguided messages about sexuality. Furthermore, opponents warned that elevating same-sex relationships to the status of marriage would undermine the importance of marriage and the nuclear family.[10]

Gay rights organizations such as the Human Rights Campaign actively sought marriage rights as a means of accessing the legal, societal, and economic privileges that heterosexual couples often took for granted. However, some gay and lesbian activists questioned the priority placed on gay marriage and proponents' tendency to present their families as similar to heterosexual arrangements. As Judith Levine wrote in the *Village Voice* in 2003, "Marriage . . . does not just normalize, it requires normality as the ticket in. Assimilating another 'virtually normal' constituency, namely monogamous, long-term, homosexual couples, pushes the queerer queers of all sexual persuasions—drag queens, club-crawlers, polyamorists, even ordinary single mothers . . . further to the margins." A better strategy for equality, these activists suggested, was to challenge a system that attached legal and economic privileges to monogamous two-person partnerships.[11]

As an advocate for gay marriage and parenting rights, O'Donnell faced cultural prejudice heightened by the recent gay marriage debates. At the same time, her public role as mother and her previous popularity with mainstream audiences granted her greater legitimacy in the public sphere than a lesbian activist might otherwise enjoy. While O'Donnell's embrace of nuclear family norms might appear to be wholesale assimilation, her political edge kept her at the margins of the mainstream.

Television Takes on LGBT Issues

Although the national political climate was hostile to gay marriage efforts in 2006, O'Donnell herself acknowledged that television offered greater avenues for queer representation than it had just a decade earlier. Fellow comedian Ellen DeGeneres parlayed the fame gained from her failed sitcom into a successful talk show in 2003 and publicly shared her life with actress Portia de Rossi. The eight-year run of the NBC comedy *Will and Grace*—on which O'Donnell had guest-starred—and the debut of Showtime's *The L Word* in 2004 made gay and lesbian themes more palatable to mainstream viewing audiences. Same-sex couples had long been fixtures on issue-oriented talk shows and increasingly factored in the casts of reality shows such as *The Amazing Race*.

However, these gay and lesbian celebrities and characters often made concessions to be accepted by mainstream audiences. *Will and Grace* couched its provocative subject matter in the close friendship of a gay man and a straight woman, rarely granting romantic relationships to the gay characters. The largely straight cast of *The L Word* offered an elite, svelte, and sexualized portrait of lesbian life. Initially, DeGeneres rarely mentioned her sexual orientation on her talk show, and she claimed that her comedy acts were not concerned with gay issues.[12]

While talk shows have historically been a key venue for gay and lesbian visibility, media scholars have questioned this genre's ability to create social change. The parade of lesbian, gay, bisexual, and transgender (LGBT) people on tabloid talk shows may serve primarily as spectacles for the audience's shock and amusement, reassuring viewers of the normalcy of heterosexuality. Less sensational hosts such as Oprah Winfrey often promote therapeutic fixes for personal relationships rather than broader solutions to societal issues such as sexism. As scholar Jane Shattuc notes, talk-show sets modeled after living rooms situate guests' conversations in the domestic realm rather than the world of work and politics. *The View*'s assumed female audience and prominent product placements make it appear less weighty than its cable news counterparts—that is, more interested in meeting lifestyle and consumer needs than swaying political opinions.[13]

O'Donnell, then, challenged expectations for gays and lesbians on television as well as the expected tone and function of *The View*. Androgynous and overweight, she lacked the glamour of lesbian characters on series such as *The L Word*. She spoke openly about her family and LGBT political issues, in contrast to the then-muted DeGeneres. As her diatribes addressed not only parenting issues and celebrity culture but also contentious political issues such as the war in Iraq, she moved *The View*'s domain from the domestic realm to the world of politics. Audiences were simultaneously intrigued and threatened by the changes she wrought.

Changing Appearances, Challenging Expectations

From the beginning, observers feared that O'Donnell's style and presentation would clash with *The View*'s. O'Donnell had been selected to fill the spot vacated by the elegant, even-keeled Meredith Viera, and she had already sparred publicly with *View* host Star Jones, who was fired before O'Donnell assumed the stage. In addition to Walters, the remaining hosts were Elisabeth Hasselbeck, a conservative mother and former reality TV star in her late twenties, and Joy Behar, a liberal comedian in her early sixties. Media pundits predicted that O'Donnell, accustomed to ruling her own talk show, might have difficulty working harmoniously as part of this ensemble.[14]

In her first appearance on *The View* in September 2006, O'Donnell, garbed in black, visibly dominated the set and the conversation. Fearing that Rosie's size and sass would overshadow the formidable Barbara Walters, *The View*'s producers reformatted the set in week one. They trimmed the legs of O'Donnell's chair, minimizing her height, and moved Walters to the opposite end of the table, placing O'Donnell beside the more petite Hasselbeck. As Rosie quipped on her blog, "My torso is so long I look like gigantor the spaceage robot. They cut 3 inches off the chair by day 2."[15] A promotional photo of the new *View* lineup with O'Donnell at the center was digitally altered to grant her a trimmer hourglass figure; O'Donnell reported on her Web site that she barely recognized the "Photoshopped" image of herself. Furthermore, her contract forbade her from cutting her hair, a rule that some reporters interpreted as homophobic.[16]

In her opening comments in September 2006, O'Donnell strategically distanced herself from her earlier politicized image. "I'm wearing high heels today because you girls are heel-wearers on this show," she remarked. "I had that crazy, crazy haircut that scared America to death, so you know, it's going to be long from now on. And," she added in a dramatic whisper, "I'm taking my medication, so everything's fine."[17]

If a shorter chair, longer hair, and quick wit weren't enough to soften O'Donnell's abrasive image, perhaps evoking parenthood would do the trick. A segment prepared for *The View* explained her four-year absence from public life as a hiatus that enabled her to become a full-time mom. "I've sorta been home with Kelli and the kids," she said, against the backdrop of a photo montage that showed her hugging her children and kissing Kelli on the cheek. "I needed to refocus."[18]

O'Donnell frequently discussed parenting and family life as a means to connect with her cohosts, both comparing and contrasting herself to the norm. When Behar announced on the season premiere that her daughter was getting married, O'Donnell cooed over pictures of the happy couple and empathized with Behar about empty-nest syndrome. Then the topic turned to weddings—namely, Rosie and Kelli's, which had been invalidated by the California Supreme Court. "We were married and then unmarried," O'Donnell said. "We'll get to that. Not on the first day." She looked at the camera and mouthed the word "lesbian" conspiratorially, to the audience's delight. When a cohost suggested that they remarry in Massachusetts, O'Donnell scoffed at the double standard: "What, are we going to do it state by state, have fifty weddings?"[19]

At other times, cohosts remarked on the significance of Rosie's revelations. When O'Donnell casually repeated a conversation with her southern mother-in-law, Behar expressed amazement. "They call you the daughter-in-law," Behar said. "They must have come a long way from Baton Rouge. That's pretty cool." The conversation that followed detailed Rosie's rough road to acceptance from Kelli's traditional, religious family.[20]

For some gay and lesbian viewers, these intimate discussions of family life were personally as well as politically affirming. The Gay and Lesbian Alliance Against Defamation recognized O'Donnell for providing "unprecedented visibility and equality in conversation" and bringing "those stories and issues into America's living rooms." Columnists on the site AfterEllen.com, a key space for debating the representations of lesbians in media, hailed the new "out and proud" Rosie:

> she regularly refers not only to her children, but also to her wife, her in-laws, her now-rescinded marriage in San Francisco, gay marriage in general . . . and how important gay civil rights are to a civilized society. . . . Wait, this is daytime TV? On ABC? Owned by Disney? . . . She exhibits every day that gays are just like everyone else: As parents they are just as concerned about their kids' safety as straights are; they're just as caring and as crafty, just as involved and as cordial and as silly and as entitled to be treated fairly. And instead of an abstract concept, gay marriage is a real issue that's serious to someone in straight viewers' lives, even if that person only comes through their televisions for an hour a day.[21]

However, the need to present gay parents as "just like everyone else" often comes at the expense of individuality. Media portrayals of same-sex families—the documentary *All Aboard* among them—tend to present them as virtuous and harmonious to counter cultural prejudices against gay parenting.[22] O'Donnell, in contrast, presented a truer picture of family life. On her first *View* appearance, she asked Hasselbeck how her child's potty training was progressing. Elisabeth complained that her daughter "tinkled" in the bathtub as they bathed together. "That's love," Elisabeth groaned, "sitting in a tub of urine with your child." Rosie upped the ante with an embarrassing story of bathing with her toddler. "I take a bath with Vivi, too," she said. "Vivi always looks at me and says, 'When am I getting my fur?'" O'Donnell contorted her face for the camera, adding, "Not soon, honey—don't throw mama into a coma."[23]

O'Donnell's participation in this intimate, self-revelatory conversation serves to connect her with her cohost and to the daytime female demographic. Yet the story also evokes culturally ingrained fears about gay parenting. Rather than de-emphasizing O'Donnell's sexuality, it draws attention to her large, queer, nonmaternal body and reminds viewers of her pivotal role in shaping her adopted daughter's sexuality and sense of self. Months after the fact, this conversation circulated on YouTube primarily as evidence of O'Donnell's vulgarity rather than her parenting skills.

Toward the end of her *View* career, O'Donnell offered another provocative take on motherhood, confessing that she sometimes cursed at her young children in moments of anger and frustration. A shocked Barbara Walters rushed to clarify, "But you always hug them afterwards, right?" While the audience cheered at O'Donnell's admission of imperfect parenting, conservative critics cited this moment as evidence of her perversity.[24]

All in the Family

Family not only was a prominent theme in O'Donnell's repertoire but also structured her relationship to *The View*. In her 2007 memoir *Celebrity Detox*, O'Donnell presents her year on daytime television as an experiment in parenting and depicts the panelists as a dysfunctional family of sorts. She claims she took on the role of celebrity cohost partly because she hoped the show's morning taping schedule would allow her to divide her day between work and home, public life and private life. Instead, she claims, the role took a toll on her family by placing her under heightened media scrutiny. Her struggles to balance professional success and parenthood parallel the challenges faced by many middle-class mothers.[25]

Her cohosts, she explained, felt more like family members than coworkers. She writes that she looked up to Barbara Walters as a mother figure, seeking support and approval that Walters was often reticent to provide. (Indeed, many media reports have similarly characterized Walters as a dignified maternal figure trying desperately to reign in her unruly, bickering children.) As I discuss later in this chapter, the final argument with Hasselbeck that led to O'Donnell's abrupt departure from *The View* seemed less a matter of political difference than one of personal betrayal.[26]

The framing of *The View* as a dysfunctional family—with Rosie as its black sheep—may have made the drama that ensued more relevant and engaging for female audiences. However, the idea that these were family struggles rather than political discussions devalued the conversation by placing it in the domestic rather than the political realm. It also masked the power dynamics and corporate control happening behind the scenes, such as pressure on the female hosts to conform to male producers' directives.[27]

Tokenism and Homophobia

Even as O'Donnell offered a sympathetic and sometimes less than flattering portrait of lesbian motherhood, she both played into and challenged expectations placed on her as the panel's token lesbian. As feminist scholars have theorized, tokenism places individual minorities in the uncomfortable position of constantly speaking for their group and being solely responsible for educating others about discrimination.[28]

Early in her *View* career, O'Donnell accused fellow talk-show host Kelly Ripa of making a homophobic remark, arguing with Ripa via conference call as her cohosts watched.[29] On a subsequent show in February 2007, O'Donnell discussed the controversy surrounding a short-lived Snickers commercial that showed two straight men accidentally kissing, reacting in horror, and tearing out tufts of their chest hair to reassert their masculinity. While Hasselbeck and Behar claimed that the commercial innocently made fun of "macho guys who are homophobic," O'Donnell defended activists' opposition to the ad. "The implication is that there is something so wrong with two men kissing that you need to do something and that two men kissing cannot be manly. In a country where the president says that gay people are not equal to the protections under the Constitution, it's very hard not to feel sensitive," she said, her voice trailing off. Yet she defended a diversity of opinion among LGBT viewers. "Not every gay person thought it was unfunny." O'Donnell herself had a neutral reaction to the ad, and her children found it "hysterical." When Hasselbeck thanked O'Donnell for helping her see the commercial in a new light, Rosie chided her for her lack of awareness. "I'm tired of being the gay police," she snapped. "That's how I feel on this show."[30]

In an earlier appearance, O'Donnell had refused to join in the grilling of Jim McGreevey, the former New Jersey governor who had hidden his sexual orientation and cheated on his wife before resigning in disgrace. She later expressed knowledge of the social pressures that compelled him to cheat. "It seemed to me he was the typical nerdy gay Irish Catholic kid. [He] couldn't come out. I get it," she wrote in *Celebrity Detox*.[31]

Warring with Donald Trump

O'Donnell wasn't quite as forgiving when it came to Donald Trump's infidelities. In her memoir, O'Donnell claims that her outburst against Trump in December 2006 was a spur-of-the-moment impulse stemming from her distaste for beauty pageants and paternalistic control of women's sexuality.[32] When Trump publicly chastised a Miss USA contestant who had been caught partying, O'Donnell sided with the young woman. She flipped her hair into a fake toupee and entertained the crowd with an unflattering impression of Trump, then offered her view. "He's the moral authority," she said, sarcastically. "Left the first wife, had an affair. Left the second wife, had an affair. Had kids both times, but he's the moral compass for twenty-year-olds in America. Donald, sit and spin, my friend," she pronounced, as her cohosts laughed uproariously. She later compared Trump to a "snake-oil salesman" who went bankrupt and cheated his creditors. In this moment, a flawed but faithful lesbian mother claimed moral superiority over a powerful patriarch—and paid a high price.[33]

Although O'Donnell joked on the show that Trump was likely to sue her, she claimed to be taken aback by the personal attacks that came her way. Trump responded by berating her physical appearance and threatening Rosie's relationship with Kelli. He pitted Barbara Walters against O'Donnell by criticizing her decision to hire the caustic comedian. O'Donnell fought back, joking at a media awards luncheon that she couldn't care less if a "balding billionaire" found her sexually attractive. "Eat me," she beckoned to her critics, grabbing her crotch. Conservatives castigated O'Donnell for her outburst, claiming that the routine was inappropriate for the occasion and offensive to the teenagers attending the luncheon.[34]

Increasingly, O'Donnell's comedic antics and political platforms were perceived as crude and out of control. Critics compiled a catalog of her worst moments: She offended Asian Americans by using the words "ching chong" to mimic Chinese speech in December 2006—later offering what some considered a halfhearted apology. She asked whether Iraqis might perceive the invading Americans as terrorists. She lent credence to conspiracy theories in March 2007 by suggesting that the U.S. government had foreknowledge of the September 11 attacks. She called for Bush's impeachment more than once.[35] Throughout her fiery stint on *The View,* she reportedly refused to wear an earpiece that would connect her to conservative producers' directives and urged her cohosts to do the same. "I am not a puppet," she wrote in her memoir. "Make TV live, truly live."[36]

The View's conversations about public policy often devolved into shouting matches, with O'Donnell on one side and Hasselbeck on the other. Although the outbursts may have been in character for O'Donnell, they defied expectations for a daytime talk show. And O'Donnell was hardly humble about her contribution to the conversation: "You've never talked about real issues until this year," she told her cohosts.[37] Conservative Fox News commentator Bill O'Reilly, who had earlier expressed a grudging respect for O'Donnell, reacted strongly to *The View*'s change of tone, accusing Rosie of turning a "coffee klatch into Al Jazeera West." Critics were clearly threatened by her role as a loud-mouthed Hollywood liberal with a live forum. As O'Reilly said: "If Rosie O'Donnell were a serious person with serious credentials, fine. I mean, if Hillary Clinton made these same comments about 9/11 [being] an inside job, you go to the bookstore and you confront her and no problem."[38]

O'Donnell's sexual orientation amplified the threat she posed to critics. Conservatives claimed that she had protected status as a lesbian, that ABC's need to demonstrate acceptance of her sexual orientation was the main reason she was not censured and fired. To the contrary, O'Donnell asserted on *The View* that her openly lesbian status made her politics more threatening, that she was seen as a large lavender menace picking on "poor little Elisabeth."[39]

Ratings and Realities

O'Donnell's escalating antics put ABC in a bind: although the feuds provided a boost for the show's ratings, Rosie's untamed tongue threatened to alienate advertisers and risked legal problems for the network. O'Donnell had been recruited partly to enhance the show's marketing appeal by performing advertising jingles and announcing product giveaways.[40] O'Reilly continually reminded his viewers that ABC is owned by Disney and that the family-friendly company should be ashamed of O'Donnell's "anti-patriotic" views.[41] Furthermore, the furor over radio host Don Imus's racist comments in 2007 provoked media outlets to police outspoken personalities more closely—and led conservatives to claim that O'Donnell herself had made racial slurs (the "ching chong" remark) and perpetuated "hate speech" against soldiers and fundamentalist Christians on a daily basis.[42]

Despite her many detractors, O'Donnell's presence was good for business. Even as her own approval ratings plummeted, *The View*'s overall viewership rose by 17 percent and increased even more dramatically among women aged eighteen to thirty-four, a key consumer group. Whether viewers loved or hated O'Donnell, they couldn't stop watching.[43]

New Beginnings

In April 2007 O'Donnell announced she planned to leave her *View* post after only a year; ABC had reportedly sought a three-year contract. Her career on the panel came to a dramatic halt the following month when a heated argument with Hasselbeck escalated to name-calling. Hurt that Hasselbeck had failed to defend her in a media interview, O'Donnell called her cohost a "coward" and accused her of "double-speak." That ABC captured the argument in a split-screen format, visually pitting the women against each other, cemented O'Donnell's decision to resign. Walters denied any role in O'Donnell's decision, and the panel show entered its eleventh season with Whoopi Goldberg as O'Donnell's replacement. (Roseanne Barr had also been considered for the role.)[44]

Rosie O'Donnell may be absent from daytime television, but she has maintained a formative presence in popular culture. She followed her abrupt *View* departure with a tell-all memoir and joined the "True Colors" celebrity tour to benefit the Human Rights Campaign. Although a proposed MSNBC news talk show with Rosie at the helm failed to materialize, NBC selected her to host a prime-time variety special in November 2008.[45]

O'Donnell also commands a presence on blogs and sites such as You-Tube, where she is alternately vilified and idolized for her personal politics. Her own Web site provides a forum that is uncensored, deeply personal, and entirely self-directed. While webcam videos show her at home without makeup and subject to the glare of unflattering lighting, Rosie posts poems and personal responses to fans in text speak, a style she claims mimics stream of consciousness. O'Donnell claims to be "detoxing" from her recent celebrity stint and relishing her return to a more domestic role. Yet her blog, comedy tours, and television guest appearances maintain a captive audience just waiting for her to resurface—out, proud, and as outrageous as ever.[46]

Notes

1. *All Aboard! Rosie's Family Cruise,* DVD, directed by Shari Cookson (New York: HBO Home Video, 2006).

2. Marc Peyser, "Rosie's New View," *Newsweek,* September 11, 2006, 50.

3. Ibid.; "Rosie O'Donnell Marries Girlfriend in San Francisco," CNN.com, February 27, 2004, http://www.cnn.com/2004/SHOWBIZ/TV/02/26/odonnell.ap/index.html (accessed November 18, 2008).

4. Rosie O'Donnell, interview by Larry King, *Larry King Weekend,* CNN, March 16, 2002, http://transcripts.cnn.com/TRANSCRIPTS/0203/16/lklw.00.html (accessed November 18, 2008); Peyser, "Rosie's New View."

5. O'Donnell interview by King.

6. "Rosie O'Donnell Marries Girlfriend."

7. Sean Cahill, *Same-Sex Marriage in the United States: Focus on the Facts* (Lanham, MD: Lexington Books, 2004), 31.

8. Human Rights Campaign, "Statewide Marriage Prohibitions," November 6, 2008, http://www.hrc.org/documents/marriage_prohibitions.pdf (accessed November 18, 2008).

9. Cahill, *Same-Sex Marriage,* 98–99.

10. Ibid., 27–38.

11. Judith Levine, "Why Gays Should Oppose Same-Sex Marriage," in *Gay Marriage,* ed. Kate Burns (Farmington Hills, MI: Thomson Gale, 2005), 78. This article originally appeared in the July 23–29, 2003, edition of the *Village Voice.*

12. Gail Shister, "Rosie Leaving 'View,'" *Philadelphia Inquirer,* April 26, 2007, D1. Shister writes that "hit daytime talker Ellen DeGeneres, who came out publicly several years before O'Donnell, avoids discussions on her show of her sexuality." For an earlier analysis, see Malinda Lo, "The Incredible Story of Ellen DeGeneres: The Rise and Fall and Rise Again of a Reluctant Lesbian Icon," AfterEllen.com, February 2004, http://www.afterellen.com/archive/ellen/People/ellen/html (accessed September 16, 2009).

13. Jane Shattuc, *The Talking Cure: TV Talk Shows and Women* (New York: Routledge, 1997), 48–49.

14. "Rosie Future May Turn Ugly," *Toronto Star,* May 1, 2006, E3.

15. Ann Marie Kerwin, "Ms. Walters' View of Rosie," *Mediaworks,* September 25, 2006, 28; Jacques Steinberg, "On 'The View,' New Face, New Dynamics," *New York Times,* September 21, 2006, E1; Rosie O'Donnell, *Celebrity Detox: The Fame Game* (New York: Grand Central Publishing, 2007), 70.

16. Marisa Guthrie, "ABC Takes Slim 'View' of Rosie," *New York Daily News,* September 1, 2006, 122; Rebecca Traister, "No Butch Hair for Rosie," *Salon*.com, July 11, 2006, http://www.salon.com/mwt/broadsheet/2006/05/02/rosie/ (accessed November 18, 2008).

17. *The View,* ABC, September 5, 2006.

18. Ibid.

19. Ibid.

20. *The View,* ABC, October 18, 2006.

21. Shister, "Rosie Leaving 'View,'" D1; Anna Wahrman, "Rosie Returns Loud and Proud on *The View,*" AfterEllen.com, November 6, 2006, http://www.afterellen.com/archive/ellen/TV/2006/11/rosie.html (accessed November 18, 2008).

22. Joy Matkowski, "Offensive Review of Rosie O'Donnell's 'Cruise,'" *Washington Post,* April 15, 2006, A13.

23. *The View,* ABC, September 5, 2006.

24. Bill O'Reilly, "Adieu to Rosie," *Creators Syndicate,* April 28, 2007, http://www.creators.com/opinion/bill-oreilly/adieu-to-rosie.html (accessed November 18, 2008).

25. O'Donnell, *Celebrity Detox,* 22.

26. Ibid., 7, 10; Tara Ariano, "Rosie's Wonderful Week," *National Post,* September 11, 2006, AL9.

27. O'Donnell, *Celebrity Detox,* 155–59.

28. For a foundational argument about tokenism, see Audre Lorde, "The Master's Tools Will Never Dismantle the Master's House," in *Sister Outsider: Essays and Speeches by Audre Lorde* (Freedom, CA: Crossing Press, 1984), 110–13.

29. *The View,* ABC, November 21, 2006.

30. *The View,* ABC, February 6, 2007.

31. O'Donnell, *Celebrity Detox,* 92–93. McGreevey appeared on *The View* on September 20, 2006.

32. Ibid., 143.

33. *The View,* ABC, December 20, 2007.

34. John Gibson, "Rosie to Leave 'The View,'" *The Big Story with John Gibson,* Fox News, April 25, 2007.

35. Jacques Steinberg, "Rosie O'Donnell Says She Will Say Goodbye to 'The View' in June," *New York Times,* April 26, 2007, E1; John Gibson, "Rosie O'Donnell Calls for Impeachment of President Bush," *The Big Story with John Gibson,* Fox News, March 28, 2007.

36. O'Donnell, *Celebrity Detox,* 57, 85.

37. *The View,* ABC, May 3, 2007.

38. Bill O'Reilly, "How Is Media Covering Elections? OK to Ambush Rosie?" *The O'Reilly Factor,* Fox News, November 1, 2007.

39. Gibson, "Rosie O'Donnell Calls for Impeachment."

40. Steinberg, "On 'The View,' New Face, New Dynamics," E1.

41. O'Reilly, "Adieu to Rosie."

42. Bill O'Reilly, "The Rosie Factor," *Creators Syndicate,* April 7, 2007, http://www.creators.com/opinion/bill-oreilly/the-rosie-factor.html (accessed November 18, 2008).

43. John Maynard, "'The View' Suddenly in Rosie's Rearview," *Washington Post,* May 26, 2007, C1; Larry King, "What Happened on 'The View' Today?" *Larry King Live,* CNN, May 23, 2007.

44. *The View,* ABC, May 23, 2007; King, "What Happened on 'The View' Today?"

45. Carlis Davis, "Rosie O'Donnell Loses MSNBC Talk Show," *People*.com, November 8, 2007, http://www.people.com/people/article/0,,20159089,00.html (accessed November 20, 2008); Michael Schneider, "Rosie to Get 'Variety Show' on NBC," *Variety,* October 1, 2008, http://www.variety.com/VR1117993209.html (accessed November 18, 2008).

46. O'Donnell, *Celebrity Detox,* 12. O'Donnell's Web site is located at http://www.rosie.com/.

8

"GABBIN' ABOUT GOD"

Religion, Secularity, and Satire on *The Simpsons*

Matthew Henry

> Many people [in America] remain convinced of God's existence but realize increasingly that the reality of their world is secular. Thus, they are constantly coming to terms with this secularity—and suffering the pangs of adjustment associated with acquiring any new status.
>
> —Robert Wuthnow, *After Heaven*

Religion is undoubtedly a prominent element of *The Simpsons,* and the highly contentious issues related to it are featured in episodes on a regular basis, either centrally or tangentially. Not surprisingly, no topic on *The Simpsons* has garnered more written commentary than religion, and the ensuing discussions have led to some of the most diverse interpretations of the show among fans and scholars alike.[1] This raises some important questions about how *The Simpsons* engages the ongoing tension between religious and secular forces in the United States. Does *The Simpsons* operate from a theological or a philosophical position? Does it promote a religious worldview or a secular one? Answering such questions, of course, is not easy and requires careful consideration of the show and its historical contexts: namely, the rise of the Religious Right in the 1980s, the increasing influence of religiosity during the 1990s, the debates over the roles of science and religion in the public sphere, and the intensification of religious fundamentalism in the post-9/11 environment. As the growing body of scholarship on *The Simpsons* attests, the show does more than simply mirror modern American life; it also regularly intervenes

Never shying away from controversial issues, *The Simpsons,* television's longest-running animated series, offers its own perspective on institutionalized religion and the American culture wars. (Jerry Ohlinger's Movie Material Store)

in the heated debates surrounding many of the issues gathered under the umbrella of "culture wars," including racial integration, affirmative action, social welfare, prayer in schools, feminism, abortion, gay and lesbian rights, and the increased secularization of society.

A truly comprehensive treatment of religion and spirituality in *The Simpsons* is beyond the scope of this chapter; my treatment here is more selective and focuses only on the Judeo-Christian tradition that informs *The Simpsons* and the various ways in which this tradition is understood, represented, and commented on within the show. In general, I concur with the view of many commentators that *The Simpsons* is, overall, a very spiritual show; faith in both family and community, as well as the compassion for others so commonly portrayed on *The Simpsons,* comes across as quite sincere. However, the fact that such positive qualities exist does not necessarily make *The Simpsons* a religious program. Although the Simpson family is associated by tradition with Christianity and Protestantism, this is modified in significant ways; in short, the "goodness" of the Simpsons is not presented as deriving solely from religion. Moreover, institutional religion (Christianity, in particular) is most often present on *The Simpsons* only to be satirized, usually via the comments and behaviors of the two representatives of religion, Reverend Timothy Lovejoy and Ned Flanders. Marge and Lisa Simpson, who are inevitably the moral centers of the show, sometimes behave in accordance with Judeo-Christian religious beliefs; however, more often than not, they each operate from a philosophical and secularized perspective. And although one can find examples of what appear to be "Christian" beliefs on the show, one must acknowledge that these examples can just as easily be seen as Humanist, since the more beneficent tenets of New Testament Christianity (compassion, brotherhood, love) run parallel to those of secular Humanism.[2]

I do not presume to speak here for Matt Groening or for the various writers and producers of *The Simpsons* regarding their personal religious or spiritual beliefs. In general, they have been reluctant to express their own beliefs, although many have stated that they are Jewish, and some have admitted in interviews to being former Catholics or atheists. Steve Tompkins, who was a writer for *The Simpsons* for three seasons and worked as a coproducer alongside George Meyer and Mike Scully, has been most overt about such affiliations: he claims that *The Simpsons'* writers are "atheist Jews or atheist Christians" and that during his tenure with the show, only two writers were "churchgoing Christians."[3] Regardless of the individual faiths of those involved in creating the show, the predominant worldview on display in *The Simpsons* is generally in accord with the worldly, progressive, left-leaning position the show takes on many issues.

One quality that has kept *The Simpsons* so successful is its chameleon-like ability to blur boundaries, and its treatment of religion is an excellent example. If one looks carefully at *The Simpsons,* one can see that alongside religion lies a faith in humankind and a moral and ethical stance that is based, more often than not, in reason and rationality rather than religious doctrine. Although I understand how the subtle humor of *The Simpsons* can prod the believer into seeing some aspect of his or her faith reflected, if not validated, I am less inclined to see the show redeeming Christianity as a faith system or, as Jamey Heit puts it, "helping Christianity retain its cultural relevance."[4] Indeed, I believe *The Simpsons* aims to question (and perhaps lessen) the authority of Christianity through its satirical attacks on institutional religion and to promote a more ecumenical, individual, and secularized worldview. In short, I believe that provocative cultural issues are brought into the world of *The Simpsons*—and into the homes of its viewers—to showcase and satirize the hypocrisy, bigotry, and narrow-mindedness of institutional Christianity and to censure the zealotry of religious fundamentalism.

Culture Wars and American Religiosity

The debate between religious and secular forces in the United States is very old, predating the establishment of the nation itself, and its intensity waxed and waned throughout the eighteenth and nineteenth centuries. The debate was given renewed life, however, in the second half of the twentieth century, partly due to the advent of television, which provided a new and powerful means by which both religious and secular groups could disseminate messages, but primarily due to the social and political upheavals of the late 1950s and 1960s. In general, since the end of the Second World War, evangelicals and religious fundamentalists have been concerned about many "secularizing" trends in the United States that have, in their view, moved the nation further toward pluralistic and relativistic perspectives. Indeed, as recent studies of religious affiliation and belief show, over the past forty years there has been a slow but steady movement away from traditional organized religions and toward a variety of more secular perspectives and activities. Currently, individuals who are not affiliated with any particular religion make up about one-sixth (16.1 percent) of the adult population and thus constitute the fourth largest "religious" tradition in the country.[5] It is, of course, these kinds of social shifts that initially inspired—and in many ways continue to fuel—the so-called culture wars of the post–civil rights era.

Some of the emphasis in these cultural debates has been on the way certain values or belief systems are reflected in or excluded from the mainstream media, including television. In a now famous study of religion and spirituality on American network television in the early 1990s, researcher Thomas Skill and his colleagues determined that religion was "a rather invisible institution" in prime-time television.[6] In a more recent study, researcher Scott Clarke showed that prime-time characters were more than twice as likely as the general public to belong to a religion other than Christianity or to embrace a more individualized "spirituality."[7] Although Clarke's study clearly indicates that religion remains "rather invisible" on prime-time network television, it also points up the fact that Christianity continues to be, by default, a "normative" religion on television, whereas non-Christian religions are overtly identified. *The Simpsons* is unique in that both Christian and non-Christian religions, as well as forms of secular spirituality, are not only visible but consciously foregrounded as important aspects of the geography of Springfield, the daily lives of many of the show's characters, and the plots of innumerable episodes.

That religion figures so prominently in *The Simpsons* is not surprising, given the context in which the show developed. Although *The Simpsons* debuted as a television series in 1990, the Simpson family was created by Groening in 1985 and was first offered to viewers as part of Fox's *Tracey Ullman Show* in 1987. Hence, *The Simpsons* appeared in the midst of the Reagan-Bush era, a time of revival and intensification of evangelical and fundamentalist religiosity in the United States. Among other things, the 1970s and 1980s were witness to the rise of the Religious Right (sometimes called the Christian Right) and the advent of the culture wars, which often (but not exclusively) involved the differing positions taken by religious and secular camps on a variety of moral and legal issues. Although a powerful evangelical tradition was in place in the United States in the earliest decades of the twentieth century, this tradition operated largely outside of the political sphere. The development of a more politically engaged evangelism began with the responses of certain fundamentalist leaders to the Supreme Court rulings in *Engel v. Vitale* (1962) and *Abington School District v. Schempp* (1963), which banned prayer and Bible reading, respectively, from public schools. Religious fundamentalists became even more visible and vocal in their criticism of secularization in the wake of the Supreme Court's decision in *Roe v. Wade* (1973). These Supreme Court rulings, in addition to other secularizing trends in the culture, provided the impetus for the formation of a host of far-right religious organizations and the rise to national prominence of their leaders—most notably Jerry Falwell, Pat Robertson, James Dobson, Don Wildmon, Louis Sheldon, Gary Bauer, Ralph Reed, and William Dono-hue—who increasingly turned their attention to national politics.[8]

The social and political influence of Religious Right leaders and orga-nizations in the 1970s and 1980s, particularly during the Reagan-Bush era, marked a significant shift in American culture. During this same period, Groening was still struggling with his *Life in Hell* comic, and many of the writers for *The Simpsons* were still honing their skills on programs such as *Late Night with David Letterman, Not Necessarily the News,* and *Saturday Night Live.* By the late 1980s, when the work of turning *The Simpsons* into a series was begun, the creators of the show were working in a context in which evangelical and fundamentalist religiosity was a dominant part of the cultural and political landscape of the United States. As George Marsden notes, "secular humanism" came to be the conceptual framework for under-standing the convergence of the many secularizing trends and thus "the code word for enemy forces in the dichotomized world" of the culture wars.[9] The tenor of this cultural conflict in the early 1990s was perhaps best epitomized by Patrick Buchanan's fiery statement at the Republican National Conven-tion in 1992. "There is a religious war going on in this country," Buchanan said, "a cultural war as critical to the kind of nation we shall be as the Cold War itself, for this war is for the soul of America."[10]

It was inevitable that *The Simpsons* would become engaged in this "war," partly because of its status as a social satire, and partly because of the con-demnation it received from conservative political and religious quarters after its debut in the spring of 1990.[11] Although *The Simpsons* does not explicitly reference Religious Right leaders or organizations, their collective influ-ence is reflected in the show in many ways, including the characterization of religious believers, such as Reverend Lovejoy and Ned Flanders, and the framing of many episodes around the hot-button moral issues that have been politicized by those on either side of the culture war debates, such as abortion and gay marriage. These and many other controversial issues make their way into the scripts of *The Simpsons* in both large and small ways, and they are often positioned within the plotlines so they directly engage with and question, if not censure, religious traditions and dogma.

The Simpsons, Christianity, and Fundamentalism

Given its regular presentation of prayer, church attendance, and other religious activities, in addition to its engagement with moral and theological issues, it is not surprising that some have called *The Simpsons* a "Christian" show. In its earliest seasons, *The Simpsons* did appear to be aligned with mainstream Protestantism, and it generally reflected the mores and behaviors typical of those following the Judeo-Christian tradition. Most notable, perhaps, was the second-season episode "Homer vs. Lisa and the 8th Commandment," which links morality and religion via Homer's desire for and Lisa's protest against an illegal cable connection. It would be much more accurate, however, to describe the worldview of *The Simpsons* as Judaic: although the generic Protestantism of Springfield does derive from a Judeo-Christian tradition, it is the Old Testament that is most frequently referred to, quoted, parodied, and satirized on the show. As Heit notes, "A general tendency within Springfield is to focus heavily on the issues of prohibition, judgment, and God's punishment that pervade the Old Testament."[12] I would argue that this is a general tendency among the writers for *The Simpsons* (many of whom are Jewish, former Catholics, or atheists), who are highlighting and satirizing the continued emphasis on God's wrath in the rhetoric of Christian fundamentalists today. Nonetheless, after the publication of Mark Pinsky's *The Gospel According to* The Simpsons in 2001, religious and political conservatives, who had initially condemned the show, reconsidered and even attempted to (re)claim *The Simpsons* for Christian believers. However, since the show is often less than flattering to religion, this reclamation came in the guise of "family values," a phrase that remains code for religious conservatism in U.S. culture. In the foreword to Pinsky's book, for example, Professor Tony Campolo claims that, "contrary to what some critics say, the Simpsons are basically a decent family with good values. They go to church on Sunday."[13] The syntax here is quite revealing: Campolo clearly implies a connection between church attendance and possessing "good values," thereby dismissing the idea that their values could possibly derive from something or somewhere else. This is a remarkably simplistic link, yet it is a central tenet of the "family values" and "pro-family" Religious Right.

As stated at the outset, *The Simpsons* has a very strong spirituality, but institutional religion—particularly Christianity—is most often present only to be satirized, most commonly through the words and actions of Reverend Lovejoy and Ned Flanders. A fine example of this satirical quality can be found in *The Simpsons'* presentation of prayer, particularly the contrasting representations of the (in)efficacy of prayer for Lovejoy and Flanders. For example, in the episode "She of Little Faith," after Homer inadvertently destroys the First Church of Springfield, Lovejoy convenes the church council to assess the damage. "Fixing all that damage is going to be very expensive," Marge says. "Yes," Lovejoy responds, "barring some sort of miracle," at which point he turns, looks heavenward, and expectantly waits a few beats. When nothing happens, he turns back and says, with a hint of resentment, "All right, we'll help ourselves . . . yet again."[14] In stark contrast, we see that Ned Flanders's prayers, no matter how trivial, are answered immediately. In "A Star Is Burns," for example, we see Ned filming a scene from Exodus for the Springfield Film Festival, using his son Todd to replicate the scene in which Moses' mother places her baby in a basket in the river. When a sudden strong current grabs the basket and threatens to send it far downriver, Ned hastily prays: "Flanders to God, Flanders to God, get off your cloud and save my Todd." Immediately, lightning strikes a tree and a branch falls into the river to block the path of the basket. "Thanks, God," Ned says.[15] Heit concedes that such scenes are "contrived," but he disregards any satirical intent by claiming that these examples suggest "that prayer, when appropriately presented, has efficacy."[16] To me, the highly exaggerated way in which Flanders's faith is portrayed seems to be an indication of satire: the writers are satirizing the presumption that, through prayer, one has the power to effect immediate change in one's physical environment.

To fully understand how and why the representation of prayer is satirical, it is important to consider the context in which it arises. Many of the religious leaders prominent in the 1990s claimed to communicate directly with God and stated that their prayers could, among other things, avert or even cause a variety of natural disasters. Pat Robertson, for example, claimed in 1995 that his prayers to God helped steer Hurricane Felix away from coastal Virginia (which happens to be where his Christian Broadcasting Network is headquartered). In due form, the writers of *The Simpsons* incorporated such cultural elements for satirical ends. Only a year after Robertson's claims, *The Simpsons* premiered an episode entitled "Hurricane Neddy," in which Ned Flanders's house is destroyed by a hurricane and he momentarily questions his faith in God. "Hurricane Neddy" is quite revealing about how the show deals with both faith and prayer. Prior to the storm, the Simpson family gathers in the cellar of their home, where Marge prays to God to spare their house. After the storm passes, they emerge to find their house intact. Pleased, Marge says, "It just goes to show you that everything will work out if you have faith." Clearly, however, that is not the case, as the Flanders house has been utterly destroyed. Ned, who considers himself a devout Christian, assumes that he is being punished by God, although he cannot fathom why—as he notes, he does "everything the Bible says, even the stuff that contradicts the other stuff."[17] Such contradictions are what the writers of *The Simpson* latch on to to satirize religiosity. In this and other episodes, it is clear that they intend to mock a number of beliefs, including the idea that the "reverent" have some exclusive access to God; the belief that God would, at their behest, micromanage the lives of individuals; and the notion that the "faithful" are treated in some preferential way.

Flanders's fundamentalism is evident, of course, from the start of *The Simpsons*. One early example is "Homer the Heretic," which aired in October 1992 and is perhaps the most widely analyzed and commented on episode of *The Simpsons*. It concerns Homer's decision to skip church and, subsequently, to abandon his faith altogether in search of a more individualized, spiritual path. Marge, positioned in this episode as a devout Christian, is understandably concerned and calls on Reverend Lovejoy to intervene, but she and Lovejoy fail to persuade Homer to return to church. Ned Flanders, who has heard of Homer's "heresy," makes it his family's mission to win Homer "back to the flock." The satirical critique of religious fundamentalism is well demonstrated in one short sequence involving Ned's missionary zeal. After trying to convert Homer in person and over the phone, Ned and his family confront Homer in his car. "Leave me alone," Homer grumbles, and speeds off. "Dad," Todd says, "the heathen's getting away." "I see him, son," Ned says, narrowing his eyes. What ensues is a high-speed car chase through Springfield. Homer, desperate to escape, sees an opportunity at a railroad crossing and accelerates his car, making it over the tracks just in advance of the approaching train. Surprisingly, Ned also accelerates rather than stopping, despite the fact that the train is now blocking the road; Ned's car safely leaps though a gap, and the pursuit continues. Given the wide range of viewing positions, it is conceivable that someone could interpret this moment as an act of "divine intervention." But to do so, one must ignore the markers of satire: the scene is highly exaggerated, bordering on the absurd. That the otherwise intelligent and caring Ned Flanders would risk the lives of his family to "save" Homer is somewhat surprising, given that Flanders is normally more mild-mannered. Considering the Flanders family's earlier harassment of Homer and their casting of him as a "heathen," not to mention the generally satirical aims of *The Simpsons,* this scene is most appropriately read as a condemnation of zealotry.[18]

Remarkably, none of the commentary on "Homer the Heretic" includes a discussion of the car-chase scene; most commentators focus instead on Ned's later efforts to save Homer in a physical sense, after Homer inadvertently sets his house on fire. Ned is seen to be doing the "Christian thing" by entering the house, risking his own life, and dragging Homer to safety. Shortly thereafter, the volunteer fire department arrives to put out the fire as Homer and Lisa stand watching. "Truly, this was an act of God," Lisa says, still invested, like Homer, in the concept of a vengeful God. At this point the flames from the roof leap over to the Flanders rooftop. "Hey, wait a minute," Homer says, "Flanders is a regular Charlie Church, and God didn't save his house." With that, a dark cloud appears above Flanders's house and, to the strains of a pipe organ, releases rain to douse the fire, after which a rainbow appears. "D'oh!" Homer exclaims. Like the scenes discussed earlier involving prayer, this is another moment that is open to multiple interpretations, highly dependent on the viewer's social position, experiences, and beliefs. One can see how a religious "believer" might read this scene in "Homer the Heretic" as affirming the idea that God plays favorites, punishing Homer for his heresy and rewarding Flanders for his faith. However, to read the text in this way is to ignore the irony and the gratuitous exaggeration and thus to miss the satirical critique.

In the final scene of "Homer the Heretic," everyone is gathered in the Simpsons' kitchen, where they discuss the "moral" of Homer's experience. Asked by Marge if he has learned his lesson, Homer replies that he has learned that God is vengeful. Lovejoy laughs and tells Homer that God didn't set his house on fire. "But he was working in the hearts of your friends and neighbors," Lovejoy says, gesturing toward Ned, Krusty, and Apu, "whether they be Christian, Jew, or . . . miscellaneous." "Hindu," Apu says; "there are seven hundred million of us, you know." "Aw, that's super," Lovejoy responds. Oddly, Lovejoy's dismissive observation and condescending reply to Apu are not examined in any of the analyses of "Homer the Heretic" either. In their essay on this episode, Lisle Dalton, Eric Michael Mazur, and Monica Siems subordinate Lovejoy's comments to a parenthetical phrase, offering no reflection on them whatsoever, yet they later claim that Lovejoy's overall view "represents the sort of generic Christianity prevalent in today's mainline Protestant churches and in most television portrayals of religion."[19]

Based on Lovejoy's attitude toward Hindus (and presumably other faiths outside the Judeo-Christian tradition), it would be more accurate to say that Lovejoy represents a generic ignorance and prejudice, which is also prevalent in certain mainline churches today—for example, in "megachurches" such as the Thomas Road Baptist Church in Virginia, the Saddleback Church in California, and the Fellowship Church in Texas—and which is clearly the target of the satire in "Homer the Heretic." In *Understanding Theology and Popular Culture,* Gordon Lynch briefly discusses "Homer the Heretic" and claims that, in the end, Lovejoy voices a "humane and tolerant vision of religion," altogether ignoring Lovejoy's rather intolerant dismissal of Apu's faith as "miscellaneous."[20] Considering how the narrative resolves itself, it is a mistake to argue, as Lynch does, that "the narrative tends towards a view that organized religion is a good thing in so far as it makes people more humane and concerned for those around them."[21] But organized religion had nothing to do with the compassion extended to Homer: he was saved by the collective efforts of Ned Flanders and the Springfield volunteer fire department, which includes Krusty the Klown, a secularized Jew who does not practice Judaism, and Apu, a Hindu who is not part of an institutionalized tradition in Springfield. It is quite a stretch to say that the humanity of Krusty and Apu is derived from organized religion and thereby to dismiss the satirical critiques of fundamentalism and intolerance offered in this episode.

The evangelical and fundamentalist aspects of the Flanders family are also satirized quite effectively in "Home Sweet Home-Diddily-Dum-Doodily," which first aired in October 1995. Due to a variety of mishaps and misunderstandings, the Simpson children are taken away from Marge and Homer by Child Protective Services and placed in foster care with the Flanders family. In the course of playing a game called "Bombardment . . . of Bible Trivia," Flanders discovers that Bart and Lisa are not baptized; after recovering from this shock, Flanders takes it upon himself to "save" the kids from their "hell-bound family" and brings them to the Springfield River for a ritual baptism. The final scenes of the episode speak powerfully of Ned's zealotry and the satirical aims of *The Simpsons.* When Marge and Homer discover Ned's intentions, they are both angry and race to the river to stop him. They arrive just in time to see Ned about to anoint Bart with a drop of holy water. "Noooo!" Homer cries, and dives toward Bart to knock him out of the way. In the process, Homer himself is hit by the droplet of holy water, at which point we hear an audible hiss, and Homer begins to writhe and thrash in the water, presumably because his demonic self is being seared by the power of God. Bart runs to Homer and says, "Wow, Dad, you took a baptismal for me. How do you feel?" Homer, in a reverent tone, replies, "Oh, Bartholomew, I feel like St. Augustine of Hippo after his conversion by Ambrose of Milan." Ned, understandably shocked, asks, "Homer, what did you just say?" "I said shut your ugly face, Flanders!" Homer yells, clearly over his momentary conversion. The ridiculousness of this scene indicates that the writers are satirizing a variety of things, including Ned's view of the world as a stark contrast between good and evil, the belief that holy water has some kind of power to fight evil, and the idea that religious conversion can be so easily attained. Above all, however, the episode is most invested in satirizing the actions of religious fundamentalists, represented by Ned, who operate out of sheer zealotry, without regard for the beliefs and values of those they condemn or proselytize.

As the seasons have progressed, the satire on *The Simpsons* has become more specifically directed against evangelical Protestantism and the religious fundamentalism this often generates, and the tone has become increasingly harsh. As Chris Turner accurately notes in *Planet Simpson*, after the first few seasons, Ned Flanders and his family became "an extended satirical study in American evangelical Christianity." According to Turner, "*The Simpsons'* writers have lost patience with the Flanders brand of fundamentalist Christianity in recent years, their somewhat playful ribbing turning into palpable disgust."[22] A fine example of this appears in the season 12 episode "HOMR," which aired in January 2001. Although the central narrative is not concerned specifically with religious issues, there are two very potent satirical scenes that express the heightened frustration with fundamentalism that Turner mentions. In one scene, we see the Flanders boys, Rod and Todd, watching a show called *Gravey and Jobriath*, a parody of the 1960s Christian claymation program *Davey and Goliath*. Here, Gravey is busily making something in the garage. "Whatcha making there, Gravey?" Jobriath asks. "It's a pipe bomb, Jobriath, for to blow up Planned Parenthood," Gravey says. When Jobriath expresses some doubt about this action, Gravey shouts, "I'm sick of your lack of faith," then lights the bomb and stuffs it into Jobriath's mouth. An explosion is heard, and Rod and Todd righteously cheer: "Yay!"[23] We also learn in "HOMR" that Homer was once quite intelligent (he became stupid after sticking a crayon up his nose). In a flashback, we see Homer explain to Ned that he has stumbled upon a mathematical proof that definitively demonstrates God does not exist. Skeptical, Ned reviews the proof, determines it is accurate, and then whips out a lighter and sets it on fire. "Can't let this little doozy get out," Ned says. The satire here ought to be clear, as it is consistent with a point raised repeatedly on *The Simpsons:* reason and rationality have the potential to undermine the belief system fundamental to Christianity. Ned recognizes this truth and, like many before him, feels threatened. So he destroys the evidence in another example of the extremes to which believers will go to maintain the mystique of religion.

The critique of religious fundamentalism is a central part of several more recent episodes, including "Thank God, It's Doomsday" (May 2005), "The Father, the Son, and the Holy Guest Star" (May 2005), and "The Monkey Suit" (May 2006). In "Thank God, It's Doomsday," a series of events leads to Homer becoming a prophet of the Apocalypse, convinced that he knows the specific date of the Rapture and determined to warn and thus save his fellow citizens. Lisa is skeptical, of course, but so is Marge, who tells Homer he is acting "crazy." Collectively, Marge, Lisa, and Bart express their concern, telling Homer they don't believe the world is coming to an end and asking him to "lighten up on the *left below* stuff." However, as usual, the residents of Springfield exhibit a group-think mentality and are quickly persuaded to follow Homer to Springfield Mesa and await the Rapture. Although Homer is an unlikely (and ultimately unreliable) prophet, they are willing to listen to his advice. On Judgment Day, Springfield's residents dutifully gather and take a bus to the Mesa. Of course, at the appointed time specified by Homer, nothing happens: there is no Rapture. Everyone waits patiently—a few minutes, then a few hours—but they finally realize the end is not coming and leave, muttering angry curses at Homer. After discovering an error in his calculations, Homer recalculates and concludes that the Rapture is due later that same day. At this point, however, no one is willing to listen to him, so Homer goes alone to the Mesa and settles in to await the Judgment. He soon falls asleep and dreams of the Rapture.

In Homer's dream, heaven is like a resort spa, complete with concierge, hotel rooms, and entertaining activities. Homer enjoys himself until he inquires about those "left below." He is then shown (on a large-screen television) an image of his suffering family, surrounded by a lake of fire and being tormented by the devil. Disturbed, Homer goes to speak to God about the situation. "God," Homer says, "you've got a first-class destination resort here—really top-notch—but I can't enjoy myself knowing my family is suffering." "Oh, don't tell me about family suffering," God replies. "My son went down to Earth once. I don't know what you people did to him, but he hasn't been the same since." The camera then pans to an image of Jesus sitting alone on a swing set, spinning aimlessly in his seat with a blank look on his face.

This is a curious moment in the episode, and it raises some provocative questions about theology and humanity. Jesus appears to be psychologically or emotionally damaged, much like a human being, which calls into question his "divine" nature. Moreover, God's comments imply that he did not send Jesus to Earth and is not aware of what happened to him there, which calls into question both the omnipotence and the omniscience of God. Finally, and perhaps most importantly, considering the concerns of the show's writers, the responsibility for the damage done to Jesus is placed on humankind—"you people," as God puts it—which could be read as a metaphorical indictment of the perversions of Christian doctrine (the harm done to the faith) or of the cruelties committed in its name (the harm done to fellow beings).

When God refuses to spare the Simpson family, Homer goes on a rampage, destroying the "resort." Like a frustrated father with an incorrigible child, God reprimands Homer and then asks him what he wants. What Homer wants, of course, is for things to return to the way they were. "To do what you're asking, I'd have to turn back time," God says. "Superman did it," Homer taunts, interestingly pitting a secular "all-powerful" being against a religious one. "Fine, mister smarty-pants," God says, "I will undo the Apocalypse." God then intones "Deus ex machina" and claps his hands, and we are returned to Homer asleep on the Mesa. "It was all just a dream," Homer says with relief, just as his family arrives. In the final scene, Homer returns to Moe's bar to be with his friends. Seated at the bar and sipping a beer, Homer quietly says, "This is heaven." At this point, the camera slowly pulls back to reveal a parodic replication of Da Vinci's *The Last Supper,* with Homer seated at the center of the iconic image in lieu of Jesus, accompanied by a chorus of voices singing "Hallelujah." This is a remarkably secular intervention into the iconic imagery of religious art, and it puts a final and clear punctuation point on the statements made in this episode: the Rapture is nothing more than the wild imagining of false prophets, and focusing so zealously on the "end-time" prevents people from appreciating and enjoying what they have in the here and now, such as a loving family, good friends, or a cold bottle of Duff.

Religious zealotry is also openly dealt with in "The Father, the Son, and the Holy Guest Star," which aired just one week after "Thank God, It's Doomsday." This episode involves Bart going to a Catholic school and being taken under the wing of the sympathetic Father Sean. When Marge questions Bart's newfound allegiance to Catholicism, pointing out that the church doesn't allow birth control, for example, Bart accuses her of "blasphemy" and offers to say a rosary for her. Homer, also displeased with Bart's behavior, is sent to intervene, but he is quickly seduced by the concept of absolution and decides to convert as well. This, of course, creates a bit of a scandal, both at home and in the community. The following Sunday, Reverend Lovejoy confronts Marge, claiming that Homer and Bart are "under the spell of a man in a pointy white hat." Marge initially tries to defend their choice as "an interest in spirituality," but Lovejoy tells her that "a different faith means a different afterlife." Frightened by this prospect, and determined to win Homer and Bart back, Marge, Ned Flanders, and Reverend Lovejoy team up for an intervention. On the ride home, Bart complains to Marge: "You're always telling me to go to church, and now that I am, it's the wrong one." Lovejoy responds, "We're here to bring you back to the one true faith—the Western Branch of American Reform Presbylutheranism." The remainder of the episode makes it abundantly clear that *The Simpsons* aims to satirize the idea of "one true faith" and the intolerance this breeds, even among Christians themselves.

In an effort to show Bart that "Protestants can be hip too," Marge takes him to a Protestant youth festival. Bart is unimpressed until he sees the Onward Paintball Soldiers tent. With gun in hand, Bart proceeds to wreak havoc, splattering a nativity scene with red paint and "shooting" Rod and Todd Flanders. When Father Sean and Homer arrive, sporting their own paintball guns, Homer is determined to show Marge that "our God kicks your God's butt." Homer then cocks and aims his gun, and everyone around him follows suit, ready for battle. At this point, Bart steps up and says, "Easy on the zeal, church-os. I've got something to say. Don't you get it? It's all Christianity, people. The little stupid differences are nothing compared to the big stupid similarities." "He's right," Flanders says, "can't we all get together and concentrate on our real enemies: monogamous gays and stem cells?" Father Sean agrees and shakes hands with Flanders. Lovejoy concedes that Bart has taught them all a valuable lesson, saying, "We Christians have been niggling over details for far too long." "Amen," Father Sean says, "and from this day forward, I hope we all learn to take Bart's message of tolerance and understanding to heart." On the heels of Father Sean's statement, we see the words "1000 Years Later" superimposed over dark clouds and set to ominous music. The camera then pans down to reveal two rival factions, both followers of "God's last prophet, Bart Simpson," facing each other on a battlefield and arguing over the message of "the holy Bartman": one group claims that he "preached a message of tolerance and love"; the other that he "preached a message of understanding and peace." With shouts of "Eat our shorts!" and "Cowabunga!" the rival groups rush into battle, and the end credits roll. The irony of the ending should not be lost on anyone, nor should the satirical critique of religious zealotry.

Voices of Reason

One of the ways *The Simpsons* offers opposition to mainstream Christianity and Christian fundamentalism is through the words and actions of the show's two most rational characters, Marge and Lisa. As might be expected, Lisa Simpson is the most overtly secular voice on the show and, eventually, the most vocal critic of institutional religion. Although Lisa was closely aligned with the Judeo-Christian tradition at the start of the series, she moves toward a more rationalist and skeptical position as the series progresses—ultimately rejecting Christianity altogether and converting to Buddhism in the 2001 episode "She of Little Faith." Lisa demonstrates along the way that her views—and I would venture to say the views of her creators—are shaped primarily by the traditions of Enlightenment philosophy, rationality, and scientific inquiry. Lisa's scientific rationality is the centerpiece of episodes such as "Lisa the Skeptic" (November 1997), "I'm Goin' to Praiseland" (May 2001), "She of Little Faith" (December 2001), and "The Monkey Suit" (May 2006). In "Lisa the Skeptic," faith and science are pitted against each other over the discovery of an unusual looking skeleton, which is quickly presumed to be the remains of an angel. Lisa is bothered that nearly everyone unquestioningly accepts that the skeleton is an angel and takes a sample of it to the Springfield Museum, where noted evolutionary biologist Stephen Jay Gould (guest starring in the episode) calls the idea "preposterous." When Gould informs the townspeople that the test results were "inconclusive" (though we later learn he never ran tests at all), Reverend Lovejoy gloatingly says, "Well, it appears science has failed again, in front of overwhelming religious evidence." Lisa, still convinced that science will prove her right, continues to challenge people's belief by offering a variety of plausible explanations for the skeleton. Frustrated, Lisa complains to her mother about the "morons" in town who refuse to listen. Marge, however, does not take Lisa's side; she is positioned once again as a believer, and she encourages Lisa to make a "leap of faith." Lisa cannot and continues to present her case with an appearance on the television show *Smartline*, where she matter-of-factly states to the audience, "You can either accept science and face reality or you can believe in angels and live in a childish dream world." Tensions run high, a mob gathers, and Lisa, the "unbeliever," is chased by the townsfolk back to the dig site where the skeleton was first found. Here they discover that the angel was merely part of an elaborate publicity stunt for the grand opening of the Heavenly Hills Mall. Lisa attempts to channel the outrage she expects the townsfolk to feel at having their faith exploited, but they don't even hear her; good consumers all, they rush headlong to the mall, having already forgotten their religious devotion. With such an ending, the writers are clearly satirizing the substitution of one religion for another—here, consumerism for theism—but it should not be forgotten that the primary concern of the episode is Lisa's rationality and faith in scientific explanation, and her view is vindicated in the end.

Lisa's rationality also figures prominently in "The Monkey Suit," which focuses more specifically on religion's general anti-intellectualism and its opposition to scientific inquiry. "The Monkey Suit" was inspired by the events leading up to the 2005 decision in *Kitzmiller v. Dover*, which settled a rancorous debate over science curricula in the small town of Dover, Pennsylvania.[24] True to form, *The Simpsons* incorporated this contemporary debate for satirical ends. "The Monkey Suit" begins with a trip to the Springfield Museum of Natural History, where Ned and his sons stumble into the Hall of Man and an exhibit on evolution. Shocked by what he sees, Ned covers his sons' eyes and confronts the docent, asking, "Excuse me, but how can you have an exhibit on the origins of man and not have one mention of the Bible?" "Oh, we do," he replies, pointing to a rather low-tech exhibit labeled "The Myth of Creation," which features the finger of God reaching down from a cloud to create a tree, a rabbit, a sheep, and Adam and Eve—all to the tune of the Doobie Brothers' "What a Fool Believes." Unnerved by the idea that his cherished beliefs are a "myth," and angered by the suggestion that he and others are descended from apes, Ned consults with Reverend Lovejoy, and the two of them approach Principal Skinner to demand that an alternative to evolutionary theory be taught in the school. The following day, Skinner tells Lisa's class that they will now be taught about creationism. Lisa, of course, protests, saying that creationism is not science. To mollify her, Skinner shows a videotape, a propaganda piece called "So You're Calling God a Liar" that provides an "unbiased" comparison of evolutionism and creationism. According to the video, the Bible was written by "our Lord," whereas *The Origin of Species* "was written by a cowardly drunk, Charles Darwin," who is shown making out with Satan. Lisa attempts to counter the slander rationally—explaining that "evolution is a widely acknowledged scientific fact and is even accepted by prominent conservatives such as George Will and the late Pope John Paul"—but as usual, she is ignored. In short order, Mayor Quimby bans the teaching of evolution in Springfield, and Lisa is subsequently arrested for conducting a secret class for the scientifically "faithful" where she reads passages from Darwin's book. At her trial, which Kent Brockman dubs *God vs. Lisa Simpson,* Lisa is represented by "ACLU appointed liberal Clarice Drummond," a clear stand-in for Clarence Darrow. Prosecuting the case is "humble country lawyer Wallace Brady." The key witness winds up being Ned Flanders, who claims that he is positive that man and ape cannot be related—that is, until Homer, trying unsuccessfully to open a bottle of Duff beer, tests Ned's patience until he blurts out: "Would you shut your yap, you big monkey-faced gorilla." Clarice Drummond uses this as a wedge and gets Ned to confess that Homer (and thereby man) could possibly be related to an ape. The judge then orders the repeal of the law banning the teaching of evolution, in a victory for reason and rationality.

Marge Simpson figures more prominently in episodes that deal with ethical issues and satirize the widespread belief in an exclusive link between religion and morality. Many people—particularly those within the Judeo-Christian tradition—have a hard time comprehending that morality and religion are not synonymous, as they have been trained to see the two as inextricably linked.[25] Marge is a Christian, and she appears to abide by the laws of that faith. But Marge is also a rationalist, and her choices do not always align with doctrine—indeed, they often contradict it. In "Homer vs. Lisa and the 8th Commandment," for example, Marge is at a loss to identify the rule she is breaking when she pilfers two grapes at the local grocery store. Lisa, at this point rather intensely focused on sin and damnation, asks Marge, "Don't you remember the eighth commandment?" "Of course," Marge replies, "it's 'Thou shall not . . . um . . . covet graven images'—something about covet." "It's 'Thou shall not steal!'" Lisa shouts. Marge's more secularist position is also seen in the season 8 episode "In Marge We Trust," in which Marge becomes the "Listen Lady" of the First Church of Springfield after Reverend Lovejoy loses interest in helping his parishioners. As she tells Reverend Lovejoy, "Sermons about 'constancy' and 'prudissitude' are all well and good, but the church could be doing so much more to reach out to people." What Marge proceeds to do is offer friendly, commonsense advice to the troubled citizens of Springfield. In short, Marge Simpson straddles the religious and secular realms, drawing on the strengths of both and using what is most appropriate from each in response to a given situation. According to Gerald Erion and Joseph Zeccardi, this quality classifies Marge as a "Christian-flavored Aristotelian."[26] Marge is a good and virtuous person, and the character traits that make her so—friendliness, honesty, compassion—are as much a consequence of adhering to certain tenets of Christianity as they are of employing reason and rationality. As the authors state, "To resolve her moral dilemmas, Marge simply allows reason to guide her conduct to a thoughtful and admirable balance between extremes."[27]

One of the finest examples of Marge's moral reasoning is in the February 2005 episode "There's Something about Marrying," which deals with the topic of gay marriage. To increase tourism and raise money, Mayor Quimby, following the suggestion of Lisa Simpson, legalizes gay marriage. As might be expected, before we see any marriages take place, we see a showdown between the religious and secular forces in Springfield, the former led by Reverend Lovejoy and the latter by Marge Simpson. As a large group of couples approaches the First Church of Springfield, Lovejoy is seen rapidly nailing a board over the door. Lovejoy explains that he cannot (more accurately, will not) perform same-sex marriages. As the dejected crowd disperses, Marge steps up to confront Lovejoy and challenge the religious viewpoint. She says, "As long as two people love each other, I don't think God cares whether they have the same hoo-hoo or ha-ha." Though couched in the language of emotion, her statement is an implicit defense of civil rights. Lovejoy responds, "The Bible forbids same-sex relations." "Which book?" Marge asks. Marge is clearly "striking a blow for civil rights," as Lisa puts it, but she is also directly challenging Lovejoy's perspective and thereby challenging the authority of religion as an arbiter of morality. The writers are also making an important point about the selective interpretation of the Bible to justify persecution. They know that viewers will be familiar with the citation from Leviticus, but for Lovejoy, it is all one book: "Which book?" he incredulously asks. "The Bible!" Lovejoy then begins to ring the church bell to silence Marge's protest. One can hear her begin to say, "But Reverend, scriptural scholars disagree on the significance of. . . ." Her words are briefly drowned out by Lovejoy's ringing of the bell, but a moment later, one can hear Marge conclude: "Jesus's teachings stress inclusiveness and compassion." Despite her best efforts and her rationality, however, Marge cannot get through to Lovejoy.

Marge's comments underscore what is fundamental to the view of religion on display in *The Simpsons:* a distinction between Old Testament and New Testament worldviews. For believers, the intolerance practiced by the pious and the religious is "justified" by scripture, but that scripture is invariably in the Old Testament. As is well known, that part of the Bible has long been used to justify slavery, abuse, torture, and the subjugation of women, among other things. In light of the social and political changes wrought by the modern civil rights movement, such texts are rarely referred to today outside of fundamentalist circles. In general, Christianity has largely shifted its focus to the New Testament, to the teachings of Jesus, and to the very virtues Marge Simpson embodies—virtues that, as she attempts to remind Reverend Lovejoy, are part of the Christian faith. Of course, the dichotomized view of the Bible presented by *The Simpsons* is an oversimplification of matters; in many ways, the New Testament is as troublesome and problematic as the Old Testament, such as its continuing support of patriarchal structures of dominance. But the creators of *The Simpsons* are simplifying things with a purpose: in this case, to condemn the recourse to fear, hatred, and violence so often promoted by Old Testament Christianity and a strictly religious worldview, and to highlight the potential links between New Testament Christianity and a more Humanistic worldview, which are evident in their shared emphases on qualities such as compassion, brotherhood, and love.

The two most sustained treatments of religious themes on *The Simpsons* are Mark Pinsky's *The Gospel According to* The Simpsons and Jamey Heit's *The Springfield Reformation*. In his final chapter (entitled "Concluding Trumpet Blast"), Heit makes his larger concern perfectly clear: "While the extent to which *The Simpsons* is critical of American Christianity suggests that the faith tradition has lost its ability to be relevant in American culture, one can see in the show's inevitable emphasis on coming together that *The Simpsons* does not give up on Christianity."[28] Pinsky expresses a similar sentiment in his concluding chapter, the title of which poses a question about *The Simpsons*: "Cloaking the Sacred with the Profane?" For Pinsky, the answer is clearly yes. However, even Pinsky acknowledges that "whether the series, once considered so antiauthoritarian, is subversive or supportive of faith is largely in the eye of the beholder."[29] Indeed it is, and one's interpretation is dependent on many factors, not the least of which is what one means by *faith*.

For all the dogmatic quoting of scripture in Pinsky's and Heit's texts, their claims boil down to three things: family, brotherhood, and love, which they find in abundance on *The Simpsons*. Does Christianity have an exclusive claim to these values? Of course not. As I note previously, the aims of mainline Christianity and Humanism run along parallel tracks, and this is reflected in many episodes of *The Simpsons*. But it is not enough to simply note that a degree of ambiguity exists and that viewers can read the show in accordance with their own beliefs. Above all, *The Simpsons* is a satire, and as such it has a particular take on elements of the culture seen to be problematic. What the show regularly satirizes are elements of a far-right religious fundamentalism, an outgrowth of Religious Right perspectives that has come to have a powerful influence in American culture. As Kevin Phillips astutely notes in *American Theocracy*, "the radical side of U.S. religion has embraced cultural anti-modernism, war hawkishness, Armageddon prophecy, and in the case of conservative fundamentalists, a demand for government by literal biblical interpretation."[30] Religious organizations such as the Moral Majority, Christian Coalition, Southern Baptist Convention, and Focus on the Family have had an enormous impact on the American political system over the past three decades: they have shaped the national conversation about the "moral issues" that have been centerpieces of the culture wars for the past forty years, and they have been very successful in prompting the populace to react to these issues with emotion rather than reason. As Phillips further argues, changes in affiliation away from mainline Protestantism and toward more "radical" sects have pushed the United States toward a "national Disenlightenment."[31]

Such righteous moralizing and anti-intellectualism are widely evident in Springfield, which is representative of America in general, and these are on display on *The Simpsons* to be satirized. The impatience with religion that has been building over many years is evident in the blunt way it is dismissed in another recent episode, "Bart Has Two Mommies," which aired in March 2006. This episode opens with the Simpson family entering the grounds of the church fund-raiser (which, according to the banner at the entrance, "Does Not Count as Church"), where they pass games such as Whack-a-Moses, Holy Roller-Coaster, and the Tunnel of Abstinence. One scene shows Lenny and Carl playing Halo Toss, a game in which they try to toss rings onto the heads of saints. Like any carnival game, it's rigged such that the odds are against the player. Frustrated, Lenny says, "Who knew saints had such big heads?" Carl asserts, "Ah, it's all a big scam." "This booth?" Lenny asks. "No, religion in general," Carl replies. Of course, it is safe to put this view into the mouths of somewhat peripheral characters rather than members of the Simpson family, even Lisa. Nonetheless, there is a thread running through the narrative of this episode—indeed, through the entirety of *The Simpsons* as a series—that underscores the idea that religion, particularly Christianity, is a sham. This lends support to the view that the critique offered by Lenny and Carl is not just the opinion of two minor characters but that of the creative voices behind *The Simpsons* as well.

Notes

Epigraph: Robert Wuthnow, *After Heaven: Spirituality in America since the 1950s* (Berkeley: University of California Press, 1998), 10.

1. This is evident in a variety of journal and newspaper articles, the numerous "academic papers" posted on *The Simpsons Archive*, and select essays in collections such as William Irwin et al., eds., The Simpsons *and Philosophy: The D'oh of Homer* (Chicago: Open Court Press, 2000), and John Alberti, ed., *Leaving Springfield:* The Simpsons *and the Possibilities of Oppositional Television* (Detroit: Wayne State University Press, 2004). The most sustained treatments of religious themes, however, are found in Mark Pinsky's *The Gospel According to* The Simpsons: *The Spiritual Life of the World's Most Animated Family* (Louisville, KY: Westminster John Knox Press, 2001) and Jamey Heit's *The Springfield Reformation:* The Simpsons, *Christianity, and American Culture* (New York: Continuum, 2008). By and large, the shorter works primarily note that religion and spirituality are regular topics on *The Simpsons.* Pinsky and Heit, however, argue that the show openly supports and, to an extent, actively promotes a Christian worldview. To be fair, both Pinsky and Heit acknowledge that *The Simpsons* routinely critiques many aspects of Christianity and regularly satirizes religious extremism, but neither author believes such criticism devalues Christianity's role in society.

2. *Humanist* and *Humanism* are highly contested terms with lengthy and varying histories. I employ the terms here with reference to the secular Humanist tradition currently promoted by the American Humanist Association and the Council for Secular Humanism, among others. In short, secular Humanism is an ethical, scientific, and philosophical outlook that rejects theistic and supernatural beliefs in favor of reason, objectivity, and scientific inquiry and is dedicated to democracy, equality, social justice, human rights, and the overall improvement of the human condition. For a concise overview, see Tony Davies, *Humanism* (New York: Routledge, 1997). For more on the Humanist project, see Paul Kurtz, *Humanist Manifesto 2000* (Amherst, NY: Prometheus, 2000).

3. John Dart, "Simpsons Have Soul," *Christian Century,* January 31, 2001, 14.

4. Heit, *Springfield Reformation,* 21.

5. The two most significant studies are the 2001 American Religious Identification Survey (ARIS), conducted by the Graduate Center of the City University of New York, and the 2008 U.S. Religious Landscape Survey, conducted by the Pew Forum on Religion and Public Life. The ARIS was based on a random telephone survey of 50,281 American households in the continental United States; the Pew Religious Landscape Survey was based on extensive interviews with a representative sample of more than

35,000 Americans aged eighteen and older. Both surveys confirm that the United States is on the verge of becoming a minority Protestant country: the number of Americans who report that they are members of Protestant churches stands at just 51.3 percent. The Pew survey also shows that although the United States is still approximately 78 percent Christian, more than one-quarter of American adults (28 percent) have left the faith in which they were raised in favor of another religion or no religion at all, and roughly one-quarter of Americans aged eighteen to twenty-nine say that they are not currently affiliated with any particular religion. See Barry A. Kosmin et al., "American Religious Identification Survey," Graduate Center at CUNY, December 2001, http://www.gc.cuny.edu/faculty/research_studies.htm; Luis Lugo et al., "2008 U.S. Religious Landscape Survey," Pew Forum on Religion and Public Life, February 2008, http://religions.pewforum.org/.

6. Thomas Skill et al., "The Portrayal of Religion and Spirituality on Fictional Network Television," *Review of Religious Research* 35 (March 1994): 265. This study was commissioned by the American Family Association in 1990. It was based on a five-week analysis of religious behaviors on prime-time shows and the examination of more than 1,400 characters on 100 different programs. It found that less than 6 percent of characters had an identifiable religious affiliation.

7. Scott H. Clarke, "Created in Whose Image? Religious Characters on Network Television," *Journal of Media and Religion* 4, no. 3 (2005): 137. Clarke's study focused only on the three top-rated comedies and dramas presented by seven networks during one week in 2002. Based on an analysis of 549 speaking characters on 42 different programs, Clarke concluded that only 32 characters in the sample (5.8 percent) could be identified as religious, which replicated the findings in Skill's study from the early 1990s. Only 25 characters could be associated with a specific religion, and of these, just 15 were Christian—exclusively Protestant.

8. Religious Right organizations included the Catholic League (1973), Focus on the Family (1977), American Family Association (1977), Moral Majority (1979), Southern Baptist Convention (1979), Traditional Values Coalition (1980), Freedom Council (1981), Family Research Council (1983), and Christian Coalition (1990). For more detailed histories of the rise of the Religious Right, see William Martin, *With God on Our Side: The Rise of the Religious Right in America* (New York: Broadway, 1996); Dan Gilgoff, *The Jesus Machine: How James Dobson, Focus on the Family, and Evangelical America Are Winning the Culture War* (New York: St. Martin's, 2007).

9. George M. Marsden, *Fundamentalism and American Culture,* 2nd ed. (New York: Oxford University Press, 2006), 245.

10. Martin, *With God on Our Side,* 325.

11. *The Simpsons* was initially seen by many religious and political conservatives as an amoral and corruptive influence in American culture. In 1990, for example, America's "drug czar," William Bennett, chastised the residents of a drug rehabilitation facility for watching *The Simpsons,* claiming that doing so would not help them reform their lives.

Chris Turner, *Planet Simpson: How a Cartoon Masterpiece Defined a Generation* (Cambridge, MA: Da Capo, 2004), 26. Later that same year, in a profile in *People* magazine, First Lady Barbara Bush referred to *The Simpsons* as "the dumbest thing I've ever seen," which touched off a brief but heated exchange with the creators of the show. Then, in 1992, George H. W. Bush unfavorably compared *The Simpsons* to *The Waltons* as he was campaigning for the presidency. James Brooks discusses these incidents at length in a supplemental featurette, *Bush vs. Simpsons,* on disc 1 of the season 4 DVD box set (Fox Home Entertainment, 2004). A brief discussion of these events also appears in Turner, *Planet Simpson,* 231–33.

12. Heit, *Springfield Reformation,* 57.

13. Pinsky, *Gospel According to* The Simpsons, ix.

14. "She of Little Faith," episode DABF02, *The Simpsons,* Fox Television Network, December 16, 2001.

15. "A Star Is Burns," episode 2F31, *The Simpsons,* Fox Television Network, March 5, 1995.

16. Heit, *Springfield Reformation,* 31.

17. "Hurricane Neddy," episode 4F07, *The Simpsons,* Fox Television Network, December 29, 1996.

18. It is worth noting that "Homer the Heretic" was written by George Meyer, an avowed atheist who was raised in a strict Catholic home. David Owen, "Taking Humor Seriously," *New Yorker,* March 13, 2000, 68. As a large body of scholarship demonstrates, authorial intent clearly does not dictate meaning, because audiences can and do decode texts in a multiplicity of ways; however, it would be remiss to ignore intentionality in a discussion of satire and to simply disregard the way Meyer's views help shape the satirical attack on religiosity in this episode.

19. Lisle Dalton, Eric Michael Mazur, and Monica Siems, "Homer the Heretic and Charlie Church: Parody, Piety, and Pluralism in *The Simpsons,*" in *God in the Details: American Religion in Popular Culture,* ed. Eric Michael Mazur and Kate McCarthy (New York: Routledge, 2001), 240.

20. Gordon Lynch, *Understanding Theology and Popular Culture* (Malden, MA: Blackwell, 2005), 153.

21. Ibid., 153–54.

22. Turner, *Planet Simpson,* 265, 266.

23. By 2001, bombings of abortion clinics were no longer commonplace; however, other forms of violence were, and they continue to be a problem. The National Clinic Violence Survey, conducted by the Feminist Majority Foundation, reports that in 2005 nearly one in five clinics throughout the country was still targeted with antiabortion violence, including "blockades, invasions, arsons, bombings, chemical attacks, stalking, gunfire, physical assaults, and threats of death, bomb, or arson." The report is available online at http://www.feminist.org/rrights/clinicsurvey.html.

24. The controversy that led to *Kitzmiller v. Dover* began in October 2004, when the

Dover Area School Board adopted a resolution providing that students in science courses "will be made aware of gaps/problems in Darwin's theory and of other theories of evolution including, but not limited to, intelligent design." *Kitzmiller* was a rather surprising replay of the debates over creationism and evolution that culminated in the infamous Scopes "monkey" trial in 1925, which seemed to mark the final defeat of nineteenth-century evangelical and fundamentalist religion. Nonetheless, at the start of the new millennium, the debate between evolutionary science and creationist belief was raging once again as school boards around the country attempted to insert creationism into science curricula or remove the teaching of evolutionary theory. In November 2004 the Dover school district announced that as of January 2005, high school biology teachers would be required to read to their students a disclaimer pointing out that Darwin's theory of natural selection is only a theory and not fact. The full disclaimer reads: "Because Darwin's theory is a theory, it continues to be tested as new evidence is discovered. The theory is not a fact. Gaps in the theory exist for which there is no evidence. A theory is defined as a well-tested explanation that unifies a broad range of observations. Intelligent Design is an explanation of the origin of life that differs from Darwin's view. The reference book *Of Pandas and People* is available for students who might be interested in gaining an understanding of what Intelligent Design actually involves." Parents of some students sued, alleging that the board's policy violated their constitutional rights under the establishment clause. Brenda Lee, "*Kitzmiller v. Dover Area School District*: Teaching Intelligent Design in Public Schools," *Harvard Civil Rights–Civil Liberties Law Review* 41 (2006): 581. For more details, see Lauri Lebo, *The Devil in Dover: An Insider's Story of Dogma v. Darwin in Small-town America* (New York: New Press, 2008).

25. Many people believe that their morality derives from religious doctrine—that is, the divine command theory—and that ethical choices can be made only with reference to religious texts and tenets. However, as James Rachels explains, this is not the case. Although the divine command theory holds great appeal, it is weak in numerous ways. Christian and secular philosophers have long wrestled with questions of doctrine and morality and have come to see the flaws of the divine command theory. First, God's commands can be shown to be arbitrary, since God could have given different commands (e.g., lying is good, rather than truthfulness). As the Enlightenment led to scientific discoveries and to a better understanding of the world and human nature, the reigning theory came to be that moral judgments are, in the words of St. Thomas Aquinas, "the dictates of reason." Many philosophers have thus abandoned a theological view of morality, hypothesizing instead that "God commands it because it is right," which leads to the conclusion that "there is some standard of right and wrong that is independent of God's will." James Rachels, *The Elements of Moral Philosophy*, 4th ed. (New York: McGraw-Hill, 2002), 49.

26. Gerald Erion and Joseph Zeccardi, "Marge's Moral Motivation," in Irwin et al., *The Simpsons and Philosophy*, 46–58.

27. Ibid., 46.

28. Heit, *Springfield Reformation,* 151.

29. Pinsky, *Gospel According to* The Simpsons, 143.

30. Kevin Phillips, *American Theocracy: The Peril and Politics of Radical Religion, Oil, and Borrowed Money in the 21st Century* (New York: Viking, 2006), 100.

31. Ibid., 103. Such a claim is not new, of course. Richard Hofstadter explored a similar theme in his seminal *Anti-Intellectualism in American Life* (New York: Knopf, 1963). Recent books that address similar concerns include Charles Freeman, *The Closing of the Western Mind: The Rise of Faith and the Fall of Reason* (New York: Vintage, 2005); Al Gore, *The Assault on Reason* (New York: Penguin, 2007); and Susan Jacoby, *The Age of American Unreason* (New York: Pantheon, 2008).

9

IT CAME FROM PLANET EARTH

Eco-Horror and the Politics of Postenvironmentalism in *The Happening*

Joseph J. Foy

Ecologically based horror films, or "eco-horror," are fright flicks in which nature turns against humankind due to environmental degradation, pollution, encroachment, nuclear disaster, or a host of other reasons. As a genre, eco-horror attempts to raise mass consciousness about the very real threats that will face humanity if we are not more environmentally cautious. The popularity of ecologically based documentaries such as *An Inconvenient Truth*, *The 11th Hour*, and *Flow* have helped spark a cinematic revival of apocalyptic tales of nature turning on humanity that were popular in the 1950s and 1970s.

Larry Fessenden, producer and director of many independent films, argues that horror movies are "cautionary tales." Fessenden's 2006 film *The Last Winter* is an eco-horror about an oil company's attempts to drill in the pristine environment of a northern Alaskan wildlife refuge. The drilling releases something that affects the psychology of the drilling team, and many of them begin to suffer what seem to be delusions that threaten the lives of the crew. According to Fessenden, such films are designed to scare us into realizing that "we don't want to be in a horror film. We don't want to wake up in a horrible superstorm . . . [or] have wars over the last drops of water."[1] According to Neda Ulaby of National Public Radio's *All Things Considered*, the purveyors of eco-horror are trying to "affect the cultural conversation" with their films.[2] In essence, eco-horror is an example of popular culture attempting to transform a marginalized, disempowered voice into a mainstream dialogue.

Although directors like Fessenden are often described as having only cult appeal, which relegates them to the cinematic fringe, apocalyptic films with environmental messages are hitting the mainstream of popular culture. For example, the 2004 blockbuster action film *The Day after Tomorrow* focuses on a heroic climatologist attempting to counteract the problems of global warming and an oncoming ice age. The sci-fi thriller *Sunshine* (2007) portrays humanity's last-ditch effort to reignite a dying sun, and even the 2008 Disney-Pixar hit *WALL-E* uses environmental themes and the effects of human consumption and pollution as a backdrop for its robotic love story. Although none of these films falls into the "horror" genre of moviemaking, their popularity has helped cult-fringe film devices such as eco-horror obtain the necessary financing and production support to achieve a more mainstream box-office appeal. One example is the 2009 film *The Thaw*, starring Val Kilmer, which uses global warming as the basis for unleashing a deadly plague that has lain dormant in the ice for thousands of years.

Joining the ranks of those spreading an ecological message on the silver screen is M. Night Shyamalan. His film *The Happening* finds its roots in creature features such as *The Creature from the Black Lagoon, Frogs, Godzilla,* and *The Swarm,* and it is one of several modern eco-horror films that are revitalizing these past warnings in an urgent, contemporary context. *The Happening* is a mainstream attempt to scare people into realizing the potentially disastrous effects of ecological encroachment and what might happen if, as Shyamalan asks, "nature one day turned on us."[3]

Eco-Horror and the Transformation of the "Cultural Conversation"

In a departure from some of Shyamalan's more fantastical films such as *The Sixth Sense, Unbreakable, Signs,* and *Lady in the Water,* the suspense generated in *The Happening* is neither mythical nor mystical. And unlike in *The Village,* in which the threat posed by the "monsters" is purely artificial, created by Covington's founders to keep its citizens from exploring the woods and discovering the world beyond, the events that transpire in *The Happening* are not manufactured. Instead, *The Happening* is a naturalist parable of what might occur if the earth began rejecting humanity as a virus. The original working title of the film, *The Green Effect,* establishes this ecological link, and in commenting on the film, Shyamalan acknowledges its eco-horror foundations. In one interview he downplays the fright factor in his first R-rated film by claiming that the seminal horror film of the century has already been made—Al Gore's Oscar-winning documentary *An Inconvenient Truth*.[4]

The Happening opens in New York City's Central Park. Two young women (Alison Folland and Kristen Connolly) are sitting on a bench reading when a scream is heard in the distance. People start clawing at themselves and drawing blood, and then everyone around them in the park freezes, and some start walking backward. One of the young women on the bench reaches up and pulls out a hairpin. Without hesitation, she jams it into her own throat. Soon, similar events begin happening in areas surrounding the park. At a construction site, a foreman (Cornell Womack) stands in horror and disbelief as the bodies of his crew come raining down from the top of a building. Suicide becomes a pandemic, breaking out in areas throughout the Northeast, as people begin shooting, hanging, and cutting themselves, while others feed themselves to lions or lay underneath the blades of a lawn mower.

Meanwhile, in a Philadelphia high school, Elliot Moore (Mark Wahl-

Ecologically based horror films, such as M. Night Shyamalan's *The Happening*, attempt to confront and transform contemporary conversations and approaches to environmental politics. (MovieGoods)

berg) is teaching a science class. He is giving a lesson about the disappearance of bee populations throughout North America, making a desperate and impassioned plea to his students to take an interest in science. He asks the students to use the scientific method to generate hypotheses about what is causing the disappearance of bee colonies. One student speculates that it could be due to a virus, while another blames global warming. After some prodding, a seemingly disinterested student, Jake (Robert Lenzi), concludes that what is going on is "an act of nature, we'll never fully understand it." It is then that the vice principal (Kathy Lee Hart) interrupts Elliot's class to take him to an emergency meeting, where he and other teachers are told that terrorists have attacked Central Park. Classes are canceled, and everyone is sent home. Elliot meets up with his wife, Alma (Zooey Deschanel), and they join his friend Julian (John Leguizamo) and Julian's daughter Jess (Ashlyn Sanchez) to catch a train to the Pennsylvania countryside, where they will presumably be safe from attack.

Events similar to those in New York City begin to occur in smaller and more remote areas, however, debunking the theory that terrorists are responsible for unleashing a neurotoxin that causes people to kill themselves. Soon other theories are developed to explain what is happening. Some blame nuclear power, while others blame the government and secret testing being performed by the Central Intelligence Agency (CIA). After separating from Julian, who catches a ride to Princeton to search for his wife, Elliot, Alma, and Jess meet the owner of a plant nursery (Frank Collison) and his wife (Victoria Clark), who speculate that the outbreak is being caused by plants. The nursery owner theorizes that plants are releasing neurotoxins into the air as a way of defending themselves against human beings in the same way that plant volatiles and terpenoids are released from herbivore-damaged plants to attract wasps that will feed on the offending caterpillars.[5] Elliot refines this theory, deducing that the plants emit a neurotoxin when they feel threatened by people in groups. Larger populations were affected first, but as the plants became more sensitive to the presence of humans, smaller groups caused the discharge of the neurotoxin.[6]

As a parable, *The Happening* provides several lessons regarding ecological awareness and sustainability. First, the film pulls together the cautions from a host of scientific, sociological, and political thinkers who have long warned against the dangers of ecological devastation. Second, it invites a comparative analysis of U.S. security policy in the global war on terror and the public policy response to impending environmental threats such as climate change, environmental exploitation, and overpopulation. Finally, its use of actual environmental issues as the basis of the eco-horror narrative provides a critical look into the current state of global ecology. Together, these combine to raise awareness and begin a dialogue that, when critically examined, can help transform the current political dialogue about domestic and global environmental policy.

We've Seen the Signs—Now It's Happening

In 1798 Thomas Malthus published *An Essay on the Principle of Population*, in which he argues that population growth occurs in a manner that tends to outstrip an ecosystem's carrying capacity—the supportable population of an organism within a given environment. Malthus suggests that unchecked populations grow at an exponential (or geometric) rate that outpaces food production, which grows only at an arithmetic rate. Shyamalan alludes to this Malthusian growth rate when Julian offers a young woman a math riddle to try to distract her from her fear. Julian asks how much money the woman would have if he gave her one penny on the first day, two pennies on the second, four on the third, and so on, doubling the amount each day for a full month. The terrified woman shouts out several low figures, none of which is right. Finally, right before they are afflicted with the neurotoxin, Julian tells her, "It's over ten million dollars. You'd have over ten million dollars at the end of the month."

Such unchecked growth, as demonstrated in the riddle, reveals some obvious problems related to populations and carrying capacity. When a population begins to outstrip food supplies and essential resources that sustain an organism within an ecosystem, something must give. According to Malthus, there are two inevitable scenarios: a human response and a natural response. The human response would be a war over scarce resources. This would likely have an impact on the population, but if it did not do enough to check the population's numbers, a natural response would result. The natural response would come in the form of famine, disease, and pestilence, such that the population would be rapidly reduced to sustainable levels (or likely well below them). In essence, the ecosystem would attack the organism, just as the human body attacks a virus in an effort to save itself.[7]

The Malthusian perspective on population is certainly present throughout Shyamalan's film. Not only is nature turning against humanity; it is prompted to do so by large population concentrations. Smaller populations are affected only after the plants develop a greater sensitivity to smaller groups of individuals. Not until right before the happening subsides, when scientists project it to be at its most intense stage, are single individuals affected. Thus, nature is responding to overpopulation and encroachment in a distinctly Malthusian manner in the film.

The concerns over a natural response to rapid population growth, resource exploitation, and ecological devastation are becoming more prevalent. With the world population in 2008 reaching over 6.7 billion, the issue of Earth's carrying capacity is becoming a serious issue. The United Nations predicts that at current rates, the population will increase by 2.5 billion by 2050, bringing the total population to 9.2 billion. Regionally, population growth is having a significant impact on some states' ability to maintain order and provide necessary services for their citizens. Nearly one-third of the total world population is concentrated in two countries—China (over 1.3 billion) and India (over 1.1 billion). Moreover, less developed countries are facing domestic and regional instability because of resource scarcity, disease, pollution, and conflict. The United Nations predicts that the population of these less developed countries will increase from 5.4 billion in 2007 to 7.9 billion in 2050.[8]

Crises resulting from ecological instability are already occurring throughout the world, and a number of analysts are predicting that current worries over energy costs and other economic concerns will pale in comparison. Current levels of consumption have stretched food supplies to the limit, and the demand for products such as corn to be used as a biofuel alternative is placing an even greater strain on supply.[9] In the United States the threat looms, but in many other countries the threat has been actualized. Food riots have broken out in parts of Africa, leading to several deaths. Riots due to food shortages are not isolated to one city or one country; they have occurred in Cameroon, Haiti, Egypt, Cote d'Ivoire, Senegal, Burkina Faso, Ethiopia, Indonesia, Bangladesh, and Madagascar. The World Bank estimates that at least thirty-three countries are at risk due to shortages in supply and price inflation.[10] Each of these instances stands as a testament to the immediate problems being caused by ecological instability, as well as microcosms of the much larger, impending global crisis.

Problems related to food production throughout the world make environmental catastrophes all the more devastating. In June 2008 the United States began experiencing violent storms and massive, record-setting flooding throughout the Midwest, affecting states such as Illinois, Indiana, Iowa,

Michigan, Missouri, and Wisconsin. The flooding throughout the Midwest not only affected those in the immediate area but also sent food prices soaring due to scarcity created when crops were destroyed. For instance, the price of corn nearly doubled from 2007 to 2008.[11]

While the Midwest was experiencing heavy rain and flooding, other parts of the country were having a heat wave that registered record high temperatures in more than fifty cities. These temperatures, reaching well above 100 degrees in some places, pose serious health threats.[12] Researchers from the Intergovernmental Panel on Climate Change (IPCC), who (along with former vice president Al Gore) were awarded the 2007 Noble Peace Prize for their work on human contributions to climate change, indicate that flooding and drought in neighboring regions are predictable outcomes of global warming. The findings of the IPCC suggest that human systems impact natural ones in a manner that increases overall warming. This warming then causes shifts in weather patterns, increasing the intensity of storms. While violent weather in one area may be creating a deluge that results in massive flooding, nearby regions may be suffering from intense heat waves that cause drought. Drought, in turn, creates problems of scarcity and increases the risk of prairie and forest fires. Thus, it is not surprising that the United States has been hit by massive flooding and drought simultaneously, given the research into the effects of climate change.[13]

In addition to droughts and flooding resulting from climate change and the overconsumption of available resources due to population growth, there are increased problems of disease. According to a 2007 report released by the World Health Organization (WHO), "In our increasingly interconnected world, new diseases are emerging at an unprecedented rate, often with the ability to cross borders rapidly and spread."[14] According to the WHO, thirty-nine new pathogens have been identified since 1967, including HIV, Ebola, and SARS. The WHO also warns that centuries-old threats, "such as pandemic influenza, malaria and tuberculosis, continue to pose a threat to health through a combination of mutation, rising resistance to antimicrobial medicines and weak health systems."[15]

The threat of a global pandemic is scarily similar to the neurotoxin outbreak in Shyamalan's film, and the spread of diseases, due in part to pollution, scarcity, waste, and lack of proper sanitation, poses an almost unimaginable threat. In "The Next Pandemic?" Laurie Garrett explores the potential outbreak of one such disease, avian flu. Making comparisons to the 1918 Spanish flu, which resulted in the deaths of 50 million people in the span of eight months, Garrett demonstrates how lethality rates result-ing from overpopulation, the rapidity of global travel, and existing health problems in developing nations could well eclipse such figures. Garrett postulates that deaths in the United States alone would soar to around 16 million, well beyond the conservative estimate of 207,000 deaths by the Centers for Disease Control (CDC).[16]

Of course, not only does nature respond in a Malthusian manner; people begin to implement a form of self-preservation that reflects the principles articulated by Malthus. When Elliot, Alma, Julian, and Jess are stuck in a small-town diner, word spreads that ninety miles to the west there have been no reported outbreaks from the neurotoxin. All the people in the diner immediately scramble to their cars to make a run for the area beyond the "hot zone." Elliot and Alma struggle to find a ride, but in numerous acts of selfish self-preservation, one car after another ignores their pleas and takes off down the road.[17] Perhaps even more illustrative of this principle of self-preservation is what happens when two teenagers—Josh (Spencer Beslin) and Jared (Robert Bailey Jr.)—join Elliot, Alma, and Jess. They make their way to a farmhouse to beg for food. At first the farmhouse seems aban-doned, but Josh and Jared see two people moving around inside, and they try to persuade the residents to give them food for young Jess. Their pleas fall on deaf ears, however, and the people inside demand that they leave. Josh becomes aggravated and begins yelling obscenities at the people inside. A gun appears out of the front door, and Josh is shot in the chest. As Jared looks on in shock and fright, another gun barrel appears out the window and fires point-blank into Jared's head. Such a lack of concern for others in light of the desire for self-preservation is a theme highlighted throughout the film, and it illustrates the human response to overpopulation described by Malthus.

The conflict and instability resulting from scarcity and attempts at self-preservation create a significant threat to humanity. In 1994 Robert Kaplan described in horrific detail actual events in the developing world related to overpopulation, scarcity, and disease, which in turn heightened the prob-lems of crime and tribalism. In a shockingly dystopian vision of the future, Kaplan describes the collapse of global governments resulting from regional anarchy and intertribal conflicts (like those witnessed in Rwanda or Darfur); the subsequent mass migration of populations to other states makes these truly transnational problems.[18] The "coming anarchy" described by Kaplan is reinforced by research into intergroup conflict and environmental instability performed by Thomas Homer-Dixon and others at the University of Toronto. Homer-Dixon summarizes the problem of the scarcity of vital renewable resources such as soil, water, forests, fish, the ozone layer, and an equitable climate by asserting that they are "already contributing to very violent conflicts in many parts of the developing world. Moreover, these conflicts may be early signs of an upsurge of violence in the coming decades—especially in poor countries—that is caused or aggravated by environmental change."[19] A decade and a half later, bearing witness to the genocide in Rwanda and Sudan, as well as conflicts in the Democratic Republic of Congo, South Africa, and Indonesia, these claims seem less an apocalyptic future than a nightmarish reality.

Threat Level Green?

It is telling that when the first outbreak is reported in *The Happening*, everyone assumes it is some type of biological terrorist attack. In post-9/11 America, it is clear why people would immediately assume so. Soon after the terrorist attacks of September 11, 2001, Americans faced the looming threat of bioterror. In October 2001 law enforcement officials in Florida discovered a case of anthrax; soon after, anthrax-laden letters were mailed to government officials and civil servants.[20] The threat of bioterrorism became a reality that struck fear throughout the United States.

The Happening invites comparisons between the U.S. response to the attacks of 9/11 and to terrorism in general and its response to the global ecological crisis, revealing a large disparity.[21] After the collapse of the Soviet Union and the end of the cold war, many Western scholars began shifting their focus to new security challenges. Many predictions, like those of Jessica Tuchman Mathews and Thomas Homer-Dixon, indicated that the biggest challenge to global security in the post–cold war world would arise from ecological instability.[22] These scholars point to overpopulation, nonsustainable growth, resource depletion, immigration, and conflict as creating environmentally based threats that could lead to large-scale war, famine, and the spread of disease. However, the global terror threat quickly pushed the concept of ecological security out of the mainstream political consciousness.

From 2005 to 2007, the National Counterterrorism Center of the U.S. Department of State reported a total of 40,225 incidents of terrorism worldwide. Of those, 19,829 (49.3 percent) resulted in the death of at least one person, and 877 (2.2 percent) resulted in the death of at least ten people.[23] The total number of deaths attributed to terrorism worldwide for this three-year period was 58,173. This means that there was a three-year average of 13,408 incidents of terrorism resulting in 19,391 deaths per year. These numbers are tragic, and there is no arguing that governments must take appropriate steps to prevent such brutal attacks. However, eco-horror films like Shyamalan's provoke a comparison of these figures to the deaths resulting from climate change.

According to studies released by the WHO, the worldwide death toll attributable to global warming was an estimated 150,000 in 2005 alone— three times the total number of deaths worldwide from terrorism in a three-year period. The WHO estimates that those numbers could double by 2030. Likewise, the WHO estimates that nearly 5 million cases of diseases contracted worldwide in 2005 can be linked to global warming, and approximately 600,000 deaths occurred in the 1990s due to "weather-related natural disasters" that are intensified by global climate change. In addition to the deaths directly attributable to global warming, the United Nations estimates that in just five countries in Africa (Kenya, Ethiopia, Eritrea, Djibouti, and Somalia), 8 million people face starvation due to drought conditions, with 15 million more at risk. Such conditions are said to be growing worse due to complications from climate change.[24]

Focusing on the United States specifically, 2,998 people were killed in the terrorist attacks of September 11, 2001, making it the worst terrorist attack in world history. Comparatively, 1,836 died as a result of Hurricane Katrina, with 1,577 of those deaths occurring in New Orleans. Although more than 1,000 more people died in 9/11 than in Katrina, the Department of Homeland Security estimates that the devastation of Katrina directly affected 1.5 million people and forced 800,000 people to relocate in the "largest displacement of people since the great Dust Bowl migrations of the 1930s."[25] Finally, in comparing the economic impact of the two events, the total cost of the attack on the World Trade Center (earnings losses, property damage, cleanup and restoration) was estimated at $33 billion to $36 billion through the first year, whereas the total cost of the damage done by Hurricane Katrina was estimated at around $81 billion through the first year.[26]

Despite the relatively comparable damage and loss of human life in these two events, the U.S. government's responses to 9/11 and Katrina were wildly dissimilar. From September 11, 2001, to December 2007, the total amount of federal money allocated to Iraq, Afghanistan, and other war on terror operations was approximately $700 billion—three and a half times more than has been spent on the recovery efforts following Katrina. Moreover, when looking at the amount of federal money allocated to combat terrorist threats versus ecological ones, it should be noted that the entire annual budget for the Environmental Protection Agency (EPA) in 2007 was $7.3 billion. This means that the EPA could operate at current levels for almost a century before equaling the total amount spent in just over five years of waging the global war against terrorism. It is also noteworthy that, according to the Office of Management and Budget, following September 11, 2001, the Bush administration worked with Congress to more than triple nondefense homeland security spending. Compare that to the budget cuts at the EPA that caused numerous research facilities to close across the United States, even after the devastation of Katrina.[27]

In addition to inviting comparisons between reactions to global climate change and responses to terrorism in the United States, *The Happening* provides interesting commentary on overt versus covert threats to American security.[28] It may be that our minds are unable to process the overwhelming reality of the millions of people directly affected by environmental disaster in the same way that we processed the horrific images of people jumping from the burning Twin Towers being broadcast on television. The enormity of ecological crises all over the world may devastate us to paralysis, and we begin to think of them as being removed from our everyday lives. As Julian remarks to Elliot in the film, "People are comforted by percentages." The events of 9/11 shocked the American consciousness in a dramatic fashion,[29] prompting a swift and fully supported response by all relevant government agencies. However, such a coordinated effort has not been undertaken by the United States to deal with the environmental threats looming at home and abroad. Shyamalan's film attempts to dramatize, through a work of fiction, the ecological threat in a manner that shocks and scares people into action so that the American consciousness is raised before it is too late.

Colony Collapse Disorder and the Politics of Postenvironmentalism

Shyamalan places his ecological nightmare in the context of recent world events when he has Elliot talk to his class about the real-world phenomenon known as colony collapse disorder (CCD). A catchall phrase used to describe the rapid decline of western honeybee populations, CCD has been attributed to pesticide exposure, inadequate food supplies, possible viruses that affect the bees' immune systems, and genetically modified foods.[30] However, despite the numerous hypotheses advanced, there is no definitive evidence that pinpoints a single cause. Shyamalan acknowledges this when he has the student in Elliot's class conclude that the bees' disappearance is an act of nature that can never be fully understood. One thing is clear from the lesson, however: the decline in bee populations is a harbinger of things to come. On the chalkboard in Elliot's classroom is a quotation attributed to Albert Einstein that reads, "If the bee disappeared off the surface of the globe, then man would only have four years of life left." Though probably not actually uttered by Einstein, the quotation goes on to explain that without bees there would be "no more pollination, no more plants, no more animals . . . no more man."[31]

The introduction of CCD in the film provides a number of important contributions to popular perceptions about ecological crises, but two in particular. First, it serves as a reminder that the "warning signs" discussed in the film are not mere fictions invented to provide a backstory. These are actual events happening right now in North America and elsewhere. Second, and perhaps most important, the discussion of the disappearance of honeybee colonies enables Shyamalan to emphasize the multiplicity of potential causes of the ecological devastation that leads to the horrific events portrayed in the film. The students provide many possible and commonly accepted explanations as to why the bees have disappeared so rapidly. Elliot praises their insights but finds reasons to challenge their assertions. He concludes the conversation by noting, "Science will come up with some reason to put in the books, but in the end it'll be just a theory. I mean, we will fail to acknowledge that there are forces at work beyond our understanding. To be a scientist, you must have a respectful awe for the laws of nature."

This discussion of CCD is reminiscent of the critique of the archaic nature of the contemporary environmental movement offered by Michael Shellenberger and Ted Nordhaus, authors of the controversial 2004 article "The Death of Environmentalism." Shellenberg and Nordhaus criticize the single-issue focus of many environmentalists who warn against the dangers of pollution, deforestation, acid rain, and more, claiming instead that the problem is much broader and more multifaceted than any one of these things (or all of them combined).[32] In their follow-up book *Break Through: From the Death of Environmentalism to the Politics of Possibility*, Shellenberger and Nordhaus expand on this critique by providing a postenvironmentalist vision of the global climate crisis. The authors contend that if humanity is to truly make progress in averting ecological disaster, we must shift focus from the so-called pollution paradigm. Instead, the world must be ready to embrace a revolutionary reevaluation of wealth and prosperity not in terms of monetary net worth or material possessions but in terms of overall well-being.[33] Elliot's agreement with his student's assertion that the disappearance of honeybee populations is a natural phenomenon that can never be fully explained by any one theory seems to raise this type of postenvironmentalist critique of single-issue ecology.

Supporting the notion that *The Happening* is a portrayal of the postenvironmentalist critique of traditional approaches to solving environmental problems is the ending of the film. In a move that is unusual for Shyamalan, he does not tie everything together through a series of flashbacks or full disclosure from any of the characters. Instead, the film ends with the audience in limbo as to what the exact cause and solution might be. Left only with the knowledge that Paris and surrounding areas are about to be hit by the same ecological nightmare, the audience takes on the role of Elliot's class at the start of the film—offering hypotheses and best guesses, but having no definitive answers to explain this act of nature.

Shellenberger and Nordhaus's postenvironmentalist critique should not be taken as a call to stop pushing for reforms and public policy designed to encourage more environmentally friendly methods of production and consumption. To the contrary, such measures would likely result from a shift in mind-set and a reevaluation of wealth in terms of a life of well-being. In fact, Shellenberer and Nordhaus have worked with many of the existing ecologically based interest groups and organizations to improve environmental quality and ecologically friendly coexistence between human beings and nature. Instead, they are calling for these groups to shift from the single-issue approach to a more culturally revolutionary method of dealing with the politics of environmentalism, which they see as the only way to produce lasting, meaningful change.

We Just Have to Be Alive When It's All Over

Having survived the ecological nightmare, Elliot and Alma find a deeper love for each other that results in a renewal of their once faltering marriage. They have taken Jess into their home, Alma discovers that she is pregnant, and their lives are being redefined in terms of what really matters. In the background, talking heads debate the phenomenon three months later, and it is evident that no one can fully account for what has happened. The movie ends with an outbreak similar to that in New York occurring in a park in Paris, France. Fade to black.

Shyamalan's apocalyptic vision is enough to scare people into thinking about what might happen if nature turned against us, but it leaves audiences with more questions than answers. Though this may be unsatisfying for some, it is necessary if we are to draw broad and far-reaching conclusions from the film. For example, in what is perhaps the most obvious environmental lesson throughout the film, Shyamalan constantly emphasizes the scientific method as a means of approaching problems. Hard science, not mysticism or faith or the paranormal, offers Elliot insight into the happenings and gives him a strategy for survival. Shyamalan seems to be directing his audience to look to science and take seriously the overwhelming research that indicates we are spiraling toward imminent ecological disaster.[34]

Shyamalan's conclusion reveals not only how easily people reject scientific claims about global ecology but also how they dismiss natural signs and warnings as isolated events or anomalies. For example, because the happenings were confined to the northeastern United States, a talk-show host (Armand Schultz) criticizes the environmental warnings proffered by his guest, Dr. Ross (Stephen Singer), as nonsense. He insists that if the events had occurred in any other place, then Ross might be believed. In the meantime, classifying the events as a natural warning against ecological exploitation and destruction should be dismissed. Because the film ends with the start of a second outbreak in France, it is impossible to tell whether people were awakened by the second disaster. However, as we look around our own world, we see more violent and destructive hurricanes, severe droughts, flooding, mudslides, tsunamis, earthquakes, diseases, food shortages, population die-offs, and colony collapse. The natural world has been offering sign after sign, but some governments seem unwilling to look at the interconnectedness of these events and recognize them as constituting a larger narrative of ecological instability.

That France is the target for the second wave of the ecological nightmare in *The Happening* offers yet another insight into the politics of environmentalism. The European Union has been very proactive in attempting to combat the problems resulting from ecological degradation.[35] However, the member states of the EU are not immune from the impending natural disaster because the politics of environmentalism requires truly global solutions. In their 2003 release *Ecological Security: An Evolutionary Perspective on Globalization,* Dennis Pirages and Theresa Manley DeGeest explain how environmental issues transcend traditional politics by transcending national boundaries. The traditional approach to political, economic, and security questions was state centered, with sovereign governments responsible for their own well-being. However, single states cannot battle environmental disaster and win, because the violent weather patterns caused by climate change will not affect only those states responsible for the most pollution or the most degradation. It takes an entirely new approach that involves multinational cooperation and solutions arising out of the interconnectedness that has emerged due to globalization. States must be willing to embrace globalization and interconnectedness to solve problems of ecological devastation and environmental scarcity, which will require a change from our traditional understanding of concepts such as national interest and security.[36]

The Happening is a warning to heed the clarion call of impending environmental catastrophe, and it provides the foundation for future social and political action. Though not clearly defined in the film, it is possible for us to draw conclusions about how to transform modern modes of living to embrace a safer and more ecologically friendly way of life.

First, as evidenced in the postenvironmentalist message of the film, environmental groups must be willing to embrace new modes of action to effectively combat the most serious threats to ecological sustainability and preservation. This does not mean abandoning the critical work these groups perform in terms of social and political reform, but it does mean that they must work more comprehensively to change the mind-set of what it means to be ecologically friendly. Mass education must be undertaken to inform people that it is not enough to change to new eco-friendly lightbulbs or to recycle their trash. Currently, people are purchasing more fuel-efficient cars, using mass transit, carpooling, and traveling less not because it is beneficial for the environment but because it is too expensive to behave any other way. The campaign to get people to use new, energy-saving lightbulbs was based primarily on convenience and saving money. People are being induced to display the right behavior, but for reasons that do not promote the long-term viability of the ecological movement. A shift in mass culture must be made to pull people away from market incentives and toward incentives of overall quality of life and well-being.

Second, security must be redefined in terms of well-being, which means taking the ecological threat as seriously (if not more so) as threats of terrorism or other more traditional defense priorities. The 9/11 Commission indicated that the single biggest threat posed by terrorists, because of the overwhelming devastation, would be for an organization like al-Qaeda to possess a nuclear device. Hundreds of thousands of people would be at risk if a nuclear device were detonated in a densely populated area, which is certainly a threat worthy of serious attention. However, we must begin to question why similar gravity and resources are not dedicated to the very real and potentially more devastating environmental disasters mentioned throughout this chapter. The CDC's conservative estimate of U.S. deaths due to an avian flu pandemic is more than 200,000, with a potential death toll upward of 16 million. Thousands of people were killed when Hurricane Katrina struck the Gulf Coast, and the displacement and destruction were nearly unprecedented in U.S. history. Looming food shortages, water and resource scarcity, and other ecological problems pose a very real international and domestic threat. Just as the government has the responsibility to take action to defend us from potential threats from terrorism, it must mobilize to prevent ecological disaster at an almost unimaginable level.

Finally, regarding issues of public health, Margaret Chan, director-general of the WHO, calls not only for increased preparedness but also for the elimination of old models of international thought in which interest is defined solely from a national perspective. Chan argues that there must be increased global cooperation and multilateralism to combat what are truly transnational problems. According to Chan, "International public health security is both a collective aspiration and a mutual responsibility. The new watchwords are diplomacy, cooperation, transparency and preparedness."[37]

Perhaps what is most needed is a reality check from the likes of a classic M. Night Shyamalan ending, such as that in *The Sixth Sense* or *Signs*, when we are pulled back through the story and shown the overlooked pieces that reveal the answer to the mystery—clues that were present all along for those who knew where to look and how to fit the pieces together. Perhaps then governments and their citizens would see the interconnectedness of human activity and the global ecosystem. In the absence of such a revolutionary shift in consciousness, eco-horror films serve as a reminder of the nightmarish future that awaits, and they may advance the type of dialogue that can truly change the cultural conversation.

Notes

I would like to thank Kevin Lee for his insights and comments on the scientific data and analysis in this chapter, and Margaret Hankenson, David Hunt, and Kristi Nelson Foy for their willingness to comment on early drafts.

1. Neda Ulaby, "'Eco-Horror': Green Panic on the Silver Screen?" *All Things Considered,* National Public Radio, June 14, 2008, http://www.npr.org/templates/story/story .php?storyId=91485965 (accessed June 15, 2008).

2. Ibid.

3. David Germain, "Shyamalan's Eco Horror Story Gasps for More Life," *Rocky Mountain News,* June 12, 2008, http://www.rockymountainnews.com/news/2008/jun/12/ shyamalans-eco-horror-story-gasps-for-more-life/ (accessed June 16, 2008).

4. Ulaby, "'Eco-Horror.'"

5. Evidence of such plant activity has been documented in botanical research. See J. Wei, L. Wang, J. Zhu, S. Zhang, and O. I. Nandi, "Plants Attract Parasitic Wasps to Defend Themselves against Insect Pests by Releasing Hexenol," *PLoS ONE* 2, no. 9 (2007), http://www.plosone.org/article/citationList.action;jsessionid=8E2BD29B6D012 8A4E556220469090D35?articleURI=info%3Adoi%2F10.1371%2Fjournal.pone.0000852 (accessed June 15, 2008).

6. Natural occurrences like that portrayed in the film are not without precedent. The neurotoxin released by the plants in the film is compared to "red tides," documented instances of algae rapidly expanding in a concentrated area. The cause of these algal blooms is indeterminate. Sometimes they seem to occur naturally, and in other cases scientists are able to link them to human activity. In either case, red tides produce toxins that can be harmful to some aquatic life and make others dangerous for human consumption. Red tides have also been known to release allergens that are carried on the wind to communities near the bloom, which can affect human respiration and cause irritation of the skin and eyes. See University of California–San Diego, "Red Tide Killer Identified: Bacteria Gang up on Algae, Quashing Red Tide Blooms" *Science Daily,* May 6, 2008, http://www.sciencedaily.com/releases/2008/05/ 080501125429.htm (accessed June 17, 2008); Lisa Sitffler, "Red Tide Bloom Follows Population Boom," *Seattle Post-Intelligencer,* April 14, 2003, http://seattlepi.nwsource.com/local/ 117413_redtide14 .html (accessed June 17, 2008).

7. Thomas Malthus, *An Essay on the Principle of Population,* ed. Geoffrey Gilbert (Oxford: Oxford University Press, 1999).

8. Population and demographic data are based on estimates through July 2008 as reported in Central Intelligence Agency, *The 2008 World Factbook* (updated June 10, 2008), https://www.cia.gov/library/publications/the-world-factbook/ (accessed June 17, 2008). United Nations estimates are based on Hania Zlotnik, "World Population Will Increase by 2.5 Billion by 2050," press release POP/952, UN Population Division, March 13, 2007, http://www.un.org/News/Press/docs//2007/pop952.doc.htm (accessed June 19, 2008).

9. Alia McMullen, "Forget Oil, the New Global Crisis Is Food," *Financial Post,* January 7, 2008, http://www.financialpost.com/story.html?id=213343 (accessed June 17, 2008).

10. Telegraph Media Group, "Food Shortages: How Will We Feed the World?" *Telegraph.*co.uk, April 22, 2008, http://www.telegraph.co.uk/earth/main.jhtml?xml=/earth/2008/04/22/scifood122.xml&page=1 (accessed June 17, 2008).

11. Associated Press, "Midwest Floods, East Coast Sizzles," *CBS News,* June 19, 2008, http://www.cbsnews.com/stories/2008/06/10/national/main4167488.shtml (accessed June 19, 2008). The floods throughout the Midwest are called "natural disasters," but some researchers believe they actually result from human action. Kamyar Enshayan, director of the Center for Energy and Environmental Education at the University of Northern Iowa, argues that research indicates that the flooding in states like Iowa is the result of human activity rather than a naturally occurring disaster. The destruction of wetlands and the transformation of the natural environment for agricultural production on a mass level have created an environment that is unable to prevent flooding naturally through absorption. See Joel Achanbach, "Iowa Flooding Could Be an Act of Man, Experts Say," *Washington Post,* June 19, 2008, A01.

12. Associated Press, "Midwest Floods, East Coast Sizzles."

13. Intergovernmental Panel on Climate Change, "Climate Change 2007: Synthesis Report," IPCC Plenary XXVII, Valencia, Spain, November 12–17, 2007, http://www.ipcc.ch/pdf/assessment-report/ar4/syr/ar4_syr.pdf (accessed June 19, 2008).

14. World Health Organization, "International Spread of Disease Threatens Public Health Security," August 23, 2007, http://www.who.int/mediacentre/news/releases/2007/pr44/en/index.html (accessed June 17, 2008).

15. Ibid.

16. Laurie Garrett, "The Next Pandemic?" *Foreign Affairs* 84, no. 4 (July–August 2005): 3–23. Garrett also argues that complicating the risks of a pandemic flu outbreak is an insufficient supply of vaccines, which would have an acute effect on less developed nations but could also pose problems for wealthier countries in Europe and North America.

17. Finally, after numerous attempts, the last vehicle stops and offers them a ride. Julian also finds a single empty seat in a Jeep that will take him to Princeton to look for his wife. He leaves Jess with Elliot and Alma, planning to reunite with them later. However, upon arriving at the university, which has been affected, he notices a tear in the fabric of the Jeep's cover. Soon after, the driver slams the Jeep into a tree, and Julian—now afflicted—sits in the middle of the road and uses a shard of broken glass to slice open his wrists.

18. Robert Kaplan, "The Coming Anarchy," *Atlantic Monthly,* February 1994, http://www.theatlantic.com/doc/199402/anarchy (accessed June 17, 2008).

19. Thomas Homer-Dixon, "Environmental Scarcity and Intergroup Conflict," in *World Security: Challenges for a New Century,* 2nd ed., ed. Michael T. Klare and Daniel C. Thomas (New York: St. Martin's Press, 1994), 290.

20. One such letter was received by former South Dakota senator and Senate Majority Leader Tom Daschle. The letter received by Daschle's office read, "You cannot stop us. We have this anthrax. You die now. Are you afraid? Death to America. Death to Israel. Allah is great." For an image of this letter and information regarding the bioterrorist threats from 2001 to 2003 in the United States, see Ralph R. Frerichs, "American Anthrax Outbreak of 2001: Introduction," UCLA Department of Epidemiology, School of Public Health, Los Angeles, http://www.ph.ucla.edu/epi/Bioter/detect/antdetect_intro .html (accessed June 16, 2008).

21. America's response to terrorism is well known and well publicized. On October 7, 2001, the United States invaded Afghanistan in an attempt to overthrow the Taliban regime and destroy support for al-Qaeda in the region. The mission in Afghanistan was also designed to find al-Qaeda operatives and leaders (including Osama bin Laden) and eradicate the infrastructure for recruitment and training. On March 20, 2003, the United States began a second front in the war on terror with the invasion of Iraq. Under the guise of eliminating the development of weapons of mass destruction (WMD), as well as the state sponsorship of terrorism, the U.S. military engaged in the overthrow of Saddam Hussein and the establishment of a democratic Iraq. The controversy surrounding the war in Iraq is entrenched in mainstream political dialogue and does not need to be rehashed here. The official reason for the initial invasion was to protect the United States from the WMD threat posed by Hussein's regime and to free the Iraqi people (George W. Bush, "President Discusses Beginning of Operation Iraqi Freedom," transcript of presidential radio address, March 22, 2003, White House, Office of the Press Secretary, http://www.whitehouse.gov/news/releases/2003/03/20030322.html [accessed June 16, 2008]). The Bush administration also made several attempts to link Hussein with al-Qaeda and the attacks of 9/11 (Dana Milbank, "Bush Defends Assertions of Iraq–Al-Qaeda Relationship," *Washington Post,* June 18, 2004, A9). However, voluminous amounts of information have been released to the contrary, including by the 9/11 Commission, members of Bush's staff, and even Bush himself (National Commission on Terrorist Attacks, *The 9/11 Commission Report: Final Report of the National Commission on Terrorist Attacks Upon the United States* [New York: W. W. Norton, 2004]; Scott McClellan, *What Happened: Inside the Bush White House and Washington's Culture of Deception* [New York: Public Affairs, 2008]; "Bush Rejects Saddam 9/11 Link," *BBC News,* September 18, 2003, http://news.bbc.co.uk/2/hi/americas/3118262.stm [accessed June 16, 2008]). By September 2005, former secretary of state Colin Powell indicated that he regretted his speech before the United Nations in which he professed the existence of a biochemical terror threat from Iraq (Steven R. Weisman, "Powell Calls His UN Speech a Lasting Blot on His Record," *New York Times,* September 9, 2005, http://www.nytimes .com/2005/09/09/politics/09powell.html?_r=1&oref=slogin [accessed June 16, 2008]). The response to the terrorist threat was immediate and far-reaching; it had hundreds of billions of dollars of resources and the full attention of the U.S. government. Joseph Stiglitz, a Nobel Prize–winning economist, indicates that the Iraq war has hidden costs

not factored in to the five-year cumulative cost of $845 billion, which is having a cooling effect on the U.S. economy. Stiglitz conservatively estimates that the war to date has cost the U.S. economy more than $3 trillion and may soon rival the $5 trillion cost of World War II (Daniel Trotta, "Iraq War Hits the U.S. Economy: Nobel Winner," *Reuters News Service*, March 2, 2008, http://www.reuters.com/article/topNews/idUSN292152742008 0302?feedType=RSS&feedName= topNews&sp=true [accessed June 16, 2008]).

22. See Jessica Tuchman Mathews, "Redefining Security," *Foreign Affairs* 67 (1989): 162–77; Thomas Homer-Dixon, "Environmental Scarcities and Violent Conflict: Evidence from Cases," *International Security* 19, no. 1 (Summer 1994): 5–40.

23. Of the 40,225 incidents of terrorism recorded, it should be noted that 16,309 (40.5 percent) of these occurred in Iraq and 2,587 (6.4 percent) occurred in Afghanistan. Office of the Coordinator for Counterterrorism, "Country Reports on Terrorism," U.S. Department of State, National Counterterrorism Center, Annex of Statistical Information, Washington, DC, April 30, 2008, http://www.state.gov/s/ct/rls/crt/2007/103716 .htm (accessed June 16, 2008).

24. Juliet Eilperin, "Climate Shift Tied to 150,000 Fatalities," *Washington Post*, November 17, 2005, A20; World Health Organization, "Climate and Health Fact Sheet, July 2005," http://www.who.int/globalchange/news/fsclimandhealth/en/index.html (accessed June 16, 2008); Integrated Regional Information Networks, UN Office for the Coordination of Humanitarian Affairs, "Food Crisis: Status and Impacts," June 16, 2008, http://www.irinnews.org/IndepthMain.aspx?IndepthId=72&ReportId=77872 (accessed June 16, 2008).

25. A full listing of the victims of 9/11 can be found at http://www.september11victims. com/september11victims/victims_list.htm (accessed June 16, 2008). The actual number of hurricane victims may be higher according to some estimates, but an exact count is impossible because of the number of missing people and the destruction of public records. See Michelle Hunter, "Deaths of Evacuees Push Toll to 1,577," *Times-Picayune*, May 19, 2006, http://www.nola.com/news/t-p/frontpage/index.ssf?/base/news-5/ 1148020620117480.xml&coll=1 (accessed June 16, 2008).

26. Department of Homeland Security, "The First Year after Hurricane Katrina: What the Federal Government Did" (updated June 9, 2008), http://www.dhs.gov/ xprepresp/programs/gc_1157649340100.shtm (accessed June 16, 2008); Jason Bram, James Orr, and Carol Rapaport, "Measuring the Effects of the September 11 Attack on New York City," *FRBNY Economic Policy Review*, November 2002, http://www .newyorkfed.org/research/epr/02v08n2/0211rapa.pdf (accessed June 16, 2008); Roger A. Pielke Jr., Joel Gratz, Christopher W. Landsea, Douglas Collins, Mark A. Saunders, and Rade Musulin, "Normalized Hurricane Damage in the United States: 1900–2005," *Natural Hazards Review* 9, no. 1 (February 2008): 29–42.

27. Amy Belasco, "CRS Report for Congress: The Cost of Iraq, Afghanistan, and Other Global War on Terror Operations since 9/11," Congressional Research Service, Washington, DC (updated April 11, 2008), http://www.fas.org/sgp/crs/natsec/RL33110.pdf

(accessed June 16, 2008); Jim Horney, Robert Greenstein, and Richard Kogan, "Katrina Relief and Federal Spending Deficits," Center on Budget and Policy Priorities (revised September 19, 2005), http://www.cbpp.org/9–17–05bud.htm (accessed June 16, 2008); Office of the Chief Financial Officer, U.S. Environmental Protection Agency, "Budget 2007: U.S. Environmental Protection Agency Summary," February 2006, http://www .epa.gov/ocfo/budget/2007/2007bib.pdf (accessed June 16, 2008); Office of Management and Budget, Executive Office of the President of the United States, "Protecting America," http://www.whitehouse.gov/omb/budget/fy2006/protecting.html (accessed June 16, 2008); Christopher Lee, "Budget Cut Would Shutter EPA Libraries," *Washington Post,* May 15, 2006, A15.

28. Prior to September 11, 2001, the worst recorded incident of terrorism in the United States was the Oklahoma City bombing in 1995, in which 169 people lost their lives. According to data compiled and reported by the FBI, there were a total of 318 acts of terrorism in the United States from 1980 to 2005, resulting in 3,178 deaths. These include a wide range of activities, including but not limited to actions of the Ku Klux Klan, abortion clinic bombings, acts of eco-terrorists and animal rights activists, the Oklahoma City bombing, and 9/11. If 9/11 and Oklahoma City are removed from that analysis as outliers, there were only 33 terrorist-related deaths, all of which were the result of domestic extremist organizations. Federal Bureau of Investigation, Counterterrorism Division, *Terrorism 2002–2005,* http://www.terrorisminfo.mipt.org/pdf/ Terrorism2002–2005.pdf (accessed June 16, 2008).

29. It wasn't until the overt, dramatic events of 9/11 that the United States was mobilized to deal with threats from terrorism. In fact, the *9/11 Commission Report* indicates that one of the most significant obstacles to preventing 9/11 was that the threat of terrorism was not part of the American political consciousness. According to the report, "As the most representative branch of the federal government, Congress closely tracks trends in what public opinion and the electorate identify as key issues. In the years before September 11, terrorism seldom registered as important. To the extent that terrorism did break through . . . it would briefly command attention after a specific incident and then return to a lower rung on the public policy agenda" (*9/11 Commission Report,* 104).

30. For research and reports on colony collapse disorder and its projected effects, see Penn State, College of Agricultural Sciences, "Honeybee Die-off Alarms Beekeepers, Crop Growers and Researchers," January 29, 2007, http://aginfo.psu.edu/news/2007/1/ HoneyBees.htm (accessed June 15, 2008); J. R. Minkel, "Mysterious Honeybee Disappearance Linked to Rare Virus," *Scientific American,* September 7, 2007, http://www.sciam .com/article.cfm?id=bees-ccd-virus (accessed June 15, 2008); Dennis van Engelsdorp, Diana Cox-Foster, Maryann Frazier, Nancy Ostiguy, and Jerry Hayes, "'Fall Dwindle Disease': Investigations into the Causes of Sudden and Alarming Colony Losses by Beekeepers in the Fall of 2006," Preliminary Report for the Colony Collapse Disorder Working Group, December 15, 2006 (revised January 5, 2007), http://maarec.cas.psu .edu/pressReleases/FallDwindleUpdate0107.pdf (accessed June 15, 2008).

31. It is likely that the quotation was originally attributed to Einstein to give it cred-ibility and add the weight of his well-established genius. Dan Shapley, a journalist with the *Daily Green*, looked into the urban legend surrounding this original statement and discovered that there is plenty of scientific evidence to support its conclusion. Therefore, even though Einstein probably did not say that the disappearance of bees would lead to the death of humankind, it is likely that if he had examined the evidence, he would have supported such a claim. Dan Shapley, "Famous Einstein Bee Quote Is Bogus," *Daily Green,* June 22, 2007, http://www.thedailygreen.com/environmental-news/latest/2782 (accessed June 15, 2008).

32. Michael Shellenberger and Ted Nordhaus, "The Death of Environmentalism: Global Warming Politics in a Post-Environmental World," essay prepared for a meet-ing of the Environmental Grantmakers Association, October 2004, reprinted online at http://www.thebreakthrough.org/images/Death_of_Environmentalism.pdf (accessed June 15, 2008).

33. Michael Shellenberger and Ted Nordhaus, *Break Through: From the Death of Environmentalism to the Politics of Possibility* (New York: Houghton Mifflin, 2007).

34. Shyamalan not only emphasizes scientific messages throughout the film but also seems to chastise the audience for the lack of public concern about the hard scientific data on problems such as climate change. In the conversation between Elliot and Jake at the start of the film, Elliot is talking about environmental issues that could have a devastating effect on all life on Earth, but Jake is bored and unconcerned. Elliot grabs his attention by noting, "You should be more interested in science, Jake. You know why? Because your face is perfect. The problem is your face is perfect at fifteen. Now if you were interested in science, you would know facts like the human nose and ears grow a fraction of an inch each year. So a perfect balance of features now might not look so perfect five years from now, and might look downright whack ten years from now." Jake, who couldn't care less about scientific research that suggests we are headed for a global catastrophe, shows immediate interest when science has something to offer about his narcissistic, self-absorbed concern for how he looks. This is a clear jab at audience members who may share Jake's lack of interest in the scientific warnings all around us.

35. For information on the steps being taken by the EU's European Environment Agency, see http://www.eea.europa.eu/ (accessed June 24, 2008).

36. Dennis Pirages and Theresa Manley DeGeest, *Ecological Security: An Evolution-ary Perspective on Globalization* (New York: Rowman and Littlefield, 2003).

37. World Health Organization, "International Spread of Disease Threatens Public Health Security," August 23, 2007, http://www.who.int/mediacentre/news/releases/2007/pr44/en/index.html (accessed June 17, 2008).

Part 3

POPULAR CULTURE AND THE DYNAMICS OF DISSENT AND SOCIAL CHANGE

10

RAISING THE RED FLAG

Culture, Labor, and the Left, 1880–1920

Jeffrey A. Johnson

Those on the Left, politically or otherwise, use a variety of cultural media to advance their goals. In the modern world, leftist ideologies are advanced in myriad ways, yet many have disseminated into popular culture. Few can overlook the radicalism inherent in lyrics from the band Rage Against the Machine, the internationally iconic image of Che Guevara posted on walls around the world, or progressive online publishing such as MoveOn.org. Yet the radicalism and left-wing politics of today, broadly conceived, are not unique in their use of cultural elements, including literature, imagery, and song, to further agendas. Radicals of the late nineteenth and early twentieth centuries used, with great competence, stylistic, societal, and media means not only to respond to a frustrating world around them but also to propagate their causes of reform.

Radicalizing the Left: The Gilded Age and Progressive Era

As the nineteenth century closed, a new era of mechanization, mass production, and speculation brought rapid and sweeping changes to the American workplace and its laborers, creating, in the words of several historians, "the seedbed of a new social and economic order."[1] The nation's new consumptive culture, far from being benevolent, placed a premium on want and wealth. While the "captains of industry" prospered, the nation's rank-and-file wage earners struggled. Across the nation industrial and agricultural laborers increasingly found themselves locked in antagonistic relationships with financiers, venture capitalists, and managers.

These conditions of a new, "modern" America allowed new challengers to emerge on the political scene. Democrats and Republicans still dominated, of course, but now there were dissenting voices that effectively argued on behalf of political "outsiders." The Gilded Age and Progressive Era (circa 1877–1918) witnessed, among others, the Populists of the 1890s and the Progressives of the pre–World War I era, parties and activists that called for sweeping economic and social reforms. However sweeping their calls, labor-minded organizers on the political Left offered some of the most radical—at times, revolutionary—agendas.

Two particular organizations, the Socialist Party of America (SPA) and the Industrial Workers of the World (IWW), arrived on the American landscape in the first years of the twentieth century. These radical organizations enjoyed considerable success at the ballot box and in local labor fights, but these successes did not come without help. The work of "labor" was not confined to simply organizing workers and holding strikes. Instead, forming a class culture, as labor historians have emphasized in recent interpretations, was equally important to working class-identity. Radical labor's agitators, inspired by the increasingly antagonistic relationship between producers and employers, were far from passive in confronting the changing world around them. And workers and their politically dissenting outlets put great emphasis on "propagandizing" as a means of educating and radicalizing the American proletariat. The SPA and IWW used, with great efficacy, a variety of cultural elements—notably, cartoons, songs, and newspapers—to propagate their message of working-class radicalism and simultaneously legitimize their causes.

Established in 1901, the Socialist Party of America became the permanent institution for socialism in the United States. Formed out of the remnants of the Socialist Labor Party and the Social Democratic Party, it offered a viable third-party challenge for nearly two decades. Although disagreements continued to arise over ideology, the party and its organizers brought a message of industrial socialism to potential voters. The SPA emerged, in the words of historian John Graham, as "*the* dominant expression of insurgent politics" in the early twentieth century. For optimistic socialists in attendance at the 1901 "Unity" convention, according to historian David Shannon, "the question was when, not if, the American people—the American working people—would see the logic of industrial history and vote the Socialist Party into office to socialize and democratize the American economy." Party members mobilized under the new banner of the SPA to organize locals, propagandize the masses, and offer candidates. Accordingly, during its first decade and a half, the SPA experienced growth unequaled in American history.[2]

Four years after the establishment of the SPA, a meeting was held that organizer and socialist William "Big Bill" Haywood called "the Continental Congress of the Working Class." Established in Chicago at that 1905 meeting, the Industrial Workers of the World, also known as the "Wobblies," preached a message of universal unionism and working-class emancipation. Among the 203 delegates sat an eclectic mix from the Western Federation of Miners, SPA, Socialist Labor Party, American Labor Union, and American Federation of Labor (AFL). The IWW emerged as a much more radical alternative, particularly over time, to the trade union organization of the AFL and the politically minded SPA. According to historian Greg Hall, the IWW had two goals, "one practical and one revolutionary." The IWW first hoped to organize workers outside of the conservative AFL, regardless of trade, gender, or race. In addition, the Wobblies preached a "one big union" philosophy that would emancipate the working class from the grasp of capitalism through such tactics as the general strike.[3]

With varying brands of socialism and propensities for radicalism, the SPA and IWW both worked diligently to create and enhance movements that represented the interests of exploited labor. For both organizations, though, working-class radicalism was not simply forged at meetings. Instead, the SPA, the Wobblies, and their activists used media and the arts to define who they were and what they thought.

Reporting the Left: Newspapers

At the head of party and labor propaganda work were newspapers and periodicals. In the same way that more "mainstream" labor organizations had publications, such as the AFL's *American Federationist,* the SPA and IWW effectively used publications to further their mission and cause. In print, a number of nationally distributed newspapers and periodicals, in addition to countless regional and local publications, publicized the socialist and unionist agenda. Nationally significant periodicals included the *International Socialist Review* (1900–1918), *Appeal to Reason* (1895–1922), and *The Masses* (1911–1917). These papers tracked, encouraged, and celebrated socialist ideology and successes as the publishers and distributors of these journals committed themselves to educating the working class. An "army of idle workers," according to the *Appeal to Reason,* was "thinking, studying, asking questions, beginning to understand the cause."[4]

The *Appeal to Reason* billed itself as a "pioneer propaganda paper," central to local organizing. "The *Appeal* Army is the backbone of the Socialist Party in America," proclaimed the Girard, Kansas, paper. Circulation varied, depending on election cycles, but it managed to break a single-issue publication record, as the staff was proud to remind readers, of 4.1 million copes.[5]

Based in Chicago, the *International Socialist Review* also played an important role in reporting regional and local events as well as in recruitment and the discussion of issues. Published in Chicago from 1900 to 1918, it offered readers a "monthly journal of international socialist thought." Yet the *Review* offered more than simply doctrine. In fact, reports of local activism and international socialist campaigns, struggles, and successes filled many of its pages.

If the *Appeal to Reason* and, to a lesser extent, the *International Socialist Review* represented, at least implicitly, Midwest sensibilities, New York's *The Masses* typified a more urban and cosmopolitan take on socialism and society. *The Masses* blended socialism with discussions of feminism, literature, race, and the arts during its publication from 1911 to 1917. Its illustrations not only celebrated the labor cause but also resoundingly attacked war and the conflict in Europe, ultimately leading to the publication's demise. What *The Masses, Appeal to Reason,* and *International Socialist Review* all demonstrated was the ability of an active socialist and radical labor press to distinguish the SPA as a legitimate alternative to the Democratic, Republican, and Progressive parties. In addition, the Left's newspapers created a sounding board for ideology and grassroots activity.[6]

Inking the Left: Cartoons

In the pages of these effective radical newspapers and journals appeared another important mechanism of socialist culture: the cartoon. Socialist cartoonists, Ryan Walker, John F. Hart, and Art Young among them, used their work with great effectiveness to both enhance and legitimize the socialist message. They mocked financiers and capitalists, celebrated candidates and electoral successes, and chided ignorant and uninformed laborers.

Ryan Walker, the chief cartoonist for the *Appeal to Reason* and later an illustrator for the socialist *New York Call,* drew countless pieces. Walker, a man Eugene Debs accurately described as "clever and resourceful," had worked as a cartoonist for the *Kansas City Times* and *St. Louis Republic* before joining the *Appeal* in 1911. He quickly became one of the more prolific cartoonists for the socialist cause, with his most popular character, named Henry Dubb, illustrating the trials and tribulations of the rank-and-file worker.[7] One 1912 cartoon for the *Appeal to Reason* depicts Theodore Roosevelt moving closer to a worker saying, "I love you as a brother! I'm Moses sent to save you from socialism." Behind Roosevelt's back, though, is a spiked club labeled "capitalism." The clever caption reads, "Speak softly and carry a big stick." For years Walker offered those who were sympathetic to socialism, and even those less sympathetic, biting critiques of the capitalist system.

Similarly, cartoonist Art Young took aim at greedy landowners and ill-informed farmers. In a 1922 illustration, a man in a top hat and suit walks away from a farmer carrying a basket full of corn labeled "the fat of the land." The farmer is shown scratching his head, left with only a pile of husks. "The Boss: Don't think; stay on the job," jabs the caption. Socialist cartoons not only pointed up labor's plight, as the Young example indicates; they also mocked labor's opponents, political and otherwise, but they sometimes attacked those who were "for labor." A *Chicago Socialist* cartoon, for example, depicts AFL head Samuel Gompers as a dog, complete with a dollar-sign tail blocking a bridge to socialism.[8]

Cartoons lampooning socialism's message and pervasiveness also appeared in the mainstream press. Spokane's *Spokesman-Review* printed a satirical look at socialism in a 1908 cartoon. The caricature depicts an ailing Uncle Sam with a neck tumor of "socialism." Meanwhile, Theodore Roosevelt, labeled "Doctor Roosevelt," stands nearby and offers an elixir of his "reform remedy" to aid Uncle Sam's "problem."[9]

The socialist cartoon served as an effective tool in educating the masses and deriding opponents. Many who were curious about socialism read articles in periodicals or even took "study courses" with pamphlets and books by Marx and Debs. But cartoons persisted as an approachable and effective device. They had a lasting legacy, too, as the political statements in cartoons pioneered new approaches. *The Masses,* some believe, originated the ubiquitous one-line cartoon popularized later by the *New Yorker.*[10]

Composing for the Left: Songs

The real work of socialists, particularly in specific communities, occurred at and around the "local." Devised as chapters, locals held meetings, distributed literature, collected dues, and sponsored events. At local meetings, another important element of labor's culture was the song. Labor songs, in the words of historian Clark Halker, served as "the cultural documents of the working class." Since the advent of the Knights of Labor in the mid-nineteenth century, songs proved important in building solidarity among a varied labor movement. They also assisted, like the socialist press, in articulating labor's objects and aspirations. The popularity of labor song-poems seemed to parallel the highs of the labor movement's success. In other words, when songs enjoyed their greatest popularity and use, labor and the SPA had their most notable successes at the ballot box.[11]

Socialists boasted a number of central tunes. In a 1901 compilation of forty-eight socialist songs, compiler and publisher Charles Kerr proclaimed, "We American socialists are only beginning to sing." And sing they did. Socialist musical compositions such as "True Freedom," "I Will Join the Party Mother," and "No Master," often sung at party encampments, typified how songs provided unity for activists. Accordingly, songs remained an important part of the political culture and gatherings. Socialists often attended local-sponsored encampments, meetings that took place over several days and nights. At this kind of event, voices also rang out. Many of the songs had Populist roots, and participants sang them to the tune of something recognizable. For instance, they sang their beloved "Red Flag" to the tune of "Maryland My Maryland." It celebrated the determined socialist spirit in its chorus: "Then raise the scarlet standard high; Within its shade we'll live and die. / Though cowards flinch and traitors sneer, We'll keep the red flag flying here."[12]

Despite their hopes for a homogeneous working-class movement, socialists did not always agree on doctrine or strategies. They were often divided into the "Reds," the most radical, class-conscious, Marxist, revolutionary socialists, and the "Yellows," who advocated gradual public ownership campaigns and held union-friendly positions. Nevertheless, socialists could agree on song. At the 1912 SPA convention, amid factionalism that helped destroy the party from within, disagreeing delegates took time to sing the "Marseillaise" and "Red Flag" during hotly contested vote counts on amendments. Although some socialists believed that socialist ideology, not song, provided the best means of understanding the relationship between capital and labor, labor songs lingered as a valuable method of disseminating propaganda and fostering culture.[13]

The IWW, too, used songs, such as those gathered in the popular *Little Red Songbook* (1916), to encourage working-class solidarity. Poets and songwriters including Joe Hill, Ralph Chaplin, T-Bone Slim, and Harry McClintock gave the Wobblies spirited and at times sarcastic tunes of solidarity. On their way to a 1908 IWW meeting, John Walsh led an "Overalls Brigade" of workers aboard a seized cattle car they dubbed the "Red Special." Holding rallies and distributing literature as they traveled east, the group sang songs from sheets they also sold. These song sheets were precursors to the titles compiled in the *Little Red Songbook*.[14]

As composers and organizers understood, song offered an approachable medium for ideology. Joe Hill, famed IWW songwriter, understood the song's power: "A pamphlet, no matter how good, is never read more than once, but a song is learned by heart and repeated over and over; and I maintain that if a person can put a few cold, common sense facts into a song, and dress them up in a cloak of humor to take the dryness off of them, he will succeed in reaching a great number of workers who are too unintelligent to read a pamphlet or an editorial on economic science." Hill did his part for the cause, penning a number of songs for the *Little Red Songbook*, including famous pieces such as "The Preacher and the Slave" and a parody of the Salvation Army's tune "In the Sweet Bye and Bye": "Workingmen of all countries unite; Side by side we for freedom will fight." Songs remained a central part of IWW culture. Even in his last years in Moscow, Big Bill Haywood welcomed guests to his hotel room, where, according to Melvyn Dubofsky, the group went "through the *Little Red Song Book* until they collapsed in a drunken stupor."[15]

Writing for the Left: Literature

In addition to newspapers, cartoons, and songs, fiction with socialist messages stood as one final piece in socialist culture. In books, poetry, and other literary forms, authors creatively mixed literature with propaganda. Utopian or broadly socialist literature, such as Edward Bellamy's 1888 book *Looking Backward*, also remained important to the popularization of socialist principles. The book tells the tale of Julian West, a late-nineteenth-century Boston aristocrat. West has trouble sleeping and constructs a basement sleeping area. When a fire destroys his home he awakes, à la Rip Van Winkle, to the futuristic Boston of 2000. The book chronicles his wonder and amazement at a society without want, one of divided labor, social and economic equality, and harmony. Organizers took this work to heart. They formed "Bellamy Clubs," and the book brought many to socialism. J. F. Mabie, one of the most active socialist organizers in Montana, explained his conversion to socialism: "In 1902 I read Bellamy's *Looking Backward*[.] I discovered myself and from that time called myself a socialist."[16]

Pieces of popular socialist fiction sometimes got their start in periodicals. The *Appeal to Reason* regularly featured implicitly political works of poetry and prose. The caliber of the authors is striking. The *Appeal* boasted works from Stephen Crane, Charlotte Perkins Gilman, Edward Bellamy, and Jack London. Upton Sinclair's *The Jungle* first appeared as a serial in the *Appeal to Reason*. In late 1904 *Appeal* editor Fred Warren took a chance on Sinclair and gave the author a $500 advance. For seven weeks Sinclair lived among Chicago's packinghouses, researching his novel about exploited workers and the unsanitary conditions. When the novel appeared in the *Appeal to Reason*'s pages in 1905, editors believed the readership doubled or even tripled. *The Jungle* came out in book form the next year, but the *Appeal to Reason* is where it got its start.

Even Portland, Oregon's John Reed, founder of and columnist for *The Masses*, became involved with celebratory travel literature. Reed (immortalized by Warren Beatty in the 1981 film *Reds*) holds the distinction of being buried in the Kremlin wall in Moscow's Red Square. As an on-the-scene chronicler of the Bolshevik Revolution, Reed provided a firsthand account of those events in his seminal 1919 work *Ten Days that Shook the World*. Reed penned the book, which boasted an introduction by Lenin in the 1922 printing, while working on assignment for *The Masses*.

Labor's Voice in Popular Culture

Through socialist newspapers, cartoons, songs, and literature, radical labor gained, in the first years of the twentieth century, a foothold as a legitimate third-party voice for labor. During this turbulent era, as historian Stephen Skowronek contends, the fight became one for power and control over new bureaucratic and administrative systems, and third-party political opportunity proliferated. Socialists had successfully positioned themselves as *the* third-party voice for American labor. Socialism in the United States achieved its greatest electoral success in 1912, when socialist presidential candidate Eugene Debs mustered 5.9 percent of the national vote. No other socialist contender in American history has managed to gain such a significant portion of the electorate's support. Even as socialists and their agenda remained fervently radical, their ideological and political positions did not hinder socialist political legitimacy. In fact, as historian Stephen Diner observes, socialists seemed unchallenged in their ability to keep "'the labor question' as a central issue in the policy debates of the Progressive Era." And it was their effective use of media and cultural representations that strengthened their movement.[17]

For socialists, Wobblies, and others on the Left, some of the very media that helped bring success proved devastating. On the eve of World War I, as suspicions mounted about "radicals" infiltrating the country, repression of leftist political dissent reached a fevered pitch as fervent patriots increasingly labeled radicals, socialists, and antiwar advocates as disloyal troublemakers. Consequently, the federal government initiated several antiradical measures. The Espionage Act of June 1917, the Trading with the Enemy Act of October 1917, and the Sedition Act of May 1918 all targeted radicals through restrictions on speech and expression. America's socialists immediately felt the sting of these events. The socialist press had always experienced some backlash. Staff at the Seattle, Washington, Public Library, for example, barred the *International Socialist Review* after a member of its board of trustees deemed the journal "hot stuff." Library officials also called the *Review*'s language "too intemperate." The "intemperate" *Review* editors had an answer. "No doubt the *Ladies' Home Journal* is safer," quipped the *Review*, "saner and milder mental pabulum for sissys in general and capitalist lackeys in particular." But by World War I, the Espionage Act and Trading with the Enemy Act had dire consequences for the socialist press. These acts authorized postal officials to deny postage to disloyal publications. By the middle of 1917 post offices regularly denied distribution to the *International Socialist Review* and *Appeal to Reason*. Later in the year authorities blacklisted approximately sixty papers nationally.[18]

Interestingly and ironically, during this famed period of the "Red scare" (1918–1919), cartoons helped demonize "radicals." During and after World War I, socialists faced continued opposition and discrimination, often in print, that portrayed them as disloyal and violent. The doors to "free government," in one 1919 *Outlook* cartoon, characterized the crackdown on radicalism, with "anarchy" and "murder" left outside. A 1919 *New York Eve-*

ning World cartoon showed the IWW digging under "industry" and "labor," leaving them unbalanced and sabotaging their work; in other words, radical Wobblies had undermined the cause of workers. Some cartoonists understood that socialism was under fire. In one *Outlook* piece, published in January 1920, a sketch of a cat, named "socialism," was bandaged with dressings labeled "expulsion" and "criticism." As the cat meowed, the caption read, "the cat with the nine lives." The era of the Red scare and the persecution that came with it sent socialists and other radical labor advocates scurrying, for good reason. The SPA and IWW saw considerable declines in membership and never fully recovered from these critiques that took the form of government policy as well as media attacks.[19]

For socialists, Wobblies, and the ranks of radical labor in the Gilded Age and Progressive Era, the connections between the use of approachable and direct media, in lieu of Marxist thought and ideology, and their political and organizational success were sizable. As much as "typical" organizing activities galvanized their leftist movements, print media, cartoons, songs, and other literature propagated their cause with great efficacy. Today, those on the Left employ literature, other published media, and cultural images for radicalization efforts—just as their activist predecessors did—to point up the strained relationship between capital and labor.

Notes

1. Richard Schneirov, Shelton Stromquist, and Nick Salvatore, *The Pullman Strike and the Crisis of the 1890s* (Urbana: University of Illinois Press, 1999), 6.

2. John Graham, ed., *"Yours for the Revolution": The Appeal to Reason, 1895–1922* (Lincoln: University of Nebraska Press, 1990), 178 (emphasis added); David Shannon, *The Socialist Party of America: A History* (Chicago: Quadrangle Books, 1955), 3–4.

3. Melvyn Dubofsky, *We Shall Be All: A History of the Industrial Workers of the World*, 2d ed. (Chicago: Quadrangle Books, 1988), 81; Greg Hall, *Harvest Wobblies: The Industrial Workers of the World and Agricultural Laborers in the American West, 1905–1930* (Corvallis: Oregon State University Press, 2001), 6.

4. *Appeal to Reason*, March 23, 1912. See also the Labor Press Project at http://depts.washington.edu/labhist/laborpress/Seattle_Socialist.htm.

5. *Appeal to Reason*, January 22, 1910, October 2, 1909; Graham, *"Yours for the Revolution,"* x.

6. See Seymour Lipset and Gary Marks, *"It Didn't Happen Here": Why Socialism Failed in the United States* (New York: W. W. Norton, 2000). The IWW also possessed a number of newspapers. Although many remained regional, some saw wider distri-

bution. The *Industrial Worker,* established in Illinois in 1906 and published from 1909 onward in Spokane, Washington, served the western United States. *Solidarity,* based in Pennsylvania and Ohio, functioned as the eastern Wobblie newspaper. Both IWW publications ably covered strikes, free speech activism, and socialist theory. See Hall, *Harvest Wobblies,* 54.

7. J. Robert Constantine, ed., *Letters of Eugene V. Debs* (Urbana: University of Illinois Press, 1995), 220.

8. Graham, *"Yours for the Revolution,"* 96, 170; Ira Kipnis, *The American Socialist Movement, 1897–1912* (Chicago: Haymarket Books, 2004), 148.

9. *Spokesman-Review* (Spokane, WA), November 6, 1908.

10. Rebecca Zurier, *Art for* The Masses: *A Radical Magazine and Its Graphics* (Philadelphia: Temple University Press, 1989), 27.

11. Clark D. Halker, *For Democracy, Workers, and God: Labor Song-Poems and Labor Protest, 1865–1895* (Urbana: University of Illinois Press, 1991), 13, 194.

12. *Socialist Songs, with Music,* comp. Charles Kerr (Chicago: Charles H. Kerr, 1901); Shannon, *Socialist Party,* 27.

13. Jonathan Dembo, *Unions and Politics in Washington State, 1885–1935* (New York: Garland, 1983), 35–37, 39, 46; Shannon, *Socialist Party,* 72; Halker, *For Democracy, Workers, and God,* 199.

14. Halker, *For Democracy, Workers, and God,* 194; Melvyn Dubofsky, *We Shall Be All: A History of the Industrial Workers of the World,* abridged ed. (Urbana: University of Illinois Press, 2000), 78. More labor and IWW songs are available at http://www.musicanet.org/robokopp/iww.html.

15. Gibbs M. Smith, *Joe Hill* (Salt Lake City: Peregrine Smith Books, 1984), 19–20; Dubofsky, *We Shall Be All* (2000), 263. See also Joyce L. Kornbluh, *Rebel Voices: An I.W.W. Anthology* (Ann Arbor: University of Michigan Press, 1964).

16. Terrence D. McGlynn, "Socialist Organizers in Montana," April 21, 1972, Typescript Vertical File, "Socialism," Montana Historical Society, 2. See also James J. Kopp, "Looking Backward at Edward Bellamy's Influence in Oregon, 1888–1936," *Oregon Historical Quarterly* 104 (Spring 2003): 62–95.

17. Stephen Skowronek, *Building a New American State: The Expansion of National Administrative Capacities, 1877–1920* (Cambridge: Cambridge University Press, 1982), 165; Carolyn Goldinger, ed., *Presidential Elections since 1789,* 5th ed. (Washington, DC: Congressional Quarterly, 1991), 122; Stephen Diner, *A Very Different Age: Americans of the Progressive Era* (New York: Hill and Wang, 1998), 68.

18. *International Socialist Review* 10 (May 1910): 1048; Ronald Schaffer, *America in the Great War: The Rise of the Welfare State* (Oxford: Oxford University Press, 1991), 13–15.

19. See http://newman.baruch.cuny.edu/digital/redscare/htmlcode CHRON/RS007 .HTM, CHRON/RS102.HTM, and CHRON/RS125.HTM.

11

IRAQ IS ARABIC FOR VIETNAM

The Evolution of Protest Songs in Popular Music from Vietnam to Iraq

Jerry Rodnitzky

Mark Twain supposedly noted: "History doesn't repeat itself, but sometimes it rhymes." In comparing the Vietnam War to the Iraq war of the past five years, George W. Bush is hardly a Lyndon Johnson, and Saddam Hussein isn't vaguely similar to Ho Chi Minh. However, Vietcong guerrilla tactics are similar to Iraqi insurgent techniques, and both wars deeply entrenched America in a foreign civil war. Indeed, the most appropriate antiwar bumper sticker cementing the two wars might read: "How Many Vietnamese or Iraqis Died in the American Civil War?"[1]

Even if the U.S. government learned nothing from the Vietnam fiasco, protesters against the Iraq war have. The anti–Iraq war protest songs rhyme with the Vietnam War protest songs in some ways, but they have their own unique style, viewpoints, rationale, and substance. They build on the past but reflect the present. For example, Iraq war protesters don't disrespect the troops in any way; they center on the commander in chief. The big difference in the two wars can be pinpointed with one name and one event—Osama bin Laden and 9/11. The simultaneous war in Afghanistan clearly involves American security, as the Vietnam War never did. Also, there is no draft now, the casualties are much lower, and the high costs of war are being paid for by deficit. Meanwhile, income taxes have actually been cut.

Protests against the Vietnam War by young college students were immersed in unspoken guilt. They were, after all, hiding behind their student deferments while the neighborhood gas station attendant had been drafted. Clearly Vietnam was no real threat to America, so many young protesters asked themselves: why didn't the draftees at least question conscription, rather than blindly cooperating with this illegitimate war? The unspoken assumption was not that the conscripts were patriotic, but that they were not very bright. Thus, on many campuses, both the ROTC and military recruiters were attacked or picketed. Many Vietnam protest songs such as "Fixin' to Die Rag" by Country Joe and the Fish presented the troops as mindless victims of an even more mindless political administration. The war seemed so pointless that many Vietnam protest songs adopted the pacifist view that all wars are stupid and immoral.[2]

Pacifism and Protest Songs

Many protest singers against the Vietnam War, such as Joan Baez, Tom Paxton, and Phil Ochs, identified with pacifism because of their involvement with Martin Luther King's nonviolent civil rights movement. Also, singing protest marchers reflected a communal pacifist spirit manifested in slogans such as "Make love, not war." However, on August 30, 1968, Baez jokingly admitted on television (on Les Crane's show) that she once told a Berkeley protest crowd: "Be nonviolent or I'll kill you."

Yet some pacifist songs of the later 1960s had double-edged lyrics that mirrored the ambivalent nonviolence common to the youthful activists. While these songs spoke eloquently for nonviolence, they also warned of "the fire next time." Behind the New Testament gentleness was a violent Old Testament image of a wrathful, avenging Jehovah. For example, Phil Ochs's songs were usually pacifist but often harbored veiled threats of violence in tone and lyrics. In "Links on the Chain" Ochs sang that past violent union struggles had taught his generation "you gotta fight" and strike "to get what you are owed." More than anyone, Ochs traced the rising youthful tides of both idealistic pacifism and frustrated violence, while suggesting the close relationships between the two.[3]

As Ochs and others moved closer to the young "New Left," they reflected the inconsistent position of antimilitarism and pacifism at home, coupled with a call for revolutionary guerrilla warfare in several developing countries. Even Pete Seeger, a pacifist in most of his songs, had joined the U.S. Army during World War II. And in his best anti-Vietnam song, "Bring Them Home," Seeger notes that he is not "really a pacifist" because if his country were invaded as Vietnam had been, you would find him "out on the firing line."[4]

Also, small, infamous groups such as the Black Panthers and the Weathermen's Students for a Democratic Society faction claimed the right to violent protest and retaliation. Yet John Lennon's 1969 pacifist hit "Give Peace a Chance" seemed to sum up the general mood of the war protesters. That same year Bobby Darin (usually nonpolitical) wrote "Simple Song of Freedom," a ringing pacifist song with the key chorus line "We the people here don't want a war." The song was covered by Tim Hardin in 1969 and became a big hit with protesters.[5]

The Iraq war has not particularly encouraged pacifism. The 9/11 attacks generally negated both pacifism and the view that small, relatively weak countries such as Afghanistan cannot be dangerous to America. And the American troops in Iraq were sometimes the same troops fighting in Afghanistan and searching for those who had supported the attack on America. Thus Iraq protest songs have centered on the political leaders who deliberately used misinformation to trick us into engaging in a stupid, unnecessary war and were now keeping us there. My purpose here is not to argue about the rationales for the two wars but to note the differences and similarities in their respective protest songs to show how they have evolved, for good or bad.

In 1965, history and the accelerating Vietnam War brought America into dangerous waters. President Lyndon Johnson had accepted the Pentagon's argument that the war could be won with large numbers of American ground troops and massive airpower. Whereas discrimination had harmed African Americans, embarrassed the nation, and fueled civil rights protest songs, the Vietnam War was lethal to young Americans black and white. The civil rights issues had been relatively simple to argue; Vietnam was far more complex and divisive. The war merged issues of patriotism, anticommunism, and world peace, and it splintered traditional American political and class alliances. The clearest division on the war was between young and old. Antiwar slogans such as "Make love, not war" and "Don't trust anyone over 30" were hardly directed toward older Americans. The war slowly destroyed Johnson's administration and his political career, and it left his successor, Richard Nixon, with a war-torn nation that he could not bring together.

Glen Campbell's cover of Buffy Sainte-Marie's 1965 pacifist song "Universal Soldier" was the best example of early public distaste for the war, as it rose to the top-ten list. Yet ironically, as the war accelerated, Campbell pointedly rejected pacifism and said, "Any man who would not fight for his country is not a real man." And later that year the California-based rock duo Jan and Dean parodied "Universal Soldier" in a song titled "Universal Coward," about a coward who ran "from Uncle Sam" and ran "from Vietnam." This was one of the few pro-war rock songs.[6]

Although specific protest songs no longer made the top-forty charts after 1965, as the antiwar movement grew, songwriters such as Phil Ochs, Pete Seeger, and Tom Paxton led the way with a stream of very specific anti-Vietnam protest songs. They also encouraged a host of younger protest songwriters. Perhaps the most controversial antiwar song was Pete Seeger's "Waist Deep in the Big Muddy." It tells the story of a 1942 army platoon being pushed by its captain to ford a dangerously deep river. The punch line notes that "the big fool" told his men "to push on." It was clearly a parable about Vietnam, and the "big fool" was obviously Lyndon Johnson. Seeger sang the song in 1967 on the *Smothers Brothers* television show, but CBS censored it because Seeger refused to omit the last verse, which tied the song to Vietnam and Johnson. In response to protests against network censorship, CBS finally permitted the song to be sung in full in January 1968 on the *Smothers Brothers*. Also on the *Smothers Brother* that year, Joan Baez was allowed to dedicate a song to her husband, David Harris, but she was not allowed to say that he was in prison for refusing the draft. In late 1968, after the *CBS Nightly News* (anchored by Walter Cronkite) became sharply critical of the Vietnam War, antiwar censorship on television was much less of a problem. Thus, on a 1969 *Smothers Brothers* show, Seeger was allowed to sing "Bring Them Home," a direct call for America to bring home its troops and end the war.[7]

Antiwar songs were generally not played on the radio because stations did not want to alienate any listeners, but protest singers continued to record them. Among the best Vietnam protest songs were two of Tom Paxton's from 1966: "Lyndon Johnson Told the Nation," which satirizes Johnson's duplicity in explaining the war to Americans, and "We Didn't Know," which compares Americans' unawareness of Vietnam atrocities with Germans who claimed they didn't know about Nazi war crimes. Also noteworthy was Holly Near's 1969 song "Hang in There," which pictures the Vietnamese rebels as long-suffering patriots, and the still popular Country Joe McDonald song "Fixin' to Die Rag." McDonald's song was featured at Woodstock, but it became even better known when it was covered by The New Bohemians on the sound track for the 1989 anti-Vietnam film *Born on the Fourth of July.* Near performed on the antiwar GI coffeehouse circuit with actors Jane Fonda and Donald Sutherland.[8]

Many antiwar songs had mixed or hazy messages. Good examples are John Lennon's 1970 "Imagine" and Melanie's 1970 "Candles in the Rain." Like Lennon's 1969 hit "Give Peace a Chance," "Imagine" is pacifist, but it also attacks nationalism, religion, and wealth in favor of universal togetherness. "Candles in the Rain" describes Melanie Safka's experience at a candlelight anti-Vietnam protest on a rainy night in the nation's capital. But since this top-forty song's vague themes of peace and brotherhood are never explicitly tied to the war, few listeners knew what it was really about, and this made it playable on national radio. Many obscure yet interesting anti-Vietnam songs were collected in *The Vietnam Songbook,* compiled by left-wing folk protest professionals Barbara Dane and Irwin Silber in 1969. It provides words and music for more than 100 protest songs against the Vietnam War.[9]

Both wars featured presidential lies and cover-ups, but since the 1990s, comedians and songwriters have felt free to attack the president, which made George W. Bush even more vulnerable than Lyndon Johnson or Richard Nixon. All three presidents were caught in the same trap. Once American lives were lost, none could admit the mistake and withdraw, because that would have been political suicide. The more soldiers who were killed, the more necessity a victory became to prove that their lives had not been lost in vain.

Yet songwriters were somewhat slower to protest the Iraq war because it followed the less costly Gulf War of 1990, the 9/11 attacks, and the controversial but very successful overthrow of Saddam Hussein in the 2003 Iraq war. The wars of 1990 and 2003 had been accomplished with relatively few casualties. Indeed, many Americans saw the interventions in the Persian Gulf as "splendid little wars"—a phrase used to describe the 1898 Spanish-American War, which also resulted in few casualties. In contrast, protesters had early on compared the Vietnam War to the catastrophic Korean War, and protest songs appeared as soon as the American "technical advisers" to the South Vietnamese army turned into American combatants.

Pro-War Anti-Protest Songs

The best-known pro–Vietnam War songs were not so much pro war as anti protester. Good examples were Merle Haggard's "Okie from Muskogee" and "Fightin' Side of Me," which crudely put down and threatened campus war protesters.[10] Most criticism of protest music has come from the political Right. And especially since 1945, left-wing songwriters have perpetuated the myth that protest songs are always humanitarian, leftist attacks against the status quo. But clearly, Ku Klux Klan political songs do not fit this description, nor do Nazi songs. In the 1960s, however, conservative country songs made popular music an ideological battleground. Today, fifty-somethings usually remember antiwar protest songs and acid-rock music, but they have forgotten 1960s conservative country songs.

Country music did not emerge commercially on records until the 1920s, so World War II was its first chance to demonstrate its fervent patriotism. And from 1941 through the 1950s, country songs uncritically supported America's troops and foreign policy. During the Korean War, country songs by popular singers such as Ernest Tubb criticized communism and championed America's hard-line cold war stance. Not surprisingly, 1960s country songs immediately supported the Vietnam War. For example, Johnny Wright's recording "Hello Vietnam" made the top country chart in 1965. It was followed by pro-war songs such as "Vietnam Blues," written by Kris Kristofferson and recorded by Dave Dudley. But Kristofferson steadily moved Left and actually recorded an anti–Iraq war song, "In the News," in 2006. Pat Boone's country recording of "Wish You Were Here, Buddy" in 1966 features a soldier in Vietnam ridiculing protesters and threatening to come looking for them after the war.[11]

The biggest pro-war hit was Sergeant Barry Saddler's "Ballad of the Green Berets." Saddler, an actual Green Beret, sang it on the *Ed Sullivan Show* in January 1966, and by March it was number one on the *Billboard* chart as a country crossover. By the late 1960s conservative songs no longer mentioned the war specifically but instead concentrated on criticizing unpatriotic protesters. The previously mentioned Merle Haggard songs are good examples, as is Ernest Tubb's 1969 tune "It's America: Love It or Leave It." "Love It or Leave It" became a popular patriotic bumper sticker during this period, but it also led to the most popular American Indian movement bumper sticker: "America: Love It or Give It Back." Perhaps the most controversial pro-Vietnam country song was "The Battle Hymn of Lt. Calley," recorded by Terry Nelson and C Company in 1971. The song defends the court-martialed Calley for his part in the 1968 My Lai massacre of Vietnamese civilians. Major record companies refused to release the song, providing certain proof that the musical struggle over the war was over.[12]

The Decline and Revitalization of Protest Songs

Protest songs in general declined in the 1970s as the Vietnam War wound down, and they have never fully recovered. In the late 1960s some singers such as Judy Collins gave up protest music because they no longer wanted to be musical political agitators, constantly facing the same audiences they recognized from the last rally. Increasingly singers began to feel that they were preaching to the choir. Even earlier, in 1965, Bob Dylan suddenly stopped writing protest songs of any kind and declared his artistic independence from movements and issues. Dylan made it crystal clear in the song "My Back Pages," which proclaims that he had oversimplified right and wrong in his earlier songs and become what he hates most—a preacher.

Also, the combination of folk music and rock, labeled folk-rock, brought hazy message songs to teenagers and the best-selling singles chart. Good examples are Dylan's "Mr. Tambourine Man" and Paul Simon's "Sounds of Silence." These were really do-it-yourself protest songs, since listeners could read many different issues into them. By saying everything, they in effect said nothing. Folk and topical music still highlighted specific issues. After 1975, however, there were few well-defined mass social movements to tie them to. Yet, ever since the 1960s, music has continued to have a mesmerizing grip on American youth. Frank Zappa said it best in 1967 when he noted that many youths are loyal to neither "flag, country, or doctrine," but only to music.[13]

Some very popular singer-songwriters of the 1970–2000 era, such as Bruce Springsteen and Billy Joel, still wrote songs with social messages. For example, in 1983 Billy Joel sang songs about victimized Vietnam troops in "Goodnight Saigon" and displaced Ohio factory workers in "Allentown." Springsteen, who personally opposed the Vietnam War, often wrote songs that highlighted problems of blue-collar Americans and became steadily more politically active. However, these constituted only a small part of their work, given their numerous songs about personal love and heartache.

A few somewhat less popular singers who had been affected by folk protest in the 1960s while growing up continued to write subtle message songs, along with some personal ones. Good examples are John Prine in the 1970s, Charlie King in the 1980s, and Iris Dement in the 1990s. All three became known as singer-songwriters or sometimes just country singers, because nobody knew what to call singers who played acoustic guitar with electronic backup bands. The generic singer-songwriter label

Celebrity musical activist and working-class hero Bruce Springsteen, known affectionately as "The Boss" to his fans, confronts politics and political power in songs such as "Born in the USA," "American Skin (41 Shots)," and "The Rising." (MovieGoods)

was also pinned on some of those who wrote lyrics with a social message or in a poetic style.

The 1985 Live Aid concert, Willie Nelson's Farm Aid concerts since the 1980s, and even Bruce Springsteen's Rock the Vote concerts in 2004 and 2008 all took place in a political vacuum. Most concertgoers went to hear famous performers play their most popular songs, not to support causes. Springsteen is likely the most politically active of these singers. Yet all these performers (now including Sheryl Crow—a surprising Obama supporter in 2008) are really celebrity musical activists, not protest singers or writers.[14]

Without famous singers to consistently champion them, protest songs mostly floundered in the shadowy, fringe folk revival nurtured by folk festivals and the coffeehouse circuit since the mid-1970s. If this movement had a starting point, it was the Kerrville Folk Festival in Kerrville, Texas, close to San Antonio. The first festival in June 1972 attracted 2,800 fans from around the United States. In 1990 attendance reached 25,000, and the festival ran for eighteen days.[15]

After 1972 protest music existed largely within this folk music movement—itself a very small segment of the burgeoning popular music industry. Although most songs described as folk music were very personal, a few touched on broad social and political problems. At least once every decade there was a song so "protesty," such as Iris Dement's "Wasteland of the Free" in 1996, that it cataloged America's faults. This 1960s flashback criticized commercial religion, schools, CEOs' pay, job outsourcing, and, more notably, the Gulf War, while supporting war resisters. It concluded that America now blamed its "troubles on the poor," a "Hitler remedy" that made America the "Wasteland of the Free."[16]

Since the 1990s folk music flourished only in coffeehouses and at small record companies such as Philo, Rounder, and later Red House. A few older, more popular folk artists such as Mary Chapin Carpenter and Emmylou Harris recorded on major labels and performed in large auditoriums, but they were usually seen as country artists. Coffeehouses were a throwback to the small 1960s folk clubs, which often featured protest songs and sprang up near college campuses in coffee shops, taverns, and sometimes churches. The performer generally received only a few hundred dollars a night and the right to sell his or her recordings.

By touring nationwide and developing personal mailing lists or Web sites, folk performers often organized small but devoted fan clubs. One cannot judge their social effect by the number of records they sold or the size of the audiences they attracted. Their songs often influenced more popular performers. Even when their songs were not covered, they may have subtly influenced socially conscious singers such as Bruce Springsteen or Willie Nelson, just as largely unknown folksingers had influenced Bob Dylan in the early 1960s.

Another genre that subtly replaced protest songs was satiric songs. By the 1980s, satire, whether on talk shows, in cartoons, or in songs, had become more politically effective than editorials or speeches in shaping mass political opinion. Perhaps the best example of musical political satire is the path-breaking Washington, D.C., group the Capitol Steps. This group originated in 1981 as sixteen young Washington staffers—male and female, Democrat and Republican. They poked fun at everything political (but especially presidents) with clever, wicked satire. They usually used popular rock music and standard tunes for political parody—a process known as adaptation. Thus Dolly Parton's hit "Working 9 to 5" became a song satirizing President Reagan's work habits, titled "Workin' 9 to 10." And "Puff the Magic Dragon" became "Dutch the Magic Reagan" (about Reagan's political magic). All subsequent presidents have received the same irreverent treatment.[17]

The folk and satiric traditions developed in the 1980s and 1990s were still the major platforms for protest songs after the overthrow of Saddam Hussein in 2003. As the United States became increasingly bogged down in Iraq's civil war, the first specific protest songs against the Iraq war surfaced. They came from coffeehouse folksingers such as Eliza Gilkyson in 2004. A year later some older, somewhat fading celebrity singers, notably Neil Young and John Mellencamp, also wrote antiwar songs, but they attracted little attention.

Gilkyson put her bright, subtle song "Hiway 9" on her 2004 CD, *Land of Milk and Honey*. The song uses an actual highway in Iraq to cleverly criticize the war and its architects. She set the pattern for many future anti–Iraq war songs. The song never mentions Bush or any specific leader by name, but it clearly identifies him with phrases such as "his daddy's kin," "chickenhawks," and "neocons" (*chickenhawks* are men who talk and act warlike but escaped combat themselves). Gilkyson never even says *Iraq* in the song. Instead, she calls it the land between "the Tigris and Euphrates," where "the white god" is going to "liberate" the population and its oil. The song also asks "whose tax dollar" will pay for the war, "yours or mine?"[18]

Gilkyson also took direct aim at Bush on her next CD, *Paradise Hotel*, with a song titled "Man of God." Again without mentioning Bush by name, she sings about a "cowboy from the "West" with a "bulletproof vest" and a "big war chest." She characterizes him as a fake man of God by comparing him with Jesus, and she accuses him of hiding "bodies" from "view" while channeling wealth toward "the chosen few." Each chorus reminds us that these are not the actions of a man of God. In an artistic way, reminiscent of Bob Dylan's protest songs, Gilkyson's two songs pioneered the style and substance of the anti-Iraq protest songs that followed. She said she felt an urgent need to write "Man of God" to separate "true Christians, who really fashion their lives after . . . Christ," from those with a "wrathful warring mentality." Gilkyson lives in Austin, Texas—a somewhat unlikely center for antiwar activity. Another irony is that her more successful folksinger father, Terry Gilkyson, the writer of "Puff the Magic Dragon" and other hits, clearly shied away from political controversy in the 1950s and 1960s.[19]

Earlier, three more well known Texas singers—the Dixie Chicks—inadvertently made themselves more famous as war protesters. At a March 2003 concert in London, England, band member Natalie Maines said, "We're ashamed the president of the United States is from Texas." The Chicks were immediately called traitors, terrorist sympathizers, and worse by many country music fans—their fan base. Chick Emily Robison thought it was part sexism, noting, "We were made into these traitorous sluts. A guy would have been an outlaw."[20] This incident also showed that many Americans considered it traitorous to criticize any American president while abroad. This geopolitical nationalism shows why Neil Young, a Canadian citizen, and Mick Jagger, a Brit, had little currency in America as antiwar singers. However, the Chicks made new fans, and their notoriety and antiwar position put them on the cover of *Time* magazine on May 29, 2006.

Country music had defended past unpopular wars such as Korea and Vietnam by identifying them with patriotism. And after 9/11 many country singers such as Toby Keith followed that tradition and supported the war with patriotic, aggressive songs that waved the flag and threatened America's enemies, including war protesters. Keith's 2002 song "The Angry American (Courtesy of the Red, White and Blue)" and his 2003 ballad "The Taliban Song" were good early examples. They were similar to the pro–Vietnam War songs but had an added urgency provided by 9/11. However, by late 2006 many country songs by popular artists began to center on tragic songs about troops who questioned the war and their loved ones left behind. Good examples include "If I Don't Make it Back" by Tracy Lawrence and "Come Home Soon" by SheDaisy. Daryl Worley, who wrote "Have You Forgotten" in 2003, supporting the war, wrote in 2006 about a soldier who just came back from a place "where they hated me and everything I stand for." These songs stop short of saying the war is a stupid mistake, but they don't voice support either.[21]

Since the 1990s, the Internet has added a new musical dimension and base. Perhaps the most well-known antiwar song distributed free on the Internet is "Talking Chickenhawk Blues," written and sung by Peter Dyer in 2003. On his Web site, Dyer notes that the song "was written as a reaction . . . to the war being led by so many people who avoided the shooting when it was their time." The song identifies Bush only as "chickenhawk #1," the "leader of the nation" who "starts wars" but "never had to go." Vice President Cheney is identified only as "chickenhawk #2," who got out of service because his wife had a child and who helped start the first Gulf War and became a "millionaire along the way." "Chickenhawk #3," described only as a "roly-poly talk-show host" who could not "enlist" because a doctor wrote a note "about some anal cyst," is obviously Rush Limbaugh, the conservative radio commentator. At last count, an Internet site listed some forty-eight little-known songs satirizing President Bush or his advisers. A good example is Chuck Brodsky's "Liar Liar, Pants on Fire."[22]

A more recent, influential, and very moving anti-Iraq song, "The Road of Good Intentions" by John Gorka, a veteran coffeehouse folksinger, became famous as an artistic YouTube video in December 2007. The subtle, poetic song doesn't mention any names but clearly blames the war in Iraq on a White House that puts out "more fiction" than "Hollywood." The video plays the song against photos of suffering Iraqis and U.S. soldiers and some of Bush and Cheney dancing with their wives. Gorka, whose father served in Vietnam, is very sympathetic to the troops. The song notes that while soldiers risk "their life and limb," the leaders who "sent them marching" can "dance the night away." The war is called a "tragic venture" that shocks you only when "the bill arrives." Gorka's song notes that on the road of good intentions, everything becomes "justified to hell."[23]

Periodically one might find a song protesting the Iraq war by the likes of Bruce Springsteen, John Mellencamp, or even a hip-hop group. But whereas the best Vietnam protest songs were by famous folksingers such as Bob Dylan and Pete Seeger, the best Iraq protest songs have been by seasoned yet relatively unknown songwriters such as Eliza Gilkyson and John Gorka. The contemporary folk performers on the coffeehouse circuit are generally more polished and innovative than their predecessors because they built on what the 1960s singers started. Several would have been famous in the 1960s, but so far, they lack a mass national audience. However, as history shows, what goes around often comes around. There may be another golden age of folk protest coming. Meanwhile, the best collection of subtle, artistic Iraq protest songs is *13 Ways to Live,* which features Eliza Gilkyson and twelve other folksingers.[24]

The group satirizing President Bush's handling of the war and his general image most effectively and consistently is the Capitol Steps. Even before Iraq, they satirized Bush as a managed president with two songs: "Son of a Bush" and "My Staff Belongs to Daddy." A song titled "Don't Go Faking Your Smart," sung to the tune of Elton John's "Don't Go Breaking My Heart," appeared on their 2002 CD, *When Bush Comes to Shove,* and questions Bush's knowledge and intelligence. Since then, *Between Iraq and a Hard Place* (2003), *Four More Years in the Bush Leagues* (2004), and *I'm So Indicted* (2005) have mercilessly satirized the Iraq invasion, Bush's problems in stabilizing Iraq, his general foreign policies, and his educational deficiencies. These clever, adaptive-style songs have become the most effective vehicle for protest songs. They are the musical equivalent of television's political satire. The Capitol Steps are the new court jesters of our era. And even when political sarcasm and satire's goal is entertainment, the main effect is often political.[25]

In the Vietnam era, protest songs found many people and conditions to blame for the war and thus were fairly complicated. Generals who advised sending troops and the silent majority of citizens were blamed, as well as presidents. In contrast, songs protesting the Iraq war blame only a managed president, his powerful vice president, and his political advisers. These songs constantly say, "Look at what those fools are doing," taking the average citizen off the hook. The Vietnam generation often took personal responsibility. Young protesters more often said, "Look at what *we're* doing." In a democracy, citizens as well as leaders are responsible. And Vietnam protest songs such as "We Didn't Know," comparing American voters to Germans who supported Hitler, make this precise point. It is a generational difference and a lesson worth learning. Many 1960s activists felt superior to older generations, both in their understanding of new issues and in their willingness to respond. The present generation doesn't feel superiority or any special responsibility for change. Most college students oppose the war but don't believe it is their job to stop it. And they don't want too much political change before they cash in their degrees. Whereas the 1960s slogan was "Don't trust anyone over thirty," for some survivors of that decade, the new slogan could be "Don't trust anyone under fifty."

The serious protest singers were on the fringes of mass culture in both eras, but their influence cannot be measured statistically, for there is a multiplier effect. The few people they inspire may be particularly vigorous and influential leaders of mass movements. And clearly, generations brought up on music can still learn things from songs—even from Bobby Darin's "Simple Song of Freedom," with its resounding chorus line: "We the people here don't want a war."

Notes

1. Historians and others have commonly attributed the "history sometimes rhymes" comment to Twain, although there is no written source for this. For an example of recent attribution, see *The Week,* July 18, 2008, 21.

2. Country Joe and the Fish, *The Life and Times of Country Joe and the Fish* (Vanguard Records, 1971).

3. Phil Ochs, *I Ain't Marching Anymore* (Elektra Records, 1965).

4. Pete Seeger, *Young vs. Old* (Columbia Records, 1967).

5. John Lennon, *Live Peace in Toronto* (Apple Records, 1969); Bobby Darin, *The Best of Bobby Darin* (Atco Records, 1991); Ochs, *I Ain't Marching Anymore.*

6. The original "Universal Soldier" is from Buffy Sainte-Marie, *The Best of Buffy Sainte-Marie* (Vanguard Records, 1968). Campbell quoted by Tom Paxton in "An Interview with Tom Paxton," *Broadside* 67 (February 1966), 8; Jan and Dean, *Folk 'N' Roll* (Liberty Records, 1965).

7. Seeger, *Young vs. Old.* On the origin and mystique of 1960s protest singers and songs, see Jerome L. Rodnitzky, *Minstrels of the Dawn: The Folk-Protest Singer as a Cultural Hero* (Chicago: Nelson-Hall, 1976), 28–39.

8. Tom Paxton, *Ain't that News* (Elektra Records, 1966); Holly Near, *Hang in There* (Redwood Records, 1973); Country Joe, *Life and Times.*

9. John Lennon, *Imagine* (Apple Records, 1971); Melanie, *Candles in the Rain* (Buddah Records, 1972); Barbara Dane and Irwin Silber, *The Vietnam Songbook* (New York: Monthly Review Press, 1969).

10. Merle Haggard, *Truly the Best of Merle Haggard* (Capitol Records, 1971).

11. Ernest Tubb, *Ernest Tubb's Greatest Hits, Vol. 2* (Decca Records, 1970); "Hello Vietnam" and "Vietnam Blues," The Deputies, *The Ballad of the Green Berets* (Wyncotte Records, 1967); Kris Kristofferson, *The Old World* (New West Records, 2006); Pat Boone, *Wish You Were Here, Buddy* (Dot Records, 1966).

12. "The Ballad of the Green Berets," The Deputies, *The Ballad of the Green Berets* (Wyncotte Records, 1967); C Company, *Wake Up America* (Plantation Records, 1971).

13. Bob Dylan, *Bob Dylan's Greatest Hits* (Columbia Records, 1967); Simon and Garfunkel, *Sounds of Silence* (Columbia Records, 1966); Frank Kofsky, "Frank Zappa: An Interview," in *The Age of Rock,* ed. Jonathan Eisen (New York: Random House, 1969), 256.

14. A good source for current musical activism is the Music for Democracy Web site, www.musicforsociety.org (accessed October 10, 2008).

15. For the beginning of the new folk movement, see "Kerrville Folk Festival," *The Handbook of Texas Online,* www.tsha.utexas/handbook/kerrville (accessed May 2, 2008).

16. Iris Dement, *The Way I Should* (Warner Brothers Records, 1996).

17. The Capitol Steps, *We Arm the World* (Capitol Steps Records, 1985) and *Workin' 9 to 10* (Capitol Steps Records, 1988).

18. Eliza Gilkyson, *Land of Milk and Honey* (Red House Records, 2004).

19. Eliza Gilkyson, *Paradise Hotel* (Red House Records, 2005); Gilkyson quoted in "Eliza Gilkyson," *Texas Music* (Fall 2005): 47.

20. Robison quoted in *The Week,* December 1, 2006, 8.

21. Toby Keith, *Unleashed* (Dreamworks Records, 2002) and *Schock and Y'all* (Dreamworks Records, 2003); new country antiwar songs noted by Michelle Cottle in *The Week,* June 29, 2007, 12; Daryl Worley, *Have You Forgotten* (Dreamworks Nashville Records, 2003) and *Here and Now* (Dreamworks Nashville Records, 2006).

22. Peter Dyer, "Talking Chickenhawk Blues," www.scroom.com/chickenhawkblues (accessed May 5, 2008); "Folksongs about U.S. President George W. Bush," www.nwfolk .com/songlists/dubya.html (accessed June 15, 2008).

23. John Gorka, "Road of Good Intentions," music video, www.youtube.com (accessed December 6, 2007). The song appeared first on John Gorka, *Writing in the Margins* (Red House Records, 2006).

24. *13 Ways to Live* (Red House Records, 2004).

25. The Capitol Steps, *When Bush Comes to Shove* (2002), *Between Iraq and a Hard Place* (2003), *Four More Years in the Bush Leagues* (2004), and *I'm So Indicted* (2005), all on Capitol Steps Records.

12

HIP-HOP AND REPRESENTIN'

Power, Voice, and Identity

Tanji Gilliam

In the introduction to *Black Popular Culture,* Gina Dent states the following: "Black Americans in the United States now have unprecedented access to cultural and economic capital. . . . We must therefore begin to analyze the relative power derived from our position as citizens, however unsatisfied, of these United States."[1] Here, Dent indirectly acknowledges that both the hip-hop and the film industries have renegotiated the status of blacks in American society. Blacks have entered these industries in increasing numbers as artists and executives, and blacks frequently inform the "subjects" of music and video projects. Furthermore, Dent introduces the notion of "power" and calls for an investigation of the various manifestations of power that oral and visual media have granted blacks in our postfilm era. She continues, "This means thinking through the hall of mirrors in which our cultural power gets projected as political power."[2]

It is important to question the lack of distinction made by the American public between cultural presence (the actual amount of time blacks spend on TV and film screens) and political presence in formal government and other significant alternative political arenas. However, I would argue that the hall of mirrors Dent refers to isn't the distorted reflection of conflated cultural and political representations alone. Hip-hop can be pervasive and political. However, the blanket generalization that all hip-hop is political is problematic. It is not necessarily wrong but troubling, because this declaration is often made without a concrete consideration of how hip-hop's politics manifests. It is my contention that hip-hop does not exist at either pole of this continuum. Instead, it often wavers in the middle. It is therefore neither entirely political nor apolitical.

Here, I explore the multiple meanings of power hip-hop represents, particularly those notions that are invested in consciously locating hip-hop politics. Hip-hop cultural production does in fact hold the potential for political empowerment. However, many critics are crippled by preestablished definitions of what political empowerment actually is.[3] When scholars interrogate political voids in hip-hop culture, they are often disappointed by the seeming divorce of cultural participants from grassroots political organizing. Again, this connects directly back to Black Nationalist models of political behavior. These critics are not satisfied with the model of media "standing in" for the political agency of artists. Furthermore, these same critics express concern about hip-hop's reliance on the commercial recording industry and other capitalist structures. Their disappointment over hip-hop's commercialism, in addition to its lack of sustained grassroots activism and formal political participation such as campaigning, voting, or registering in a political party, discourages them from conceptualizing hip-hop as a political movement rather than as an artistic and cultural phenomenon.

Hip-hop culture responds to former pitfalls of representation in rather progressive ways. First, it presents a more balanced picture of class among its representatives than did earlier black cultural models.[4] Second, hip-hop artists deliberately manipulate ideas of authenticity. Last, the "burden of representation," as scholar Kobena Mercer terms it, is consciously affirmed in a manner that sometimes advances group interests and critiques the inequalities of black class disparities.[5] When Lani Guinier notes, "By critically examining certain fundamental assumptions about representation, I hope to revive our political imagination," the representation she refers to has to do with the politics of the vote.[6] Likewise, when Guinier discusses a politics of representation, she calls for a revolution of formal political structures. Formal and cultural political concerns meet in hip-hop, with respect to black cultural representation. Guinier argues specifically for "group representation" in the wake of a society "deeply cleaved by issues of racial identity."[7] Although racial groups and cultural groups are certainly not analogous formations, I think Guinier's theory can and should apply to hip-hop culture as well.

Adam Krims suggests that although rap music has historically been identified as a fundamental "element" of hip-hop culture, we should look at it now—in its late, "commodified," and "globalized" form—as "media content" exclusively.[8] Here Krims attempts to separate industry rap productions from hip-hop culture. Krims's investment in rap music as an "impure" product is troubling, particularly because it romanticizes underground or noncommercial rap, and it unfairly divorces commercial rap artists from the culture that reared them.[9] It separates the two arenas of music production and circulation as if they always reflect competing interests. Rap produced within the context of music and other media industries does not always reflect *all* the concerns of the greater hip-hop community; however, it is unlikely that any one hip-hop artist represents the culture in a comprehensive way. By referring to rap as "impure," Krims extends this logic to challenge the "realness" of rap representations and to deny the cultural convention of rap as "something that represents." Hip-hop's stake in self-representation often leads to the (mis)representation of various "cultural truths" because of its misuse of authenticity and the real.

Hip-hop's representin' results in part from rappers' desire to identify regionally. Rap music, and hip-hop culture more broadly, is identified as an outgrowth of urban black and Latino communities. Rappers' desire to represent these cities and, more importantly, specific neighborhoods within them, results from both an awareness of New York City as the center of hip-hop culture and an attempt to carve out representational space for other locales. Also, the representation of particular "hoods" stems from an acknowledgment that local and national politicians have often abandoned these neighborhoods, and artists feel a sense of commitment to put their "forgotten" communities back on the map. An excellent example is Lil Wayne and Robin Thicke's "Tie My Hands," a message rap–R&B song about Hurricane Katrina. Lil Wayne, a New Orleans native, raps,

> They try tell me keep my eyes open
> My whole city under water, some people still floating
> And they wonder why black people still voting
> 'Cause your President's still choking
> Take away the football team, the basketball team
> Now all they got is me to represent New Orleans, shit
> No Governor, no help from the Mayor
> Just a steady beating heart and wish and a prayer
> Let's pray![10]

Among the many signal elements of these bars is the agency he attributes to athletes and rappers as hip-hop cultural representatives of their regions. He also critiques national, state, and local governments, representing George W. Bush as "your President" despite his own U.S. citizenship.

Often, hip-hop's investments in representation and authenticity involve the presentation of the individual self and the representation of cultural groups, including religious groups, gangs, hip-hop "crews," and the like, with which the self is identified. This process of self-representation heralds authenticity as a way to foster self-esteem and to validate cultural affiliations. For instance, rapper Rakim, in his song "Mahogany," raps about a counterpart black female "moon" to personally self-identify as a "sun [son]," a reference to the Five Percent ideology that the black man represents the sun and the black woman the moon.[11] Therefore, Rakim identifies a female Five-Percenter as his partner to authenticate himself as a male member within the Nation of Gods and Earths culture. Rakim raps to Mahogany, "Come to me so we can glow in the dark." He tells her, "You can represent the moon / as long as I keep ya in tune." Although Rakim informs Mahogany, "I'll tell ya who ya are and why ya here," he really enables his own self-representation, telling the audience who he is and why he is there, while clearly representing the Five Percent Nation's masculinist cultural norms.

In the mid-1990s the language of representin' came to the fore of hip-hop culture. In Jay Z and Notorious B.I.G.'s "Brooklyn's Finest," for instance, representin' is about locating the geographic origins of rappers. The lines "Brooklyn represent ya'll" and "Representin' BK to the fullest" are pronouncements that mark the two emcees as natives of that particular borough.[12] Similarly, on rapper Raekwon's "Heaven and Hell" he announces, "Big Booth represent the Q [Queens]."[13] When rap group Outkast became the first to break commercial rap music produced by southern emcees, they established a larger southern representation. In their single "Slump" the chorus states, "I'm strictly dressin' Dirty Dirty / Gonna represent it to the T-Top / Born and bred up on the street top / Get to the money and the sweet spot / And forever hollerin' 'Hootie Hoo!' when we see cops."[14] Here, Outkast begins by representing the "Dirty" South to the "T-Top" (the fullest). They also flesh out a portrait of their southern environment by representing drug trafficking locales, specific environments where they are meeting police with resistance.[15]

In similar moments, rappers seek to identify with various community blights. Masta Killa, for instance, admits that he "represent[s] the school of the hard knocks and glocks."[16] "The school of the hard knocks" is an

Big Boi (left) and Andre 3000 (right), members of the hip-hop duo known as Outkast, frequently invoke political messages in their music as well as embody a representation of life in the South. (MovieGoods)

important phrase that was popularized in the hip-hop culture of New York ghettoes, which comments critically, albeit simply, on the collapse of the public education system and the subsequent role the inner-city streets play in the "raising" of children. The phrase derives, however, from Ralph Albert Parlette's book *The University of Hard Knocks: The School that Completes Our Education,* published in 1919.[17] When Masta Killa represents "the school of the hard knocks and glocks," he locates himself in a gun-ridden community and essentially reestablishes himself, as his name already does, as an agent of that violence. In 2Pac's "Life Goes On" he represents for victims, likely of gun violence—"dead homiez" and "niggas doin' life" in prisons.[18] Rapper Nas uses the trope of representation to announce his taste in alcohol: "Heine[ken] dark drinker, represent the thinker."[19] Here, "dark" simultaneously represents a beer and the rapper's racial identity.

Explicit markers of race and ethnicity are rare, however, when it comes to representin' in hip-hop. More often we get cultural referents, such as the one outlined earlier by Rakim's "Mahogany," that allude to racial or ethnic representations. Implicit black cultural referents are plentiful, and they often take the form of lyrical and musical samples. These more indirect referents work to establish "insiderism" and often police the borders of the hip-hop (inter)national community. Frequently, these cultural samples are used to reinforce the community descriptors and examples of urban criminality referred to earlier. The Wu-Tang Clan's "Clan in the Front" evidences this. On this single, they identify Wu-Tang member GZA as "the one who just represent the Wu-Tang click / With the game and soul of an ol' school flick / like The Mack and Dolemite who both did bids." Here, GZA is represented along a black cultural continuum with black pimp characters from 1970s blaxploitation films. Although he is not linked to them by voiced referents to his sexual activity, The Mack and Dolemite are celebrated because they were incarcerated, another experience that hip-hop particularly commends. Through the citation of these two figures from film history, GZA's ethnicity, gender, and sexual orientation are represented, and he is identified as a black American heterosexual male. Furthermore, hip-hop is represented here as an art form connected to black film and black male actors and comedians.[20]

In these and other ways, hip-hop's cultural and community references seek to establish local and national identities for the culture. Codes of all varieties—linguistic, behavioral, and ideological—are developed, exhibited, and embraced as a means of crafting a hip-hop nation. As Bakari Kitwana notes, "By the early to mid-1990s hip-hop's commercialized element had black kids on the same page, regardless of geographic region. In this hip-hop friendly national environment . . . multi-platinum sales for rap artists were routine . . . and hip-hop expressions like 'blowin' up,' 'representin'' and 'keepin' it real' worked their way into the controversial language of black youth around the country." As Kitwana notes, the politics of representation, pronounced by the mass marketing of hip-hop lexicons such as representin' itself, assembled a national identity for what he refers to as the hip-hop generation.[21] Although he notes that this happened "regardless of geographic region," it is important to point out that nationalism in hip-hop developed, in rather interesting ways, because of hip-hop's persistent regional representin'. As New York discontinued its reign as the only mass-marketed urban landscape in hip-hop culture, rappers from other cities such as Los Angeles, Atlanta, and New Orleans began to "represent" their hoods in their rhymes, radio spots, album and press photography, and video promotions of all varieties, including TV interviews, music videos, and documentary films. Although this regional pride seemingly created beefs between various rap regions, evidenced by the notorious East Coast–West Coast rivalry or even southern rappers' relentless struggle to gain notoriety and credibility, it also fostered and nurtured a hip-hop nation. As hip-hop cultural participants began to notice that emergent urban centers in the rap game were very similar to one another, the greater culture developed a sense of shared cultural background with black and Latino communities across the nation. For some better-informed participants, this extended to global oppressed communities.[22] Although these regional identifications are connected to cultural nationalist trends in hip-hop culture, particularly as a result of their shared "linked fate" rhetoric, regional representation may have had an even greater effect on the development of nationalism in hip-hop than explicitly nationalist ideologies such as those espoused by groups such as Public Enemy or Queen Latifah or the Islamic nationalism of artists such as Rakim and The Wu-Tang Clan.[23]

Although it is difficult to measure the difference between the influence of regional representation and that of cultural nationalist rap on hip-hop nationalism, it is worth noting that a review of the vinyl album artwork for sixteen of the forty-three classic rap albums demonstrates the importance of regional representation for the artists. This 37 percent represents albums by thirteen of the twenty-eight artists or groups (almost 50 percent) included among the classic emcees. The albums can be divided between New York and New Jersey rappers (ten) and Los Angeles ones (six).

The back of Jay Z's *Reasonable Doubt* lists the previously discussed "Brooklyn's Finest." Main Source's *Breaks the Atom* contains a shout-out to their "New York Posse." A Tribe Called Quest's *People's Instinctive Travels and the Paths of Rhythm* has several cartoon city backdrops with the names of East Coast artists and activists De La Soul, Jungle Brothers, Zulu Nation, The Violaters, and Latifah, as well as tags for the illustrators Paige Hunyday and Bryant Peters, graffitied on top of them. Mobb Deep's *The Infamous* lists the song titled "Q.U.—Hectic," an acronym for Queens University, which represents their Queens education and terrain. Eric B. and Rakim's *Paid in Full* shows B. on the backside in a New York sweatshirt.²⁴ Big Daddy Kane thanks New York City urban radio stations WBLS and 98.7 KISS on the back of *Long Live the Kane*. Nas's *Stillmatic* cover foregrounds the artist against the New York skyline (in a New York hat), as does Slick Rick's *The Great Adventures of Slick Rick*. The cover of Nas's first-edition *Illmatic* features a sepia-toned image of the artist as a child superimposed on a photograph of the Queensbridge Housing Projects, where he grew up. Queensbridge is located on Long Island and is the largest housing project in North America.²⁵ The back features another photograph with the projects in the background, as well as the album "chapters" "40 side north" and "41st side north," representing the avenues on either side of one of the Queensbridge buildings—likely the one he grew up in. Whereas the tenth anniversary vinyl reissue of *Illmatic* has the same image on the cover, now in black and white, the new back cover features contemporary contact sheet–style images of the artist returned to Queensbridge, also in black and white to create a "classic" look. Views of Riverside State Penitentiary and the Ben Franklin Bridge in New Jersey make up the foreground and background, respectively, on the back cover of the Fugees album *The Score*. The photograph is a striking negative image created by black photographer Marc Baptiste.

This trend continues all the way on the other side of the nation. Ice Cube's *AmeriKKKa's Most Wanted* cover features six legible Los Angeles and Los Angeles Raiders hats among an endless crowd of black males standing in the background behind his image in the foreground. Los Angeles's Orpheum Theatre and the Anjac Fashion Building are also in the background, on the South Broadway block his entourage is standing on. Similarly, The D.O.C. wears a Los Angeles Kings hat and LA T-shirt on the cover of his album *No One Can Do It Better*. Alan Light's liner notes on Cube's *Death Certificate* further narrate the black and Korean tensions that climaxed in the wake of the 1992 Los Angeles riots, which Cube expresses in his lyrics to "Black Korea." Light also notes that "after Los Angeles started burning . . . it could never again be denied as a social force." The very title of N.W.A.'s *Straight Outta Compton* signifies. Dr. Dre's *2001* lists the title of his single "Some L.A. Niggaz." Finally, 2Pac, who is not even from California but experienced a sort of regional rebirth following Suge Knight's Death Row Records contract, holds up a "W" sign for the West Coast on the cover of *All Eyez on Me*. Notably, with respect to the linked fate of American inner-city hip-hop participants, Pac also shouts out "all [his] komradz in every borough of every city of every state," in his "thanxs."

In rapper-producer Dr. Dre's "Let Me Ride," he represents for Southern California cities such as Los Angeles, hip-hop's second prominent regional center.[26] "Let Me Ride" includes scenarios of both armed robbery and murder, but Dre is careful to disassociate himself from the gang activity for which Los Angeles is notorious. "But I don't represent no gang bang," Dre raps, "Some niggaz like lynching but I just watch them hang." Here the historical "markers" of African American heritage are present, but in a disturbing way. By connecting gang activity in Los Angeles to lynching in the South, Dre distances himself from white male perpetrators of lynching but aligns himself with white southern lynch mobs by announcing that he "watches them hang." In many ways, Dre fashions himself in this instance as the deviant spectator, less guilty than the lynchers who are actually enacting the violence, but less than innocent because he does not intervene to save the victim.

Comparatively, one photograph in Richard Wright's *Twelve Million Black Voices* depicts a lynched black male in the foreground and a mob of at least thirteen white males in the background standing proudly and looking stoically at the camera. The man located directly behind the lynched male is impeccably dressed in a three-piece suit and tie with a matching, modified beaver hat. The suit, at least for me, is what Roland Barthes defines as the photograph's "punctum," the "accident that bruises." This man in the suit, with his arm leaning against the tree the lynched man is hanging from, is the only one "dressed up" for the occasion. Similar to the suit and the man wearing it, Dre's privileged arrogance represents an unconscionable "sting" for the listener. Malcolm X notes that southern lynchings were spectacles where whites were witnessed "getting their kicks, the thrill, while they [did] it." He contrasts this form of murder with that committed by blacks by stating, "We kill because we need to, either for food or to defend ourselves." Of course, blacks do commit murder for reasons other than self-defense, but X writes the notion of spectacle out of black homicide.[27] In his lyrics, Dre articulates both homosocial (within the group that witnesses the violence) and heterosocial (outside the group that commits the violence) representation, as well as regional Los Angeles representation. This position he carves out for himself is in stark contrast to Malcolm X's depictions.

Significant to the sense of nationalism derived from the exploitation of inner-city ills is the collective cultural critique of state apparatuses that fostered some of these realities in the first place, particularly regional police departments and national government administrations. S. Craig Watkins notes, "The ghettocentric imagination . . . produces representations of the urban ghetto as a theatre for state coercion and militarization."[28] When Dr. Dre asserts an analogy between gang violence and state-sanctioned lynching, then, he is correct.

I previously discussed a "politics of representation" that serves as an umbrella, if you will, for the "burden of representation" and for what Tricia Rose defines as a "crisis of representation." Therefore, if the politics of representation incorporates all the various politicized types of representation that black cultural participants engage, the burden of representation is but one of these types, and the crisis of representation is another. This crisis is related to what Watkins identifies as the stake the American news media and politicians have in the mass-marketed representation of black deviance. Just as rappers function as community spokesmen for crime and violence, Rose reminds us, "monopolistic tendencies in commercial enterprises seriously constrain access to a diverse flow of information."[29] Therefore, despite the fact that many rappers critique drug and alcohol abuse and lament violence, commercial industries fail to support critical artists in the same ways they financially endorse those glorifying these behaviors. This process is a frightening effort on the part of the police, politicians, corporate America, and, notably, a host of "regressive" rappers and hip-hop consumers.[30] The crisis of representation that Rose outlines goes back to the idea of "interests" and presents a specific divide between the predominant voices presented in mainstream media and those whose interests receive adequate representation in these same "corridors of power."[31]

"It's Yours"

Two "classic" hip-hop singles—Nas's "The World Is Yours" (1994) and Jay Z's "Dead Presidents" (1996)—are connected not only by the T La Rock "It's Yours" sample that informed the former song's title but also by the greater investment in capitalism the two raps represent, helping us to understand the more problematic forms of representation in hip-hop culture.[32] Although both these songs exhibit accomplished lyricism and production, and both singles contributed significantly to the rappers' still rising prominence as culturally celebrated ("Greatest Rappers Alive") and financially successful artists, the greed they articulate represents a larger politics of capitalism with which hip-hop culture is obsessed. These two songs are excellent examples of how songs can be artistically and financially viable but politically regressive. Nas's song begins:

> Nas: I'm out for presidents to represent me!
> Say what?
> I'm out for presidents to represent me!
> Say what?
> I'm out for dead presidents to represent me!

> T La Rock: It's Yours!

"The World Is Yours" begins with a modified twelve-bar, standard blues format "remixed" with a call-and-response conversation. "I'm out for presidents to represent me," he calls. "Say what?" the song answers. This refrain repeats. Then, slightly differently, "I'm out for dead presidents to represent me!" "Dead presidents" refers to those whose faces appear on dollar bills of various monetary increments. Following this call and response, "The World Is Yours" mixes in a T La Rock sample, "It's Yours." From the first seconds of "The World Is Yours," the song conveys the musical and lyrical sophistication of a rap classic, borrowing and using not only the musical tropes of twelve-bar blues, call and response, mixing, and the rap sample but also illustrating a rap lyric standard of new linguistic phrasings to symbolize popular items. In this case, of course, "dead presidents" is introduced as new African American vernacular English (AAVE) lexicon for representing money.

The narrative of the song promotes Nas and other black males taking over the world by capitalistic exploits. Nas establishes himself as a deviant black male ("Aimin' guns in all my baby pictures") who incites resistance with housing police and provides a musical sound track for thieves and murderers. Nas does express some disaffection with the image he represents. "I need a new nigga for this black cloud to follow / 'Cause when it's over me it's too dark to see tomorrow," he explains, loosely addressing his own dissatisfaction with the bleak realities of his existence. When he notes, "I need a new nigga for this black cloud to follow," he is willfully calling for his present hardships to be visited on another black person. More explicitly, Nas raps, "The fiend of hip-hop has got me stuck like a crack pipe." The rather astute formal elements of this statement demonstrate its meaning. Hip-hop is personified in this statement as a crack user. Nas's own subjectivity as a rapper is described with the simile "stuck like a crack pipe." Therefore, Nas might be arguing that his investment in capitalism, articulated by his desire to have "dead presidents," or money, "represent" him, is actually a forced agency that he is stuck in.

Forced or not, the larger investment in capitalism and its companion evils that Nas articulates is quite troubling. Elsewhere, Nas rhymes, "And I'm amped up / They locked the champ up / Leaving my brain in hand-cuffs / Heading for Indiana / Stabbing women like a phantom." Here, Nas announces his disapproval that heavyweight boxing champion Mike Tyson was locked up in Indiana for raping Desiree Washington. His avowal of Tyson's innocence is similar to that of other prominent black male celebrities and religious leaders.[33] Furthermore, Nas announces his hypothetical plan to go to Indiana, the site of Tyson's crime, and "stab" women, a double entendre for a physical assault by knife and an aggressive act of male sexual penetration.

Nas's misogyny is linked to capitalism because his dissatisfaction with the verdict in Tyson's case likely results from the far too pervasive opinion that black women are out to "trap" prominent black male athletes, rappers, and other celebrities. Therefore, when black women and other economically marginalized women of all races come forward with allegations of sexual assault against prominent male athletes and entertainers in particular, the American public often critiques those allegations as being efforts made by those women to get monetary awards.[34] Nas's investment in capitalism, as it may foster the financial benefit of himself, Mike Tyson, and other black male celebrities, extends to a regressive gender politic. This causes him to either deny the possibility that Tyson may actually be guilty, or worse, to advocate for a culture that would ignore rape as a crime worthy of punishment.

Jay Z's "Dead Presidents" begins with another revision of the twelve-bar blues format by sampling Nas's hook: "Presidents to represent me / I'm out for presidents to represent me [two times] / I'm out for dead fucking presidents to represent me."[35]

Nas: Presidents to represent me!
Jay Z: Rock
Nas: I'm out for presidents to represent me!
Jay Z: On! Rocafella yo
Nas: I'm out for presidents to represent me
Jay Z: The saga continues
I'm out for dead fucking presidents to represent me!

Throughout his single, Jay Z brags of capitalist success. "I'm still spending money from '88," he boasts, then refers to himself as "The Dead Presidential Candidate," a title that collapses formal political power into solely economic power. For Jay Z, "'Nough dollars make sense [cents]," and "Dead Presidents" advocates an upward mobility that has historically left black elites (rappers notwithstanding) sharply divided, economically, from the black masses. Jay Z compares himself with other rappers by challenging, conventionally, "Mic machet(ed) your flow / your paper fall slow like confetti / mine's will steady grow." Finally, when Jay Z announces, "Dead presidential / politics as usual," he signals the most popular form of hip-hop politics historically addressed by emcees and possibly by the surrounding culture as well—that of contemporary capitalism. If black cultural representation has always been about mass-marketed symbols of black life, hip-hop representation is often about black males "cashing in" on that market.

Elsewhere, however, the representational politics that hip-hop offers is more progressive. Consider, for example, Sarah Jones's "Whose War?"[36] Although "Whose War?" is arguably a spoken word recording and not a rap record, I still believe it is an important case to introduce here because of the interesting ways she too samples Nas's recording "The World Is Yours."[37]

> I want a President to represent me!
> I want a President to represent me!
> I want a President to represent me!
> I want a real President to represent me!

Sarah Jones begins, like both Nas and Jay Z, with an almost identical, remixed twelve-bar blues, call and response refrain: "I want a President to represent me!" and she answers, "I want a real President to represent me." Jones's exchange of the words "dead" and "real" is especially significant here. As previously discussed, there is a preoccupation with "realness" inside black cultural representations, Jones notwithstanding. When Jones calls for a "real" president to represent her, she is speaking specifically about the failures of actual American presidents, present and former, who have failed to address her adequately as a black female progressive. Instead of asking, "Whose world is this," as Nas does, she uses the remixed phrase, "Whose war is this?" to voice opposition to the current war in Iraq initiated by President George W. Bush. "Look under 'W,'" she remarks, "it stands for war instigator." She extends her critique to the inner-city, crack-era Reaganomics "wars"; the

U.S. support of apartheid; and the first Iraq war promoted by George H. W. Bush. Jones also refers to the "corporate ties" and news media monopolization of wartime. And finally, Jones opposes the Bush-supported war against the pro-choice position. "No W. should decide when and whether we have to give birth / Not when the executioner can't even spell what a human life is worth," Jones mocks. Throughout the song, she advances progressive politics that are racialized, classed, *and* gendered.

Furthermore, Jones remixes the language of war to address a politics of representation. Conservatives call for a "divide and conquer and divide some more" approach that negates the political strategies of community and collectivity that black historical oppositions have, at least theoretically, offered up. What Jones supports instead, and what she attempts to effect when addressing her largely black public, is unity and the fair representation of black political concerns.

The politics that Jones advances is an enactment of formal politics. Although Jones did not explicitly campaign against Bush's reelection in 2004, the subtext for her argument, "I want a real president to represent me," and the timeliness of her recording (during the 2004 election season) supported these politics.

"My President"

Fast-forward four years, and Young Jeezy and Nas's "My President" is on the airwaves, prematurely celebrating Barack Obama's victory as the forty-fourth president of the United States. The song was written in June 2008 and features the two black male rappers, principally Jeezy, critiquing Bush's "stolen" ascendancy in Florida, as well as the war in Iraq and its oil-centered motivations, and proposing Obama as the realization of Dr. Martin Luther King's "dream." The video was recorded after election day and was set in front of the famed Ebenezer Baptist Church. Uncompromisingly reminiscent of Spike Lee's video for Public Enemy's "Fight the Power," which aired nearly twenty years earlier, the crowd is armed with placards supporting the newly elected Obama, along with Malcolm X, Gandhi, and deceased rappers Jam Master Jay, Pimp C, and Biggie Smalls.

The song's lyrics and video imagery are a mixture of Black Nationalist rhetoric, self-aggrandizement (as the song chiefly represents for Jeezy himself), and capitalist braggadocio. The hook, "My President is Black / My Lambo[rghini] is blue," simultaneously champions Obama's historic win and Jeezy's celebrated victory as "the first nigga to ride through [his] hood in a Lamborghini." "I'm important too," Jeezy admits. At the same time Jeezy presents himself alongside Obama, he also questions the general representation of contemporary emcees. After shouting out black historical figures such as Jackie Robinson and Booker T. Washington, he questions his listeners, "Oh you ain't think I knew that shit?" The hypothetical query reflects an earlier bar in which Jeezy interrogates the position of emcees as politicians: "Just because you got opinions, does that make you a politician?" Throughout the song it seems as though he answers by presenting himself and Obama as pop icons, although he admittedly wrestles with the significance of Obama's presence in American government at such a critical juncture in history, given the state of the American economy (the album the song appears on is entitled *Recession*). Nas's verse in the song calls for putting Obama's face on the $5,000 bill (dead presidents), and there is imagery that supports this as well graffitied onto the platform Jeezy stands on in the video. The closing title states: "Pray for Barack and Family."

Whereas hip-hop does not always challenge its investments in American capitalism, it does argue for fairer access to American wealth, particularly for black and Latino males. Cultural theorists critique black male capitalism in hip-hop culture, but it warrants mentioning that these same black male capitalists are in fact constituting the ethos of the economic system by allowing the poor to get richer while the rich get richer as well. Black female rappers such as Lil Kim, Foxy Brown, and Trina respond similarly. Although there are certainly other more progressive economic ideologies, these platforms are not as well marketed.

Hip-hop has been introduced by Chuck D as the "black CNN" and by Selwyn Hinds, former editor in chief of *Source* magazine, as a "lens" to the black American world. It has been more than thirty years since hip-hop's birth in the South Bronx, and it shows no signs of fading; in fact, despite the current "hip-hop is dead" rhetoric, it has grown into a global phenomenon. New extensions of hip-hop performance, including Reggaeton, krumping, hyphy, and digital (MP3) DJing, are constantly emerging. With the ever-growing prominence of hip-hop cultures around the world, new definitions of hip-hop politics continue to emerge as well. Hip-hop provides a research framework for interrogating black diasporic national, gender, racial, and class politics, and the national, gender, racial, and class politics of hip-hop scholars relates to the desire to produce the work and to see that work, like that culture, advance.

Through the process of research and critique, we can improve on the current state of hip-hop politics and black contemporary politics in general. Central to these efforts will be changing the nature of black representations as they currently exist. Although hip-hop presents several ideas for the development of a political consciousness, very little work has been done to imagine how we might organize these ideas into collective action. If we advance the politics of hip-hop culture so that it does not oppress any members of the hip-hop generations, the youth who are continuing to grow up in the culture can be even more affirmed by its existence.

I began my own path as a hip-hop scholar, like all others who do work in the field, by insisting on the legitimacy of hip-hop as a topic. This was an important and vital step for my intellectual development and professional growth. However, hip-hop scholarship has taken on new meaning for me now. I want to use it to affirm the cultural identities of hip-hop heads because I know that despite the past and present deficiencies in hip-hop politics, the culture has the potential to effect change in the lives of marginalized American youth and young adults.

Notes

1. Gina Dent, "Black Pleasure, Black Joy: An Introduction," in *Black Popular Culture,* ed. Gina Dent (Seattle: Bay Press, 1992), 15.

2. Ibid. Dent notes, "In the year of the televised trial of four Los Angeles police officers for the beating of Rodney King, and in the wake of such cataclysmic public events as the Anita Hill–Clarence Thomas confrontation, it has become increasingly clear that black criticism will have to begin to make use of the more sophisticated cultural analyses that depend on understanding the complexities of video imaging, the dynamics of representation and reception theories" (ibid., 5–6).

3. Yvonne Bynoe states, "There have always been members of the Hip Hop generation that have understood the importance of political activism. In that respect nothing has changed. What continues to be problematic for this generation is that by and large, despite numerous get out the vote initiatives, and the variety of issues impacting them, young Blacks are still not voting in great numbers." Shawn Collette, "Q&A: Yvonne Bynoe," *Black Collegian Online,* http://www.black-collegian.com/issues/2ndsem07/ campus_midterms_3.html (accessed October 23, 2008). Others scholars likewise restrict their definitions of the political to voting and other exercises of formal politics. Although he repeatedly identifies his subject as an unidentified "cynic," "maudlin," and

"coward," Stanley Crouch name-drops 2 Live Crew before generalizing the hip-hop generation as "knowing nothing of heroic engagement" and shamelessly denying the feverous sanguinity of the Constitution's founding fathers. Stanley Crouch, "Blues to Be Constitutional: A Look at the Wild Wherefores of Our Democratic Lives as Symbolized in the Making of Rhythm and Tune," in *The Jazz Cadence of American Culture,* ed. Robert G. O'Meally (New York: Columbia University Press, 1998), 157.

4. Whereas rapper-executives such as Jay Z and Sean "Puffy" Combs gross $86 million (2007) and $50 million (2005), respectively, and other hip-hop celebrity musicians such as DJ Mark Ronson make as much as $400,000, a host of teachers, activists, independent artists, radio personalities, and others base their careers around hip-hop and make significantly less. As for the categorization of these hip-hop personalities as representatives, I think it can be demonstrated by their various public politics. Jay Z has had ten *Billboard*-topping albums. Sean Combs sponsored a highly marketed "Vote or Die" campaign. Mark Ronson is a three-time Grammy Award–winning producer and has performed on Jimmy Kimmel's and Conan O'Brien's shows. However, activists, teachers, independent artists, and radio personalities also represent the culture for their communities and in many cases are involved in public school education, boycotts, election campaigning, voting initiatives, and so forth. Some examples include the National Hip-Hop Political Convention in Newark, New Jersey (2004); the University of Hip-Hop Chicago Public Schools initiative; and the many activist efforts of Poetess Media, founded by longtime 92.3 (The Beat) Los Angeles radio personality and former rapper The Poetess. "Who Makes How Much: New York's Salary Guide, 2005," *New York Magazine,* September 18, 2005, http://nymag.com/guides/salary/14497/; Lea Goldman, "The Top Earning African-American Stars," *Forbes*.com, February 4, 2008; "News," Mark Ronson: Version, http://markronson.net/.

5. Kobena Mercer, *Welcome to the Jungle: New Positions in Black Cultural Studies* (New York: Routledge, 1994), 90, 91, 240.

6. Lani Guinier, "Groups, Representation and Race Conscious Districting: A Case of the Emperor's Clothes," in *Critical Race Theory: The Key Writings that Formed the Movement,* ed. Kimberlé Crenshaw, Neil Gotanda, Gary Peeler, and Kendall Thomas (New York: New Press, 1995), 227. Here, Guinier is supported by Kimberlé Crenshaw, who argues that "voting is related to some notion of actual representation . . . depending on how one views society, democracy, and the historic significance of racial disenfranchisement, the appropriate relationship between voting and representation can be defined to require anything from representation at large to full proportional representation" ("Race, Reform and Retrenchment: Transformation and Legitimation in Antidiscrimination Law," in *Critical Race Theory,* 105). Both these examples suggest that the formal political act of voting is an act of "real" and perhaps even "ultimate" representation.

7. Guinier, "Groups, Representation and Race Conscious Districting," 206.

8. Adam Krims, *Rap Music and the Poetics of Identity* (Cambridge: Cambridge University Press, 2000), 2.

9. Tricia Rose notes in "Feminism and Hip Hop" (presented at the Hip-Hop and Feminism Conference, University of Chicago, April 2005), that although critics hail "underground" or noncommercial rap as hip-hop's cultural savior, much of the same investments in capitalism, patriarchy, homophobia, and other ills exist in the "underground" realm. Krims, for instance, goes so far as to suggest that capitalist rap should be "obscured or obliterated" (*Rap Music and the Poetics of Identity*, 71). Although I would certainly critique the rampant capitalism in hip-hop, I would not suggest that this capitalism exists only in mainstream hip-hop, nor would I recommend its obliteration. I would call for a balance in hip-hop culture, for both commercial and noncommercial artists, and for the presentation of more democratic economic systems, but to completely eradicate capitalist hip-hop would mean silencing the often legitimate concerns of economically marginalized groups, however personalized and exaggerated.

10. Lil Wayne and Robin Thicke, "Tie My Hands," *Tha Carter III* (Motown Records, 2008).

11. Eric B. and Rakim, "Mahogany," *Let the Rhythm Hit 'Em* (MCA Records, 1988). The Five Percent Nation of Gods and Earths developed in the mid to late twentieth century as an offshoot of the Nation of Islam. It is practiced mostly in black, inner-city communities and among black male prison populations. The foremost tenets of the Nation of Gods and Earths are that the black male is God and that the black family should consist of the black man (as the leader and the knowledge), the black woman (as the partner and the wisdom), and the black child (as the cultural continuation and the understanding). See Earnest Allen Jr., "Making the Strong Survive: The Contours and Contradictions of Message Rap," in *Droppin' Science: Critical Essays on Rap Music and Hip Hop Culture*, ed. William Eric Perkins (Philadelphia: Temple University Press, 1996), 159–91; Melvin Gibbs, "ThugGods: Spiritual Darkness and Hip Hop," in *Everything but the Burden: What White People Are Taking from Black Culture*, ed. Greg Tate (New York: Harlem Moon, 2003); Harry Allen, "Righteous Indignation," *Source: The Magazine of Hip-Hop, Culture and Politics* (March–April 1991): 48–53.

12. Jay Z and Notorious B.I.G., "Brooklyn's Finest," *Reasonable Doubt* (Roc-A-Fella, 1996).

13. Raekwon the Chef f. Ghostface Killer and Blue Raspberry, "Heaven and Hell," *Only Built for Cuban Linx* (Loud/RCA Records, 1995).

14. Outkast f. Backbone and Cool Breeze, "Slump," *Aquemini* (LaFace, 1998).

15. Surprisingly, classic West Coast albums from this same period, such as *The Chronic* and *Doggystyle*, do not use the idiom *representin'*. Perhaps it had not yet traveled such a distance. The only exception would be 2Pac's *All Eyez on Me* (Death Row, 1996).

16. Raekwon the Chef, "Wu-Gambinos," *Only Built for Cuban Linx*. Masta Killa appears on the single, although the album does not credit him as a guest artist.

17. In the book, Parlette represents the University of Hard Knocks as a metaphorical institution where society learns all life's lessons by encountering and overcoming

"bumps" or challenges. Ralph Albert Parlette, *The University of Hard Knocks: The School that Completes Our Education* (1919; reprint, Charleston, SC: Bibliobazaar, 2006).

18. 2Pac, "Life Goes On," *All Eyez on Me.*

19. Nas f. Large Professor, "One Time for Your Mind," *Illmatic* (Columbia, 1994).

20. Rudy Ray Moore was a stand-up comedian, recording artist, and actor who used rhyming to tell stories of various urban characters and narratives. He was also the main character in the film *Dolemite.* When he passed in 2008, Snoop Dogg was quoted as saying, "Without Rudy Ray Moore there would be no Snoop Dogg," as a small testament to his influence and the film's influence on hip-hop entertainers and the greater constituency. Moore also referred to himself as the "Godfather of Rap" because of the number of rap artists who sampled his material. He also rapped, "rappin' and tappin' is my game!" in his 1976 film *The Human Tornado* (directed by Cliff Roquemore, DVD, Xenon, 2002), a *Dolemite* sequel, during the early, precommercial years of rap history. Douglas Martin, "Rudy Ray Moore, 81, 'Dolemite' Star, Precursor of Rap, Dies," *Chicago Tribune,* October 22, 2008.

21. Bakari Kitwana, *The Hip Hop Generation: Young Blacks in African-American Culture* (New York: Basic Civitas Books, 2002), 199. Kitwana identifies those born between 1965 and 1984 as the "hip-hop generation" and also distinguishes three subgroups within this population (xiii, xiv). I refer to three generations of hip-hop cultural participants, the primary difference being that I account for young people born from 1985 to the present as well.

22. Dr. Dre, "The Day the Niggaz Took Over," *The Chronic* (Death Row, 1992). Dre samples an anonymous male talking about the common heritage of blacks or "niggaz" in Los Angeles and those in South Africa "suffering from apartheid and shit." On "Survival of the Fittest," from *The Infamous . . . Mobb Deep,* Havoc of Mobb Deep compares his Queens neighborhood to Vietnam.

23. *Linked fate* is a term used most often by political scientists to express black people's sense of a shared political and economic destiny. The idea of black linked fate is a core belief of Black Nationalism, and the idea of gender and racial linked fate is a core belief of black feminism. See Andrea Y. Simpson, *The Tie that Binds: Identity and Political Attitudes in the Post–Civil Rights Generation* (New York: New York University Press, 1998), 3. As an additional example of the intranational linked-fate discourse in hip-hop culture, Biggie Smalls opens the song "Everyday Struggle" (*Ready to Die* [Bad Boy Records, 1994]) by empathizing with an anonymous "you" about the economic depression in that person's neighborhood, which in his construction is comparable to his Brooklyn neighborhood. Throughout the song he parallels his own neighborhood with ones in Maryland and parts of the South where he and his girlfriend go to buy and sell drugs. Also he talks about how his friend was murdered in some town he had never heard of.

24. Comically, on the 1997 platinum reissue, Eric and Rakim's 1987 era "dookie-gold" chains and medallions are made to appear platinum. Special thanks to Dr. James

Peterson for pointing this out to me in my hip-hop literature course at the University of Pennsylvania Upward Bound Program in 2002.

25. Dan Barry, "Don't Tell Him the Projects Are Hopeless," *New York Times*, March 12, 2005.

26. Dr. Dre, "Let Me Ride," *The Chronic*.

27. Richard Wright, *Twelve Million Black Voices* (New York: Thunder's Mouth Press, 1941), 45; Roland Barthes, *Camera Lucida: Reflections on Photography* (New York: Hill and Wang, 1981), 27; Malcolm X, *Malcolm X on African-American History* (New York: Pathfinder, 1967), 51.

28. S. Craig Watkins, *Representing: Hip Hop Culture the Production of Black Cinema* (Chicago: University of Chicago Press, 1998), 215.

29. Tricia Rose, *Black Noise: Rap Music and Black Culture in Contemporary Music* (Hanover and London: Wesleyan University Press, 1994), 29.

30. I borrow the term *regressive* from the in-depth interview I conducted in March 2005 with Dr. Melissa Harris-Lacewell, associate professor of politics and African American studies at Princeton University, in which she adamantly supported the belief that hip-hop is political but also admitted that its politics is not always "progressive" and is, at times, "regressive and conservative." Tanji Gilliam, "That Crack in the Concrete: Hip-Hop, Politics and the Archive in Black Urban Video Culture, 1989–2004" (PhD diss., University of Chicago, n.d.).

31. Rose, *Black Noise*, 29.

32. Nas, "The World Is Yours," *Illmatic*; Jay Z, "Dead Presidents," *Reasonable Doubt*; T La Rock, "It's Yours," *It's Yours* (Def Jam, 1984).

33. See Aishah Simmons's film *No!* (DVD, Afrolez Productions, 2006), which addresses the cultural history of black intraracial rape and features archival footage of Louis Farrakhan and other black ministers' celebration of Mike Tyson's release from prison.

34. Interestingly, years later in his song "Coons Picnic (These Are Our Heroes)" (*Streets Disciple* [Columbia, 2004]), Nas blames basketball player Kobe Bryant for the sexual assault charges brought against him by a female hotel clerk in Colorado. Nas addresses Bryant: "You can't do better than that / the hotel clerk who adjusts the bathroom mat / Now you lose sponsorships that you thought had your back." However, Nas's critique of Bryant did not develop because of concerns over his sexual politics. Nas is more concerned with Bryant's racial politics and uses the verse to represent him, along with other popular black male celebrities, using the historical stereotype of the "coon." It is significant, however, that when Nas challenges Bryant's compromised financial status after the scandal (specifically with respect to the withdrawal of contracts for product endorsements), he blames Bryant instead of the woman who accused him of sexual assault.

35. Later in 2001, when Jay Z and Nas embarked on a fierce lyrical beef, this sample became a way for Nas to establish Jay Z's emulation of him. In Nas's "Stillmatic" (*Stillmatic*

[Columbia, 2002]), he challenges, "Remove the fake king of New York / You Show Off / I count dough off / When you sampled my voice." Jay Z counters in "The Takeover" by rhyming, "Yeah I sampled your voice / you were using it wrong / you made it a hot line / I made it a hot song." In doing so, Jay Z addresses his artistic and market superiority. He continues, "And you aint get a loan homie / you was getting plugged in / I know who I paid god / Searchlight publishing." Jay Z challenges that Nas was "raped" or "plugged in" (robbed) by Searchlight Publishing when Jay Z paid to use his sample. The homophobic reference to anal sex is disconcerting but not surprising, given the culture's rampant disdain for gay males. In an artistically astounding performance of this and other songs on *MTV Unplugged, No. 2.0* (MTV, November 18, 2001), Jay Z, along with The Roots band and vocalist Jaguar Wright (both of whom matched or outperformed Jay Z in terms of musical ability), inserted musical performances of Nas's singles "Oochie Wally," "N.Y. State of Mind," and "Streets of New York" just to insult him further. Because of the live-music format, Jay Z did not have to pay Nas to sample his work in this way, despite the fact that Jay Z produced a CD of the *Unplugged* performance.

36. Jones is an actress, playwright, and poet who has appeared on the HBO series *Def Poetry Jam*. She is the recipient of Tony and Obie awards and is the first UN ambassador and official spokesperson on violence against children. Her notoriety increased significantly when the commercial release of her poem (set to music) "Your Revolution" was censored by the Federal Communications Commission and Jones became the first artist to sue the agency over censorship. She fought victoriously to overturn the ruling. See "Bio," Sarah Jones Online, http://sarahjonesonline.com/.

37. The distinction between spoken word and rap music is somewhat muddied, and it is often left to the performer to identify his or her work. Additionally, contemporary black spoken word artists often expose a relationship with rap music because of the common cultural antecedents of the two genres and the literary and performative similarities inherent in their crafts.

13

"Things in This Country Are Gonna Change Pretty Fast"

Dissent, Mobilization, and the Politics of *Jericho*

Isabel Pinedo

> This government is corrupt and illegitimate. . . . It lied about who attacked us so it could seize power.
>
> —Heather Lisinski, "Patriots and Tyrants," *Jericho*

Five years after the September 11 attacks, a television series imagined a large-scale nuclear strike against the United States. Witnessed from the small Kansas town of Jericho, a mushroom cloud appears on the horizon in the direction of Denver. Like the 1983 telefilm *The Day After,* set in Lawrence, Kansas, *Jericho* is a nuclear narrative that portrays the country devastated by an attack. But unlike the cold war–themed *The Day After,* in which the attack emanates from a foreign state, *Jericho* depicts a homegrown terrorist attack masterminded by a faction of the U.S. government, intent on a covert coup d'etat.[1]

The nuclear attack is used to sow panic and social disorder, which allows a new government, the Allied States of America (ASA), to install itself over roughly half the country, west of the Mississippi. The new president is allied with Jennings & Rall (J&R), a giant conglomerate whose subsidiary, Ravenwood, is assigned to help the military reinstate order. The series resonates with several recent events, including the 9/11 attacks. In the pilot episode, the mushroom cloud on the horizon stands in for the devastating blow to the nation, later referred to in the series as the "September attacks." Its full extent is revealed obliquely in the second episode, "Fallout," as Hawkins, a newly arrived resident of Jericho who knows more than he is telling, places pushpins on a map of the mainland: Denver, Atlanta, Chicago, Philadelphia, San Diego. The camera lingers on the pushpins in the drawer as, in a heart-sinking moment, Hawkins's hand returns to it again and again and again.

Jericho was also influenced by Hurricane Katrina, when a delinquent government response and mismanagement led to social breakdown and reliance on private security contractors such as Blackwater. In the show, survivors flee the FEMA camps, where provisions are scarce and conditions dangerous. Residents of the fictional town hang on the fleeting images of a television transmission about the attacks, just as we did after 9/11 and Katrina. Here, the producers tap into "the idea of being a spectator to a disaster, while not quite being part of it," so familiar to us from these experiences.[2]

Last, the show resonates with Iraq, most obviously in the government's reliance on private security contractors to maintain services and in the town of Jericho's experience of occupation in the second season. Less obvious is the parallel with the "retaliatory" strike against a foreign state by the government, under false pretenses. In the case of *Jericho*, Iran and North Korea are falsely blamed for the September attacks. The critical narrative themes of the series resemble real-world events: the fallacious case made by the U.S. government for the invasion of Iraq; the erosion of democracy for the sake of security, instigated by the Patriot Act; the privatization of government functions.

But verisimilitude has its limits on network television. By locating the story in a town that was not hit and is strategically placed to avoid fallout, the producers avoid the body horror and bleak tone of earlier apocalyptic dramas such as *The Day After* and *Testament* (1983). *Jericho's* critical narrative themes play out the "what if" scenario through the action genre. Genre elements lend sufficient distance to the depiction of a postapocalyptic world to permit the audience to take pleasure from the show, to which its loyal fan base can attest. Thus the program, at least temporarily, staves off the box-office failure of the recent spate of films about Iraq. The producers of the program acknowledge the real-world political correlates of *Jericho*. So do the fans.

When CBS canceled the series after one season, fans mobilized online to demand a second season. Modeling the protest campaign specifically on a pivotal line in the season 1 finale and, more generally, on the program's insistence on the need to fight for democracy, fan activists convinced the network of the value of their loyal viewership, which led to an abridged second season. It is here that we most clearly see the series' relevance to viewers not merely as entertainment but as a model for politics. Yet without its strong genre-centered entertainment elements, the series would not have developed a loyal following.

Jericho as a Post-9/11 Action Genre Narrative

Like many action films since the 1990s, *Jericho* is an action serial that integrates elements of melodrama. The stunned residents of Jericho, cut off from communication and aid, find themselves struggling for survival and trying to make sense of what happened, although survival changes from literal survival in season 1 to the survival of a democratic society in season 2. Jake Green (Skeet Ulrich), a prodigal son with a dubious past, returns home after five years for what would have been a brief visit had the attacks not occurred. He and Robert Hawkins (Lennie James), a recent arrival who claims to be a former St. Louis police officer, are the heroes whose hypermasculine efforts drive the action.

In the first season, the action revolves around securing resources such as food and fuel for the coming winter. This pits town residents against a criminal gang, rogue mercenaries, and, most important, the neighboring town of New Bern, which has a munitions factory and is desperate to appropriate resources. The season 1 cliffhanger, "Why We Fight," leaves the two towns poised for armed conflict. Jericho is outnumbered and underequipped, but the residents, including refugees who have sought shelter there, are prepared to fight for their home. Melodramatic elements are interspersed and include romantic triangles, family estrangement, and heightened emotionality. The abridged, seven-episode-long second season jettisons most of the melodramatic elements revolving around intimate relations to focus on action elements and accelerate the narrative development. The action in season 2 pits Jericho against the new government based in Cheyenne, Wyoming, as embodied by the military, private contractors, and top-ranking government officials.[3]

Jericho negotiates its action elements in both conventional and unconventional ways. Conventionally, it presents fast-paced violence as entertaining spectacle and as the solution to seemingly insurmountable problems. Action elements, including torture, chase sequences, explosions, and shootouts, are used to create suspense. Although women play a substantive role in the narrative, including wielding guns and undertaking risky missions, the action is largely male centered, and men are responsible for most of the violence and intrigue that drives the narrative. Violence and danger are aestheticized through framing and lighting, starting with the mushroom cloud that looms on the horizon and changes everything.

Though these scenes create suspense, they are enjoyable to watch and place the heroes at the center of the action. Consistent with the action genre, Jake and Hawkins are "men masquerading as supermen" with remarkable physical abilities and special skills, such as the ability to fly a plane, drive a tank, or kill with one blow. Neither the violence nor the solutions are realistic, and both are escapist in tone. The escapist elements balance out the elements of realism and clear a space for pleasure.[4]

Some of the suspense centers on moral ambiguity. Throughout most of season 1, both Jake and Hawkins are presented as morally ambiguous characters. Jake's sordid background and the reason for his estrangement from his father, as well as Hawkins's unexplained knowledge about the attacks and his store of military supplies, which he keeps secret even from his wife, throw their moral caliber into question. Though there are hints in season 1 that Jake was involved with Ravenwood and may have been involved in the death of a friend in town, it is not until season 2 that we learn the true extent of Jake's guilt for which he is atoning.

Similarly, it is late in season 1 (episode 18, "A.K.A.") that we learn Hawkins's backstory, as he relates it to Jake. He is a CIA undercover agent who, with his handler Sarah Mason, was assigned by Thomas Valente (Daniel Benzali) of Homeland Defense to track the nuclear bombs that were eventually used in the attacks. The bombs had been brought into the country by the U.S. government, after the military in the satellite republics of the former Soviet Union put them on the black market. A few years back, a shipment went missing en route to the federal storage facility. "Those warheads were converted into twenty-five small, high-yield devices," Hawkins tells Jake. In an attempt to prevent the attacks, he infiltrated the terrorist cell that had acquired the devices, but the mission failed; Sarah betrayed him, as we later learn. Twenty-three bombs were detonated and killed 15 million people, though his intelligence prevented the attack on New York. Hawkins is in possession of the undetonated bomb, which can be used to prove that Iran and North Korea were not behind the attacks. It's the "smoking gun" that can expose Cheyenne's involvement in the attacks, and that is why the government is trying to track Hawkins down.

When Hawkins reveals all this to Jake, it forges the partnership that becomes the central relationship of season 2. Much to its credit, the series avoids homophobic humor, which the action genre typically uses to mediate the homosocial bond of the male buddy relationship. Furthermore, the centrality of the African American Hawkins is not at the cost of his subordination. This is a departure from the biracial buddy dynamic, which tends to render nonwhite characters subordinate to their white counterparts. Until the season 2 finale, when Hawkins is wounded, he often leads the action and plays the omnipotent action hero on an equal footing with Jake.[5]

Even more unconventional for the action genre, there is a surprisingly high level of realism to the mythology of the show. The larger political conflicts *Jericho* depicts refer to a recognizable social reality. The political cause of the enemy, who is homegrown, is recognizable and intelligible as a neoconservative agenda, although *Jericho* leaves the audience to fill in some of the gaps.

Jericho as Political Dissent

Over the course of twenty-nine episodes, the story of the conspiracy, before and after the attacks, unfolds as the residents of Jericho fight against the forces of tyranny in the new government. At the opening of season 2, the town becomes an occupied territory. The army puts a forcible end to the battle between Jericho and neighboring New Bern. Major Edward Beck (Esai Morales) is the officer in charge. He arrives with orders from Valente, now head of Cheyenne's Department of Homeland Defense, to suppress the "border skirmish," restore order, and hunt down a terrorist—Sarah Mason. Valente incorrectly believes she succeeded in her mission to kill Hawkins and take possession of the bomb and is now hiding from him. She is in fact dead. When Beck's investigation does not yield quick results, Valente orders Ravenwood, under the command of John Goetz (D. B. Sweeney), to return to "administer" Jericho, so Beck can devote his attention to hunting the terrorist.

Jake, whom Beck appoints sheriff, objects to Goetz's command, telling Beck that Goetz is responsible for a massacre in the town of Rogue River and for several murders in New Bern, the subject of earlier episodes. Beck counters, "What I heard is that a sanctioned government contractor attempted to enter this town and you opened fire, killing one of his men." Goetz taunts Jake by alluding to his own troubled history working for J&R

in Iraq. It is here that Jake's backstory is finally revealed, when he confides in his brother Eric (Kenneth Mitchell).

> JAKE: One day in Iraq our convoy was ambushed. A couple of our guys were killed. We had no rules of engagement, and we had seen the village they fell back to, so we just, we just went in. And we started shooting. After it was done, there were six gunmen dead along with four bystanders. One of them was a twelve-year-old girl. [Long silence.] The only reason I tell you this is because there were no repercussions. None. The army had no authority over us; the police didn't. Most of the guys, they just went back to their jobs. The company? The company wanted it quiet, so it was. . . .

> ERIC: Jake, this isn't Iraq.

> JAKE: Maybe. Maybe, but the rules are the same.

Ravenwood, as a private contractor, is above the law in the ASA, as private contractors are in Iraq. Although this episode, "Jennings and Rall," aired on February 26, 2008, the plotline was in the works months before Blackwater, a private security firm, was in the news concerning its involvement in the deaths of seventeen Iraqi civilians on September 16, 2007. Ravenwood is fashioned after Blackwater, which, along with other private contractors such as KBR, operates in Iraq with little government oversight and with immunity from prosecution under Iraqi law, thanks to Paul Bremer, who issued Coalition Provisional Authority Order 17. This has led to enormous resentment among the Iraqis, for it does nothing to discourage violence against Iraqi civilians by frightened contractors.[6]

Jericho subjects Americans to conditions of occupation that include economic monopoly, lack of due process, and violence. Ravenwood, J&R's private army, enforces the company's monopoly as supplier to merchants, farmers, and clinics. With monopoly comes price gouging. Businesses that fail to comply and seek goods on the black market are closed down. When residents get word that, contrary to official reports in the media, the Hudson River virus has jumped the Mississippi, Dale Turner (Eric Knudsen), the town's principal trader, secures the generic vaccine through unsanctioned channels. Acting to enforce J&R's stranglehold on the town, Goetz relies on an informant to identify who is behind the contraband. He arrests Dale, a teenager, and intends to send him to "prison with no judge, no trial, nothing," as Jake puts it in "Oversight." Jake asks Beck to intercede. He secures Dale's release by labeling him crucial to the hunt for a terrorist, the only way to trump Ravenwood's authority.

J&R exercises not only economic monopoly but also information monopoly; in Orwellian fashion, it rewrites history to suit its political agenda. Its revisionist history textbook, *A New America: A Comprehensive History,* is issued to schools. In "Condor," schoolteacher Emily Sullivan (Ashley Scott) complains to the mayor: "The section after World War II is called 'The Decline and Fall of the First Republic.'" Eric elaborates: It "talks about how the United States died because we got weak. That the Cuban Missile Crisis was a failure because we didn't attack the Russians; that we pulled out of 'Nam in '75 too early. I mean, it goes on!" This book expresses the aggressive militarism and prointerventionist stance of neoconservatism, associated with both the Republican Party and the Bush administration. The title even evokes the name of the influential neoconservative think tank Project for the New American Century.

The residents of Jericho are appalled by these and other changes instituted by J&R. They finally revolt after Goetz commits murder to cover up his embezzlement, a violation for which, unlike the murder of civilians, J&R has zero tolerance. When they attack J&R headquarters with Molotov cocktails, the show presents insurgency in a sympathetic light. The corporation's tyranny and violence provide the moral alibi necessary to frame the insurgents' violence as righteous. Indeed, the show has prepared us for this by having Valente label Hawkins, who is a righteous man, a terrorist, as well as with the episode titled "One Man's Terrorist," which implies the tagline, "is another man's freedom fighter."

There is little sympathy in the United States for any facet of the insurgency in Iraq, including for people who have been radicalized to resist occupation by incidents such as the massacre of civilians by Blackwater. The mainstream media, which fail to differentiate between the different threads of resistance to coalition forces, is in part responsible for this. For *Jericho* to present insurgency in a sympathetic light by showing the injustices perpetrated by occupation forces is akin to what post–World War II "problem pictures" did when they cast white actresses to play "mulatto" female characters who could "pass" as white. When such a character was subjected to racist violence, the white audience could identify with her, and the film elicited sympathy for (white) victims of racism. Whether this sympathy extended to black victims of racism is unclear, but that was the problem picture's socially conscious intent.[7] Similarly, not all viewers who sympathized with the residents of Jericho would see the parallels with Iraq or extend their sympathy to any of the antioccupation insurgents. Nevertheless, it was a bold move. And it was not their only one.

Jericho raises the specter of the United States occupied by private contractors working for a firm with covert ties to top members of the administration intent on subverting democracy for political and economic gain. Like Blackwater and KBR, the fictional Ravenwood operates with impunity. Moreover, the employees of these firms, operating in war zones, are in effect mercenaries whose loyalty is not to the nation but to the profitability of the firm. KBR, until 2007 a subsidiary of Halliburton, had ties to Vice President Cheney (chairman and CEO of Halliburton until 2000) and other top members of the Bush administration. Likewise, Ravenwood is a subsidiary of Jennings & Rall, a major donor to the political career of President Tomarchio, who once worked for J&R. Cronyism characterizes his administration; his cabinet and advisers are drawn from J&R. Halliburton is even named in "The Day Before," the episode that first suggests Jake's involvement with Ravenwood. A prospective employer asks Jake, applying for a job as a pilot, which independent contractor he worked for in Afghanistan and Iraq: "Halliburton? Blackwater?"

Halliburton and Blackwater were among the major recipients of the Bush administration's commitment to the privatization of government services, including war. KBR has received more than $20 billion since the Iraq war began; Blackwater, $1 billion. Both these firms were politically connected to the Bush administration, which was extremely receptive to allowing corporations to set policy, as was the case with Cheney's energy policy report.[8]

Jericho's "what if" scenario takes this reality further. The Cheyenne government holds a Constitutional Convention to rewrite the basic law of the land. J&R is at the core of this process. In "Patriots and Tyrants," Jake characterizes it as J&R building its "own private country," to which Gray Anderson (Michael Gaston), Jericho's mayor, responds: "And when it's done, I don't think there's anything that this government is not going to have the power to do in the name of national security," an assessment that echoes concerns raised about the Patriot Act.

Jericho's political subtext is critical of the Bush administration's "culture of deception." Its doppelganger, the Cheyenne government, promotes lies and misinformation to further its neoconservative agenda. Government officials propagate the lie that the attacks were backed by North Korea and Iran (elements of Bush's "axis of evil"). The casus belli not only deflects attention from their own complicity but also empowers them to wage war. Any evidence to the contrary is censored or met with retribution. As coproducer Matt Federman put it, "Essentially, the press has been neutered. Not unlike our own press in this world." Details about the Bush administration's "culture of deception" have emerged from former insiders, most recently from former press secretary Scott McClellan. *Jericho* merely exaggerates our government's misdeeds. Both the Cheyenne government and ours exploit a sneak attack to enlarge the power of the presidency. They make false allegations to justify an invasion. They rely on private security contractors without holding them accountable for their actions in a war zone. They stifle dissent and erode civil liberties.[9]

Like the Morse code message that opens every episode, the program embeds a political code that enriches the meaning of the show and makes it relevant to our lived political reality. Episode titles allude to real-world political situations: "One Man's Terrorist," "Casus Belli," "Coalition of the Willing," "Why We Fight," "Patriots and Tyrants." As star Skeet Ulrich comments on the season 2 DVD, "Everything felt very pertinent and relevant to what the country—our country was dealing with and what . . . our country in *Jericho* is dealing with. It sort of meshed in a weird way."[10]

At the start of the second season, executive producer Jon Turteltaub publicly acknowledged both the political nature of the show and the calculated risk this entails on broadcast television: "People, and by people I mean our bosses, probably prefer to not get all political. But that said, *Jericho* is not ignoring the political and social landscape." Likewise, Skeet Ulrich commented: "I feel like we were really making a statement to some extent. You always want to hold up a mirror, but you don't want to let people know you're doing it. Hopefully it's just enough for people to draw the parallels."[11] Fans drew the parallels, as evidenced by online fan discourse about the show and its meanings.

Fan Activism and the Mobilization of Dissent

On the Web site Television without Pity, fans took note of the political parallels and filled in the gaps in blogs and postings. *Jericho* had the distinction of being "the only scripted CBS [show] to have its own recap page on [the] popular chat site Television Without Pity." Recappers are professional fans who have turned their fandom, specifically the writings they produce about a show, into a source of income. One recapper who covered seventeen episodes, including all of season 2, Stephanie Vander Weide (aka "Keckler"), expressed her unadulterated enthusiasm for the show in the last recap: "I love that I'm totally dumb where this show is concerned! I love that I can't predict it!" Thus, she identifies the series' surprisingly effective dense plotting as a key component of the pleasure it affords fans.[12]

When Keckler interviewed Lennie James (Hawkins), she expounded on the compelling nature of the show:

> One thing that a lot of our *Jericho* posters seem to have in common is that we are completely obsessed with the show, but part of us is still wondering, "Why? What is it about this show that is so compelling?" Recently, I was at a grocery store—I don't even know how this came up, I think I made a joke about growing beets in my bathtub—and the checker said, "Do you watch that show, *Jericho?* I think it's the most important show on television!" So, what do you think it is about this show that has the power to compel and excite?

James ultimately said he did not know, but the generous helping of political commentary sprinkled throughout Keckler's recaps, especially in the more politically explicit season 2 episodes, seems to suggest that she did.[13]

In keeping with the self-described "snarky" tone of the Web site, Keckler uses humor to draw parallels—sometimes directly, sometimes allusively. Her take on the television news broadcast circulating the story about Iran and North Korea's involvement was succinct: "Lying liars who LIE!" an allusion to Al Franken's book *Lies (And the Lying Liars Who Tell Them)*.[14]

Bush and Cheney come into her direct line of fire. When Emily objects to the revisionist history books and asks, "How should we handle this?" Keckler quips: "Well, first, get Bush out of office." Her comments, embedded in program descriptions, reveal and pass on her command of political affairs: "Hawkins . . . [says] that Valente is in the Cheyenne government now, but Hawkins doesn't know in what capacity. Vice Prez? Dude can't look like Dick Cheney for nothing. And where are the Cheneys from? CHEYENNE!"[15]

Halliburton, KBR, and Blackwater are named several times, with a coating of humor: "Jake with his Ravenwater-Blackwood background." She notes, "[President Tomarchio's] cabinet and advisory board are lousy with former J&Rs. 'At the highest levels, that government and this company are one and the same,' Smith [Hawkins's inside informant] reveals. Oh, the Halliburton of it all!" Other times, the connections she draws take on a more sober tone:

"Oh, those 'sanctioned government contractors'—they're so impudent with their murder and their multiple Halliburton/KBR rape cover-ups. I wonder if the Allied States of America finds rape and torture acceptable during times of war."[16] And, like newspaper critics, she connects Jericho to occupied Iraq. When Jake declares that the contractors answer to no one, "Eric tries to say that Jericho isn't Iraq. Don't fool yourself, Eric; the Usurper President is Paul Bremer, and you all are the beaten-down insurgents."[17]

Keckler's reading of the show received explicit support from Steve Scaia, executive story editor and writer. In an e-mail, Scaia described himself as a "huge" fan of her recaps, adding, "You liked the things we worked the hardest on." He and cowriter Matt Federman tried to give her a shout-out, naming one of the characters "Trish Keckler," but it did not get clearance, presumably because someone by that name lived in Kansas. Keckler notes the irony of the timing. "When writers/executive producers of a show I recap finally write me with glowing praise, it would have to be a doomed show."[18]

The cancellation of *Jericho* incited heated protest and debate about the reasons for it. Of the 115 comments posted on the Internet Movie Database, two attribute its cancellation to the critical political nature of the program. On March 26, 2008, newmoonofsedona (U.S.) posted, "It's definitely NOT the ratings," a comment that was rated as useful by 74 percent of the users (83 out of 112) who rated it. S/he objects to *Jericho*'s cancellation and attributes CBS's lack of promotion for the show to government pressure to pull it due to its thinly veiled references to real-world events.[19]

> This was a true reality show and not like the other drivel they push on us as such. I believe, as many other fans do, that the show was canceled by pressure from the U.S. government. (Oh, you naive ones, do you really think there is no censorship here in the U.S.?) It is too close to what is going on with references to Blackwater (Ravenwood) and Halliburton (Jennings and Rall) that make one think that these supposed patriots are NOT GOOD! This is true. This show has won awards, has had a large outcry of fans, bringing it back and was NEVER PROMOTED by CBS. Instead we get these idiotic things like "Big Brother" (hmmm. . . . who is the real big brother?). . . . That this shows [*sic*] scenario, which involves the CIA, Homeland Security, etc., is just not appreciated by this administration and that is the REAL reason it was canceled. . . . Its canceling is in line with Dan Rather's firing, whist [*sic*] he had been

on CBS for DECADES, as soon as he mentioned some unflattering FACTS about G. Bush's military record, POOF, he was gone. . . . The so-called "Patriot Act" is anything but, and more like a reneging of our freedoms in the Bill of Rights![20]

CBS's scheduling strategy was to air the first half of season 1 from September through November 2006, then air the second half from February through May 2007. During the three-month hiatus, a different show was aired rather than repeats of *Jericho*. Here, CBS seems to have been following ABC's lead, which NBC also followed. This strategy resulted in audience loss in the spring not only for *Jericho* but for *Lost* and *Heroes* as well. But in addition to the long hiatus, *Jericho* had to contend with the fact that in the spring it was scheduled against Fox's ratings powerhouse *American Idol*, something the more established *Lost* did not have to face in 2007.[21]

Another factor that adversely affected *Jericho*'s ratings is that its "fiercely loyal" audience often viewed the show on DVR or online. *Jericho* "consistently [ranked] as the CBS scripted program whose [audience] grew by the largest percentage when DVR playback [which is factored into the ratings when viewers play it back within a few days after broadcast] was included. Such a [statistic] indicates a sizable [audience] went out of its way to make sure it didn't miss an episode." The cancellation of the show led not only to a multifaceted protest campaign to bring it back but also to a spirited critique of the Nielsen ratings system as unreliable in the digital age.[22]

The millennial generation, also referred to as the Internet generation, is more likely to watch online, and this group constitutes a key component of *Jericho*'s viewership. Millennials are also more receptive to criticism of the government from a leftist perspective. According to a study by the Center for American Progress, which defined millennials as those aged eighteen to twenty-nine, "Millennials mostly reject the conservative viewpoint that government is the problem, and that free markets always produce the best results for society"— the linchpin of the neoconservative drive to privatize everything, including the military. "Millennials are more likely than other age groups to disapprove of George W. Bush's handling of his presidency, which could be fueling a rejection of the larger conservative agenda and driving [their] support for progressive policies." This is a population for whom *Jericho*'s dystopian depiction of the neoconservative agenda might be particularly appealing.[23]

The millennial generation is net savvy and likely to be engaged in "prosumer" activities such as blogging, posting to forums, and creating video mashups. The successful online campaign to save *Jericho* from cancellation featured Web 2.0 activism: videos posted to YouTube, Web sites devoted to sharing information and mobilizing volunteers, and, in a deal with Amazon, a drive to send *Jericho* DVDs to U.S. soldiers in Iraq and Afghanistan. One campaign took its cue from the "Why We Fight" episode, which uses a quote from the Battle of the Bulge. When the American commander of the outnumbered and underequipped forces was asked by the Nazis to surrender, he responded, "Nuts!" This was also Jake's response to New Bern's siege of Jericho and the fans' response to CBS when the show was canceled. The online campaign resulted in the delivery of more than twenty tons of nuts to CBS. On the season 2 DVD extra "Nut Job," Nina Tassler, president of CBS Entertainment, credits the campaign as having "a profound influence on [their] decision" to renew. After the campaign succeeded in bringing about a second season a mere three weeks after cancellation, the SaveJerichoCoalition site asked, "How does it feel to make history?" These words were echoed in the series finale, when Hawkins asks Jake, "How does it feel? . . . Making history," in what Keckler calls "one of the sweetest shout-outs to fandom ever."[24]

Among the most creative strategies deployed in the campaign were videos produced by fans. In an act of digital poaching, some denounced CBS by visually aligning the network with New Bern, as Jericho gets ready to take it on in battle, or with Valente, as Hawkins spies on his forces. One of the best approaches, however, takes a different tack. In "Dear CBS," LisiBee positions the network as the recipient of a Dear John letter. She recounts the travails of their on-again, off-again relationship and poses *Jericho* as the epitome of their closeness. Feeling betrayed at having it taken away, she attacks CBS where it really hurts: "I hope your ratings shrivel up and fall off."[25]

Fans like LisiBee are taking affective marketing, which tries to forge an intense attachment between program and consumer, and turning it back on the network. Fan engagement is valued not only for ratings but also because engagement is assumed to cross over from program to ad, making viewers more attractive to advertisers and thus serving network interests. However, it also empowers fans to make demands on networks. They own the show. And the narrative of *Jericho*, which centers on the moral imperative to resist tyranny and protect democracy, provides a model for fan activism.[26]

Fans rightly celebrated their power to have the show reinstated. Their desire for renewal prevailed for a time, and a dissident perspective on political affairs aired on network prime time. It is fitting, given that *Jericho* endorses citizen engagement and the importance of dissent, that they made their voices count. And by depicting real-world events from a progressive perspective, *Jericho* was able to expand the terms of political discourse and make a political intervention.[27]

The *Jericho* campaign was both a victory for fans and a symbolic victory for democracy and dissent; as fans claimed, it was a demonstration of the power to change history. Some might argue that this form of fan activism is a distraction from real-world politics rather than an engagement with it. But what if the tactics for engagement with a politically inflected program cross over to real-world politics? Look at the strategies and tactics of the Obama presidential campaign—specifically, the way it combined centralized Web-centered action (fund-raising, distributing speeches, recruiting volunteers) with decentralized forms of organizing (YouTube videos that turned viral, such as the one featuring Obama Girl)—all working toward a common goal. This was the political repurposing of tactics developed to make demands on entertainment. Fans developed these tactics to make successful demands in the relatively low-stakes, high-pleasure realm of entertainment.

The *Jericho* campaign demonstrates the engagement of the millennial generation, whether or not they were fans of *Jericho*. This form of social engagement, widespread in the millennial demographic, set the stage for the Obama campaign, which so effectively mobilized the engagement strategies of the Internet generation. Organizing of the sort that mobilized around *Jericho* allowed people to develop a novel set of interventions that was then harnessed and redirected toward overtly political ends by the Obama campaign, constituting a form of political innovation that not only engaged more voters and deepened investment in the political process but also elected this country's first African American president. After eight years of a failed Bush presidency, Obama was elected with the hope that "things in this country are gonna change pretty fast."[28]

Notes

My thanks to David Gallagher for urging me to watch *Jericho* and for valuable comments on an earlier draft. I am indebted to Heather Levi for her careful reading and help in thinking through the more difficult aspects of this chapter.

1. Despite an allusion in the episode title "The Day Before," executive producer and writer Stephen Chbosky has said that *The Day After* was not an influence. Given

the subject matter, however, comparisons are inevitable.

2. Eric Goldman, "Paley Fest: Jericho," 2007, http://tv.ign.com/articles/773/773164p1.html (accessed June 25, 2008).

3. The episode title "Why We Fight" alludes to the series of World War II propaganda films (largely directed by Frank Capra) commissioned by the federal government to rally support for U.S. participation in the war. It also refers to the 2005 antiwar documentary by Eugene Jarecki, which argues against the preemptive strike policy of the Bush administration in Iraq.

4. Mark Gallagher, "I Married Rambo: Spectacle and Melodrama in the Hollywood Action Film," in *Mythologies of Violence in Postmodern Media,* ed. Christopher Sharrett (Detroit: Wayne State University Press, 1999), 213.

5. Ed Guerrero, "Recuperation, Representation, and Resistance: Black Cinema through the 1980s," in *Framing Blackness: The African American Image in Film* (Philadelphia: Temple University Press, 1993), 113–56.

6. Jeremy Scahill, "Blackwatergate," *Nation,* October 22, 2007; Jeremy Scahill, "Blackwater's Private Spies," *Nation,* June 23, 2008; Brian Stelter, "A TV Show Hopes to Cover a Lot of Ground in Postapocalyptic Kansas," *New York Times,* February 12, 2008.

7. Films with "passing" narratives in which the mixed-race character is played by a white performer include *Pinky* (1949) and *Imitation of Life* (1959).

8. James Risen, "Army Overseer Tells of Ouster over KBR Stir," *New York Times,* June 17, 2008; Jeremy Scahill, "Blackwater's Bu$Ine$$," *Nation,* December 24, 2007; Michael Abramowitz and Steven Mufson, "Papers Detail Industry's Role in Cheney's Energy Report," *Washington Post,* July 18, 2007, A1.

9. Federman quoted from commentary on the *Jericho* episode "Condor" (DVD, Paramount/CBS, 2008); Scott McClellan, *What Happened: Inside the Bush White House and Washington's Culture of Deception* (New York: PublicAffairs, 2008).

10. *Rebuilding Jericho* (CBS Paramount Home Entertainment, 2008).

11. Quoted in Stelter, "TV Show Hopes to Cover a Lot of Ground."

12. Rick Kissell, "*Jericho* Gets a Jolt," *Daily Variety,* June 11, 2007, 5; "Patriots and Tyrants" recap, 5, Television without Pity Recaps, http://www.televisionwithoutpity.com/show/jericho/recaps.php (accessed June 15, 2008) (hereafter, citations denoted "recap" are from this Television without Pity Web site).

13. Stephanie Vander Weide, "Intercept: TWOP Blows Lennie James's Cover," 2008, http://www.televisionwithoutpity.com/show/jericho/the_lennie_james_interview.php (accessed June 15, 2008).

14. "Reconstruction" recap, 4; Al Franken, *Lies (and the Lying Liars Who Tell Them): A Fair and Balanced Look at the Right* (New York: Dutton, 2003).

15. "Condor" recap, 4; "Reconstruction" recap, 16. While serving as a U.S. representative for the state of Wyoming, Cheney actually lived in Casper, not Cheyenne.

16. "Condor" recap, 10; "Termination for Cause" recap, 4; "Jennings & Rall" recap, 1, 4; Stelter, "TV Show Hopes to Cover a Lot of Ground." In the J&R post, "rape cover-

ups" is linked to an abcnews.com article about a female KBR employee who attempted to bring rape charges against male KBR employees for an incident that occurred while she was working in Iraq. It seems that the impunity provision applies here as well.

17. Internet Movie Database, "*Jericho* User Comments," http://www.imdb.com/title/tt0805663/usercomments (accessed June 20, 2008).

18. Stephanie Vander Weide, "The Fall of Jericho," 2008, http://www.grubreport.com/alacarte/jericho.html (accessed November 17, 2008).

19. Internet Movie Database, "Losing *Lost* and Other Hit Shows," Studio Briefing, May 2, 2007, and "*Jericho* Rises," Studio Briefing, June 7, 2007, http://uk.imdb.com/title/tt0805663/news?year=2007 (accessed September 21, 2009).

20. Dan Rather's lawsuit against CBS unearthed evidence to support his allegation that when the network commissioned a panel to investigate his work on the *60 Minutes* segment about Bush's National Guard service, "network executives used Republican operatives to vet the names" of potential panelists. The panel's purpose seems to have been to mollify Republican conservatives and to pressure Rather to step down as anchor of the *CBS Evening News*. See Jacques Steinberg, "Rather's Lawsuit Shows Role of G.O.P. in Inquiry," *New York Times,* November 16, 2008.

21. Internet Movie Database, "Losing *Lost* and Other Hit Shows" and "*Jericho* Rises."

22. As noted earlier, the campaign to bring *Jericho* back garnered a seven-episode second season, but not a third. The series was dropped due to weak ratings, but fans did not surrender, and SaveJericho spun off SaveJerichoAgain.

23. David Madland and Amanda Logan, "The Progressive Generation: How Young Adults Think about the Economy," 2008, http://www.americanprogress.org/issues/2008/05/progressive_generation.html (accessed June 25, 2008).

24. "Patriots and Tyrants" recap.

25. LisiBee, "Dear CBS," 2007, http://www.youtube.com/watch?v=4k9qtVve09A (accessed November 17, 2008).

26. For a discussion of affective marketing, see Henry Jenkins, "Buying into American Idol: How We Are Being Sold on Reality TV," in *Convergence Culture: Where Old and New Media Collide* (New York: New York University Press, 2006), 59–92.

27. After *Jericho* was canceled a second time in 2008, efforts to revive the show continued. Fans insisted that their viewership counted, and they hoped to find a home for new episodes on cable. That hope grew bright when *Friday Night Lights* was saved by an NBC-DirecTV deal, which provided for initial airing of the new season to DirecTV subscribers in the fall, followed by an NBC airing the following spring. Although Comcast expressed interest in a similar deal with CBS, no deal was brokered. This was followed by buzz about a feature-length film, an idea fueled by executive producer Jon Turteltaub in a January 15, 2009, interview with *IF Magazine*, http://www.ifmagazine.com/new.asp?article=7427.

28. barelypolitical, "I Got a Crush.On Obama," 2007, http://www.youtube.com/watch?v=wKsoXHYICqU (accessed November 30, 2008).

14

It's Not Funny 'Cause It's True

The Mainstream Media's Response to Media Satire in the Bush Years

Carl Bergetz

At the start of the new millennium, a phenomenon began troubling members of the mainstream national news media (imprecisely but efficiently shortened here to MSM).[1] They were becoming increasingly defensive about their ratings, image, and standing in the community inside and outside the Upper East Side. A perception existed—mainly among the MSM—that the MSM was under attack.

Of course, the MSM had been assailed before and lived to report on it. The confrontations have typically come from technological changes, manifested in competing alternative media outlets.[2] From print to radio to television to cable, the old guard has substantially subsumed each new threat into the protean MSM agglomeration. Even the wild World Wide Web, teeming with bloggers living in their moms' basements and writing in their pajamas, has not been immune, as the MSM has copied, co-opted, or otherwise moved erstwhile indie writers out of their parents' homes and into some classier sleepwear.[3]

But during the Bush years, a different threat to the MSM emerged that needed no technological advancement. It was something truly no-tech, something as old as the Romans, something powerful enough to shake the very idea of the MSM itself: clowns. Yes, clowns were breaching the MSM gates. At least that was a conclusion drawn from a 2004 Pew Research Center study on viewing habits, which showed a growing number of people getting their news from clowns (more precisely, "satirists") on *Saturday Night Live*, *The Daily Show*, and similar after-hours comedy programs.[4]

Will Ferrell's parody of President George W. Bush on *Saturday Night Live* continues a long tradition of late-night satire's strong influence on popular perceptions
of political figures. (MovieGoods)

A roiling feud between satirists and MSM news personalities (more precisely, "journalists") was poised to explode into an all-out war in 2004 and divert our attention from the real threat in Afghanistan. Journalists alleged that satirists were encroaching on their turf and generating cynicism about democracy. But the satirists were fighting back, contending that journalists were abdicating their professional duties.

In keeping with the "Comedy Rule of Three," this chapter examines (1) some notable satirical jabs thrown at the MSM in the past decade, (2) the response from the MSM to those punches, and (3) the effect of this conflict on the satirical and journalistic professions.[5]

Whose Job Is It Anyway?

The contention that late-night comedy is somehow replacing serious news has been studiously debunked.[6] Simply put, if people didn't get the news, they wouldn't get the comedians' jokes. And if people laugh in such situations, the laughter is purely symptomatic of the same nervous energy that elicits giggles of fear when real clowns who wear makeup appear in circuses and nightmares. Here is the truism: satirists need journalists. When journalists fail to do their job (i.e., aggressively pursuing the truth and holding powerful politicians to account), satirists can't do theirs (i.e., satirizing politicians). And then the Republic is put at risk. Seriously.

The job of the journalist is arguably the most important to the proper functioning of our democracy.[7] In its ideal, the press seeks the truth, objectively yet aggressively, and holds those in power to account for that truth.[8] Getting at the truth is a difficult and daunting task, particularly in times of strife.[9] Indeed, while America has a history of enshrining the press's importance to democracy, it also has a countervailing history of chilling the press's effect.

Thus, even the greatest of superheroes (to wit, Superman, a serious journalist in his day job) would have difficulty measuring up, but through earnest pursuit of the ideal, the press earned the public's trust during the twentieth century. As such, the words on the pages of the *New York Times* and other national papers were implicitly truthful; America's network news was serious, dignified business (albeit not too profitable); and "Edward R. Murrow" became a synonym for the journalistic ideal itself.

However, a funny thing happened on the way out of Watergate. The MSM at the time may have won the battle against Nixon, but Nixonian politics won the war. As much as he derided the press as liberal elites, Nixon understood that politics could be theater, and the MSM could serve as its stage. In 1968 Nixon and his team, including a young Roger Ailes (future Fox News mastermind), developed a media plan that focused on emotion and impression, not reason, and cast people in unidimensional, broadly drawn roles for a narrative that audiences could easily follow.[10] Television could serve as a proscenium arch, within which a political theater could be performed. MSM journalists, in time, would become theater critics. Instead of reporting and commenting on policy, the MSM critiqued performances that the campaigns scripted. In so doing, the MSM helped facilitate "caricature campaigns."

Ironically, a courageous press that had exposed Nixon's corruption slowly devolved into what Nixon's team had scripted—an MSM whose reality slipped away from its ideals and the public's expectations. And whenever the distance between reality and ideals opens wide in any industry, another group of professionals has the job of filling the gap: satirists.

Satire is an art in which "human . . . shortcomings are held up to censure by means of ridicule, derision, burlesque, irony, or other methods, ideally with the intent to bring about improvement."[11] As Twain, Mencken, and others have shown, politicians have always been needful subjects of satire throughout American history. However, whereas the distance between political ideals and reality was always somewhat apparent and became painfully clear during Vietnam and Watergate, the gap between journalistic ideals and reality was relatively minor. Consequently, satire directed at the MSM was less prevalent.

That's not to say news parody was nonexistent. In the early 1960s the BBC produced the influential and controversial *That Was the Week that Was,* a comedic sketch show that goofed on topical stories.[12] In the United States the late 1960s saw *Rowan and Martin's Laugh-in* (1968–1973) and *The Smothers Brothers Comedy Hour* (1967–1969) satirize political events. *Laugh-in* specifically had overt news parody routines, including "*Laugh-in* Looks at the News" and "News of the Future." And of course, since 1975, "Weekend Update" on NBC's *Saturday Night Live* (*SNL*) has parodied television news.

But in most instances, the faux news provided a framing device to poke fun at the politicians and celebrities in the real news. To the extent these programs ridiculed television journalists, much of the comedy was mockery of either all-too-serious commentators or stereotypical local newsreaders.

Take, for instance, Ted Knight's dim, sexist, and pompous Ted Baxter from *The Mary Tyler Moore Show* or Chevy Chase's goofball anchor on *SNL* or Paddy Chayefsky's "angry prophet" of the airwaves Howard Beale in *Network*.[13] These characters worked because they played against the general perception of journalists as dignified, fearless seekers of truth. *Network*'s mad-as-hell Howard Beale and his corporate puppeteers still had a backroom of sagacious newsmen. Behind the blowhard Ted Baxter was a serious Lou Grant pushing his staff to uncover material so that he could spin off his own dramatic program. And while the childish Chevy Chase could mock her to hilarious effect, Jane Curtin was not going to be deterred from her earnest editorializing on the environmental dangers of aerosol cans.

But during the Bush years, the MSM (and perceptions and expectations about it) began to change. The distance between journalistic ideals and reality widened in the run-up to the Iraq war, with contrived shout-fests spreading like contagion around MSM cable outlets, anemic inquiries about the casus belli further spinning the spin of the Bush administration, and reporting on politics generally turning into caricature coverage.

The prophecy of Chayefsky (and Nixon's own Roger Ailes) was being fulfilled (perhaps self-fulfilled, in the case of Ailes). The MSM was not so much losing ground to satirists as it was stepping away from its ideals; therefore, satirists were not encroaching on any territory not already ceded. Rather, incrementally, journalists were joining the campaign carnival, and someone needed to tell the audience—and the MSM itself.

Crossfires and Hardballs

In 1999 comedian Jon Stewart became the host of Comedy Central's *The Daily Show* and turned the show's aim toward political issues and figures.[14] After several years of success, including the presciently titled "Indecision 2000" segment on that year's presidential election, *The Daily Show* became a leader in late-night comedy and, according to the Pew study mentioned earlier, an alternative news source.

Not long after the MSM's hackles rose up, and ABC's *Nightline* host Ted Koppel confronted Stewart at the July 2004 Democratic National Convention to grouse about the MSM's potential obsolescence. "A lot of television viewers—more, quite frankly, than I am comfortable with—get their news from . . . *The Daily Show*," Koppel charged, as if reading straight from the Pew study. He then complained about Stewart's contention that the convention was "like a product launch." Stewart corrected him: "Not 'like a product launch'—it is a product launch." Stewart emphasized that Koppel, as a serious journalist, could get more accountability and speak more truth to power without humor because of his "credibility and gravitas." Koppel rained on the wishful thinking and ended the exchange by saying, "You're finished."[15]

Stewart saw the dynamic differently from Koppel and other MSM mandarins: satire wasn't displacing news; news was displacing itself with unserious newslike product, playing far too large a role in the political theater. Now Stewart was taking aim at the MSM itself.

Stewart took his case directly to one of the premier MSM theatrical stages: CNN's *Crossfire*. Ostensibly there to promote his new book, Stewart nearly immediately made a plea to Tucker Carlson and Paul Begala to "stop hurting America" (actually, to "stop, stop, stop, stop hurting America"). And of course, he wasn't referring just to Carlson and Begala but to all similar programs—Stewart listed "*Crossfire* . . . or *Hardball* or *I'm Gonna Kick Your Ass*," the last of which could have been the name of any number of Fox News's Beale-like programs.[16]

Stewart overtly called on the MSM to fulfill its "responsibility to the public discourse" and live up to its ideal, suggesting, tongue only partially in cheek, that its members "come work for us." Poignantly and humorously, he implored, "See, the thing is, we need your help. Right now, you're helping the politicians and the corporations. And we're left out there to mow our lawns." If democracy was going to work, the press needed to hew more closely to its ideals.

Carlson fought back, chastising Stewart for his questioning of politicians and "suck[ing] up to" presidential hopeful Senator John Kerry. Carlson essentially claimed that Stewart had the same duty as the press. If Stewart was going to interview politicians, he was encroaching on journalistic territory and needed to assume journalistic responsibilities. In other words, satirists couldn't have their pie and throw it too.

However, Stewart disagreed. His job was to entertain. The MSM had a more serious and important job for our country, but it had become "theater": "You're part of their strategies," Stewart stated, and "[you could] actually get politicians off their marketing and strategy." Carlson sat in disbelief.

CARLSON: Is this really Jon Stewart? What is this, anyway?

STEWART: Yes, it's someone who watches your show and cannot take it anymore.

Instead of the newsman being "mad as hell" at politicians, the satirist had had enough of the newsmen. And near the rancorous end of the discussion, Stewart betrayed why the target of today's satire is moving from politicians, whose failure to live up to ideals we have come to expect, to the MSM, which until relatively recently had engendered the opposite expectation. When asked which candidate for president, Kerry or Bush, "would provide better material" for comedy, Stewart responded: "The absurdity of the system provides us the most material. And that is best served by the sort of theater of it all, you know, which, by the way, thank you both, because it's been helpful."

Stewart's lambasting of CNN's signature program preceded its cancellation by only a few months. Whether his appearance caused the end of *Crossfire* is unclear, but statements from interested parties show that Stewart's jibes had some effect. The first spin from CNN came shortly after the show when former host Robert Novak said he didn't think Stewart was funny and called him "uninformed." James Carville, Democratic strategist and CNN contributor, admitted that Stewart was funny but a "pompous ass."[17] However, after Bush's reelection, Carlson was dispatched from CNN to MSNBC, and *Crossfire* was canceled. CNN/US president Jonathan Klein said his network wanted to leave behind "head-butting debate shows." On the subject of Stewart's appearance, Klein said he agreed "wholeheartedly with Jon Stewart's overall premise."[18]

Whatever effect Stewart may have had on one corner of the MSM block, he clearly had more work to do elsewhere. In a *60 Minutes* interview just weeks after the CNN confrontation, Stewart chastised the CBS News program for failing to verify Dan Rather's story about Bush's National Guard service or the lack thereof.[19] But Stewart put that controversy into perspective for the MSM: "I can't believe that the National Guard memo scandal is the only scandal in four years that has gotten elevated to the state of having a 'gate' attached to it. 'Rather-gate.' For God's sake, we launched a war based on forged documents. That doesn't get a 'gate.' How do you not get a 'gate' out of that?"[20]

The contrast between the MSM's investigation of Watergate and its role in the lead-up to the Iraq war provides evidence of the problem Stewart was highlighting. In Watergate, journalists courageously pursued the truth and, in so doing, exposed governmental corruption and the grievous distance between our political ideals and our political reality. In the Iraq war, journalists were not aggressive or courageous and, in some instances, played into the theater created by the politicians. When the truth finally leaked out, drip by painful drip, the MSM exposed another chasm between ideals and reality—its own.

Loaded Colbert

If politicians and the MSM had become one meta–political theater, then Stewart had become the meta-critic—observing and commenting on the theater actors (the politicians) and the theater critics (the MSM). *The Daily Show* did this by surrounding a bemused Stewart with faux journalists who displayed no acquaintance with journalistic ideals. One such phony reporter, Stephen Colbert, took the satire a step further, leaving behind any reality-based mooring and conveying his satire in character at all times. His program, *The Colbert Report,* delivered something novel: method satire.[21]

Tossing aside any pretense of objectivity, courage, dignity, or self-reflection, Colbert's never-out-of-character character was everything Stewart had been deriding. Each night his studio became the nadir of the modern MSM. But on April 29, 2006, Colbert ventured out of his den to attend the White House Correspondents' Association dinner, and the bar for satirists everywhere was raised.

This junket is usually a low-temperature roast, with the comic host kidding the press and the president. However, Colbert, the method satirist, addressed the dinner guests without any winks or nods and illustrated the problem of the MSM playing in the political theater. He first chastised the media for recently reporting on "secret prisons," which he said had been kept "secret for a very important reason: they're super-depressing." He then "commended" them for their dereliction of duty in the previous five years and reminded them of their role: "But listen, let's review the rules. Here's how it works. The President makes the decisions. He's the decider. The press secretary announces those decisions, and you people of the press type those decisions down. Make, announce, type. Just put 'em through a spell check and go home. Get to know your family again. Make love to your wife. Write that novel you got kicking around in your head. You know, the one about the intrepid Washington reporter with the courage to stand up to the administration? You know, fiction!"[22] With these lines, he sent a missile into that gap between the ideal of an intrepid press and its MSM reality. The reaction (or lack thereof) to Colbert's appearance has been fairly well chronicled, but not without some dispute. Many Colbert fans and progressive bloggers hailed

Colbert's combination of bomb throwing and sniper fire at the administration and the MSM. Some made allegations that the MSM, smarting from the assault on its lack of courage in the face of the Bush administration, ignored his direct hits in its subsequent coverage of the event.[23] In fact, over the next few days, ABC's *This Week,* CNN's *American Morning,* and the NBC, ABC, and CBS morning programs each referenced the dinner and Bush's comic stylings but made no mention of Colbert's routine.[24] The *New York Times* initially didn't make any reference to it either. Eventually it was covered far more broadly by the MSM, but many journalists and commentators, including Carlson on his new MSNBC show *Tucker,* deemed it "unfunny." The *Washington Post*'s Richard Cohen called the act "rude."[25]

Interestingly, Ana Marie Cox, a former independent blogger who later became a writer for *Time,* scoffed at the significance of the speech and theorized, "Comedy can have a political point but it is not political action."[26] However, her own point is suspect. The allegations that the MSM refused to cover Colbert's speech, true or not, resulted in far more coverage—or at least more coverage of the allegations of noncoverage—than would have resulted had the allegations not been made. And since the MSM plays a large role in the political theater that voters follow and to which they respond, comedy, in this case, was political action.[27]

Of course, how much "action" it caused is speculative. Columnist Frank Rich called the performance a possible "defining moment" of the 2006 midterm campaign.[28] Whether Colbert's wise tomfoolery inspired some voters to help return Congress to the Democrats later that year is of course unknowable (as Colbert might say, it feels like it did). His routine certainly coincided with a wave of books and articles about the Bush administration's secrets and spinning during the Iraq war and the war on terror and just how derelict the MSM had been. And from the tone of the blogosphere, Colbert's roast emboldened those critical of the press to press on, and it may have even emboldened the press itself into some action.

But, as the next election cycle displayed, satire is a dish best served continuously.

The Bitch Is Back

The 2008 election offered opportunities for the MSM to seek the truth from a clean slate of power seekers, to avoid playing a part in the political theater, and to expiate the failures of the now-waning Bush era. One problem:

the Clinton era was returning. Despite the throng of hopefuls, coverage of election 2008 focused for much of 2007 on Hillary Clinton, and although her proposals and achievements were covered, the MSM repeatedly fell into re-covering old memes and perpetuating a caricature campaign tinged with sexism.

From her days as first lady to her Senate run, Clinton had been caricatured simultaneously as an undeserving beneficiary of her husband's achievements and as a tough, heartless Machiavellian. Certainly, many male politicians have benefited from connections to successful spouses and family members, and many more have displayed calculated heartlessness without so much as a peep from the press. But for this female politician, the caricature meant one thing: it could be hinted at many different ways, but, recalling Barbara Bush, they all rhyme with "rich."

At the start of Clinton's presidential run, ABC's Charles Gibson kept the meme alive when he asked her, "Would you be in this position were it not for your husband?"[29] Around that same time, MSNBC's Chris Matthews repeatedly referred to Clinton as "uppity."[30] Later in 2007 and in early 2008 the comments kept coming, and they kept getting stranger. MSNBC personalities in particular emitted egregious examples of sexist caricature coverage. Matthews and Tucker Carlson each used weird allusions to "castration" when talking about Clinton. Mike Barnicle drew cackles from the boys on MSNBC's *Morning Joe* when he said Clinton looked "like everyone's first wife standing outside a probate court." David Shuster questioned whether Clinton had "pimped out" her daughter Chelsea in the campaign. And Matthews infamously opined, "The reason she's a U.S. senator, the reason she's a candidate for president, the reason she may be a front-runner is her husband messed around."[31] Perhaps in this climate, even Senator John McCain, a man with a tough, irascible reputation and an extremely wealthy spouse, felt it acceptable to commend a supporter's question as "excellent" when she asked him, "How do we beat the bitch?"[32]

Interestingly, most of these incidents happened during a television writers' strike, when late-night comedy programs were either on hiatus or without scriveners. So it was fitting that a writer, from NBC no less, would return to punch the MSM in a place that rhymes with "guts."

Tina Fey, the first female head writer of *SNL* and creator of the critically acclaimed comedy *30 Rock,* assumed *SNL* hosting duties on February 23, 2008. The cold open was a satire of a presidential debate between Clinton and Senator Barack Obama. CNN's Campbell Brown, John King, and others in the MSM were deemed "in the tank" for Obama, tossing him softballs and dismissively deriding a shrewish Clinton.[33] Later, during the "Weekend Update" segment, Fey humorously harangued the sexist caricaturing of Clinton as a "bitch." With the memorable line "Bitch is the new black," Fey satirically "took back" the word and made it a badge of honor for people who "get stuff done."[34]

Of course, the extent of the MSM's "bitchiness" toward Clinton and supportiveness of Obama could be debated endlessly; such criticisms are always something of a Rorschach test.[35] Nonetheless, as with most good comedy, a truth was at the core. In the wake of the episode, Howard Kurtz of CNN and the *Washington Post* noted that a study from the Center for Media and Public Affairs found that from December 16, 2007, to February 19, 2008, "the three network newscasts aired reports that were 84 percent positive for Obama and 53 percent positive for Clinton."[36] Further, after Obama secured the nomination, some members of the MSM admitted to sexism in their coverage.[37] But most pertinently, like Stewart and Colbert, Fey and *SNL* had again called out the MSM for playing in the political theater as opposed to reporting aggressively to get beneath the simplistic campaign narratives.

The question of sexism and caricature coverage continued to rear its head like Vladimir Putin over Alaskan airspace after McCain announced that Governor Sarah Palin would be the GOP's first female vice presidential nominee. In the few days between her national introduction and her nomination acceptance speech on September 3, 2008, the MSM had little opportunity to investigate her, allowing the McCain campaign to script a narrative of a tough but sexy "maverick." In a speech that bitterly mocked Obama, Palin drew her own caricature broadly, joking that the difference between a "hockey mom" (as she described herself) and a "pit bull" (as her speech portrayed her) was "lipstick."[38]

The next week Obama claimed in a stump speech that McCain and Palin represented more of the same, referencing the old saw that you could put "lipstick" on a pig, but it was still a pig.[39] Perhaps because of his use of the word "lipstick," the McCain campaign, through adviser Carly Fiorina, decried Obama's comment as "sexist."[40] Later that week ABC's Charles Gibson interviewed Palin, and her performance caused some people to wonder whether she offered much more than pit bull rhetoric and lipstick. In particular, Palin's answer to Gibson's question about the "Bush doctrine" made it appear that she had never heard the term.[41]

Just a few days later, Fey debuted her now-famous impression of Palin on the 2008 season premiere of *SNL*.[42] In an opening sketch that paired her with Amy Poehler as Clinton, two forms of sexism were illustrated—"bitch" contra "bimbo."

> CLINTON/POEHLER: But, Sarah, one thing we can agree on is that sexism can never be allowed to permeate an American election.
>   . . .

> PALIN/FEY: So, we ask reporters and commentators, stop using words that diminish us, like "pretty," "attractive," "beautiful."

> CLINTON/POEHLER: "Harpy," "shrew," and "boner shrinker."

But beyond that dichotomy, the sketch, like Fey's previous bit on *SNL,* wound up punching the MSM in the same old place:

> PALIN/FEY: So, in the next six weeks, I invite the media to be vigilant for sexist behavior.

> CLINTON/POEHLER: Although it is never sexist to question female politicians' credentials. Please ask this one about dinosaurs. So, I invite the media to grow a pair. And if you can't, I will lend you mine.

The sketch called on the MSM to be more aggressive in its quest for the truth—or, for that matter, any information—about Palin, a relative unknown with a significant actuarial probability of becoming the leader of the free world.

So, did the MSM take Poehler/Clinton up on the offer? Although the McCain campaign made Palin remarkably unavailable to the press, she did agree to a series of interviews with CBS's Katie Couric in late September 2008. Refusing to be part of the strategies or theater of a caricature campaign, Couric was appropriately aggressive (more so than typical MSM inquiry in the Bush years), asking follow-ups when answers seemed deficient and forcing Palin off her talking points. The result was so risible that on September 27, 2008, Fey was back with Poehler on *SNL* parodying the interview, letting the sketch write itself.[43]

After this one-two punch from the satirists and a journalist, Palin's lack of qualifications was apparent. Almost immediately, even many conservatives began acknowledging the problem,[44] and by election day, polling showed that a majority of the public considered Palin unqualified to be vice president.[45]

Couric got to Palin in numerous ways (Palin later said she was "a bit annoyed with some of the questions").[46] But Couric (like Fey and Poehler) was just doing her job—a critical endeavor when faced with a campaign intent on creating caricatures and keeping reality from the electorate. For instance, Carl Cameron of Fox News had uncovered even more embarrassing stories about Palin, but they were embargoed, like Palin herself, and not open to public disclosure until after the election.[47]

The Nation of Networks

Over the past decade, a pattern has emerged in the discourse between satirists and MSM journalists. As opposed to the politicians they have historically targeted, satirists have more recently aimed their fire at the MSM for falling short of its expected responsibilities relative to those politicians. Comedians such as Stewart, Colbert, Fey, and Poehler have satirized members of the MSM for contriving confrontations that were more broad comic theater than dignified political debate, for lacking the courage to uncover the truth, and for partaking in caricature coverage of politicians.

In response to these satirical attacks, the MSM has had moments of denial, acknowledgment, and change. Of course, some in the MSM still haven't gotten the joke—or the truth behind it. After former Bush press secretary Scott McClellan explained that "the national press corps was probably too deferential" to the Bush administration on the decision to invade Iraq and that the "country would have been better served" had the "liberal media" lived up to its reputation,[48] one would expect acknowledgment and change to be forthcoming.

However, when the anchors of the three main MSM newscasts appeared on NBC's *Today Show* in 2008 and were asked whether the media had abandoned its responsibilities in the lead-up to the war, Charles Gibson actually said, "It was just a drumbeat of support from the administration. And it is not our job to debate them. It's our job to ask the questions." Not surprisingly, only Couric admitted the MSM could have been more aggressive.[49]

Given the cultural and economic changes of the past generation, expectations of a return to the journalistic ideals of Murrow are as unrealistic as they are unfair. The MSM has become a player in the political theater because so much of politics has indeed become theater, because the public has grown to view the world in theatrical terms, and because the MSM is part of a complex corporate entertainment industry. So now we have comedy programs with thick slices of news, and news programs with small helpings of humor, such as Keith Olbermann's "Worst Person in the World" segment on MSNBC's *Countdown*.[50]

The line has blurred, and there is no going back. As newsman–entertainer–angry prophet Howard Beale harangued, "We are in the boredom-killing business. If you want truth go to God, go to your guru, go to yourself because that's the only place you'll ever find real truth. But man, you're never going to get any truth from us."[51] However, to say that no truth can be offered, extracted, or expected is in itself not true. Some narrowing of the distance between journalistic ideals and reality is not impossible and should be demanded, given the importance of the MSM to democracy. If the past eight years have taught us anything, it is that real live humans, not caricatures, feel the ramifications of any dereliction of duty, whether by our government or by our press. Political theater has entertainment value, but at some point the show must stop and real life must go on. And when it does—as satirists such as Stewart, Colbert, and Fey point out through their funny business—the press must engage in the unfunny business of courageously demanding that those in power not simply put on a good act for the public, but act for the public good.

Notes

Over the centuries, satire has been a literary and artistic form providing an outlet for voices of dissent, particularly in political discourse. As such, despite all the laughter it engenders, satire has been a subject for serious study. See Robert C. Elliott, *The Power of Satire: Magic, Ritual, Art* (Princeton, NJ: Princeton University Press, 1960); Dustin Griffin, *Satire: A Critical Reintroduction* (Lexington: University Press of Kentucky, 1994). In recent years, political satire has proliferated in the electronic media, taking aim at both those media and the politics they cover. The interplay of satire, politics, and media has, not surprisingly, become a growing area of inquiry. See Stephen E. Kercher, *Revel with a Cause: Liberal Satire in Postwar America* (Chicago: University of Chicago Press, 2006), exploring sociopolitical satire during the advent of the television era; Russell L. Peterson, *Strange Bedfellows: How Late-Night Comedy Turns Democracy into a Joke* (New Brunswick, NJ: Rutgers University Press, 2008), analyzing the effect of political satire on public perceptions of government in the new millennium; Jonathan Gray, Jeffrey Jones, and Ethan Thompson, eds., *Satire TV: Politics and Comedy in the Post-Network Era* (New York: New York University Press, 2009). This chapter contributes to this critical area of study by examining recent, notable examples of satire of mainstream media political coverage and analyzing its effects to see whether the satirical jabs have prompted any change in the intended targets.

1. The term *mainstream media* is frowned on by some media types, particularly those in the alternative media of the blogosphere who are typically dissatisfied with other people's wordsmithing, especially when those other people are in the mainstream. Markos Moulitas considers the term to be pejorative, designed to exclude bloggers from the mainstream and perpetuate the GOP's Svengali-like sway over public discourse. See Markos "Kos" Moulitsas, "'MSM' vs. 'Traditional Media,'" *Daily Kos,* August 15, 2007, http://www.dailykos.com/storyonly/2007/8/15/1023/64571 (accessed August 17, 2008). To be more precise and less pejorative, this chapter's focus is on televised national news networks, programs, and personalities. Of course, such an agglomeration is not specific enough, as it presumes a monolithic creature that moves slowly and speaks ominously with one voice, which is patently untrue. This creature speaks with two voices: Internet newsman Matt Drudge's, and everyone else who lives in the world he rules. See Mark Halperin and John Harris, *The Way to Win: Taking the White House in 2008* (New York: Random House, 2006). However, if this bipolar planet and every newsperson and news program in it were individually referenced, this chapter would be exceedingly unwieldy.

2. In fact, the MSM was spawned by technology. As the nation became networked through radio and then television, the monolithic nature of the MSM was enabled.

3. In an August 21, 2007, episode of his program on *CNN Headline News,* commentator Glenn Beck ridiculed the possible influence of bloggers: "I mean, they all live in their mom's basement anyway, so what difference does that make?" See Glenn Beck, *CNN Transcripts,* August 21, 2007, http://transcripts.cnn.com/TRANSCRIPTS/0708/21/gb.01 .html (accessed December 1, 2008). In September 2004 former CBS News executive and current CNN/US president Jonathan Klein, appearing on Fox News, infamously made the following comparison between traditional journalists and bloggers: "You couldn't have a starker contrast between the multiple layers of checks and balances and a guy sitting in his living room in his pajamas writing." See "How the Blogosphere Took on CBS' Docs," *Special Report w/ Brit Hume,* Fox News, September 17, 2004, http://www .foxnews.com/story/0,2933,132494,00.html (accessed December 1, 2008).

4. Pew Research Center for People and the Press, *Cable and Internet Loom Large in Fragmented Political News Universe,* January 11, 2004, http://people-press .org/report/200/cable-and-internet-loom-large-in-fragmented-political-news-universe (accessed December 1, 2008).

5. "Monologue," *Saturday Night Live,* February 23, 2008 (season 33, episode 5). The "Comedy Rule of Three" was expressly demonstrated by Steve Martin and Tina Fey with a trio of stage slaps.

6. Russell L. Peterson, *Strange Bedfellows: How Late-Night Comedy Turns Democracy into a Joke* (New Brunswick, NJ: Rutgers University Press, 2008), 39–43. Peterson

dissects the Pew study, explains how it has been quoted and interpreted selectively, and theorizes that it was used by various people to feed a largely MSM-driven narrative that serious "traditional news" was under attack from unserious, cynical rabble-rousers.

7. Joyce Appleby and Terence Ball, eds., *Jefferson: Political Writings* (Cambridge: Cambridge University Press, 1999), 271. In a letter to Judge John Tyler on June 28, 1804, Thomas Jefferson wrote: "No experiment can be more interesting than that we are now trying, and which we trust will end in establishing the fact, that men can be governed by reason and truth. Our first object should therefore be to leave open to him all the avenues of truth. The most effective hitherto found, is the freedom of the press."

8. Although no enforceable laws exist regarding journalistic ethics, the Society of Professional Journalists (SPJ) and the Radio-Television News Directors Association (RTNDA) both have ethical codes. These codes embody a certain ideal to which the news media should aspire, emphasizing key virtues such as dignity and courage. According to the RTNDA, electronic journalists should "guard against oversimplification of issues or events," "treat all subjects of news coverage with respect and dignity," and "respect the dignity and intelligence of the audience as well as the subject of the news." The SPJ urges journalists not to "highlight incidents out of context" but rather to "show good taste" and "avoid pandering to lurid curiosity." The SPJ also says that journalists should be "courageous in gathering, reporting, and interpreting information" and should "be vigilant and courageous about holding those with power accountable." The RTNDA highlights the need to "continuously seek the truth" and "pursue truth aggressively." In addition, both codes are replete with admonishments to truth, impartiality, and the distinction between reporting and editorializing. The SPJ's *Code of Ethics* originated from the American Society of Newspaper Editors in 1926. The code went through several iterations, and the present version was adopted in 1996. See http://www.spj.org/ethicscode.asp (accessed December 1, 2008). The RTNDA's *Code of Ethics and Professional Conduct* was adopted on September 14, 2000. See http://www.rtnda.org/pages/media_items/code-of-ethics-and-professional-conduct48.php (accessed December 1, 2008).

9. See the Alien and Sedition Acts of 1798; Espionage Act of 1917; Sedition Act of 1918; *Schenck v. United States,* 249 U.S. 47 (1919) (establishing the "clear and present danger" test); *Brandenburg v. Ohio,* 395 U.S. 444 (1969) ("imminent lawless action").

10. See Joe McGinniss, *The Selling of the President* (New York: Penguin Books, 1988), 26–29, 37–39, 67. See also Neil Gabler, *Life: The Movie* (New York: Vintage Books, 1998), 108–9.

11. Robert C. Elliott, ed., "Satire," *Encyclopaedia Britannica,* 2004.

12. *That Was the Week that Was* aired on the BBC in 1962 and 1963, featuring David Frost and writers John Cleese, Graham Chapman, Roald Dahl, and Peter Cook, among others. An American version of the show aired from 1964 to 1965 and featured, at various points, Gene Hackman, Mike Nichols, Elaine May, Buck Henry, Alan Alda, Woody Allen, and Steve Allen. These programs drew from the late 1950s–early 1960s improvisational comedy and satire movements in London (e.g., Peter Cook's *Beyond*

the Fringe stage show) and Chicago (e.g., Compass Players and Second City). In turn, these shows and acts helped give rise to NBC's *Saturday Night Live.*

13. *Network* was directed by Sidney Lumet, written by Paddy Chayefsky, and produced by MGM/UA in 1976. The script can be found in *The Collected Works of Paddy Chayefsky: The Screenplays Vol. II* (New York: Applause Books, 1995). In Chayefsky's story, a struggling network has its entertainment division reprogram a dreadfully serious and money-losing news program over the objections of a dreadfully serious newsman who had worked with Edward R. Murrow, Walter Cronkite, and other dreadfully serious newsmen. So a live audience is added, as well as a soothsayer, a gossip, and "an angry prophet denouncing the hypocrisies of our times" as lead anchor. With that angry anchor, Howard Beale (who, incidentally, is certifiably mad), screaming at the camera, the program becomes a hit.

14. Stewart took over hosting duties from Craig Kilborn, who had hosted the show since 1996. With the assistance of writers Ben Karlin and David Javerbaum from the satirical newspaper *The Onion,* Stewart aimed the show's comedic arsenal away from celebrity and human-interest stories and toward more political targets.

15. Dana Stevens, "Battle of the Network Anchors," *Slate,* July 30, 2004, http://www .slate.com/id/2104473/ (accessed December 1, 2008). Koppel failed to appear on *The Daily Show* as scheduled the next day, but the two eventually patched things up. However, his concerns may have had a dab of justification: Disney, the parent company of ABC, contemplated canceling *Nightline* in early 2005 in favor of more tabloid-like fare. See Scott Collins, "Signs that *Nightline*'s Days May Be Numbered," *Los Angeles Times,* February 7, 2005, E1, http://articles.latimes.com/2005/feb/07/entertainment/et-nightline7 (accessed December 1, 2008).

16. This and following quotes from transcript of Jon Stewart interview, *Crossfire,* CNN, October 15, 2004, http://transcripts.cnn.com/TRANSCRIPTS/0410/15/cf.01 .html (accessed December 1, 2008).

17. Lisa De Moraes, "Jon Stewart, Again in the Crossfire," *Washington Post,* October 19, 2004, C7, http://www.washingtonpost.com/wp-dyn/articles/A43775–20040ct18 .html (accessed December 1, 2008).

18. Bill Carter, "CNN Will Cancel 'Crossfire' and Cut Ties to Commentator," *New York Times,* January 6, 2005, http://www.nytimes.com/2005/01/06/business/media/ 06crossfire.html (accessed December 1, 2008). For all CNN's talk about ending the "head-butting," CNN's *Headline News* hired conservative head-butter Glenn Beck for an hour-long slot just a year later. Despite his ideological and temperamental resemblance to Fox News's Bill O'Reilly and Sean Hannity, Beck's style was described by *Headline News*'s president as "cordial" and "conversational, not confrontational." Michael Learmonth, "CNN Names New Headliner," *Variety,* January 17, 2006, http://www.variety .com/article/VR1117936232.html?categoryid=1238&cs=1&s=h&p=0 (accessed December 1, 2008). CNN's Headline News Network, though primarily a purveyor of loops of straight news stories throughout the day, showcases an evening cast (includ-

ing Beck and Nancy Grace) who could play understudies to the head-butting stars on Fox News's prime-time gallery. Perhaps not surprisingly, Beck has since migrated to Fox News.

19. The memoranda supporting the Bush-gone-AWOL story were later shown to be forgeries, a gaffe that, incidentally, was exposed by the pajama-wearing, basement-dwelling bloggers at the conservative Powerline.com (and originally defended by former CBS executive and current CNN president Jonathan Klein). See "How the Blogosphere Took on CBS' Docs."

20. "Jon Stewart Roasts Real News," CBSNews.com, October 24, 2004, http://www.cbsnews.com/stories/2004/10/21/60minutes/main650690.shtml (accessed December 1, 2008).

21. Few examples of such method satire exist. Perhaps the progenitor of this unique role was Pat Paulsen, who made six tongue-in-cheek runs for president between 1968 and his death in 1997. He heralded himself as "just a common, ordinary, simple savior of America's destiny" and got his start on a comedy-variety show with strong doses of political satire: *The Smothers Brothers Comedy Hour.* If this sounds all too similar to Colbert, think again: Paulsen believed not in the right to bear arms but in the "right to arm bears," a position that places him squarely at odds with the arctophobic Colbert.

22. Stephen Colbert, speech at White House correspondents' dinner, April 29, 2006, transcript at http://politicalhumor.about.com/od/stephencolbert/a/colbertbush .htm (accessed December 1, 2008). Colbert's video segment at the end of the live routine intimated how one courageous though frail journalist (Helen Thomas) could put fear into the minds of politicians and hold them accountable.

23. Peter Daou, "Ignoring Colbert: A Small Taste of the Media's Power to Choose the News," *Huffington Post,* April 30, 2006, http://www.huffingtonpost.com/peter-daou/ignoring-colbert-a-small_b_20092.html (accessed December 1, 2008).

24. "Media Touted Bush's Routine at Correspondents' Dinner, Ignored Colbert's Skewering," *Media Matters for America,* May 1, 2006, http://mediamatters.org/items/200605010005 (accessed December 1, 2008). Russell Peterson further details the claims and counterclaims about the alleged MSM blackout on Colbert's satirical sniping. See Peterson, *Strange Bedfellows,* 6–9.

25. Richard Cohen, "So Not Funny," *Washington Post,* May 4, 2006, http://www.washingtonpost.com/wp-dyn/content/article/2006/05/03/AR2006050302202.html (accessed December 1, 2008).

26. Ana Marie Cox, "Was Stephen Colbert Funny?" *Time,* May 4, 2006, http://www.time.com/time/nation/article/0,8599,1191093,00.html (accessed December 1, 2008).

27. See Michael Scherer, "The Truthiness Hurts," *Salon,* May 1, 2006, http://www.salon.com/opinion/feature/2006/05/01/colbert/ (accessed December 1, 2008). Scherer wrote, "Colbert's jokes attacked not just Bush's policies, but the whole drama and language of American politics, the phony demonstration of strength, unity and vision."

28. Frank Rich, "Throw the Truthiness Bums Out," *New York Times,* November 5, 2006, http://select.nytimes.com/2006/11/05/opinion/05rich.html?_r=1&oref=slogin (accessed December 1, 2008).

29. Transcript of Hillary Clinton interview on *World News with Charles Gibson,* ABCNews.go.com, January 22, 2007, http://abcnews.go.com/WNT/story?id=2814240& page=1 (accessed November 30, 2008).

30. Katie Heimer, "Hillary Clinton and the Media: From Intelligent and Fair to Appallingly Sexist and Pointless," NOW.org, March 15, 2007, http://www.now.org/issues/ media/070315hillary_media.html (accessed November 30, 2008).

31. David Brock, "The Time for Apologies Has Passed," *Media Matters for America,* February 8, 2008, http://mediamatters.org/items/200802080012?f=s_search (accessed November 30, 2008). Matthews and Shuster later apologized for their remarks, and MSNBC suspended Shuster for a time.

32. Marc Santora, "Pointed Question Puts McCain in a Tight Spot," *New York Times,* November 14, 2007, http://www.nytimes.com/2007/11/14/us/politics/14mccain .html?_r=1&ref=politics&oref=slogin (accessed December 1, 2008).

33. "CNN Univision Democratic Debate," *Saturday Night Live,* February 23, 2008 (season 33, episode 5). This sketch was reportedly written by Jim Downey.

34. "Weekend Update," *Saturday Night Live,* February 23, 2008.

35. Casey Greenfield and Jeff Greenfield, "How Now, Ol' Man MSM? A Father-Daughter Smackdown over Sexism and the Media Coverage of Hillary Clinton," *Slate,* June 17, 2008, http://www.slate.com/id/2193755 (accessed December 1, 2008).

36. Howard Kurtz, "'Soft' Press Sharpens Its Focus on Obama," *Washington Post,* March 3, 2008, C01, http://www.washingtonpost.com/wp-dyn/content/article/ 2008/03/02/AR2008030202476_pf.html (accessed November 30, 2008). Although many stories about Obama had been covered, particularly by the Chicago press, they didn't get much national MSM "traction" on the first go-round.

37. Katharine Q. Seelye and Julie Bosman, "Media Charged with Sexism in Clinton Coverage," *New York Times,* June 13, 2008, http://www.nytimes.com/2008/06/13/us/ politics/13women.html?ref=politics (accessed November 30, 2008).

38. "Palin Comes out Throwing Punches," CNNPolitics.com, September 4, 2008, http://www.cnn.com/2008/POLITICS/09/03/rnc.day/index.html (accessed December 1, 2008).

39. "'Lipstick on a Pig': Attack on Palin or Common Line?" CNN.com, September 10, 2008, http://www.cnn.com/2008/POLITICS/09/10/campaign.lipstick/ (accessed December 1, 2008).

40. Barbara Lippert, "Fey Chic," AdWeek.com, October 13, 2008, http://www .adweek.com/aw/content_display/creative/critique/e3i5c4d8ac24396d86e36d65494e6 3dea46 (accessed December 1, 2008).

41. Seth Colter Walls and Sam Stein, "Palin's ABC Interview: Stumped on Bush Doctrine, Seems to Contradict McCain on Pakistan," *Huffington Post,* September 11, 2008,

http://www.huffingtonpost.com/2008/09/11/palins-abc-interview-stum_n_125818.html (accessed December 1, 2008).

42. "A Non-Partisan Message from Sarah Palin and Hillary Clinton," *Saturday Night Live,* September 13, 2008 (season 34, episode 1). This sketch was reportedly written by Seth Meyers, Tina Fey, and Amy Poehler.

43. "CBS Evening News," *Saturday Night Live,* September 27, 2008 (season 34, episode 3). In one part, the sketch uses Palin's actual answers nearly verbatim.

44. Linda Feldmann, "Doubts about Palin Grow, Even among Conservatives," *Christian Science Monitor,* September 30, 2008, http://features.csmonitor.com/politics/2008/09/30/doubts-about-palin-grow-even-among-conservatives/ (accessed December 1, 2008).

45. Michael Cooper and Dalia Sussman, "Growing Doubts on Palin Take a Toll, Poll Finds," *New York Times,* October 30, 2008, http://www.nytimes.com/2008/10/31/us/politics/31poll.html (accessed December 1, 2008).

46. "Palin Says She Doesn't Regret Couric Interview," CNNPolitics.com, November 12, 2008, http://www.cnn.com/2008/POLITICS/11/12/palin/ (accessed December 1, 2008).

47. Faiz Shakir, "Fox's Carl Cameron: Palin 'Didn't Understand that Africa Was a Continent,'" *Think Progress,* November 5, 2008, http://thinkprogress.org/2008/11/05/palin-africa-continent/ (accessed December 1, 2008).

48. Scott McClellan, *What Happened: Inside the Bush White House and Washington's Culture of Deception* (New York: PublicAffairs, 2008), 156.

49. Glenn Greenwald, "Network News Anchors Praise the Job They Did in the Run-up to the War," *Salon,* May 28, 2008, http://www.salon.com/opinion/greenwald/2008/05/28/gibson/print.html (accessed December 1, 2008).

50. Throughout the Bush years, MSM news programs aired some humor—for example, MSNBC's *Hardball* featured a "Hardball Sideshow," ABC's *This Week* had its "Funnies," and Fox News's *The O'Reilly Factor* showcased an occasional "Miller Time" piece with comedian and former *SNL* "Weekend Update" anchor Dennis Miller. By including "comedy" bits on news programs, the MSM is mixing a little "sauce for the goose" with a dab of "can't beat 'em, join 'em."

51. Chayefsky, *Network,* 183.

15

GENDER, THE FINAL FRONTIER

Revisiting *Star Trek: The Next Generation*

Diana M. A. Relke

Star Trek departed this galaxy in 2005 when *Enterprise*, the last of the five television series, was canceled after only four seasons due to poor ratings. The sci-fi television audience of the new millennium had moved on. We had become globalized, postmodernized, posthumanized: we now preferred something edgier—something darker, less predictable, less high-minded— and definitely something less humanist. But we were also discovering that humanism—that quintessential white, Western, masculine construction of subjectivity—could not simply be discarded like last season's unfashionable overcoat. As Neil Badmington notes, "Humanism has happened and continues to happen to 'us' (it is the very 'Thing' that makes 'us' 'us,' in fact), and the experience—however traumatic, however unpleasant—cannot be erased without trace in an instant."[1] So it's hardly surprising that we are haunted by afterimages: *Star Trek* in syndication across the cable TV universe. More revealing, the release of an eleventh feature-length film in 2009 suggests that rumors of *Star Trek*'s death may have been exaggerated. This chapter looks back at an earlier resurrection miracle—the one that returned *Star Trek* to television screens as *The Next Generation* after eighteen years in the wilderness.

My own engagement with *Star Trek* began in 1988, when *The Next Generation* was in its second season. Teaching a course in gender imagery in popular culture, I found those early episodes full of teachable moments. Were these episodes an accurate reflection of second-wave feminism's progress in consolidating its achievements of the 1970s? Or could they be read as

For many, Dr. Beverly Crusher (Gates McFadden) is a hero of popular feminism. A single mother, career medical officer, and scientist, she transforms traditional notions of gender and ideas of a feminine ethic. (MovieGoods)

reflective of the feminist backlash of the 1980s and a deepening ambivalence about women's aspirations? What did it mean that the Starfleet men were so studly and the women so femme? Was the blackness of the black actors intended—however unconsciously—to say something about the status of the characters they played? And where were the black women? Interestingly, the answers to these questions changed over the next five years, not just because students were changing with the times but also because *The Next Generation* was evolving—and so were its critics.

In 1994 *The Next Generation* completed its seventh and final season. That fall, while surfing the Internet, I splashed upon an article on *Star Trek* in the online journal *Postmodern Culture*. The article reaffirmed my decision to stay as far away from paranoid academic interpretations of *Star Trek* as I did from those sophisticated misinterpretations of Madonna as a feminist that were ubiquitous in the 1990s. In that article, literary critic Valerie Fulton rolled out the heavy artillery—namely, Foucault and Derrida—to tell us what every adolescent Trekkie already knew: namely, that *Star Trek* is made in America, by Americans, and thus exhibits a uniquely Americocentric point of view.[2] After stating the obvious about the racism, sexism, and American imperialism that *Star Trek* could be seen to reinforce, Fulton went on to analyze a particular episode of *The Next Generation* that features Mark Twain as one of its characters and sets about proving to us that "*Star Trek* encourages its viewers to contextualize [Twain's] work in a way that undermines the full complexity even of those aspects it engages." This observation was hardly illuminating, since as Harold Bloom had told us, every textual borrowing is inevitably a map of misreading. Perhaps the only way to capture the "full complexity" of any text is to photocopy it.

Articles like Fulton's were making me exceedingly uncomfortable with some of the ways in which cultural studies scholars were approaching popular culture. *Star Trek*, like virtually all television drama, is a laughably easy target for Foucauldian analysis and Derridian deconstruction. Killing a fly with a sledgehammer is not merely an abuse of the fly; it is a ludicrous misuse of the hammer. Surely, Foucault and Derrida were meant for tougher things! More disturbing, Fulton's article provided the dominant critical establishment with even more ammunition against postmodernist cultural studies. Her article could be deployed as "proof" that postmodernist analysis offers nothing but a convoluted and jargon-ridden way of saying what traditional "high-culture" scholars have always known—that popular culture is a simpleminded and contemptible form unfit for academic decency.

What Fulton sidestepped completely was the possibility that *Star Trek: The Next Generation* may well have been conceived as a legitimate response to certain varieties of postmodernism itself—those ahistorical, apolitical, and relativistic varieties that used to trickle down from the lofty academy and into popular magazine articles, self-help literature, and advertising—in short, those varieties of postmodernism that, purporting to critique contemporary culture, actually helped construct it. Here is what Peter McLaren had to say about that emergent postmodernist culture and its subjects in the closing decade of the old millennium:

> The rapture of dislocation, disruption and displacement of the citizen/subject brought on by what has been called the postmodern condition has ushered in a view of de-objectified identity in which the secure, autonomous agent of history . . . has been sheared away from its former originating anchor points to be revealed as perpetually in composition. We are living at a time of moment-to-moment

apocalypse; we are in the future anterior where we feel nostalgia for a time that has not yet arrived and whose realization is structurally impossible. . . . The new postmodern self is patterned on the cathedral of capitalism, that sanctuary of consumption where we find a strange convergence of our fragmented identities in the signifying structure of global amusement culture which we know as the shopping mall. The shopping mall self (the self as the rhetorical effect of image value) has become the quintessential model of panic identity.[3]

Given this construction of the late-twentieth-century postmodern subject, trapped as she is between a history that's up for grabs and a future that's structurally impossible, is it any wonder that *Star Trek,* with its postconsumerist, post-postmodernist vision of a future that cherishes the supposed best of the past while rising above the worst, was enjoying such unprecedented popularity?

The Next Generation was conceived in the mid-1980s. This was a period characterized by a postmodernist critique that dismantled the master narratives of our culture, its institutions, and its codes yet still ended up being complicit with them because it had no program for change. Indeed, in its celebration of moral and ethical relativism, it often refused to take a stand on issues of human oppression and social injustice and hence played right into the hands of the Reagans and the Thatchers—not to mention all the bank presidents and corporate executives we did not have the opportunity to mistakenly vote for. *Star Trek* creator Gene Roddenberry leaped into this intellectual vacuum with an alternative to that pastless, futureless, malaise-ridden postmodernist present. Whatever the limitations of his vision, it seemed to me grossly unfair that it should now be shat upon by the very intellectuals whose own lack of vision probably contributed to its creation in the first place.

I did not exclude feminism from my indictment of the postmodernism of the 1980s. The women's movement of the late 1960s and 1970s had left many of us in search of new ways of being women and men, but by about 1982, just as we were beginning to take the women's movement seriously as a possible source of answers to this search, feminist scholars in large numbers began abandoning the search as naively and hopelessly essentialist. These feminist postmodernists were so busy producing esoteric deconstructions of terms such as *patriarchy, gender,* and even *feminism* itself that they forgot about actual, embodied women and men. They swooned over Lacan, the ladies' man who awarded tenure to the phallus as the universal signifier, and they listened raptly when Derrida, in his deconstruction of women and men as merely linguistic categories, proclaimed, "I am a woman." In the wake of this abandonment, the search for gender alternatives fell in part to popular culture, including television, which took up that task as best it could. So I found it unsurprising that Mr. Roddenberry's starship *Enterprise* had been commissioned to "seek out" not "new worlds" or "new civilizations" but rather new forms of masculinity. If these new forms were a bit too reminiscent of the old forms, postmodernism had no one to blame but itself.

It's easy for us academics, with all our sophisticated training, to take cheap shots at *Star Trek,* but if you were teaching a course in popular culture during the height of *Trek*'s popularity, you took those shots at your own peril. There were more Trekkies among students than you might imagine, so it was far more rewarding to help them toward a more complex understanding of why they were watching it. For me, getting students to help me figure out why I was watching it was even more rewarding. Today, I still find that the best approach to *Star Trek,* as to all mainstream popular culture, is to begin with the simple observation that if popular culture told us things about ourselves we didn't want to know, popular culture wouldn't be popular for long. If *Star Trek* had overturned all the myths of gender by which we live our lives, we would not have tuned in, and corporate sponsors would have withdrawn their support.

In other words, even if Roddenberry had been the most radical of feminist television writers, he would have been obliged to remain within the severe limits placed on television by both its audience and its sponsors. Perhaps this is why all ships in the *Star Trek* universe are referred to as "she," while all Starfleet officers, whether male or female, are addressed as "Sir."[4] Yet the original pilot episode of the original *Star Trek* in 1966 featured a highly rational woman as second in command on the *Enterprise.* Roddenberry created her to balance out his passionate and impulsive starship captain. But he was coerced by the network to scrap that pilot and create a new one in which the logical Mr. Spock of the planet Vulcan replaced the Earth woman as executive officer. The network's excuse was that acceptance of a woman of intelligence and authority was too much to ask of the American public; an extraterrestrial was supposedly more believable.

What Roddenberry succeeded in retaining in his second pilot was a communications officer who was not only female but also black. Back then, in those prefeminist days, I was no fan of television and had even less interest in the silly genre of science fiction, yet I can distinctly remember sitting up and taking notice. This was an important first for television in an era when we had little understanding of the relationship between racism and representation and had not yet invented the word *sexism*.

The point I'm making is that no matter how limited Roddenberry's depiction of gender equality was in the original *Star Trek* and continued to be in *The Next Generation,* his instincts about the inevitability of women's professionalism and authority earned *Star Trek* a substantial female following. In the context of this alone, it was easier for female Trekkers to forgive Roddenberry for *The Next Generation*'s three regular female characters—all of whom are caretakers and good listeners and thus function as a feminine context within which masculinity can be showcased more strikingly. Unlike other action-adventure series, most of which exclude women as important central characters, there is no need for *Star Trek* to feminize one or two male characters to underscore the exemplary masculinity of its heroes.

It's a simple matter to see Dr. Crusher, Counselor Troi, and bartender Guynan as measuring up to the long-standing stereotype of women as exclusively nurturant. This gives us an excellent excuse to dismiss *The Next Generation* as hopelessly sexist. It's an equally simple matter to dismiss it on the grounds of racism, for *Star Trek* can be seen as merely translating racial issues to the level of humanoid species, so that, for example, the odious, profit-mongering, physically diminutive race known as the Ferengi is no longer a critique of the excesses of Western capitalism but rather is analogous to the Japanese. Undoubtedly, *Star Trek* fans of the 1980s and early 1990s who worried about the globalization of unfettered capitalism leaned toward the former reading, while fans who resented Japan's unrivaled economic prosperity in those decades would have favored the latter. However, it seems to me that there is more racism in the latter interpretation than there is in the Ferengi themselves. Thus, it's more interesting and perhaps a bit more challenging to get *The Next Generation* to yield more useful and congenial meanings.

To return to the question of feminine caretaking, it's not caretaking per se but rather the feminization of it that's the problem. Forty years of feminist scholarship has by no means convinced everyone that caretaking is not genetically encoded in women. It could be useful to keep this in mind when looking at *The Next Generation*'s three female characters. Of the three, only Crusher is human, and one could argue that she comes by her caretaking skills largely through medical training, not genetics. Troi's exaggerated feminine intuition—her empathic power—is attributed to her nonhuman genetic inheritance, as is Guynan's facility for listening to the troubles of her customers, for she's described as a member of a mysterious race of listeners. For all we know, Roddenberry and his team were on some level aware that if men in the twenty-fourth century still longed atavistically for a genetic guarantee of these stereotypically feminine qualities in their women, they would have to leave home to find it.

So does genetically encoding caretaking exclusively in nonhuman races, thereby feminizing them, make *The Next Generation* racist? As with the capitalist Ferengi, it depends on who's doing the interpreting.

If you had eavesdropped on the many Internet newsgroups devoted to *Star Trek* at the height of its popularity, as I was wont to do, you would have had a pretty good idea of what appealed to women viewers. To them, as to many of my students, Beverly Crusher was the superwoman of popular feminism: a single mother, a career officer, and a scientist in her own right. The fact that actress Gates McFadden's face harkens back to Hollywood goddess Greta Garbo didn't hurt either. As for Counselor Cleavage, as male Trekkers liked to call Deanna Troi, viewers had little respect for this character until the show's last season, when she finally donned a regular Starfleet uniform, passed the bridge officer's exam, and was promoted to the rank of commander. Actress Marina Sirtis, who plays this character, said that these long-overdue changes had a miraculous effect on the writers of subsequent episodes, who suddenly began putting intelligent lines in her mouth. As for Whoopie Goldberg's Guynan, even Captain Jean-Luc Picard defers to her superior wisdom. Moreover, the fact that Goldberg went public with her belief in *The Next Generation* as transcending dysfunctional attitudes toward gender and race encouraged women viewers to overlook Guynan's reinforcement of the antique stereotype of women as the possessors of darkly mysterious superhuman (or subhuman) powers.

It is important to point out that although women in the *Star Trek* universe have freedoms not enjoyed by many in the show's female audience, these characters are permitted to exercise that freedom only in the service of Starfleet's hierarchical, almost priestly order. In this way, they are reminiscent of medieval nuns, who escaped the oppression of marriages of convenience and multiple life-threatening pregnancies by opting for the celibate life. So long as they remained in the service of the patriarchal church and its male priesthood, these women could learn to read and write, pursue scholarly interests, and even rise to relatively powerful positions within their religious orders. Marriage to a mortal man is hardly a sacrifice when you're married to Christ, the bridegroom who never disappoints. Many of these religious must have regarded themselves as among the most liberated and fortunate of women. And given the alternatives, they probably were. Similarly, when we compare Crusher, Troi, and Guynan with some of the females we encounter among alien civilizations scattered throughout *Star Trek's* galaxy, females whose status is more like that of most contemporary Western women, these Starfleet nuns appear remarkably liberated and fulfilled.

For many female Trekkers, Starfleet was the patriarchal order, but minus its abuses and excesses. Similarly, for Roddenberry, the United Federation of Planets was the United States of America, minus its excessive militarism, its xenophobia, and its economic injustice. Here is how science fiction author and *Star Trek* fan Ursula Le Guin described *The Next Generation* on the occasion of its final episode:

> *The Next Generation* never had a simplistic concept of Us/Nice/Real People vs. Them/Ugly/Villains. Of course, there are bad guys out there. When the Klingons turned into real people, the Romulans and Cardassians were waiting; but they keep turning into real people too. . . . Violence, on *The Next Generation,* is shown as a problem, or the failure to solve a problem, never as the true solution. This is surely one reason why the show has such a following. . . . On the *Enterprise,* we see the difference of racial and alien types, gender difference, handicaps, apparent deformities, all accepted simply as different ways of being human. In this, *The Next Generation* has been light-years ahead of its predecessors, its imitators, and practically everything else on TV.[5]

Indeed, seen in this way, *Star Trek* becomes a highly refined interpretation of the American Dream fulfilled. Roddenberry subscribed to the belief that the founders had left a viable blueprint for a "more perfect union," but Americans were far from realizing its promise. An eternal optimist about the future, he could hardly be described as a voice of political dissent, but he did believe in the inspirational power of utopian vision, and he believed in the American potential for achieving the Good Society. But Roddenberry was no different from the vast majority of American patriots who did not—and still do not—recognize that, like patriarchy, the American Dream itself is the problem. This is why Le Guin's positive reading of *The Next Generation* can be countered by equally convincing negative readings.

But if the United Federation of Planets were merely America writ large, there would not have been such pronounced international interest in it. For many non-American viewers, the Federation's allusion to the United Nations was at least as obvious as *Star Trek*'s Americanism. For that reason, I find it more useful to view the *Star Trek* universe as the fulfillment of the goals of Western humanism—which is truer to Roddenberry's stated intentions than the oppressive American imperialism attributed to his vision by its postmodernist critics. Despite the plot's utter dependence on space technology and the quantities of technobabble written into every episode, scientific knowledge in *The Next Generation* is merely technical; science serves the practical necessities of everyday life and work aboard the *Enterprise,* and basic technological literacy within the Federation is taken for granted. The humanities, in contrast, are represented as a higher form of knowledge and the real avenue to truth and wisdom. Picard is the embodiment of this higher, more valuable knowledge, and he is often contrasted to the rest of his bridge crew, who, though they all possess scientific and technological expertise, pale in comparison to Picard, who knows his history, his archaeology, his Shakespeare, his Mozart, and his Plato. Like Leonardo's *Vitruvian Man,* the famous sketch that serves as the emblem of humanism, Picard is the measure of all things. Indeed, he is the image of man in his ideal form.

Picard represents Soul, which appears on the middle rung of early humanism's five-rung universal hierarchy as translated from Plato by Renaissance humanist Marsilio Ficino. Above Soul, Ficino put God in first place and the Angels in second; below it, he put Quality in fourth place and the Body in fifth. Quality gave man the dignity that differentiated him from lower forms of matter, and I use the term *man* advisedly, for Ficino defined dignity in part as masculine beauty. The soul in its Western humanist incarnation may have been what inspired this insight from Le Guin: "The Borg [a race of technologically determined cyborgs] was a great embodiment of Evil—mechanical evil, absence of soul. Hence the power of the episode where Picard, the very soul of the *Enterprise,* became a Borg: anybody, even the best man, can lose his soul. This is a genuinely scary idea, a mature concept."[6]

Again with reference to the humanist fondness for hierarchy, the Starfleet chain of command, which draws on Anglo-American naval tradition, is only the most obvious hierarchical structure. Masculinity in *The Next Generation* is also constructed hierarchically and is measured on a reason-emotion scale that mimics Ficino's five-rung model. Again, Picard is halfway between top and bottom because he is central and most ideally human; he represents the near-perfect integration of reason, which is highly valued, and emotion, which is also valued but only when under the control of the "higher" faculty of reason. Lieutenant Commander Data, the totally unemotional android, is the perfect embodiment of reason and reason's highest achievement, while Lieutenant Worf, the Klingon warrior, takes up his position at the bottom, where he represents volatile emotion. In the spaces between these three we can slot Commander Riker, who is next to Picard in human perfection but is also a stud, with a girl in every spaceport, and Lieutenant Geordie LaForge, who is a genius in quantum mechanics but can't get a date.

If we turn the hierarchy on its side, it becomes a spectrum along which the five masculine ways of being run from superhuman at one end to subhuman at the other. I find it significant that hyperrationality and violence are represented as remote from the human ideal at the center: Data flatters us with his desire to be more like us in our spiritual and emotional complexity, while Worf earns our respect largely in direct proportion to his success in curbing his aggressive impulses. Despite the glaring absence of homosexuality in this five-category spectrum, as an orderly representation of multiple masculine subjectivities, it might be precisely what many male viewers of *The Next Generation* still find attractive, as it provides them with a simple (if oversimplified) tool for measuring what it is to be a heterosexual man in gender-obsessed humanist culture.

Women fit into *The Next Generation* in the same way they fit into humanism. But where *do* they fit? We find a clue in humanist Lorenzo Valla's Renaissance tract *De Voluptate,* which redeems from medieval Christian condemnation the value of earthly pleasure: "Only pleasure is the authentic good of man. All the other goods can be reduced to pleasure. It is the end that nature herself has indicated to man, furnishing him also with the means of obtaining it. Courtesans and harlots are more deserving of humankind than holy and chaste virgins."[7] Clearly, in Lorenzo's view, courtesans, harlots, and virgins are the *objects* rather than the *subjects* of pleasure. They are not the deserving; they are what man deserves—or, more accurately in the case of withholding virgins, what he *does not* deserve. Similarly, the excellent medical and psychotherapeutic services of the nurturant Crusher, the empathic Troi, and the commiserating Guynan are no less than what the men on the *Enterprise* deserve. Female admirals, of which there are many in *The Next Generation,* get to remain on Earth and keep the home fires burning.

To my mind, the most successful female character in *The Next Generation* is K'Ehleyr, the half-human, half-Klingon mate of Lieutenant Worf and the mother of his son. She is an accomplished and respected Federation ambassador to the Klingon Empire, and she harbors no illusions regarding the Klingons' propensity to cloak their violent practices in claims of honor, glory, and duty. She is as fierce as she is tender, as intelligent as she is beautiful, as autonomous as she is relational. Thus she embodies the best of both genders. Consequently, there is no continuing place for her within the humanist structure that gives *The Next Generation* its gender coherence, and she therefore appears in only two episodes. In response to her brutal murder by the treacherous Klingon Duras, we are so swept away by our admiration for her that, unlike Captain Picard, we are in complete accord with Worf as he crosses the thin line of his restraint, gives in to his Klingon rage, and kills Duras in a violent duel. In other words, K'Ehleyr is one of those female figures whose primary function is to render justifiable the ultimate expression of traditional masculine power.[8]

At the opposite end of the feminine spectrum is the character of the telepathic extraterrestrial Lwaxana Troi, the hormonally crazed, menopausal mother of Deanna. Whereas characterization in *The Next Generation* is encoded and hence decoded according to the conventions of realism, Lwaxana's character is rendered in the exaggerated conventions of burlesque comedy and hence comes across as a tasteless sexist joke. She is not only the bane of her daughter's existence but also a sexual predator who functions as justification for the latent misogyny of the scripts she inhabits. In addition, as she repeatedly reminds us in her imperious way, she is the daughter of the Fifth House, holder of the Sacred Chalice of Rixx, and heir to the Holy Rings of Betazed. She is also notorious for her rude and dismissive remarks about other humanoid species. Thus, as the exaggerated focus of elitism and racism, she draws our attention away from these qualities as they exist in their normative form in the other characters. Indeed, in one episode Captain Picard and the other officers, whose male protection she seeks, can abandon her with impunity to a repulsive and lecherous Ferengi kidnapper.

Whereas many father-son relationships are explored throughout the series with dignity, sensitivity, and compassion, the crudely comedic conflict between Lwaxana and Deanna represents the only mother-daughter interchange to receive sustained treatment in *The Next Generation*. Thus, in striking contrast to the multiplicity of diverse father-son interchanges, the Troi burlesque becomes by default the implicit paradigm case for all mother-daughter relationships. However, in fairness to the *Trek* writers, as the series progressed, the burlesque was muted, Lwaxana's character was rendered less misogynistically, and her relationship with Deanna was given more complexity. However, she never entirely rose above her initial depiction as an embarrassment to the feminine gender. Perhaps this is why, unlike K'Ehleyr, Lwaxana enjoyed a continuing place in the *Star Trek* saga, appearing in episodes of the later *Deep Space Nine* series. However, some might claim that this had more to do with the fact that Majel Barrett, the actress who played Lwaxana, was the wife of the late Gene Roddenberry and the custodian of his lucrative *Star Trek* empire.

The Next Generation is not merely a useful device for introducing into the classroom a critique of the gender-encoded discourse of Western humanism; it is more obviously useful for deconstructing the binary opposition of high versus popular culture, for Roddenberry and his team consciously created *The Next Generation* as the legitimate heir to both. Roddenberry sold the original *Star Trek* to the network by calling it "a wagon-train to the stars," and indeed, *The Next Generation* contains multiple allusions to the Hollywood western. Six-guns have become phasers, horses have become starships, and saloons proliferate along the final frontier. Gambling has evolved into the more civilized activity of the weekly poker game in Commander Riker's quarters; although nothing so crass as money changes hands, the high-risk stakes of American frontier exploration are repeatedly evoked in the allusion to poker as analogous to the chancy adventure of space exploration. Cheek by jowl with these elements of the Hollywood western are elaborate allusions to William Shakespeare, Charles Dickens, John Masefield, Mark Twain, Agatha Christie, and Arthur Conan Doyle. Picard's reverence for Shakespeare is rivaled only by his love of a pulp fiction novelist whose private eye character Dixon Hill is Picard's holodeck alter ego. Two American cultural studies scholars identify Dixon Hill as an allusion to the novels of Philip K. Dick.

I came across this reference to Philip K. Dick in an unpublished conference paper by Sarah Hardy and Rebecca Kukla entitled "Staging Narrative and the Narrative Stage: Exploring Space on the Starship *Enterprise*." A postmodernist reading of *The Next Generation,* but unlike the Fulton article mentioned earlier, this paper is completely free of paranoia. Instead, Hardy and Kukla explore space within the starship *Enterprise* in much the same spirit as its Starfleet crew explores the interstellar space outside of it. Hardy and Kukla begin by noting that "an episode in which the *Enterprise* becomes a sentient being makes explicit its ongoing role as a protagonist in the *Star Trek* saga." They go on "to take the *Enterprise* as an example illustrating the thesis that fictional spaces can constitute and control the forms of subjectivity . . . they contain." They also note what I believe to be a most important observation for anyone trying to understand the phenomenal appeal of *Star Trek:* "The importance placed upon the purely physical character of both the old and the new *Enterprise,* by both the show's creators and the audience alike, is evident from the publication for fans of whole books of extraordinarily detailed 'blueprints' for each ship. Viewers know, and have proven that they want to know, a great deal about the technological capabilities, physical workings, and spatial and functional divisions of each *Enterprise.*"[9]

As someone who sleeps beneath a two- by four-foot glazed cutaway representation of the *Enterprise-D,* I exemplify audience fascination with this object as the most important protagonist in *The Next Generation.* Perhaps for the whole viewing audience, no less than for me, the *Enterprise* is analogous to the self, in that it contains a multiplicity of interacting subjectivities. Male or female, there is no character on the bridge of the *Enterprise* who cannot be experienced as a projection of some aspect of the self, some fragment of subjectivity in a dynamic relationship of oscillating harmony-conflict-resolution with all other fragments. I think Carl Jung would have been well pleased with the *Enterprise* and would have embraced it as yet more evidence in support of his theory of archetypes—in contrast to the cultural critics who have denounced the *Enterprise* for its crew of stereotypes.

Perhaps the most intriguing aspect of this character called *Enterprise* is her vivid imagination expressed through that most wonderful of all twenty-fourth-century technologies, the holodeck. Representative of the ship's rich fantasy life, the holodeck is evidence of the *Star Trek* creators' belief that not even the galaxy is a large enough arena for the human imagination. The holodeck is an excellent metaphor for introducing into the classroom an analysis of the human propensity for discursively constructing reality, for that process is analogous to the transformation of energy into matter. One only has to speak to the voice-activated holodeck computer to create a simulation of any environment of any shape in perfect detail. The fact that no hologram can exist outside the holodeck in its material form can be used to suggest that reality as discursively constructed by any one individual or group is always subject to impingement by other realities.

Indeed, in their discussion of the holodeck as providing individual crew members with the opportunity to realize the kind of fantasies that most viewers feel constrained to keep under wraps, Hardy and Kukla note, "Although the holodeck doors are not kept locked and anyone can enter anyone else's fantasy at will, people's antics on the holodeck are clearly treated as personal business and beyond judgment." This leads them to conclude that "the holodeck challenges our distinction between the included and the excluded, the contained and the out of bounds, at the physical, cultural, and normative levels." Thus, "in each case, the narrative presence of the holodeck makes the provocative claim that we can imaginatively extend our world into an open, accessible space, containing even those possibilities which must be excluded from everyday life and traditionally understood space-time. Yet at the same time, the holodeck is used in several episodes to problematize and reveal the limits of the myth of a radically inclusive space."[10]

What is permissible and what is out of bounds is constantly being renegotiated where the holodeck is concerned. Just as Data, that other marvel of twenty-fourth-century technology, gives his android offspring the chance to choose its own gender and species identity, the holodeck implies this potential as well. Indeed, Data takes his offspring to the holodeck to "try on" several thousand available subjectivities before a holographic mirror. Although, with the exception of Data himself, no character has actually been transformed into the so-called opposite sex, many characters use the holodeck as a temporary escape from the restrictions—gender and otherwise—of real space-time, and the holodeck computer instantly adjusts and responds to these alternative subjectivities. Thus, the holodeck is useful for initiating a classroom discussion about the construction of subjectivity and the fluidity of representation.

In an episode called "Conundrum," contact with an alien probe leaves the *Enterprise* crew and the ship's computer with amnesia. The crew can only guess who they are by interpreting external clues in the context of their emotional self-awareness, which is all they have left of their identities. Thus Data, who has no emotional awareness and just happens to be behind the bar in Ten-Forward when the probe strikes, assumes that he is the bartender and begins to act accordingly. Commander Riker and Ensign Ro, who, under normal circumstances, are constantly at odds with each other professionally, interpret the tension between them as sexual. Worf interprets the Klingon ceremonial sash he wears as signifying his status as ship's captain. This seems to make sense in the context of his aggressive warrior feelings, for the computer's reprogrammed memory tells them that the Federation is at war with a race called the Lysians, and their orders are to attack and destroy the Lysian Central Command. But more fragmentary evidence retrieved from the computer soon corrects them as to the proper chain of command. Picard resumes his place as captain, and the crew proceeds to carry out its mission of destruction. In the end, it's a variation on the humanist balance of reason and emotion that saves the day. Picard's ethical instincts, working in tandem with his finely honed logic, tips them off: they are the victims of an insidious plot. An unscrupulous race called the Satarrans has inflicted this pastless and futureless condition on them in an attempt to use the *Enterprise* as a weapon to destroy the Lysians, with whom the Satarrans are at war.

On the surface, this episode appears to be one of the sillier ones, yet it can be seen as an apt analogy for the postmodern condition as described in the passage by McLaren quoted earlier. Like the *Enterprise* crew, we have been transformed from humanist to postmodern subjects: robbed of our past, and without a vision for the future, we are helpless and vulnerable to perpetual, moment-to-moment manipulation by the ideologies that circulate through and around us like some invasive, malevolent force. We have only this highly misinterpretable, malaise-ridden, discursively tangled present to guide our trajectory, which is just as likely to be toward destruction as toward preservation. Is it any wonder, then, that Roddenberry's vision of the future as not merely ensured but enhanced by the triumph of the humanist spirit enjoyed such phenomenal appeal?

Like all the other permutations of the *Star Trek* saga, *The Next Generation* was not conceived as a subversive text, as, for example, *All in the Family* and *M*A*S*H** were iconic texts of the much more liberal and liberating decade of the 1970s. Nor was it conceived in staunch support of the status quo. The humanist assumptions on which it rests ensure that for every progressive idea that appears to inform it, there are at least two others that seem disappointingly conventional. What's important about *Star Trek* is the loyalty it inspired in its millions of active fans, who refused to be marginalized for their textual preferences, either by the gatekeepers of high-cultural taste or by a postmodern present in which meaning is eternally deferred. And although there are far fewer Trekkers among the students in our gender studies and cultural studies classrooms these days, they have by no means disappeared completely. Indeed, at the time of this writing, they eagerly await the release of the eleventh feature-length *Star Trek* film.

Clearly, much has changed in the *Star Trek* universe since *The Next Gen-*

eration. Though its humanist framework remains intact, it has undergone postmodernization in many of its details. In terms of gender, we've had *Voyager,* with its tough female captain, its even tougher female chief engineer, and a cyborg whose technological prowess is one up on the kick-ass women of Japanese cyberpunk. This trio of Alpha Babes cruising the Delta Quadrant provided an opportunity to study how *Star Trek's* gender imagery evolved. Although *Voyager* did not enjoy the same level of popularity as *The Next Generation* or even *Deep Space Nine,* this had less to do with its feminine troika than with *Voyager's* competition—namely, the several other space-fiction series for which *The Next Generation* had blazed the way into prime time. Nevertheless, *Voyager* had a substantial female fan base whose loyalty almost certainly played a role in preventing the series' cancellation when, in its third season, ratings took a dangerous dip. What made the humanist character of Janeway important was not so much her admirable projection of female authority as the opportunity she gave the writers to explore the limitations of humanism in a posthuman universe.[11]

As a key to what might be generalized as the dominant Western psyche, *Star Trek* rivals the legends of King Arthur. Its translation into such languages as Hindi and Japanese suggests that, for better or worse, it may also rival Coca-Cola and McDonald's as a globalizing phenomenon. For that reason alone its potential for generating multiple readings needs to be exploited in our cultural studies classrooms. It is available in seemingly eternal syndication, beaming into households across North America and perhaps beyond, offering us a way to approach gender issues as we negotiate the cultural terrain between humanism and the posthuman. Not to take advantage of it would be to miss a powerful opportunity to deconstruct and reconstruct the cultural myths by which we are destined to live our lives.

Notes

1. Neil Badmington, "Theorizing Posthumanism," *Cultural Critique* 53 (2003): 10–27.

2. Valerie Fulton, "An Other Frontier: Voyaging West with Mark Twain and *Star Trek's* Imperial Subject," *Postmodern Culture* 4, no. 3 (1994), http://muse.jhu.edu/login?uri=/journals/postmodern_culture/v004/4.3fulton_v.html (accessed February 8, 2009).

3. Peter McLaren, "Predatory Culture and the Politics of Education," *Cultural Studies Times* 1, no. 3 (1995): 7–10.

4. In the later series, *Star Trek: Voyager,* Captain Kathryn Janeway resists this Starfleet tradition, instructing her subordinates to call her "Captain" or, in a pinch, "Ma'am." I strongly suspect that the writers—trapped by the gender binaries of humanism—were anxious to avoid overmasculinizing *Trek*'s first female captain. It's worth noting, however, that in a few episodes in which the plot requires Janeway's authority to be emphatically reinforced, one or more of her officers can be counted on to "slip" and address her as "Sir."

5. Ursula Le Guin, "My Appointment with *The Enterprise,*" *TV Guide,* May 21, 1994, 13.

6. Ibid.

7. Nicola Abbagnano, "Renaissance Humanism," in *Dictionary of the History of Ideas: Studies of Selected Pivotal Ideas,* vol. 4 (New York: Scribner, 1973), 133.

8. To my knowledge, K'Ehleyr has received no sustained attention from feminist critics of *Star Trek.* I find this regrettable, for as an attractive hybrid, she can be read as a positive alternative to those other hybrids—the technologically determined Borg. But at the time of her appearance in *The Next Generation,* the writers were still hewing closely to Roddenberry's humanist philosophy. Any really interesting experiments with the posthuman potential locked up in *Star Trek*'s androids, holograms, cyborgs, and other boundary-dwelling species would have to wait until *Voyager.*

9. Sarah Hardy and Rebecca Kukla, "A Paramount Narrative: Exploring Space on the Starship *Enterprise,*" *Journal of Aesthetics and Art Criticism* 57, no, 2 (1999): 177, 180.

10. Ibid., 182–83.

11. I discuss this at length in *Drones, Clones, and Alpha Babes: Retrofitting* Star Trek's *Humanism, Post-9/11* (Calgary: University of Calgary Press, 2006).

CONTRIBUTORS

CARL BERGETZ is adjunct professor at John Marshall Law School.

PAUL A. CANTOR is the Clifton Waller Barrett professor of English at the University of Virginia. His *Gilligan Unbound: Pop Culture in the Age of Globalization* was chosen by the *Los Angeles Times* as one of the best nonfiction books of 2001. He has written widely on pop culture, including essays on *The Simpsons, South Park, Star Trek, 24,* the western, and film noir.

PETER CASTER is assistant professor of English at the University of South Carolina Upstate. He is the author of *Prisons, Race, and Masculinity in Twentieth-Century U.S. Literature and Film* as well as articles published in *English Language Notes, The Drama Review,* and other journals. He is currently coediting the collection *Black Masculinity in U.S. History and Literature, 1790–1945.*

TIMOTHY M. DALE is assistant professor of political science in the Department of Social Change and Development at the University of Wisconsin–Green Bay. His research interests are in the fields of political theory and American politics, with a particular focus on civic engagement, diversity, and democratic theory. He is coauthor of the book *Political Thinking, Political Theory, and Civil Society.*

JOSEPH J. FOY is assistant professor of political science at the University of Wisconsin–Waukesha. He is editor of and contributing author to *Homer Simpson Goes to Washington: American Politics through Popular Culture,* which was selected for the John G. Cawelti Award for the Best Textbook/Primer on Popular and American Culture for 2008 by the Popular Culture Association/American Culture Association. Foy also contributed essays on the ethics and rationality of counterterrorism in *Steven Spielberg and Philosophy* and on power and the transvaluation of ethical standards in *The Philosophy of the X-Files.*

TANJI GILLIAM is postdoctoral fellow at the Center for Africana Studies at the University of Pennsylvania and the artistic director of Oil House Productions.

PHILLIP W. GRAY is lecturer in the American Studies Programme at the University of Hong Kong. He has published articles in *Humanitas* and *Politics and Religion* and is the author of the book *Being in the Just War: Ontology and the Decline of the Just War Tradition.*

BETH WIELDE HEIDELBERG is assistant professor at Minnesota State University, Mankato, where she teaches urban planning, historic preservation, downtown revitalization, urban design, and historic urban development. Her research focuses on the depiction of public servants and government officials in narrative film. Other research interests include the connection between historic (specifically Roman) architectural techniques and their modern adaptations and the application of historic urban design in modern American settlement.

MATTHEW HENRY is a member of the faculty at Richland College in Dallas, Texas, where he teaches courses in composition, African American literature, and cultural studies. He has published essays in *African American Review, Critique, Popular Culture Review, Studies in Popular Culture, Journal of Popular Culture,* and *Teaching English in the Two-Year College.* His research focuses on *The Simpsons* and American culture, and his essay on gay identity in *The Simpsons* appeared in *Leaving Springfield:* The Simpsons *and the Possibility of Oppositional Culture.*

JEFFREY A. JOHNSON is assistant professor of history at Providence College in Rhode Island and is a specialist in late-nineteenth- and early-twentieth-century labor and political history. He is the author of *They Are All Red Out Here: Socialist Politics in the Pacific Northwest, 1895–1925.* Johnson has served as a fellow at the W. E. B. DuBois Institute at Harvard University, the Montana Historical Society, and the U.S. Military Academy at West Point.

SARA R. JORDAN is assistant professor in the Department of Politics and Public Administration at the University of Hong Kong. Some of her earlier publications appeared in *Public Administration, Administrative Theory & Praxis,* and *Public Administration Review.*

KATHERINE LEHMAN is assistant professor of communications at Albright College in Reading, Pennsylvania. She previously served as a visiting assistant professor in American studies and gender studies at the University of Miami in Florida. Her current book project explores representations of single women, feminism, and sexuality in television and film in the 1960s and 1970s.

ISABEL PINEDO is associate professor of film and media studies at Hunter College, City University of New York. In addition to her book *Recreational Terror: Women and the Pleasures of Horror Film Viewing,* she has published articles in the *Journal of*

Film and Video, Paradoxa: Studies in World Literary Genres, and *Battlestar Galactica and Philosophy.* She is currently working on a book on death, torture, and terrorism in television and film after 9/11.

DIANA M. A. RELKE is professor of women's and gender studies at the University of Saskatchewan. She teaches courses in science fiction and technoculture and is the author of *Drones, Clones, and Alpha Babes: Retrofitting* Star Trek's *Humanism, Post-9/11.*

JERRY RODNITZKY is professor of history at the University of Texas at Arlington, where he specializes in recent American cultural history. His books include *Minstrels of the Dawn: The Folk-Protest Singer as a Cultural Hero, Jazz-Age Boomtown, Feminist Phoenix: The Rise and Fall of a Feminist Counterculture,* and *Lights, Camera, History: Portraying the Past in Film.* He is a founding and advisory editor of the journal *Popular Music and Society* and an advisory editor for *Journal of Texas Music History.*

DAVID SCHULTZ is professor at the Hamline University School of Business. He is also a member of the Hamline University Department of Criminal Justice and Forensic Science and is a senior fellow in the Institute of Law and Politics at the University of Minnesota Law School. Schultz is the author of twenty-four books and more than seventy articles on various aspects of law, ethics, public policy, and the media and politics.

JAMIE WARNER teaches political theory at Marshall University. Her research interests revolve around nontraditional forms of political communication, especially political parody and political humor. She has had work published in *Polity, Popular Communication, Politics and Gender,* and the *Electronic Journal of Communication.* She is currently working on a book-length manuscript titled "Political Culture Jamming: Parody, Politics, and Humor in the American Public Sphere."

INDEX